THE STYLISTICS OF FICTION

THE STYLISTICS OF FICTION

A literary-linguistic approach

M<small>ICHAEL</small> J. T<small>OOLAN</small>

ROUTLEDGE

LONDON AND NEW YORK

First published in 1990
by Routledge
11 New Fetter Lane, London EC4P 4EE

Simultaneously published in the USA and Canada
by Routledge
a division of Routledge, Chapman and Hall, Inc.
29 West 35th Street, New York, NY 10001

Printed and bound in Great Britain by
Biddles Ltd, Guildford and King's Lynn
Photoset by Rowland Phototypesetting Ltd
Bury St Edmunds, Suffolk

British Library Cataloguing in Publication Data

Toolan, Michael
The Stylistics of Fiction: a literary-linguistic approach.
1. Fiction in English.   Criticism of applications in stylistics
I. Title
823'.009

ISBN 0-415-03168-0

Library of Congress Cataloging in Publication Data

Toolan, Michael J.
The stylistics of fiction: a literary-linguistic approach/
Michael J. Toolan.'
p.   cm.
Bibliography: p.
Includes index.
ISBN 0-415-03168-0
1. Faulkner, William, 1897–1962. Go down, Moses. 2. Faulkner,
William, 1897–1962 – Style. 3. Faulkner, William, 1897–1962 –
Language. 4. Stylistics. 5. Fiction. I. Title.
PS3511.A86G639   1990
813'.52–dc20   89-10396

in loving memory of my mother
Catherine Elizabeth Toolan

CONTENTS

ACKNOWLEDGEMENTS

This book began life, too many years ago, as a doctoral thesis at the University of Oxford. I am grateful to those at Oxford and, in my undergraduate years, Edinburgh University who introduced me to Faulkner or stylistics, and encouraged my stumbling efforts to relate the two: Christopher Butler, Norman Macleod, Colin Nicholson, Faith Pullin, and James Thorne. I particularly value the criticisms of my former supervisor, Roy Harris, whose penetrating commentaries on linguistics and linguistic theorizing, of whatever stripe, continue to be for me a rich source of intellectual invigoration. Additionally, the following, in one way or another, have shared their ideas with me, taken the trouble to read and comment upon my work, and engaged in the disjointed dialogue of academic enquiry with generosity and patience; my warm thanks go to them all: Rukmini Bhaya Nair, David Birch, David Butt, Ronald Carter, George Dillon, and Talbot Taylor. Students at the University of Washington and the National University of Singapore, whom I have attempted to persuade of the merits of stylistics, have provided invaluable feedback, ranging from the sharply sceptical to the hearteningly enthusiastic. Literal feeding, rather than figurative feedback, is just one of the essential ways in which my wife, Julianne Statham, has supported me. Her contribution to this book – like that of our children – is immeasurable, and deeply appreciated.

All references to *Go Down, Moses* in this study are to the original Random House edition of 1942 (photographically reproduced in the Modern Library (1955) and Vintage Books (paperback, 1973) editions). I am most grateful to Random House, Inc., and Chatto & Windus Ltd, holders of the copyright to *Go Down, Moses* in the United States and Britain respectively, for permission to quote from the novel.

xi

1

STYLISTICS AND ITS DISCONTENTS; OR, GETTING OFF THE FISH 'HOOK'

STYLE AND LITERARY LINGUISTICS

The concept of style has had a troubled history in the modern period. Both within and outside literary study, it has commonly been argued that we use the term 'style' without knowing its meaning. Most of us have little difficulty in using words like 'style' and 'stylish' in everyday discourse, to refer to some characteristic of a person or thing which we find distinctive and pleasing. But the status of the judgement usually remains unexamined. When we speak of style in Milton – or McEnroe – are we merely spontaneously asserting the presence of some quality which is subjectively perceived and unanalysable, that is, making a purely arbitrary personal evaluation or 'witnessing'? In this opening chapter I want to sketch the wider background of orthodox literary and linguistic studies, particularly as these bear on influential theorizations of such key notions as style, stylistics, literature, and linguistics.

By way of a beginning, we might consider a question that arises with regard to the specific domain of *literary* style, namely whether style is a linguistic topic, part of the linguistic description of a text, or chiefly a topic in literary criticism and appreciation of a text, hence largely subjective.

It may be a clarification rather than a distortion to posit two such divergent responses to style, for such deepseated conflict underlies much of the wrangling between linguists and critics in their various contributions to this controversial question during the last twenty years. Too many of the contributors have preferred, for whatever reason, to adopt a combative stance in the face of their alleged antagonists, and have indulged in a destructively extreme dialecticalism of debate. Too few have noted, as Roger Fowler did long ago

1

(Fowler 1971), the considerable community of interests of style students, whether from the literary or linguistic camp, and their common intellectual and cultural ancestry in nineteenth- and twentieth-century philology.

However, in the last fifteen years or so a new polyphony of contending approaches, subdisciplines, and agendas – a renewed sense of lost or multiple directions, the sceptic might suggest – has emerged. So many formerly cast-iron and irrefutable distinctions, in both linguistic and literary criticism, are now acknowledged to be disconcertingly vulnerable to challenge (see, for example, McLain 1977). After Derrida, it seems, every binary categorization one cares to think of is vulnerable to deconstruction: speech versus writing; poem versus novel; dialogue versus narrative; character versus incident; and, perhaps, linguistics versus literary criticism. In the domain of linguistics, the Chomskyan generativist epoch promoted the claims of a number of universalizable characteristics of language and, more important, promised that the theory might eventually provide a full description of a native language-user's competence. But linguists now increasingly acknowledge both the narrowness, in practice, of the microlinguistic turn that generativism took, and the theoretical uncertainty of even such fundamental distinctions as that between competence and performance (early critics included Gross 1979; Koerner 1983). There is renewed debate about what constitutes a language, and how linguistics relates to communication (Harris 1980; Pateman 1983a; Itkonen 1984). Many of the post-Saussurean categories of linguistic theory, supposedly fundamental, are now seen to contain quite arbitrary suppositions. Perhaps the most notorious of these are those surrounding Chomsky's idealized conceptualization of the homogeneous speech community whose members know their language perfectly. The stronger objection to this is not that it is an idealization – all theory idealizes in some respects – but that it presents, as a workable conceptualization, a construct which stipulates homogeneity and perfect knowledge of a phenomenon which, definitionally, needs to be characterized in terms of heterogeneity and difference. As Love (1981) has suggested, Chomsky's idealization may be no more useful than the concept of a square circle (on these issues, see also Love 1988). Many recent studies argue quite explicitly for the need to attend anew to the observed phenomena of linguistic behaviour, in all their seemingly chaotic diversity, and notwithstanding the difficulties for modelling and description that this involves (see

Harris 1981, 1987; Milroy 1980; Le Page and Tabouret-Keller 1985; Romaine 1983, 1988; Hudson 1980).

The crisis in literary studies is as acute. Many literary scholars continue to assert that artistic literature is different in kind from 'ordinary' language, and that there is a sharp divide between the two types of discourse. This view is often held in conjunction with the familiar New Critical verdict on form and content: in ordinary language form and content are separable, statements are often synonymous and paraphrasable, but in verbal art content is never paraphrasable, nor separable from form.

To anyone with a vocational interest in literature it is difficult to resist some of the pull of New Criticism, which both mystifies the production of artistic literature and makes the poem itself a sacred mystery. New Criticism is, technically, utterly defunct, universally dismissed as a theoretical dinosaur; but the kinds of critical practice that it privileged are still widely adhered to, and the preoccupation, in theory, with Lacan, Lyotard, Foucault, Bakhtin, etc., has done little to shift that adherence. Like high priests of former times, a special elect group with apparently sole rights to approach and interpret the venerated texts for and to the common faithful, New Critics were instrumental in clearing and occupying a particular space in the sociocultural terrain. Theirs was perhaps the first professionalization of literary study; and the chief benefit of this professionalization was that, for a time at least, there was renewed consciousness, in some sections of the societies affected, that literature was important. Of the problems that arose, one was the familiar characteristic of a profession to become hidebound in its thinking, self-perpetuating, swift to close ranks in the face of criticism, resistant to consideration of fundamental premises. I have cited two of these – that literature is essentially different from ordinary language use, and that it is non-paraphrasable. Neither of these can be plausibly defended today without substantial reformulation (for various arguments against seeing literary language as a special language, see Pratt 1977; Lodge 1977; Fish 1980).

In place of the unmaintainable absolutes of the linguistics and literary criticism of a generation ago, new relativist tendencies have emerged. Linguistics may be a science, in that it pursues knowledge which may be formalized and generalized about the way people have and use language, but it is much more a social science than a pure one. The generative linguists' pursuit of rules and representations of

3

competence, expressible in abstract terms akin to those of mathematics, has often been conducted to the neglect of many of the most interesting characteristics of language (see Gross 1979; Koerner 1983). Among some linguists at least, there has latterly been a noticeable redirection of attention away from narrow abstractions and towards the actual dynamics of language as our chief resource in the achievement of interpersonal communication and the negotiation of individual goals. Even those uncritical of the theoretical assumptions and idealizations of generative linguistics widely recognize that in the contemporary world there are many other applications of linguistic expertise, of pressing concern, to make demands on linguists' intellectual energy: 'language universals in government and binding theory' must accept 'complex-sentence comprehension in the very old' and 'pragmalinguistic guidelines for the questions formulated by immigration officers' as equally legitimate research topics.

In light of these changes in theory and practice, a recent paper by Mary Louise Pratt, surveying the unreally utopian nature of contemporary linguistic idealizations and modellings, is of particular interest. Over and over again, she argues, problematic phenomena, heterogeneity, and difference are marginalized or silenced altogether by prevailing models of egalitarian homogeneity: 'Disorders . . . are almost automatically seen as failures or breakdowns not to be accounted for within the system' (Pratt 1987: 51). Instead, models of 'imagined communities' are constructed, 'speech communities with their own boundaries, sovereignty, fraternity and authenticity' (56). This has persisted even in sociolinguistics, Pratt argues, despite the 'empowering' effect of, for example, Labov's imagined community of black English vernacular speakers, or early feminist accounts of 'women's language'. These have value as far as they go, she concedes, but adds:

What the 'subcommunity' approach does not do, however, is see the dominated and dominant *in their relations with each other* – this is the limitation imposed by the imaginings of community. . . . Social difference is seen as constituted by distance and separation rather than by ongoing contact and structured relations in a shared social space. Language is seen as a nexus of social identity, but not as a site of social struggle or a producer of social relations. (Pratt 1987: 56)

In the cases of both Labov and Bernstein, for example, though the former is utopian and the latter dystopian in their view of the community dialects they examine (so that black English vernacular is presented as no problem, British working-class verbal culture as nothing but a problem), the upshot of both treatments is to legitimize the assimilationist practices of the dominant culture: in both cases, via bidialectalism, the out-group code can be learned and maintained alongside the already acquired one. As Harris notes of Bernstein (Harris 1980: 96) – and this reflects the non-conflictual nature of most such modellings – one thing Bernstein is concerned to deny is that, for instance, middle-class English children and working-class English children speak different languages. For Bernstein the codes relate to linguistic performance only, and not to linguistic competence. In making this compromise in support of the idealized community of potential homogeneity, as Harris notes, much of the force of Bernstein's theory is dissipated: difference is asserted, but only surface difference.

While there is much in Pratt's proposal for a 'linguistics of contact' that one might accept, certain questions remain open. First, she does not demonstrate – although she clearly implies it – that analyses which highlight 'the hierarchical and conflictive web of social relations' shaping any encounter between individuals (subjects) in a divided and stratified society *cannot* be produced using the linguistics of community. In fact, it is hard to image how a linguistics of contact itself, a linguistics focused on conflict, contrast, and difference, can operate without a linguistics that models community in some way. Conflict, contrast, and difference are – clearly – relational terms that cannot signify without their implicit counterparts: harmony, identity, and sameness. One 'unravelling' of the speech-community notion that may be attractive is that proposed by Milroy (1981), who argues for a sociolinguistic modelling that captures the intricate, intersecting, and overlapping networks of cultural and linguistic relation which individual speakers construct, in the process making diverse acts of identity (see Le Page and Tabouret-Keller 1985) with a spectrum of other speakers. But for those concerned to emphasize the workings of 'gross' categorizations, such as class or gender domination, the social-networks model may be unattractive, since it does less to dramatize the effects of such larger factors.

If linguistics has begun to embrace a much broader field of enquiry, beyond abstract rule formulations, literary criticism has also

developed along lines other than the indirect reinforcement of normative values (criticism as refined and 'improving' conversation; for an
ingenious but controversial revaluation of the notion of 'conversation'
in humanistic discourse, see Rorty 1982). Influential critics are
those who acknowledge and analyse the cultural conventions and
conditions affecting what a society admits as artistic literature, the
intricate network of (often binary) categorizations, privileging one,
excluding or marginalizing the other, investing with voice here,
silencing there – the complex but substantial (shifting) system of
values and significations on the basis of which meanings and evaluations are made. Artistic literature is thus newly attended to, in such
studies, as continuous with all other language uses, even while lacking
the immediate communicational function or illocutionary force of
most language use.

At the same time, however, it seems clear that in some ways
literature does remain unlike much everyday language use – not just
in its high status within a society, but in such features of construction
as the degree of revision that writers apply to their texts. Following
Ochs's distinctions between various types of planned and unplanned
discourse (Ochs 1979), literature might be treated as 'written to be
read, then rewritten to be read'. The writing of literature is often
highly self-conscious, and this reflexivity may reach a point where
there can be said to be a focus on the message for the message's own
sake (Jakobson 1960). But such radical reflexivity is a potential
rather than a necessary condition. Lodge's important amendments
to Jakobson's claims are worth holding in mind: thoroughly
message-focused literature is literary language at its most material
and metaphorical, but a great deal of literature is (read as) less
thoroughly self-focused, more other-focused, more conventionally
referential, communicative, and, to use the Jakobsonian term,
metonymical. Mention may be made here of Attridge's excellent
reassessment of Jakobson's seminal 'Closing statement: linguistics
and poetics', and the commitment therein to 'objective' linguistic
explanations of poetic language (Attridge 1987). As Attridge shows,
Jakobson's own orientation towards objectivist analysis of the palpable form (Jakobson refers to the latter as the 'message', although
'text' would be a more usual label) means that his 'functions' and
functionalism are of a severely attenuated kind:

> [The] avoidance of any appeal to the reader, and to the values or
> expectations he or she brings to the text, is part of a wider elision of

the cultural determination of literature itself, in its many changing and differently interpreted forms, though the word 'function' remains like the ghost of these excluded possibilities. (Attridge 1987: 20)

STYLE AND THE BI-PLANAR MODEL OF LANGUAGE

Whatever the degree of metaphoricality of a particular literary text, the standard treatment of that text's style has fitted well with the equally standard model of language as a fixed bi-planar system mapping forms on to meanings. This theory, reinvigorated by Saussure in the twentieth century, propounds that two essential levels in language production and description are those of surface linguistic forms (morphological/phonological) and underlying semantic contents. A general principle is asserted, namely that surface forms are systematically and predictably relatable to underlying abstract semantic contents.

This bi-planar model has long presented itself as an irrefutable foundation of western linguistic study, with the consequence that many of the discussions of linguistic topics I shall draw on have themselves been shaped and coloured by at least latent bi-planar assumptions. Indeed, the 'new' twentieth-century science of linguistics is bi-planar to its Saussurean roots and is only now experiencing, in any widespread and consequential way, a painful, resisted process of demythologizing (see especially Harris 1981 and 1987; T. Taylor 1980). There are many facets to Harris's critique of orthodox bi-planar linguistic theorizing, and it would be perilous to attempt a summary here. What follows are brief descriptive remarks on Harris's objections, and on some features of his contrasting, 'integrationalist', perspective. For Harris the two interrelated assumptions of the contemporary language myth are that language is telementational in function (that words convey speaker A's thoughts, along the linguistic channel, to hearer B), and that this telementation is guaranteed by the fact that a language is a fixed code (the thoughts in the various heads of members of a language community are firmly linked to the verbal symbols in use, thanks to a fixed, collective code). Such a scenario of determinate telementation has been instrumental to the spread of the idea that human linguistic activity is machine-like, made possible by complex cerebral mechanisms, and eventually open to mechanical replication, when sufficiently intelligent computers are

7

designed. Such assumptions, however, run counter to the whole purpose of language and our everyday experience of its situated unpredictability. Over against bi-planar decontextualizations and mechanicalities, Harris insists upon the routine unexpectedness of language use, its everyday creativity (not the impoverished sense of creativity – rule-bound rearrangements of predetermined units – allowed in standard approaches), and the cotemporal integratedness of verbal and non-verbal activity. Some representative extracts from Harris (1981) are offered below:

> The basic principle which an integrational linguistics will be concerned to give adequate expression to is that language is continuously created by the interaction of individuals in specific communication situations. It is this interaction which confers relevance upon the participants' past experience with words; and not, as orthodox linguistics would have us believe, past experience (that is to say, mastery of 'the language') which determines the communicational possibilities of their present interaction. (Harris 1981: 167)

> The central indeterminacy of all communication is indeterminacy of what is meant. . . . Insofar as what is meant is determinate, it can be only a provisional determinacy, relativised to a particular interactional situation. (167)

> If language is a game at all, it is a game we mostly make up as we go along. It is a communication game in which there is no referee, and the only rule that cannot be bent says that players shall improvise as best they can. . . . An integrational linguistics would be concerned with the analysis of this improvisation as a function, simultaneously, of relevant past experience and a current communication situation. It would, however, give priority to the latter. . . . What is important from an integrational perspective is not so much the fund of past linguistic experience as the individual's adaptive use of it to meet the communication requirements of the present. (187)

The limitations of stylistic theory predicated upon a conception of language as determinate telementation are amply exposed in Taylor (1980). There it is persuasively argued that the entire enterprise of structural stylistics, from Bally onwards, has been built on the flimsy foundations of bi-planar linguistics, and has accordingly been doomed to repeat the contradictions and arbitrary analytical moves first perpetrated by Bally. In a thorough critical review of work in structural stylistics from Bally through Jakobson and Riffaterre to the generativist stylisticians, Taylor concludes: 'The guiding principle throughout the development of structural stylistics has been linguistic reductionism. This principle holds that the effects produced in verbal communication have their causal source in observable features of the expression-plane' (T. Taylor 1980: 104). Furthermore, Taylor notes, these produced stylistic effects are claimed to be shared uniformly by all readers:

> The assumption that stylistic content is inter-subjective has surfaced in every new specification. This is the assumption that a message communicates the same content to each of its addressees. The content actually *belongs* to the message. . . . Were this not to be true – so the argument goes – there would be no sense in speaking of a message *communicating* at all. (104–5; original emphases)

Taylor charts the failures of successive models to specify these proposed stylistic effects, arguing that, ignoring the disabling theoretical assumptions of bi-planar identical telementation which undermined their work from the outset, each theoretician in turn has claimed some sort of privileged access to unobservable mental events. In practice, such theorists were simply developing new ways of talking about mental experience, rather than properly characterizing mental experience:

> The result is a rather curious cause–effect study where the cause is supposed to be observable, but the identification of the effect remains a question of guesswork, tradition, and some rather autocratic theory-making. The empirical study of how language 'gives' us what we 'get' in communication continues to be frustrated by the impossibility of analysing just what it is we all do indeed 'get'. (106)

Taylor urges that stylisticians – and linguisticians – adopt a new concept of communication, which would hold that in our perception and interpretation of speech events we are, individually, 'heavily influenced by situational, experiential, emotional, and social factors' (107).

A theme of such critiques of the fixed-code telementational orthodoxy in linguistic theorizing is that all models which claim to identify and predict fixed correlations between form and meaning in language

9

behaviour tend towards error. We have no independent grounds for predicting meanings: these are always, from an integrationalist perspective, context-bound, individual-bound, and provisional. Analysts may therefore need to be content with reporting and understanding (apparent) uses. Relatedly, any stylistic theory of reading is doomed if it claims to capture, prescribe, or predict on the basis of what a particular stylistician 'does and thinks'. (The latter formulation echoes Sapir's succinct early definition of culture as what a society does and thinks, and seeks to emphasize that stylistics itself is a cultural activity and a culture-bound practice.) A stylistics model is a way of reading, a particular stylistician's preferred way of reading, and is as partial or contingent as any written grammar or dictionary. The latter, like objectivist stylistics, tend to invoke the protection and authority of 'impartial description' and 'educated usage'; but they are ultimately shaped by particular individuals and particular interests.

With those preliminary orientations in view, what is meant by 'a stylistic reading of *Go Down, Moses*'? What is the status of this process and product; and what might be the justification – linguistic or literary? To the extent that these questions are premised on a view of linguistics as a scientific study of a fixed bi-planar structural system, and on the received orthodoxy of literary criticism that it is the sensitive open-minded pursuit of *the* richest interpretation of the work as well-wrought icon of significations (an interpretation which is somehow the inalienable property of the text rather than of the reader), the questions may be misleading. Conventional – prevailing – linguistics and criticism have both miscast the relations between the individual and the community. Linguistics has assumed that meanings and interpretations are or can be shared, just as words seem to be. And professional criticism, while paying lip-service to the facts of private individual reading and interpretation, typically proceeds – through teaching, examinations, and publishing – to disallow much of the rich variety of proffered readings, to foster in readers a self-censorship of the 'eccentric' reading, and to privilege one (perhaps two or three, if it's a classic text) allegedly rich and widely accepted interpretation. Both enterprises suppress the active role of the individual addressee in verbal communication. A stylistics that does not face and challenge these facts about the disciplines which spawned it will simply be furnishing orthodox critical practice with another instrument (linguistics) with which to enforce its authoritarian and repressive readings of literature.

10

So as to resist both the objectivist and fixed-code tendencies of linguistic analysis and the discounting of variant interpretation practised by traditional criticism, I propose that stylistics be viewed as a way rather than a method – a confessedly partial or oriented act of intervention, a reading which is strategic, as all readings necessarily are. The attraction of the 'way' of stylistics lies in its attempt at public-ness, even as it acknowledges private-ness, unpredictability. If that is an unhappy compromise, it is not easy – from this perspective – to conceive of a happier one or a less compromised happiness. If we reject the privileging of undecidability of the wilder deconstructionists (Derrida himself seems not to be of their number), engaged in their private revels of pure textuality, we must inevitably grapple with (though we may avoid succumbing to) what Norris (1982: 113) has called 'the normative constraints of effective communication'. Be she never so radical in her reading, the critic's published interpretation of a text is necessarily norm-shaping, norm-creating. The acts of publication, inviting readers to read your views, entail struggling to compel or persuade readers to privilege your reading of a work over theirs – or at least to engage with your reading and (too often) submit to it through exhaustion, inertia, pressure of other demands. Hence the professionals' double-bind: damned if they do not publish, by effecting little intervention in their intellectual communities (to say nothing of the pressure to publish or cease to be professionally engaged), they are damned if they do publish, vulnerable to the complaint that their writing is authoritarian and prescriptive, coercive of readers and students.

In the circumstances, what is essential is a renewed self-critical awareness of the provisionality of one's reading, of the roots of description in rhetorical persuasion, and of the heterogeneity of cultural myths and tastes that contribute to the constitution of 'the literary' and the academic discipline of literature. Those cultural myths and tastes should not be characterized as arbitrary in the sense of random or beyond explanation (in the way that the arbitrary matching of the utterance of the sounds in [dag], in American English, with the concept 'dog', is beyond explanation). Rather they are undoubtedly motivated, but by a background of contingent circumstances rather than logical factors or timeless essentials of the human condition. Renewed awareness of the provisionality of interpretations, held up – but also held, trapped – in a complex net of contingently motivated assumptions and discriminations, should

bring with it a renewed recognition that behind the bland nominalization 'the literary profession', a term without a referent, stands the
reality of a process, an activity maintained in innumerable ways
around the world: professing literature.

A stylistic reading is, in part, an artefact shaped by the adopted
model and theory; but there is no alternative to this. There is no
absolute or essential reading of *Go Down, Moses*, since there are no
absolute context-free models or theories. Interpretation and persuasion are always at work. Paul B. Armstrong has put the case with
admirable succinctness:

> The presuppositions of any interpretive method are both enabling
> and limiting. They give us a vantage point from which to construe
> the work – a specific place of observation, without which knowing
> would be impossible. They also furnish a set of expectations with
> which to pose questions to a work that would otherwise remain
> silent, and they provide guidance and inspiration as we begin to
> make guesses. But presuppositions are at the same time limiting
> because in opening up a work in a particular way they close off
> other potential modes of access. Every interpretive approach re-
> veals something only by disguising something else that a competing
> method with different assumptions might disclose. (Armstrong
> 1983: 343)

Interestingly, both Fish (1980) and Armstrong (the latter explicitly
following C. S. Peirce) appeal to the notion of the 'interpretive
community' and communal agreement, as a ground for justifying
continued adherence to particular interpretative presuppositions.
For Fish, discussed more fully in the next section, interpretations
derive from, and are validated and sustained by, particular communities of interpreters: groups of indefinite extent from whom
derives and in whom resides the authority (provisional, local, com-
munity-bound) for such readings. That, says Fish, is all the authority
ye have or need to have.

This clearly rejects one dominant set of myths in traditional
western modes of literature study, namely that authorial intentions
are crucial, the major goal of study, and that there is an ideal, 'full'
reading of any text, like a Platonic form, in relation to which the
dissonant versions of contending critics are only approximations.
But the alternative position Fish sketches (Fish 1980) is in need of
much more presentation and critique. It is never made clear just what

12

these 'interpretive communities' are, where they are, how they are constituted, influenced, and changed. If one thinks of groups in the world to which one might readily attach the label 'community' – the community of Latter-Day Saints, Bristol's West Indian community, the European Economic Community – each such grouping is bound together, in the public imagination, by nominal adherence to a public and retrievable set of shared commitments, practices, and experiences. The world at large is well aware that these communities exist in some sense, and is aware that members of such communities manifest (freely or under duress) a preference for certain values or practices rather than others. Consequently, erstwhile members of these communities can opt out, explicitly and publicly withdraw from such affiliations, and the communities themselves may dissolve or divide under the pressure of conflicting interests: class, gender, nationality, and so on. Whether Fish's 'interpretive communities' exist at all, simply in the sense that, by standards of public accounting, the 'Bristol West Indian community' may be said to exist, remains to be demonstrated. There are perspectives from sociolinguistics, social theory, and cultural criticism that may be helpful here, including the following: Goffman (1971, 1981), Halliday (1978), Berger and Luckmann (1967), Said (1982), Foucault (1972), Giddens (1979), and Anderson (1983).

Those sceptical of Fish's notions that the authority of interpretations rests with communities and that interpretation is all often ask what these acts of interpreting are interpretations *of*. For those wedded to a goal of comprehensive description of the 'interpretative competence' of an interpretative community, there is the awful prospect of an infinite regress (the loadedness of the word 'regress' here should not be ignored), of reading as entering the abyss. Once a belief is unpicked, its interpretative roots specified (to the extent that this is possible), it ceases to be the *fons et origo* of one's interpretative practices – those identified roots now are, instead. In the view of Knapp and Michaels (1982) this points to the irrelevance of theory to practice; for practice is guided by true belief, and that, they argue, cannot be held and unpicked at the same time. Similarly, Armstrong (1983: 348) has written, probably with intentional understatement: 'There is something a priori about accepting any set of presuppositions as our hermeneutic point of departure.' Countering Knapp and Michaels, Walter Davis (1984) has argued that a degree of reflexive critique of one's interpretative groundings is both possible

13

and relevant. One wonders if the dispute does not hinge on what is felt to be useful and relevant critique: while, with Knapp and Michaels, we might accept that we cannot 'do' critical interpretation and simultaneously reflect on its grounds, yet, with Davis, we might hold that a subsequent interrogation of the principles, rationales, and strategies we appeared to be guided by in our critical practice is possible, and that such a diachronic perspective is useful, in that we learn the logic of the lessons of our past interpretative practice.

What, then, of stylistics, and its interpretative foundations in language description? Cannot language description, like any other descriptive-cum-interpretative base, be unpicked, analysed, dissolved? In principle, yes; but not in practice, if we continue to want to see poems as a public discourse that can be in some sense and to some degree shared by diverse readers. The pull of convention, collectivity, normativity, social cohesion, and accommodation interacts dialectically with individualism and consciousness of self.

LITERARY LINGUISTICS AND ITS CRITICS

Literary linguistics, or linguistic criticism – the gathering of linguistic information about a literary text, and the use of that information in critical interpretation of the text – has aims and practices related to those of many stylisticians. But it is to be contrasted with some of the stylistics of the 1960s, and Jakobsonian poetics, in the relative modesty of its programme and expectations. The weaknesses of earlier versions of stylistics have been amply noted in recent years (e.g. in Fowler 1975 and 1979). What is newly clear is that close study of the language features of a text may often be valuable to the literary critic, but that such study can never supplant interpretation and criticism more broadly conceived (not least because stylistics itself entails various interpretative and critical assumptions, which too often pass unnoted). In this study I want to demonstrate in addition that familiar procedures such as simple frequency counts, comparisons with norms (chiefly those derived from the text's own 'economy'), and so on are also of value, so long as those norms are not canonized as absolutes, and so long as the linguistic statistician remains mindful of all the contextual variations and influences affecting the textual form. Earlier studies that might be claimed to lie within such a tradition include Spitzer (1948), Halliday (1964, 1971), and Bronzwaer (1970).

14

During the past twenty years, in the field of linguistics applied to literature, a story of frustration seems to have predominated, a showing and telling of what stylistics cannot do. In the more recent past the story has seemed in danger of final resolution, with stylisticians caught helplessly on the Fish 'hook' – the accounts, reprinted in Fish (1980), of how more-objective-than-thou stylisticians have traded shamelessly on unexamined and indefensible assumptions, assumptions without which the attractions of stylistics are, to say the least, considerably diminished.

In 'What is stylistics and why are they saying such terrible things about it?' Fish criticizes the work of Milic (1967), Ohmann (1971, 1972), and Thorne (1965, 1970) for its fondness for mentalist and interpretative leaps. Transformational grammar, Fish argues, is particularly conducive of bad stylistics: 'For since its formations operate independently of semantic and psychological processes (are neutral between production and reception) they can be assigned any semantic or psychological value one may wish them to carry' (Fish 1980: 77). He sees no comfort in contextualization: that way leads only to a geometric expansion of rules to the point of chaos. He turns to Halliday's influential article on transitivity and agency in the language(s) of Golding's *The Inheritors* (in Chatman 1971) to argue that in Halliday, just as in Milic and others, there are the same unproven assumptions that 'syntactic preferences correlate with habits of meaning' (Fish 1980: 82) and that the yoking of grammar to interpretation is not arbitrary. By way of refutation of these allegedly suspect moves, Fish suggests that, instead of what he sees as Halliday's Darwinian interpretation of the supplanting of the primitive people by the more sophisticated tribe within the novel, there could be an Edenic view of the innocent non-manipulative state of the former group.

To this, however, one might assent enthusiastically, arguing that both interpretations are supported by the grammatical contrasts Halliday notes. By prevailing conventions and community preference, the potential infinity of possible interpretations is discounted by most readers, constrained by a desire for sharedness of literary experience. With that constraint at work, along with many other socially sustained conventions and evaluations, certain interpretations may, with or without dialectical negotiation, be arrived at and sanctioned by a particular community occupying a particular sociohistorical position. In the western liberal-humanist academic communities to which Fish and Halliday both belong, the Edenic and Darwinian 'approaches' to *The Inheritors* are elements in the two major perspectives on this novel. Literary linguistics does not adopt the assumption that *the* meaning is in the syntax, as Fish portrays it as doing, but rather makes the assumption that syntactic (and lexical) characteristics (a less ambiguous term than 'preferences') themselves often carry meanings. And the rationale for these meanings can often be corroborated independently. Fish's general case, however, against any totalizing stylistic account or characterization of a text remains persuasive; and he rightly emphasizes that different contexts yield different meanings.

One wonders, however, whether Fish would still take the sceptical line concerning stylistics that he formerly adopted towards Halliday and others. More recent writings point to his conceding that stylistics, like any other constraining set of interpretative strategies, proceeds on assumptions that are not merely unproven but unprovable. Unless one adopts the early Chomskyan view that syntax is independent of meaning, autonomous of semantics, there is nothing to stop the analyst assuming that variations in syntax, like variations in lexis or pronunciation or clothes, may convey an intended meaning from an addresser to an addressee. I doubt that Fish would any longer question this. But what he might and I must question is whether a particular syntactic variation, in general or on a particular occasion, will necessarily convey an identical import to all readers. If we reject the identical-import assumption, then the interpretative or explanatory power of syntactic stylistics seems to be nil. There is some restoration of power, however, if, maintaining our distrust of the facile reductivism of the identical-import assumption, we yet counterpose to it the recognition that syntax like lexis is a part of a necessarily public enterprise, language, necessarily sustained by means of habitual and conventional imports for its syntax, lexis, and so on.

Fish's view is that the reader is always 'already oriented in the direction of specific concerns and . . . expectations': in a character-istically bald assertion of the reader's alleged omnipotence, and temporarily blind to the dialectical practice in which the reader's assumptions and those of the text interact, he declares that the reader manipulates the text, and never the reverse. With such premises, the need for an 'affective stylistics' specifying the reader's assumptions, expectations, and so on, in the face of any particular word or verbal pattern, is quite clear.

16

But even this affective-stylistic model carries with it its own arbitrarily privileged method and presuppositions, as Fish lucidly exposes in his book, *Is There a Text in this Class?: The Authority of Interpretive Communities* (1980). By gathering together, in sequence, his major articles over the previous ten years, the book presents a clear picture of Fish's marked shift in critical emphasis away from the 'self-sufficient' text, in favour of the reader's experience of the text, as a developing, temporally extended process of actualizing meanings. It is also a shift away from treating the reader as mere instrument, a key for unlocking text-bound meanings, towards revaluing that reader as in dynamic relation to the text, bringing to it his/her own expectations, which in turn enter into the reader's construction of text-related meanings. Fish's reader is thus engaged, active, and responsible.

Much of this is most sharply set forth in the introduction to the book. Here Fish grapples again with formalism, concluding that a critic's interpretative principles (e.g. that readers are performers of interpretation) are too often self-fulfilling prophecies, inducing a particular focus on certain formal features which can then, by a sleight of hand, be named as the 'true and initial' source of the produced interpretation. It is interpretative strategies which give texts their shape, but such strategies are not individual (as might lead to an anarchic pluralism of readings) but 'community property' (1980: 14). They are sustained or authorized by 'interpretive communities', made up of 'those who share interpretive strategies not for reading but for writing texts, for constituting their properties' (1980: 14). Reader-response criticism itself, then, is more accurately a rewriting (by readers) of texts, on the basis of a shared interpretative orientation. Steven Mailloux articulates the shift in his own thinking, as well as that of Fish, from an 'innocent' reader-response criticism to an 'aware' focus on interpretation, when he summarizes thus:

> It is true that reader-response criticism claims to approximate closely the content of reading experiences that are always assumed to pre-exist the critical performance. But what in fact takes place is quite different: the critical performance fills those reading experiences with its own interpretive moves. Like all critical approaches, reader-response criticism is a set of interpretive conventions that constitutes what it claims to describe. (Mailloux 1979: 107)

Although Fish does not state this explicitly, his thesis appears to be analogous to one model of how a natural language works. All competent users of a language, it is often thought, share a remarkably complex interrelated and interdependent set of interpretative conventions for expressing and constituting their shared world (not truly a code, since there is no 'message' prior to this 'code'). This is the grammar that no grammar or linguistics book has ever adequately captured. So far so good, but the picture is perhaps more complicated than it has been painted to be by Fish and others. For there is plenty of evidence to call into question both the idea of language communities as discrete, sharply bounded groups, and the idea that competence is 'full' and largely guided by innate predispositions. Competence in a language, in actuality, is often noticeably differential, subject to various constraints on its full acquisition; and the assumption that there is an evident and necessary arrival at shared usage, conventionally agreed patterns of interpretation and signification, all by some marvellously egalitarian process of induction, also seems far from the truth. As in life, so in language in general, so also in the language activity of literary criticism in particular, we have differential access to the formulation and invocation of interpretative strategies.

What Fish's *Is There a Text in this Class?* signally lacks is the extended discussion of the nature of interpretative communities which his theory requires. Members of the same community will necessarily maintain stability of interpretations 'because they will see (and by seeing, make) everything in relation to that community's assumed purposes and goals' (1980: 15). There is not so much an individualized literary competence (as in Culler 1975) as a normative perspective and a shared, communal competence. The term 'community' is an attractive one, connoting a cohesive, caring fraternity of equals. But is it an accurate description of the sort of group which confirms and sustains any critical reading? More specifically, do all communities merit approval (presumably not), and how do they change or become changed? Or would the theory claim that communities do not change, rather that new communities come into existence? The same difficulty emerges here as in the Saussurean idealized community sharing a common *langue*: no account is advanced as to how the evident changes in community and in *langue* actually occur – a silence that fosters the suspicion that any such accounting would expose the inadequacy of the prior conceptualizations of *langue* and community. We need much more information about the several roles played by readers, authors, and texts in the shaping and changing of interpretative communities. It seems too naïve to suppose that all community members are equally free to lobby for revisions in interpretations, since there is ample evidence that hierarchies of power, influence, patronage, intelligence, access to the channels of dissemination of views, and adeptness at and interest in persuasion exist. It is easier to rehearse such general observations than to assess in detail the different factors involved, but a necessary beginning is an acknowledgement that diverse and opposed interests are involved, that criticism involves intellectual resistance and struggle. The objection to Fish that comes from Cain (1981: 86) is along such lines: 'His theory lacks a politically charged vocabulary, which would reveal "interpretation" to be a system of difficult, even violent, exchanges, with forced entrances of new communities and exclusions of old ones.' The analysis might well benefit from an orientation which was receptive to recent arguments in sociology for a 'conflict methodology'. On the other hand perhaps too much is made of the idea of interpretative conflict amounting to 'violent exchange'. Personalities apart, interpretations themselves and the whole tenor of literary discourse seem far more typically characterized by a spirit of polite and co-operative negotiation.

In short, Fish's book has been an invaluable corrective to the objectivist mentalist tendencies that stylistics had long nurtured (since Bally), tendencies which came to maturity in work of the 1960s. Introducing the second of the book's two chapters on stylistics, Fish writes: 'Here I assert that the act of description is itself an interpretation and that stylistics is never even within hailing distance of a fact that has been independently (that is, objectively) specified.' Most stylisticians, it seems, are now quite prepared to renounce claims to any such 'objective specification of facts', so that the impact of the reproof is considerably reduced. However, looking again at Fish's formulation, it may be worth reflecting upon whether, as Fish assumes, *independent* specification and *objective* specification amount to the same thing. For a conception of stylistics such as my own does persist in the fond hope that independent specification of linguistic forms and communicative functions, as suggested (certainly not ordained) by preferred, habitual, and conventional usage, is some guide to both formulaic conformity and creative departure in verbal art. As soon as the word 'independently' is used, we must ask, 'independently of what?', since the claim of independence is necessarily made in relation to certain interests or factors rather than others, these others often effecting veiled determinations of description. In the case of stylistics, the *dependence* on the analyst's linguistic descriptive system, and the dependence of this upon the analyst's understanding of what a language is and does, are the declared, public, and – perhaps – corrigible groundings.

From his literary perspective Fish attacks the 'strong theory' stylistics of Jakobson, Riffaterre, and Ohmann which Taylor (1980) has challenged from a linguistic one. One objection is to various claims that the phonology of particular poems is mimetic of their sense – stylistic games which are said to be just too easy to play. For such passages alone the book should be recommended reading for anyone contemplating linguistic study of literary texts. Fish rightly argues that the stylistician's focus on a particular phonological or syntactical pattern in a text is itself an interpretative act. As I hope to have suggested, this in itself does not constitute an overwhelming argument to stop doing stylistics unless (1) that interpretative act is shown to be incoherent or ill grounded, or (2) more coherent interpretative acts are presented, and preferably both.

No such moves are made in the book under discussion. We are reminded that any description we offer is an imposed interpretation, that responses are occasioned by interpretative frameworks which themselves are products, not 'real', objective *ur*-sources, because there are no such things. No more than Archimedes can we find one firm spot on which to stand so as to move the earth. To the troubled question 'What, then, is interpretation an interpretation of?' Fish cheerfully assures us we cannot finally know the answer: we must (will, inevitably) carry on, not quite as before, more aware that we are necessarily interpreting interpreting.

The question of interpretative groundings that Fish raises is also approached by Dillon, from a Whorfian perspective. Dillon argues that stylisticians make a claim which roughly parallels a Whorfian one, namely that 'analyzing the structure of a literary work can yield insight into the way the work conceptualizes experience (or "the world of the poem")' (Dillon 1982: 73). The crucial issue in such a claim, he notes, concerns what kind of knowledge such formal analysis is taken to yield. The first thing Dillon emphasizes is that neither Whorfianism nor stylistics is so mechanical or arbitrary a procedure as Fish pretends. All such analysts are intent on grasping a 'fashion of speaking' (of a culture, or an author), the linguistic patterning when viewed as comprehensively as possible, no matter how atomic the intermediate stages of analysis – the focusing on forms and elements – may appear. Intrinsic to this effort of generalization will be varying conclusions due to varying interpretative assumptions:

> The characterization of the unique fashion of speaking is as much a product of the interpreter's art as the characterization of the culture's world view. This art in both instances is largely intuitive and cannot be reduced to a method. (1982: 74)

Dillon rightly dismisses the idea that stylistics can be a discovery procedure for finding interpretations or a means of validating an interpretation, and suggests that such imagined scientific purposes – discovery, validation – should not be applied to this activity.

> One engages in formal analysis to specify and articulate one's own response and perhaps to share it with others. . . . The proper response to a successful piece of stylistic analysis would be 'I see' and not 'You've proved your point'. (1982: 75)

Ironically, by contrast with this innocent reliance on the interpreter's touch, there is much shrewd calculation, even method, in Fish's version of the business of criticism. That business is 'to establish by political and persuasive means . . . the set of interpretive assumptions from the vantage of which the evidence (and the facts and the intentions and everything else) will hereafter be specifiable' (Fish 1980: 16). Again, it is striking that Fish writes of a 'vantage', that Armstrong – in the passage I quoted on p. 12 – writes of an interpretative 'vantage point', and that others speak of a *point d'appui*: all recognize that the given perspective or frame is both advantageous and a taking advantage. Determining our interpretative codes seems to be the project Culler has in mind when he writes of a 'systematic poetics' or 'a semiotics of reading' (Culler 1981). Such a semiotics of reading has not emerged, he complains, because time and time again, from Frye to Mailloux, writers have slipped – or retreated – from reading theory back to traditional interpretative criticism (see also the valuable recent survey of reader-response criticism and theory in Freund 1987). The former is descriptive and systematic, the latter attempts to adjudicate and persuade. Of course Fish would be eager to remind those who claim such a distinction that every description is an interpretative strategy of persuasion. However, as I have tried to argue earlier, that game is just too easy to play. It is keeping the

21

politics of interpretation at a removed level where, in the words of Mitchell, 'the infinite regress of understanding can be contemplated the way abysses usually are – as thrilling landscapes of the sublime' (1982: vi). It is itself the adoption of a particular interpretative strategy, in which a strictly limited reflexivity and self-criticism are adduced.

If Fish has by and large declined to explore the groundings we adduce from our interpretative codes, many others, it should be emphasized, have begun that work, from a perspective that is semiotic in a broad sense. Emphases vary greatly, but contributions that range from the cultural semiotics of Barthes and Eco, through the work of Culler, Mailloux, Foucault, and Lotman, and, from a linguistic perspective, Halliday, may be noted. Particularly innovative has been feminist criticism and its uncovering of interpretative groundings (see, for example, Gilbert and Gubar 1979; Moi 1985; Modleski 1982).

However, Fish remains one of his own most responsive readers, and he continues to revise the text of his own critical theory. In the course of a discussion of continuities in the thinking of J. L. Austin and Derrida, he has emphasized the consequences of a politics of interpretation, a semiotics of reading, not merely for selected seventeenth-century literary texts but also for 'pieces of the world':

> Communications of every kind are characterized by exactly the same conditions – the necessity of interpretive work, the unavoidability of perspective, and the construction by acts of interpretation of that which supposedly grounds interpretation, intention, characters, and pieces of the world. (Fish 1982: 700)

His most comprehensive recent reflections on many of the issues involved come in an essay entitled simply 'Consequences' (Fish 1985), where he reiterates the pragmatist point that only belief, and not theory, underwrites action and critical practice. By theory, he is concerned to emphasize, he means any general hermeneutics – such as Chomskyan linguistic theory – aimed at an invariant, context-free system (e.g. of rules) that will mechanically or algorithmically characterize linguistic competence. There are many so-called theoretical exercises that are not theory in this comprehensive sense – local hermeneutics or rules of thumb, as Hirsch (1976) terms them, rather than 'rules'. Rules of thumb are context-sensitive 'insider's tips' as to how agents might proceed in their making of interpretative decisions; and contemporary stylistics and narratology, it would seem, are exemplary ragbags of such historicized rules of thumb.

While Fish's critique of stylistics is part of a wide-ranging exposé of the fallibility of interpretative groundings, the strictures of E. D. Hirsch are focused chiefly on problems in the philosophy of language, as they inform or undermine stylistics. Significantly, these two critics of certain types of stylistics are by no means in agreement with each other concerning quite fundamental critical and theoretical issues. In *The Aims of Interpretation* Hirsch offers a defence of synonymity, and a concomitant attack on what he sees as a basic assumption of stylistics, that 'a difference in linguistic form compels a difference in meaning' (Hirsch 1976: 50). He adds: 'The object of my attack is simply the false methodological optimism that seeks in stylistic analysis a reliable system of interpretation' (50). As such, Hirsch's arguments against the strong form of linguistic determinism are a valuable corrective, involving some exposure of the fallacies underlying the literary doctrine of inseparability of form and content. Hirsch cites Humpty Dumpty's joust with Alice over the asserted synonymity of *glory* and *a nice knock-down argument*, and other celebrated cases, to argue for the possibility of occasional substitutability of different forms with identical meanings.

However, in rejecting the strong Whorfian hypothesis of linguistic determinism and the strong-theory stylistics of Jakobson and others, Hirsch is drawn to an equally implausible extremism of his own, a methodological pessimism where total fluidity of the relations between meanings and forms obtains. In his drive to expose the folly of absolute formalism (of a kind almost never practised today) Hirsch ascribes to stylisticians a belief not merely in the connectedness of form and meaning but in the priority of form over meaning. The stylistician is said to assert that 'form compels meaning' (1976: 10). This is a serious misrepresentation of how literary linguists think and proceed, for there are vast differences between analysing compulsions and analysing interrelations.

Hirsch is chiefly of interest for his remarks on the concept of style – a notion sufficiently intractable of definition and sufficiently variously understood as to have prompted an avoidance of its use or even of its derivatives, *stylistics* and *stylistician*, among contemporary literary linguists. Hirsch assumes that style equals meaningful form, and adds:

23

> If style . . . is *defined* as the system of linguistic traits which do participate in higher-level meanings, then the postulate that style is part of meaning becomes an empty tautology which simply states that style is part of meaning whenever it is part of meaning. One simply begs the question at issue to define style in advance as actualized meaning. (Hirsch 1976: 58)

Hirsch's question here is essentially the following: on what grounds can we identify and separate certain parts of form as participating in higher-level meanings, hence style, as distinct from other parts of form which are not meaningfully distinctive? This is the old search for principles for selecting or identifying key meaningful language traits. That debate has never satisfactorily gone beyond Spitzer's (1948) hunch-and-circle, Riffaterre's (1959, 1960) super-reader, or the informed intuitions of Ohmann and others, for reasons which the earlier discussion of the fallaciousness of bi-planar reasoning about language should have made clear. There can be no guarantee that what a particular reader 'gets out' of a text can be matched unproblematically, and without attention to the specific unique context of that reader and reading, with what linguistic forms 'put in' (T. Taylor 1980). Language behaviour is typically and intrinsically (not merely on rare occasions) too creative and innovative for literary linguistics (or any other type of linguistics) ever to be able to furnish a codebook for the definitive decipherment of discourse. If it were not thus creative, we would be revealed as mere machines designed so as to process texts, using a programme which had temporarily been mislaid. That, however, is not remotely akin to actual differing experiences of texts.

In attacking the 'false methodological optimism' of strong-theory stylistics, Hirsch is prone to an equally false methodological pessimism: 'Stylistics cannot be a reliable method of determining meaning, nor a reliable method of confirming an interpretation, but neither can any other method perform those feats' (Hirsch 1976: 72). As should become clear in succeeding chapters, the emphasis on 'reliability' or on 'method' or on 'confirmation' is not strictly appropriate to stylistics, which is better thought of as a loose confederation of interpretative strategies in pursuit of a strategic interpretation of a text. Practising stylisticians will concede Fish's point that their interpretative moves are inextricably bound up with their stylistic ones, that all stylistics is based on a set of interpretative assumptions of the value and validity of linguistic and structural description. In a sense, one person's interpretative moves are as good as the next one's. That would be sufficient defence of stylistics for some. In addition, however, it might be argued that stylistics is also attractive since its moves are relatively inspectable, and the basis of its moves, linguistic description (especially traditional, surface-, rhetoric-oriented description), is a relatively public and widely accepted characterization of a language as it is understood to operate in many domains besides the literary.

If stylistics can be a useful orientation (not truly a method) from which to approach texts, this may particularly be the case with regard to extended literary texts, like novels, which create their own context of situation, which are revised and rewritten according to various strategies (i.e. are objects of conscious composition), and where formal differences are much more consistently felt or expected (by readers) to be functional than they would be in ordinary language. To say as much is not, however, to restore the formalist illusion of a fundamental contrast between ordinary language and literary language: the contrast between literature and other discourses lies not in essential properties – and especially not in essential linguistic properties – of the texts themselves, but in the habitual and conventional differences in the ways in which readers apprehend those texts. Those texts are literary which we take to be literary – by talking about them, our readings, and the authors in certain distinctive ways (playing the language game of literary appreciation).

If we grant, with Fish and Hirsch, that literary linguistics may be a procedure for confirming interpretations or reconstructing meanings, rather than a method of constructing meanings, it may be appropriate to note the sort of achievement possible with weak-theory (or 'rule-of-thumb') stylistics in practice. One of the best examplars of this is Bronzwaer's monograph, *Tense in the Novel* (1970). I discuss this work briefly below. It is one of the studies in literary linguistics nearest my own approach in intent, expectations, and, to a degree, procedure, while having been less widely discussed than, for example, the work of Halliday, Ohmann, or Milic.

While conceding the chaotic confusion of stylistic theories current in the late 1960s, Bronzwaer retains a sense of the value of concepts such as norm, deviation, and context, all of which are central to my approach here. He recognizes, as I do, that Riffaterre fruitfully extended the concept of context in emphasizing that with regard to a literary text (particularly an extended one such as a novel or epic) context is bi-scopal: any specific stylistic device may be related both to co-textual norms and to extratextual norms or expectations. As Bronzwaer comments: 'It is no longer only an outward set of characteristics with which the text under study is compared; it is primarily an *internal* set of characteristics distinguishing a text from all other texts' (1970: 27). The authority, as it were, of such internal norms or standards is certainly one of the striking properties of literary texts, setting them apart from all other kinds of text – where any particular text is standardly treated as a token to be evaluated in the (external) context of text types. In literature, uniquely, while individual texts can be identified as tokens of culturally enshrined types in many respects, yet they retain or are granted the licence of counting as unique types in their own right. This distinction is reflected in, for example, Carter and Nash's (1983) emphasis on the relative 'sovereignty' of the literary text. This dual status of the literary text (now token of a generic type, now unique type without tokens) underlies recent observations by Birch and O'Toole concerning the touch of both genre and the individual author in the construction of style:

> Our stylistic choices . . . are partly determined by the norms of the socially appropriate genre for these functions. And yet we do recognize a personal style in texts of language as much as in the way an individual plays tennis, conducts an orchestra or orchestrates a commercial takeover. Certain tendencies occur regularly or are foregrounded deliberately so that we recognize them as a kind of 'trade mark' of the individual. Style functions, then, both to class a text among other texts – generically – and to give it an unmistakably individual flavour. (Birch and O'Toole 1988: 1)

While Bronzwaer leans towards a Riffaterrian, intratextual, analytical approach, my own will combine intratextual and extratextual study, both micro- and macro-textual norms; its findings may be more generalizable as a result. However generalizable, stylistics must defer to criticism, in Bronzwaer's view, when it comes to evaluative interpretation. He quotes Leech on this point, while stressing that the linguist and the critic are two distinct roles which may be assumed by the same person:

> The linguist is the man who identifies what features in a poem need interpretation (i.e., what features are foregrounded), and to some

extent (e.g., by specifying rules of transference) what opportunities for interpretation are available; the literary critic is the man who weighs up the different possible interpretations. (Leech 1969: 225)

The objection to this must be that linguistics is quite as oriented and evaluative as literary criticism. What should surprise us and make us suspicious is not the prospect of a single scholar filling two roles, those of linguist and critic, but the assumption that textual analysis can ever avoid incorporating, simultaneously, these two tendencies. It is only a longstanding separation of professional domains that leads us to imagine that linguistics and criticism are essentially distinct, rather than interconnected aspects of a single activity.

The core of Bronzwaer's study is an exploration of the use of preterite verbs and present-time-reference adverbs in passages of free indirect discourse. He finds these used in novels and some types of journalism where 'a change from a less subjective to a more subjective perspective' (Bronzwaer 1970: 47) is intended, and suggests that such 'involvement . . . through identification with and adopting the perspective of an "Aussagesubjekt"' (48) is a technique of empathy. He particularly examines the empathetic effects of free indirect discourse in Iris Murdoch's *The Italian Girl*.

One conclusion, implicit in Bronzwaer's work, is that different texts may use somewhat different formal and lexical means in the fashioning of free indirect discourse; and a general principle of identification is that passages of free indirect discourse contrast locally (in syntactic or lexical character) with adjacent narrative text. This hypothesis is amply tested in the course of my analysis of varying patterns of formal features of the narrative, and of narrative depictions of character, in *Go Down, Moses*. The formal regularities I examine appear correlatable with fluctuating narratorial perspective, a dramatic interplay of empathies, and ironizing 'echoic' mentions, arguably more complex and satisfying than a more mechanical narrative switching between direct speech, indirect record, and free indirect discourse. In short, a particular goal of the stylistics reported below will be the provision of specific textual evidence charting the shifting narratorial alignments with the chief characters, more subtle and fluid than canonical free indirect discourse.

But I have wider goals too: to show that a stylistics of fiction is feasible; that linguistics can be both pleasing and useful in textual study; and that linguistic analysis, in its own systematic way, can afford us glimpses at least of the depth of Faulkner's craft.

27

2

LITERARY LINGUISTICS AND CRITICAL THEORY

THEORY AND RHETORIC

This chapter attempts several distinct but related tasks. The first task is to review some recent arguments in literary-critical theory, especially as they bear on the theory and practice of stylistics. The second is to express some reservations about orthodox stylistics and its overdependence on the principles of structural linguistics. The third task is to argue that the denial of intentions and referentiality in certain forms of poetics, if maintained, will continue to leave that poetics in an absurd and trivial position. Ultimately, I want to rescue stylistics from the intellectual scrapheap, but believe this can be done only if misleading claims to its status as an autonomous, self-validating discipline are avoided.

Stylistics – or linguistic criticism, or literary linguistics – must be seen to be a way of reading (not a method), whose shaping orientation (not an exclusionary obsession) is a systematic and analytic attention to the language of the text. The usefulness of setting a boundary between linguistic and non-linguistic matters, in the study of text and discourse in particular, is doubtful. It is more relevant to emphasize that stylistics is a reading of literature that attends to the language in the process of pursuing interpretative ends and assumptions well beyond the methods of conventional stylistics. Such a coming-clean about what stylisticians have long done covertly should be embarrassing only to those who cling to the illusion of stylistics – and, more fundamentally, linguistics itself – as objective, autonomous sciences. The newer stylistics tends to dismantle the neat compartmentalizations, which are often so convenient, into different approaches to literary and discoursal study. But those 'clarificatory' dissections are equally often a misrepresentation, treating different models and emphases as though they were necessarily disjunct: there is, for example, no theoretical incompatibility between my notion of stylistics and Lacanian, Marxist, feminist, or historical criticism (no more than are these frameworks always necessarily at odds with each other).

Two relatively recent critiques of literary theory, critiques which prompt consideration of the possible relevance of such theory to stylistics, are a useful starting-point for discussion: Christopher Butler's *Interpretation, Deconstruction, and Ideology* (1984) and Terry Eagleton's *Literary Theory* (1983). Butler's guiding assumption is that, as far as a theory of interpretation is concerned, what is important and in many ways determining is 'not some notion of truth to the meaning of the text' but 'pragmatic ends'. These pragmatic ends, he argues, are those of 'competing intellectual frameworks', such as Marxism, liberalism, and moral individualism, which seek to win the allegiance of 'different interpretive communities'. At some fundamental level, he concludes, interpretations are grounded on the (provisional, shiftable) bedrock of our sets of beliefs about ourselves and the world. The role of belief is not argued for all that explicitly in Butler's book, but it seems to be the logical conclusion of his exposure of the arbitrary positions and exclusions adopted in the schools of criticism he examines. One of Butler's most telling points is that texts do not in themselves require or prescribe the interpretative moves we make on them; that rather 'the text alone under-determines its own context of interpretation'. Critical moves, it is argued, are not defensible on logical grounds or because they are required but simply because they are reasonable responses given the stimulus of various culturally favoured or salient ideological commitments.

The role of belief is more fully explored by theorists such as Stanley Fish (discussed in chapter 1) and, most interestingly, Knapp and Michaels (1982). Fish, we have seen, identifies belief as always the provisional grounding of our interpretative strategies and inclinations. However, perhaps fearful of heterodox chaos, he suggests (as Butler does) that the centripetal pull of the persuasive rhetoric of the various interpretive communities assumed to exist makes each of us members of one party or another. He also claims that unravelling or unpicking those beliefs brings no liberation from this collective subjective determinism, for henceforth some other anterior or more removed principles will be the grounds of our interpretative activity.

29

This view involves the widely applicable principle that unpicking a rationale never leads to irrationality or chaos, but only to a deeper rationale that enabled the unpicking to proceed.

Knapp and Michaels have pursued this issue less cheerfully, perhaps, confronting the readers of the journal *Critical Inquiry* with the argument that the uninspectability of interpretative groundings should lead us to turn away from theory altogether. It should be added immediately that the thrust of Knapp and Michaels's critique is not a thoroughgoing anti-intellectual nihilism. One of their arguments is rather that what masquerades as theory in our interpretative sense-making of texts and the world is better seen and studied as practice. As one might have predicted, detractors have not been slow to suggest that the very claim that theory is only disguised practice is itself a theory.

This is not the place for a full review of Knapp and Michaels's powerful and provocative argument; I shall simply note that they argue for dispensing with theory, at least as prosecuted by intentionalists like Hirsch and textualists like de Man, on the grounds that both discourse in gulfs or margins that are their own illicit creations. For Knapp and Michaels, de Man's theory rests on the false assumption that there is some gulf between language and language-harnessed-to-speech-acts, while Hirsch assumes that textual meaning and authorial intention are distinct, and treats the latter as a ground from which to work towards the former. Against Hirsch and others, they insist that textual meaning is simply the author's intended meaning, that the intentionalists' project is thus valueless (because incoherent) and irrelevant (because it has no genuine bearing on critical practice). Their elegantly argued and potentially devastating critique has not – and not surprisingly – gone unchallenged in subsequent issues of *Critical Inquiry*; but the unrepentant duo look to have had the better of the argument so far. Interestingly, at the opening of their essay Knapp and Michaels specifically mention stylistics as one of the practices they do not intend to critique (this exclusion is clarified in Fish (1985) in terms of rule-of-thumb theorizing; all three neo-pragmatists in effect view stylistics and narratology as essentially practices, not comprehensive theoretical 'explanations', more akin to rhetoric than to logic).

Knapp and Michaels are relevant here, since although they dispute the assumption that 'theoretical accounts of intention' are of any use to interpretation they do not question the necessary principle of intentionality *per se*. On the contrary, they would not dissent from this formulation by Fish:

> One cannot read *or* reread independently of intention, independently, that is, of the assumption that one is dealing with marks or sounds produced by an intentional being, a being situated in some enterprise in relation to which he has purpose or a point of view. This is not an assumption that one adds to an already construed sense in order to stabilize it but an assumption without which the construing of sense could not occur. . . . Intention like anything else is an interpretative act; that is, it must be construed. (Fish 1982: 205)

The important question of intentionality will be returned to. It is perhaps what prompts Butler to hint at the desirability of a shift from Derrida to Foucault, that is, towards a historically contextualized rereading; for their part, Knapp and Michaels might be seen as urging a parallel shift from Saussure to Peirce, that is, from an orientation that treats semiotics as uniform and arbitrary to one that sees it as variant and pragmatically motivated.

It is very probable that such a conclusion is acceptable to Terry Eagleton, whose *Literary Theory* (1983) upbraids much contemporary theorizing for its flight from ideology, politics, and history, even as it blindly reinforces a reactionary ideology, politics, and history. Eagleton's view is that there can be no *intrinsic* definition of Literature, no specification of what it is and what it is not that is not itself culturally grounded. Unlike most texts in that it lacks an easily specified context of situation, an explicit conventional use (like hotel brochures, insurance agreements, and medical reports), Literature can only be delimited, controversially, by some extrinsic definition. One such characterization of what currently counts as Literature might be the following: 'Literature comprises those context-detached texts that the middle classes feel ought to be read, and even re-read.'

Eagleton's argument that Literature is an ideological construct rather than an ontological essence is also an important strategic move. Literature (capitalized) is different from and narrower than literature, and the major task becomes that of understanding how we read what we read, why we read just these texts, and why we read just these texts in just these ways. These are at once more fundamental and more answerable questions, since they are explicitly geared to the concrete experience of actual readers and communities, than the impossible ones that try to specify the essences of literature and literariness.

Understanding how we read what we read – whether Shakespeare or a zoology textbook – involves exploring the rhetoric of discursive practices: 'reading . . . to see how (the) discourse is structured and organized, and examining what kind of effects these forms and devices produce in particular readers in actual situations' (Eagleton 1983: 205). Arguing for rhetoric in preference to the 'suburban moral ideology' of liberal humanism and the sterile and culpable claims of clinical detachment trumpeted by formalism, Eagleton reminds us that, in its major phase,

> [Rhetoric] saw speaking and writing not merely as textual objects, to be aesthetically contemplated or endlessly deconstructed, but as forms of *activity* inseparable from the wider social relations between writers and readers, orators and audiences, and as largely unintelligible outside the social purposes and conditions in which they were embedded. (1983: 206)

Although Eagleton's proposal is a revaluation (to use a Leavisite word) of an ancient and allegedly neglected activity, it is at least arguable that his rhetoric or discourse theory has many similarities with what I take to be the proper business of literary linguistics. He is quick to add that his rhetoric would draw on formalism, structuralism, reception theory, deconstruction, psychoanalytic theory, and liberal humanism, as appropriate, but always with a view to how they clarify the *effects* of discourses on particular positioned readers, caught in multiple webs of power and desire.

The congruence of this project with that of literary linguistics may be clearer if it is acknowledged that there may be different kinds of effects: immediate, removed, particular, or general. These effects are not examined merely because they are there, however, but because, for a socialist like Eagleton, it is important to see how they fail or succeed in playing a part to bring about a transformation of a divided society and an exploitative social order. (While the neo-pragmatists insist that theory has no consequences, the consequences and effects of practices – stylistics, criticism, 'reading' – are everywhere.) This is the ultimate rationale for his 'discourse theory' or 'cultural studies', and it is one that hardly differs in kind from those of all interpretative frameworks. While he is critical of the liberal-humanist approach, with its implicit assumption that – roughly – literature study makes you a better person, the socialist position is but an alternative and more dramatic specification of betterment. As Butler argues, every ideological position, including the deconstructive one, carries an implicit claim of superiority of insight afforded by its way of interpreting text and world. Different frameworks privilege different issues as their priority, as the focus of their enhanced knowledge: class (Marxist criticism), gender (feminist criticism), or the moral consciousness of the individual (liberal-humanist criticism).

Where others have written of belief, Eagleton talks of politics, but it amounts to the same thing, and, one may be beginning to fear, uneasily, this brings us to the same impasse: which framework is the 'correct' one, do we choose impartially, can we change our framework, and how?

> There is no way of settling the question of which politics is preferable in literary critical terms. You simply have to argue about politics. It is not a question of debating whether 'literature' should be related to 'history' or not: it is a question of different readings of history itself. (Eagleton 1983: 209)

Once again, the extrinsic referential move, which takes us far from speechless veneration of the verbal icon, is necessary, inescapable, already made. However, to Eagleton's reminder that 'it is a question of different readings of history itself' it might be added that the readings we so formulate are or can be graced with reason and compassion. Eagleton would be the first to acknowledge that readings of history and political assessments are complex and uncertain phenomena; the same cannot always be said for the neo-pragmatists. Fish, especially, often seems to conceive belief as certain, a definite, subject-oriented grounding (a grounding until it is theorized and understood, in terms of some comprehending belief); here belief is never 'half-belief', intermittent, varying in strength. As a result, interpretative conformity to what particular beliefs sanction seems too mechanical, leading Norris to conclude, in a useful essay on new pragmatism and critical legal studies, that 'the pragmatist argues away the very grounds for seeking an informed, rational consensus on . . . any . . . topic of debate' (Norris 1988: 147).

The fear of interpretative impasse can and should be allayed. The briefest self-critical reflections should remind us that, in fact, over time, we do quite naturally (but perhaps not effortlessly) come to adjust and change our judgements of different frameworks: we change or modify our reading frames as and because our politics change, just as, imperceptibly but increasingly visibly, languages change. It is common to suggest that political consciousness changes by a means of a process of dialectical and continuous revision of postions; and this image seems to have been carried over into deconstruction, where there is much emphasis on the unending oscillation of readings, the next unravelling the former.

While this may not be wrong, it perhaps promotes an inaccurate picture of giddy progress, where every revision is a radical reformulation. An alternative and more plausible picture emerges when due emphasis is given to the centrality of creative sense-making in our language behaviour – when we are seen as rational individuals reconciling different interests in particular circumstances. Here lie the seeds of a response to the 'impasse' concern for impartial evaluation of approaches. For, just as Harris reminds us that the language-bound theorist 'has ultimately no leverage to bring to bear on understanding language other than such leverage as can be exerted from the *terra firma* of his own linguistic experiences' (Harris 1981: 204), so we may suggest that our political and interpretative assumptions and practices are quite locally rooted in our own developing (and so changing) experience.

REFERENTIALITY

One consequence of local rootedness is contact with local dirt. It is widely accepted that there is no wholly innocent 'newcomer' to criticism; whatever the level, no 'beginning student' is a classless, sexless, tasteless, and colourless *tabula rasa*, but an already contaminated, prejudiced, purposeful harbinger of ideological commitments. Yet these very facts have been exploited by the 'autonomous text' critics for their own purposes. Yes, they have enthusiastically agreed, the world is sordid and we readers are sordid, but the truly artistic text achieves an immaculate transcendence, is incorruptible. It speaks to an ideal order of things – there lies its only referentiality – not to the common order already too much with us.

And they may insist on the strict irrelevance and inconsequentiality of literature to concrete history by pointing to its apparently negligible 'civilizing influences' on readers of whatever persuasion. We have all read the propaganda from various critical camps (from Arnold to Leavis to Belsey) proclaiming the egalitarian revolution in thought and human relations, the enlarged personal and social sensibility prompting moral uplift, and so on, but the world of actuality often seems strangely impervious to these manifestos. Sometimes it's hard to see particular describable consequences at all.

Since, with Eagleton, I have argued that literature is a notional category for a kind of writing that defies an easy and direct assignment of its use and context of situation, it would not now be appropriate to counter this telling point with any vulgar principle of direct application. Dickens's novels are not necessarily to be read as a policy document or veiled pamphlet about the workings of the nineteenth-century Poor Laws. Arguments over 'errors of historical fact' within them, over whether such and such a law or treatment prevailed in such and such a year, thus may or may not be to the point. A principle of referentiality must simply claim that Dickens's narratives, like all others, are necessarily taken to be a plotted commentary on particular assumed topics. Readers necessarily assume references are being made, and they have to take up references. In the case of Dickens, a consequence of one frequent kind of referential uptake of his assumed topics is the view that the novels compel critical reflection on the living conditions of poor people in England at a time when nascent industrial capitalism was bringing enormous wealth to a powerful minority. The point is not that this particular referential uptake is 'correct', but that some sort of uptake is essential.

A major theoretical source of strength of the anti-referential position seems to lie in a widespread view of metaphor and the metaphoricality of literature. Literature, on this view, is metaphorical to its roots, a figurative heterocosm, where no necessary relation to 'the real world' is involved. It is entirely appropriate, then, that views of metaphor should be the first interpretation-shaping topic that Butler chooses to explore.

Following many other theorists, Butler suggests that in interpreting metaphors we look for likeness *in certain specific respects* between the figurative term or focus and its co-text. He proceeds to talk in terms of the literal and the metaphorical, using a conventional binary opposition which is perhaps inappropriate as a theoretical distinction. Literal meaning is no more exalted or intrinsic a category than the excessively authoritative and prescriptive label for the standard sense and the standard usage – the association of meanings and expressions established in the authorized dialect.

All text requires interpreting, making sense of, postulating the relevance of. The descriptive anomalies or foregroundings that constitute metaphors (as these present themselves in relation to the assumed background referential norms) simply invite further interpretative work than usual. And this interpretative work may be best thought of not as a switching back and forth between two modes, literal and metaphorical, but as a continuous and developing sense-making relative to a postulated and revisable purpose, to relevance in the given context. The inevitable consequence of the position that referentiality is plural is that so too are metaphor and anomaly. Indefinitely many different kinds of anomaly or making-strange (relative to the beholder's sense of the automatized, 'transparent', and prosaic) may be attested and be felt to need interpreting by different readers.

A less mystificatory view of metaphor, then, proposed from a variety of perspectives (e.g. both deconstructivist and linguistic), suggests that there is metaphor in all language, although the metaphoricality is typically 'dead' (or metaphor that we readers are not alive to). Metaphor pervades all language and human behaviour, and, as Lakoff and Johnson's work suggests (1980), certain culturally salient metaphors powerfully direct much of our habitual thinking. Metaphor is the foregrounding of the ever-present potential in our language behaviour for creative risk-taking along Saussure's associative axis, an attempt to break free from the normative predictabilities of the established public paradigms in analogy, exemplification, and description.

The way in which we use metaphor, in literature as everywhere else, is no more than a special instance of the way in which we use language, and here again Harris's integrational-linguistic emphasis on a dynamic, provisional, creative sense-making of particular interactants in particular circumstances, informed by previous experience and an understanding of the conventional use of the language, is very useful. Metaphor interpretation is an enhanced form of that creative sense-making, where no specifiable meaning or intent can be attached a-contextually to particular utterances. If we allow that world and language are different (and heterogeneous) entities, the interpretation of metaphor is as problematic and inescapable as the positing of referential ties. We must reject the prevailing myth in much stylistic and linguistic work that there is an unproblematic algorithmic procedure (in our heads, or in our dictionaries, or at least somewhere – the community?) for matching the tokens of our language with concepts in our heads. Speech, thought, and world are different but profoundly interdependent domains: we are obliged to relate them, but the relating is neither automatic nor impossible. As meta-phor, para-phrase and trans-lation suggest, there is always a difficult crossing to effect.

One reflection of our rational assumptions that communication is possible but not a mechanical certainty can be seen in all the conversational techniques we have for monitoring each other's talk. But monitoring a situation, similarly, in no way guarantees that all problems are spotted. It rather reflects our proceeding in good faith on the assumption that each of us is working at grasping the intended meanings of the other (no matter how hostile we may be towards that other or their messages) and that an approximation towards these intended meanings is possible. Making sense is then by definition the (uncertain) ascribing or inferring of intended meanings. This emphasis on intentionality, like the related one on referentiality, may at first glance appear unpalatably reactionary. But that is fair criticism only if, in addition to emphasizing the inescapability of intention and reference, one proceeds under the illusion that both issues can be finally determined, at least in broad terms, for any given text – as Hirsch seems to do (see Hirsch 1967 and 1983).

If intentionality and referentiality have been rarely discussed by theorists of stylistics, then that has been to the detriment of the approach and has led to a host of questionable practices. Unfortunately, when these topics have been examined by theorists of poetics, their influential conclusions have often been disastrously wrongheaded. Chief culprit here is Michael Riffaterre, whose work might otherwise appear to be a brilliant bridge of diverse disciplines; it has been reprinted in anthologies both of stylistics and of post-structuralist criticism, and his theories have been examined by many (besides Butler (1984) and Thurley (1983), see Fowler (1981: 129 –41) and chapter 4 of T. Taylor (1980). However, while there are many viable and theoretically coherent links between literary linguistics and post-structuralism, Riffaterre's work in this area needs to be handled with care, since it is built on peculiarly shaky theoretical ground(s).

This can be seen in Riffaterre's notorious article on 'Interpretation and descriptive poetry: a reading of Wordsworth's "Yew Trees"', perhaps his most influential article of the 1970s (Riffaterre 1973). This begins unobjectionably as an unpicking of the interpretative convention of verisimilar representation, of 'nature poems' as faithful records of actual scenes (to be evaluated in terms of their success in that task). This Aunt Sally is easily knocked down, but Riffaterre then adopts the equally wrongheaded assumption (even in the midst of some astute conventional literary analysis) of the fundamental non-referentiality of the poetic text.

Riffaterre's paper is a strikingly vivid example of an authoritarian structural stylistics, here embarrassed by the jargon of componential semantics. Despite brief nods towards a genuine reader-cum-text sense-making, and just as Fish did in the early 1970s, he claims that the overwhelming focus of attention, privileging of authority, and basis for analysis is the text itself. Riffaterre argues for a series of remorselessly structuralist principles of equivalence, tautology, and oxymoron, of repeatedly actualized semantic features in strings of words, interrelating and pointing back to a core or kernel sentence from which, in some less than clear way, the full poem is generated. That, says Riffaterre, is how interpretation should work. The pre-scriptivism is breathtaking: 'Interpretation must, then, be a state-ment of these [semantic] equivalences. . . . Such a reading, by defi-nition, allows the reader no freedom of choice in his understanding of descriptive details' (Riffaterre 1973: 114). Riffaterre's reader is no longer either super or average, but more like an ill-disciplined child with weak powers of concentration: 'The starter, the system com-ponent which triggers the sequence, must have stylistic features that make it so compellingly noticeable that the reader's attention is kept under control and his further decoding of what follows is firmly directed' (114).

However, perhaps the most concise expression of Riffaterre's anti-referential structuralism is the following sentence: 'The represen-tation of reality is a verbal construct in which meaning is achieved by reference from words to words, not to things' (1973: 107). This is an instructively confused version of Saussurean structuralism, blending the unexceptionable with the absurd. Riffaterre's claim is that the referentiality of literary meaning, the assumption that the yew trees and the Azincour, and so on, of Wordsworth's poem are to be related to any 'actual' yew trees or Agincourt, is fallacious *because* meaning is achieved by reference from words to words, not to things. There lies the confusion: what Saussurean structuralism actually says is that meaning is achieved by the differential *relation* of words to other words. It would never talk of one word *referring* to the rest of the

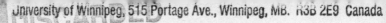

LITERARY LINGUISTICS AND CRITICAL THEORY

system, for the simple reason that reference is understood as a postulated denotative tie (effected by the language-user) between words and things. Saussure fathered a tradition which turned away from the messy variant interests and concerns of individual speakers using language to get things done. However, as Firth insisted, it is incoherent to enquire into language use without attending to the (hypothesized) context of situation. The sentence from Riffaterre plausibly maintains that 'meaning is achieved by language'; but it cannot be used to sustain the much stronger and implausible claim that 'existence is achieved by language'.

The referentiality issue is inevitably broached by Butler in his critique of Riffaterre:

> The language the poet uses is the very same language (it could not be otherwise) with which in purely referential contexts we may talk about trees or any other of the subjects of Wordsworth's poem. . . . The language of the poem only counts as systematically related because it selects and develops features (of trees or anything else) that are taken to be systematically related in the external world. (Butler 1984: 51)

My only reservation with this would be with its counterposing of the language and the external world, when in practice the two are interdependent and interdetermining (Butler's reading of Halliday, who emphasizes that one's language is one's most powerful and pervasive semiotic, might have drawn him closer to this latter view). And Butler rightly emphasizes, *contra* Riffaterre, that the Romantics' attitudes to natural religion, what we take Azincour to mean, and so on, are of 'considerable historical and ideological importance' (52). If the limits of our language are the limits of our world, then texts cannot be in the world without being of it, and the only correspondence we can attempt to inspect is the correspondence of the use of a term or description on some particular occasion to its conventional usage.

Usage, however, is notoriously multiple, as a simple instance from 'Yew Trees' may remind us. Riffaterre argues at one point that 'drew their sounding bows' suffices to make 'Azincour' a battle, while 'bows' suffices to set the incident back in the Middle Ages. But texts are never 'sufficient' in the way Riffaterre claims; they characteristically under-determine context. As far as 'drew their sounding bows' goes, there seems nothing to prevent an intelligent reader who knows nothing of the Battle of Agincourt from supposing that here is a reference to some modern (not medieval) Festival of Folk Fiddle (are not violin bows made of yew?). The broader point to be made is that, as the double designation Agincourt/Azincour suggests (G/Z?), our accounts of events will always be plural. The mention of Azincour we take to be an invitation to understand 'Azincour' as relevant to its co-text, but mere mention does not prescribe which facts and usages, of all those the word might reasonably call to mind in the reader, are the ones to keep in view. Readers do still have to do their own interpretative work – or have others do it for them.

The same misconception as Riffaterre's emerges early on in Geoffrey Thurley's breathless survey of all the ills that theory is heir to:

> 'To mean' means to relate a beholder and a beheld. In the case of the map of the (London) Underground, the description will make no sense unless the recipient latches on to the fact that the notches on the longer lines indicate stations, and that the stations are geographically related much as they are physically related on the map: Acton Town is farther away from Hammersmith than either is from Brook Green, and to get from Acton Town to Hammersmith without using the Underground will probably take you through a place called Brook Green. (Thurley 1983: 18)

Anyone who knows the London Tube knows that much of this is wrong and irrelevant. Newcomers to London, armed only with tiny maps of the Underground in their pocket diaries, soon learn that beyond the occasional very general distinction (King's Cross is somewhat north of Charing Cross, etc.) the map is worse than useless for helping one to get around the city at ground level. But then that is not its purpose: the map is relevant less to the actual geography of London than to the routes and connections of the Underground trains. It makes sense in those terms alone. Who's to say that Farringdon is more related to the Barbican than to the Angel 'in the world'? The map simply indicates that 'on the Tube' this is so, since Farringdon and Barbican are adjacent on the Circle line, while the Angel can be reached from either only by changing at Moorgate or St Pancras. Similarly, how you get (and are implicitly advised to get) from the Barbican to the Angel *on the Tube* has little relevance to how you might do so by any other means of transport.

So Thurley's picture of how the Tube map 'means' is mistaken. That in itself would be a trivial problem were it not that he proceeds to use the map analogy in an attempt to expose the folly of Frye, Iser, and various others who, he claims, have emphasized either the subjectivity of response to works of literary art or the need to study the reader's aesthetic response to a text. With staggering reductivism he claims that understanding the map is just like understanding a text, that we cannot properly have a variety of understandings of a text any more than we can of the map. But this simply begs the question of purpose. The map is usually used for very easily specified purposes, a signposting of the train routes. Its functional relevance is clear, and viewed in those terms we would agree that anyone who consulted the map and deduced that they could travel from the Barbican to the Angel without changing trains would have 'misunderstood the map'.

But how is this analogous to art interpretation, where no single functional relevance is prescribable? Tube maps have a conventional purpose, but even this can be easily set aside if we choose to view the picture as an op-art work, a sinuous blend of gradated, regimented linearity subverted by the unpredictable curves and diagonals, primary colours on a white background with overly *lisible* names, a pictorial and iterated critique of the alienating mechanical predictability of urban relations, etc. etc. (For a much wittier art-reading of a non-literary text, see Eagleton's fresh look at the Tube notice 'Dogs must be carried on the escalator', in Eagleton (1983).) Since composing the above sentences I have read Paul Theroux's *Sunrise with Seamonsters*, in which he justly remarks: 'The map of the London Underground is by almost any standards a work of art – a squint turns it into late Mondrian – but it also has great practical value' (Theroux 1985: 281). No particular practical value, or conventional purpose, can be assigned as the permanent or essential characteristic of any literary text.

In literary art there is typically adopted a counter-convention to what we think of as normal practice: a convention that no single purpose shall be specified for the text. Perhaps only this convention separates literature from advertising, parables, and propaganda. Mark Twain's famous warning at the opening of *Huckleberry Finn* – 'Persons attempting to find a motive in this narrative will be prosecuted; persons attempting to find a moral in it will be banished' – is partly memorable because no one playing the literary-critical language game observes these injunctions. What we do accept, however, is that we probably won't all find the same moral(s) in the story. Again, potential diversity of imputed purpose or intention and diversity of possible effects are always present in language behaviour, if we are only willing to see this. In Harris's words, language is 'a communication game in which there is no referee, and the only rule that cannot be bent says that players shall improvise as best they can' (Harris 1981: 186).

THE ROLE AND STATUS OF LITERARY LINGUISTICS

Turning his attention to stylisticians in particular, Thurley chastises them with the familiar reproof that their declarations of emancipating criticism from subjectivity and impressionism are hollow, that their commitment to setting criticism on a scientific and objective basis has never been honoured. His criticisms here are true but, I trust, outdated. No practising literary linguist can justly deny the partiality and incompleteness of stylistics; most, I take it, would recognize their work as 'positioned' and thus subjective. Incorporating a particularly high value on the linguistic structuring and phenomena of the text into their reading framework, they see stylistics as part of a particular value-laden way of reading. Objectivity is hardly the goal, but discussing texts within a public discourse of widely understood vocabulary, a language expressing models and frameworks which are applicable to a range of texts (not just those deemed literary), it promotes a colloquy and a discipline, if not yet a science.

Stylistics also serves quite different purposes for different people; among these I would emphasize two particular purposes.

First of all, for students of English literature for whom the language is not a native tongue, and for those not already sensitive to the craft and effects of different ways with words, stylistics is an aid in the grasp of certain kinds of structuring, craft, and effect. (It obviously cannot, however, supply outsiders with the insider's encyclopaedic cultural knowledge, which we may feel is necessary for reading Milton or Ted Hughes or whomever.) This, I concede, amounts to what linguists in education might call a deficit theory of stylistics, and it courts the condemnation often (and rightly) heaped on such proposals in rather different circumstances. But I do believe that reading and writing about complex texts are skills, and that literary linguistics can be an invaluable crutch or catalyst for those who are less adept. There remain many graduate teachers of English (to say nothing of their students) who lack the procedures – and procedural confidence – even to get started on their own communicable assessment of a Stevens poem or a Heaney sonnet. For them stylistics may be a crucial enabling device. I believe stylistics is also particularly useful in second-language settings, where, as students of the language, both teacher and students are likely to have already some of the necessary familiarity with standard descriptions of the language.

Second, although many readers do not need stylistics in their progress to rich and suggestive interpretations, those interpretations remain interesting to stylisticians (at least, to those who don't simply dismiss all critics from Leavis to Bayley as subjective intuitionists). Such stylisticians adopt the premise that if Ricks, Kermode, Booth, or Eagleton has arrived at a particular interpretative commentary on the text (as broadly interpreted as this may need to be) that commentary is not likely to be arbitrary. On the contrary, it should be possible to 'work back' from particular interpretations (valued by the – or some – community as insightful and judicious) to the language of the text itself, so as to gain a better understanding of how discourses achieve their effects, and of how language works. This orientation – often my own – is towards the writer's *assumed* craft or *techne*, the superior effectiveness of their use of language. Note that what emerges here, in addition to interest in the (political) 'effects on readers' adopted from Eagleton, is an interest in the *how* of writing: stylistics is useful not only for faltering readers but for failed writers too. There are clear and important relations with analysis of the techniques and rhetoric of less exalted types of language use: analysis of the language of courtroom speech, of political talks, of popular scientific articles, of students' essay-writing, and so on.

The relation of the text to the world, and in particular the 'real and everyday world' that 'we' all know and which we often assume to be denoted and illuminated by elements in the text, will always be a key problematic for interpretation and theory. If there is a fixed, deter-minate external world, known to all of us as the same set of entities, and if we agree that literary texts necessarily relate that world (in no matter how troubled and agonistic a way) and relate *to* that world, then here lies a gold standard by which we can assay the metals of a text, assign values, and establish fixed rates of exchange. It would make for a simpler world, and a simpler text-life. As things currently are, we are often quite unsure of the text–world relations, and of whether we readers are supposed to produce or consume. The calibration of our extratextual experience with our experience of the text, and the matching of these against what we understand to be other people's views of the world, is a continually varying exercise; as a corollary, so is evaluation and interpretation. Between all such related positions, the negotiated rates of exchange shift unpredictably. (The latter metaphor has been explored brilliantly by Malcolm Bradbury in his recent novel, *Rates of Exchange*.)

However, if one exchange rate is more crucial to us and more controversial than any other, I would suggest it is the referential one, concerning the linking of words and things. Having nothing to say to the radical sceptic (except 'I don't believe you'), I take the view that there is a considerable world of objective entities outside my consciousness and prior to my language. My (limited) contact with the blind and deaf suggests that they share with me a similar raw perception of the existence of trees. My two-year-old daughter too is well aware that trees exist, though she has not yet learned their name(s). Having claimed this much for the independent existence of substantial entities, I hasten to add two riders:

1 Very much – perhaps the more interesting part – of our 'world' is not of the above nature, but rather comprises complexes of objects, or abstract principles, ideas, and evaluations, which can scarely have an existence prior to and independent of human intervention, by way of fabrication, conceptualization, and so on.

2 Much more crucially, this postulated independent existence of trees, cats, and so on, is a wholly different claim from that of independent *meaning*. Because I take trees to be an independent fact of the world, regardless of our language and cognitive practices, this does not imply that we all (even within the same language) have or should have a shared sense of what a tree is or means. Meaning cannot inhere in 'the thing itself' but must be an assessment negotiated by particular individuals (meaners) on a particular occasion through their shared semiotic system (e.g. a language).

A long-familiar traditionalist approach to reference is that of Ogden and Richards (1923), as represented in their famous semiotic triangle. This celebrated icon of early-twentieth-century language theory has the linguistic symbol (phonetic or graphetic) positioned at one of the base angles of a triangle, the concept or thought denoted by it at the apex, and the real-world referent relevant to the symbol and the thought at the other base angle. The two lines linking the apex to the base are solid, asserting that there is a 'causal' and systematic relation between symbol and referent *by way of* the conceptual system.

By contrast, the base line itself, the direct link between symbol and referent, is a broken one: there is, it is emphasized, no direct or unproblematic relation between words (forms) and things.

Many students of linguistics will have reflected long on the mystery of Ogden and Richards's famous dotted line. It is a nicely suggestive and ambivalent pictorial representation, like the duck-rabbit, since on one view a dotted line gestures pretty explicitly towards the 'virtual' unbroken line it implies. On the road, a broken line is hardly less adequate than an unbroken one, as far as establishing the boundaries of lanes is concerned. On the other hand we may view the discontinuous line (especially by contrast with the adjacent solid ones) as expressive of fracture, hesitancy. From Ogden and Richards's point of view, nothing much hinges on these reflections: they chiefly wished to emphasize the irrelevance of looking for direct connections between trees and the spoken or written expressions we may use to refer to them. By contrast, they wished to emphasize that, concerning meaning and reference, the relations between forms and concepts were non-arbitrary, motivated, and systematic, that a language consists in a principled and mutual determination of symbolic forms and concepts.

Where the richest difficulties lie, perhaps, are with the third side to the triangle, where concepts are connected to things by means of a solid line. For Ogden and Richards, here too relations are causal and unproblematic. But Saussure's position is significantly different; in his view referential indeterminacy is one of the uncertainties that emerges as soon as one moves from the collective psychological world of forms and concepts (*langue*) to the individualist material world of things and experience (as reflected in *parole*). For Saussure, the line between mental token and real-world referent would have to be a broken one. But more cannily, perhaps, he never invoked this fragile triangulation imagery. He has two alternative mantraic icons with which to mesmerize the suggestible: these are the sign as a sheet of paper, the planes of *signifiant* and *signifié* occupying either side of that sheet, so that the plane of forms cannot be cut into (or adjusted, or anything) without inevitably effecting a commensurate influence on the plane of concepts. Alternatively he wrote of the domain of linguistic structure as like the interface between water and air, the only place (allegedly) where we can examine in a systematic way the mutual influences on each other of these vast, mobile, and 'chaotic' powers, water and air (or, by analogy, the substances of speech sound and mind). For only at this interface does inspectable form emerge from these domains of uninspectable substance. The beauty of both images is that they seem to have intrinsically just the two dimensions Saussure needs to reinforce his bi-planar perspective. Neither image has room for the world of actually existing things that the margin or interface of signs presumably relates to. On the key question of reference, the *Cours* is eloquently silent.

The reason for the silence has been made abundantly clear in Harris's recent critique of dominant linguistic theory and practice. The silence is explained by the radical inability of structuralist linguistic method, whether of the Saussurean, Bloomfieldian, or Chomskyan variety, to recognize and cope with the fact that 'the central indeterminacy of all communication is indeterminacy of what is meant' (Harris 1981: 167). It can neither acknowledge nor cope with this, since the enabling fiction of modern linguistics, that a language is a fixed, bi-planar system for effecting the telementational transfer of thoughts between its users, orients them in entirely the opposite direction.

It needs to be emphasized anew that, while we have grounds for supposing considerable overlap in our conventions of using particular words to refer to particular things, there can be no guarantee that we always refer to the same things by the same words, nor is it reasonable to suppose that we each assign the very same sense or meaning to a word. Just as it is not necessary for a monolingual Chinese-speaker and a monolingual English speaker to carry an identical meaning for the different forms *hwoche* and *train* respectively in order that translation can be effected, similarly, intralingually, it is not necessary (or verifiable) that you and I carry an identical meaning for the word *democratic* (or *Azincour*).

STYLISTICS AND DECONSTRUCTION

In this discussion of critical theory, referentiality, intention, and meaning, and their significance for literary linguistics, I have so far made little mention of deconstruction, which has developed its own iconoclastic unravellings of these principles. As a focus for some remarks on these topics I shall refer to deconstructionist essays that appear in the same post-structuralist anthology, *Untying the Text* (Young 1981), as does the Riffaterre paper examined earlier. The first of these is Barthes's 'Textual analysis of Poe's "Valdemar"'. Barthes views text as an ongoing signifying practice, alert to the moment-to-moment creativity of meaning-making in language practice, and one that does not issue or conclude in 'understanding' (in the sense of 'full' comprehension or the unproblematic transfer of information from one unified subject to another). All 'endings' are now seen as a breaking-off rather than a conclusion, a breaking-off of the provisionalizing dialectic of *signifiance*. A text can 'float free' from its actual origins, its shaping voices; rather than a space where structure is observed, it can be seen as a space where structuration (by the reader) is enacted and continues. A largely unpredictable and mobile engagement with the text is thus urged.

In the course of Barthes's record of his structuration of 'Valdemar', reference is made to a number of 'codes', with the instruction that these codes do not comprise a system or grammar; rather they appear to be a rhetorical strategic device, invoked so as to be put in question, disintegrated, undermined. This looks like an ingenious gesture towards accommodation within the double-bind of interpretative circularity (as articulated by Fish and others), all too familiar to stylisticians. Thus Barthes promises, 'we are going to locate the avenues of meaning', while adding, 'our aim is not to find *the* meaning, nor even *a* meaning of the text' (in Young 1981: 135), turning a blind eye to the certainty that once the 'avenues' are in place interpretation will tend to be channelled in pre-ordained directions towards pre-scribed goals. What Barthes does, then, is not 'wrong': interpretative strategies – be they those of stylistics, or textual analysis, or whatever – are a way of reading, and human beings are always strategists finding or making a way. It is simply that Barthes is not always open about the predeterminations, the working assumptions, on which his activities of *signifiance* build.

A major working assumption – at first glance paradoxical – of several of the psychoanalytically oriented studies in Young's collection is that every interpretation of a text, no matter how freely it floats by contrast with a 'normal' reading, is a repression. These essays break with traditional 'applications' of psychoanalysis to literature and are, rather, textual analyses that are 'undecidably psychoanalytic or literary' (Young, in Young 1981: 175). They involve startling rereadings of Freud, Joyce's *Portrait*, Tennyson, and others – and equally startling recastings of the role of repression, narcissism, interpretation, and the repressive function of reading in a certain way. For Jeffrey Mehlman, for example, the wish-fulfilment believed – in early Freud – to be the core and 'key' to the secret of dreams is itself the crucially significant repression, a reduction of the mobile textuality of the unconscious to the fixity of interpretability.

Defensible as these positions are, they sometimes do not make clear, for their own purposes, that repression is not necessarily undesirable. Selective repression is inescapable, and often the only healthy and rational response to a super-plenitude of possibilities or significances. The two papers in Young's collection by Barbara Johnson are, however, instructive in their evidence for the inevitability of analytical framing in the rereading that is critical practice. Of the first of these papers, on the 'interestedness' of Barthes's famous reading of Balzac's 'Sarrasine', Young comments in his preface:

> A sense . . . of the necessarily reductive nature of interpretation leads her to trace the tactics of Barthes's own 'writerly' reading of a 'readerly' text, and to discern a curious homology between Barthes's own critical concerns and those of the story that he analyses. The collapse of the metalinguistic distance that Johnson describes is, however, perhaps equally appropriate for her own text. (Young 1981: 162)

Johnson's second paper pursues the practice of a similar inescapable strategy of framing, as enacted by Derrida on Lacan on Poe (and of course by Johnson on all of these), one upshot of which, as she acknowledges, is to place the reader in 'a vertiginously insecure position' (227). The heart of the unresolvable oscillation of views that Johnson explores is reached, I think, in the following passage:

> It would seem that the theoretical frame of reference that governs recognition is a constitutive element in the blindness of any interpretative insight. And it is precisely that frame of reference that allows the analyst to frame the author of the text he is reading for practices whose locus is simultaneously beyond the letter of the text and behind the vision of its reader. (228)

It is interesting to contrast Johnson and Derrida with Thurley, who rejects all that Lacan and (especially) Derrida read into or out of Poe's 'The Purloined Letter', confident in his hard-facts empiricism: 'It is a mere rhetorical device that Poe refrains from telling us what was in the letter to bother the queen. . . . More, we don't *need* to know: it is enough that the queen and the blackmailer know' (Thurley 1983: 142).

It is evident that this is simply the adoption of one critical stance, and the dismissal of another, without argued defence. Just how we can confidently dismiss certain facts as mere rhetoric (and how cheap is the price of that word for Thurley, in contrast to its high value for others), unnecessary, a 'refraining from telling' rather than a productive repression, is not made clear. The impasse between Lacan, Derrida, and Thurley has, as Johnson's position suggests, no final resolution within its own terms. The reflexive critique can in principle continue to oscillate between dialectically revisionist alternatives. But we can and will expect a critique of a particular reading to be a detailed inspection and unravelling, not merely a polemical rejection: the critique must persuade us, but it will do so as a suggestive and illuminating rhetorical move, or as articulating the facts as we see them, not on the grounds of 'correspondence to *the* facts'.

Are we obliged, however, to continue the discourse within its own endlessly provisional terms? Are we to be continually persuaded of new interpretations? How we choose to answer these questions is finally up to us, our perceived interests, purposes, and faiths. These are not intrinsically arbitrary or 'irresponsible' (is Marxist criticism or psychoanalytic criticism arbitrary?), but it may be that we are never in that co-ordinate-free space or uncharted ground, stripped of conditionings, where we can impartially weigh and choose among 'competing' frameworks and interpretations. What we can do, however, is press on open-mindedly, rationally, prepared to confront our own faith and framework with alternative ones, and prepared to have others read texts differently from ourselves.

This in turn does not mean we proceed embarrassedly clutching our own interpretative 'bag', knowing it to be full of the perishable fruit of interpretative conventions, attending the moment when we can dump it in favour of some radically different nourishment. The history of our changing selves and ideologies is never so flip as it might appear in the absurdist portrait of perpetual revision that is sometimes painted. Indeed, this issue – just how, diachronically, we ever come to move from one framework towards another (given the powerful determinations supplied by particular norms, conventions, and frameworks) – has been seriously neglected in much modern theory. There seems at least some truth, for example, in Eagleton's complaint that some forms of post-structuralism involve a 'hedonist withdrawal from history', and that Derrida, nothwithstanding the possible *political* impulses underlying his deconstruction, has been 'grossly unhistorical, politically evasive, and in practice oblivious to language as "discourse"' (Eagleton 1983: 148).

Johnson's essay also involves a demonstration of a general principle of post-structuralism: its semioclastic denial of the separateness of writing and reading, or of text and interpretation. It asserts that interpretation or criticism has long masqueraded as an 'other', detached, an impartial analytical language through which to analyse 'data', trading on a claimed metalinguistic distance (between itself and its target text) that does not and cannot exist.

Analogies are possible, I believe, with two other aspects of inter-pretative repression: those that emerge in our response to the metaphoricality of language and in stylistics. In everyday language, I suggested earlier, as in literature, there is a potential metaphoricality. By and large we overlook it, since it simply isn't in our interests, when we're buying vegetables, giving directions to motorists, arranging a baby-sitter, etc., to focus on the message for the message's own sake. We neglect the materiality and metaphoricality of language in favour of other interests.

In literary linguistics too, to the extent that interpretation appeals to a particular system of linguistic description and analysis, the inadequacies, blind-spots, and exclusions of that system may be neglected. But even here there is always the possibility of the decon-structive double-movement or oscillation, where the reading of a text through a particular linguistic perspective fosters a revisionary criti-que, even a dismantling, of that perspective. Covertly or overtly, this has gone on in much recent work in stylistics, and seems the only way in which the enterprise can remain alive and interesting rather than a mechanical mapping of description on to text. It entails what Fowler has called an interdisciplinary relationship, where the two subjects, poetics and linguistics, are experienced 'in a state of mutual critique' (Fowler 1981: 162). The analyses produced become (echoing Mehl-man) undecidably linguistic or literary. They will be as determined and repressive as any entering into words, but such discourses will not be *pre*determined. For me the original (if I dare use the word) repression is a productive and enabling one: the narrowing of interests and intentions that is necessary if we are to begin writing (or reading). The business of getting started on interpretation (or the unravelling of interpretation) is itself, as Butler would say, an attending to particu-lar interests and pragmatic ends. Deconstructionists differ from the rest of us interpreters not in kind but in the degree to which they are prepared to unravel our habitual repressive reading processes. If they sometimes appear to be like Ulysses' Penelope, always busy inside their texts, weaving and unravelling, that appearance should not lead us to overlook the fact that, like hers, their moves are prompted by extratextual interests and ends.

In short, in language perhaps more vividly than anywhere else, there are no origins: no original meanings, no original forms, no original signs, no original intentions. There are no origins but we have to make a start on things (interpreting, reacting, evaluating). The idiom 'to make a start', with its constructivist emphasis, is startlingly apposite.

What deconstructionists like Johnson might call the framing effect of frames, on readers, authors, and texts, inevitably has its counterpart in linguistics: context. Linguists the world over respond to questions about grammaticality with the hedge 'It depends on the context', paying lip-service (or protection money) to a principle which their entire discipline is designed to ignore: from Saussure through Bloomfield to Chomsky, the discipline has striven to marginalize referentiality, *parole*, indeterminacy of what is meant, performance, all the aspects of language behaviour which would shed (flickering) light on what it is to mean and understand in context. There are dissenting voices, of course (Firth is one), but these are typically placed at an inaudible distance, since, like the revised stylistics I propose, they carry merely the unsatisfactory promise of a patchy, localized way rather than a comprehensive methodical account.

Besides Firth, mention might be made here of another profound student of language and cultural behaviour, long marginalized by mainstream linguistics. The emphases we have arrived at, on provisionality and the context-basedness of description-cum-interpretation, on the inescapable ethnomethodological positionedness of analysis and modelling of the norms and habitual conventions in verbal interaction, can all be related to the thinking of Edward Sapir. It was Sapir who memorably declared that 'Language is a guide to "social reality"', that 'it powerfully conditions all our thinking about social problems and processes'. I believe a Sapirian perspective in stylistics might lead us to recognize, modifying Sapir, that

Language [study] is a guide to 'social [textual] reality'. . . .It powerfully conditions all our [stylistic] thinking about social

51

[textual] problems and processes. Human beings [stylisticians] do not live in the objective world alone, nor alone in the world of social activity as ordinarily understood, but are very much at the mercy of the particular language [interpretative linguistics] which has become the medium of expression for their society [interpretative community]. (Mandelbaum 1949: 162)

And we must come to see that our linguistics tends actually to define our textual experience for us 'by reason of its formal completeness and because of our unconscious projection of its implicit expectations into the field of experience' (Sapir 1931).

We must, of course, avoid being the worst sort of passive determinists in the face of these difficulties. Whorf certainly never was. True to his profession (I mean insurance, not linguistics), he reminded the linguistic and world community of the dilemmas Sapir had described, and urged us to take out calibrational protection against possible mishaps. As in metaphor, discussed earlier, so in the explosive atmospheres of gasoline drums perceived as 'Empty', so in all intra- and interlingual interaction, where we proceed in our descriptions of conditions in varying degrees of ignorance, there are risks involved, risks of communicational breakdown with serious consequences. The rational response to these risks is not to avoid them by forsaking metaphor, gasoline, and speech, but to mind how we go. Whorfian protection, like insurance, brings no certainty that mishaps won't still sometimes occur. But at least there is then an intelligent, reflexive awareness of potential problems, difficulties, and unexamined assumptions.

Sapir's development is instructive for literary linguists, since the trajectory of his thinking shows him moving far away from his early position, that of a standard structuralist, where language was analysable form, easily separable from the vagaries and variabilities of cultural content. By his final years a quite different view has emerged, under the pressure of repeated critique of his previous assumptions: he now views language and culture as a mutually determining unity, the one not really comprehensible except by means of the other (on Sapir's intellectual career, see Hymes (1983), especially pp. 150–61). His reorientation is a model for what is needed in stylistics, if we are to break free of the misconceptions sustained by a homogenizing form–content bi-planarity adopted uncritically from orthodox linguistics. There is a persistent reluctance to theorize within much stylistics:

many stylisticians would rather 'get on' with 'practical' analyses of texts – as if such a response did not itself reveal adoption of a partial theoretical position.

What future is there for a stylistics of social discourse, or cultural rhetoric? Is it to be found in a development of the critical linguistics propounded by Fowler, Hodge, and Kress? Or of the Foucaldian literary linguistics begun by MacCabe and others, itself a more systematic prosecution of Raymond Williams's project? Can it join hands with the attempted revival of formalism apparent in the work of Banfield (1982) and T. Austin (1984)? It is no doubt too early to tell. However, if we take literature to be a uniquely valued social semiotic, then it is simply a misdirection for literary linguistics to attempt to explore the discoursal mediation of language and society without addressing the large issues that are involved: issues of power, control, self, gender, class. Thankfully, there is a vast and growing literature on these topics, even from language scholars, in relation to which stylisticians and their work must now find an intertextual position.

From this overview of stylistics and theory I turn in the next chapter to some previous studies of Faulkner's style, since the major part of this book may be viewed as a literary-linguistic extension of those studies.

3

APPROACHING FAULKNER'S STYLE

In this chapter I briefly survey the observations of previous commentators on Faulkner's style, and discuss some of the assumptions about style that lie behind those observations. I then turn to the literary-linguistic perspective adopted here, and the procedural dilemmas which bedevil any textual analysis but which are especially apparent in the face of the rich expanse of a novel. I go on to explain in some detail the assumptions and methods which underpin the stylistic analyses offered in later chapters. I conclude with a version of my own critical interpretation of the novel, and the interpretative choices that are entailed. These interpretative choices concern what we take to be the novel's themes, and which stylistic and narratological features are most salient to the distinctive construction of those themes.

LITERARY AND GRAMMATICAL EVALUATIONS

One of the earliest style critics of Faulkner was Conrad Aiken, who noted that Faulkner's sentences

> parallel in a curious and perhaps inevitable way, and not without aesthetic justification, the whole elaborate method of deliberately withheld meaning, of progressive and partial and delayed disclosure, which so often gives the characteristic shape to the novels themselves. It is a persistent offering of obstacles, a calculated system of screens and obtrusions, of confusions and ambiguous interpolations and delays, with one express purpose; and that purpose is simply to keep the form – and the idea – fluid and unfurnished, still in motion, as it were, and unknown, until the dropping into place of the very last syllable. (Aiken 1939: 650)

Some touchstones of Faulkner criticism emerge here: the alleged withholding of meaning, delayed disclosure, calculated obtrusions, and the assumed intent to keep the form or idea 'in motion'. A major qualification one should add, however, concerns whether there truly is – or that Faulkner wanted – a final, definitive 'dropping into place' of syllables or meanings. Faulkner's own remarks about what drove him to keep writing, and the ambivalence of the narrative or characterological closure even in those novels where it is nominally achieved (e.g. *Light in August, As I Lay Dying*), would suggest otherwise.

Just three years after Aiken's essay, Alfred Kazin delivered his famous verdict:

> In the end one must always return to Faulkner's language and his conception of style, for his every character and observation are lost in the spool of his rhetoric, and no more than they can he ever wind himself free. That rhetoric – perhaps the most elaborate, intermittently incoherent and ungrammatical, thunderous, polyphonic rhetoric in all American writing – explains why he always plays as great a role in his novels as any of his characters to the point of acting out their characters in himself; why he has so often appeared to be a Laocoon writhing in all the outrageous confusions of the ineffable; why he has been able, correlating the South with every possible point of view, every shade or extremity of character, and to persuade us of none. (Kazin 1942: 462)

Kazin's marvellous rhetoric here – of which, notwithstanding the impaired grammaticality of its close, Faulkner himself would surely have been proud – makes his view entertaining even if not wholly plausible. It is likely that much of Kazin's resistance to Faulkner comes from his personal preference for a more directed rhetoric, highly referential and involving explicit commentary on the topic of discourse. But what is remarkable in Kazin's criticism is that it touches upon many of those features of Faulkner's style which I shall claim to be prominent in the narrative of *Go Down, Moses*. Thus Kazin writes of Faulkner (the narrator?) as 'acting out [the] characters in himself'; of the texts as intense entrapments of author and characters in the former's rhetoric; and of Faulkner 'writing in many styles, to project every possible point of view' (462). Reflecting his preference for that style which persuasively presents a single paraphrasable view, Kazin closes by noting that Faulkner's rhetoric fails to persuade. In my own interpretative commentary I hope to show that such an alleged failure can easily be seen as a type of success. Despite these possible objections to Kazin's conclusions, his criticism of Faulkner, published in *On Native Grounds* in the same year that *Go Down, Moses* appeared (1942), remains one of the most discerning responses to his style.

A final quotation from the early style critics of Faulkner comes from Warren Beck's celebrated article on the writer's point of view (Beck 1976). First published in 1941, it makes some of the points which, against Kazin's view of Faulkner as the intruding egotistical narrator, I adopt as critical underpinnings to a stylistic approach to the narrative sections of *Go Down, Moses*. Beck writes:

> Not often, however, does Faulkner speak in his own right, out of the omniscience of third-person narrative, for he is devoted to dramative form and to the perspective it supplies, and most of his stories are told largely through the consciousness of participant characters. And even when Faulkner speaks, through third-person narrative, he usually keys his utterance to the mood of the scene and makes himself the lyrical mouthpiece of his characters' experience. Consequently, it is not possible to comprehend Faulkner's point of view from separate quotations but only from implications in his novels as wholes and from positions of his various characters in relation to these implied themes. (Beck 1976: 6)

After these influential early assessments, it is something of a surprise to find that only a handful of useful essay-length style studies of Faulkner appeared in the 1950s and 1960s. The first of these was Karl Zink's article, in which he argues that Faulkner's prose is like the syntax of speech. He characterizes the sentences thus:

> Physically they are often characterized by unusual length, by patterns of involuted dependent elements, clause modified by clause, by phrase, with dependencies as far removed, sometimes, as three and four degrees. They make little use of the period; the basic end stop for predications is the semi-colon. The comma and the parenthesis, the dash and the colon serve to distinguish and to extend dependencies to great lengths – frequently, it must be admitted, with what seems perversity. Frequently, a very simple syntactical pattern such as a single subject with a multiple predicate will carry a governing rhetorical pattern for half a page or more; the subject need not recur with each verb; verbs may or may

not be correlated by conjunctions; verb phrases may themselves become involved with cumulating subordinations; or subordination may be cut ruthlessly to free the verbs for rapid movement in the passage. (Zink 1954: 393)

On reflection, many of the practices Zink notes ('the subject need not recur with each verb') are not unique to Faulkner but are common in much written text. But the prevailing tenor here is representative of views in the 1950s and 1960s: discomfort with the seemingly wilful difficulties of text-processing that the writing presented, and a preoccupation with those difficulties, rather than any positive consequences that might be derived.

Writing in 1957, Riedel claimed that the mature style of Faulkner often created merely a meaningless collage (Riedel 1957). These 'life sentences', with their multiple parentheses and recursive right-branching to assimilate more clauses and phrases were, he said, 'perverse in syntax' and had 'little regard for reference of pronouns or other grammatical decencies' (462). Perhaps going even further than Kazin, he saw these sentences as strategies in an attempt to compel rather than persuade the reader. However, while Riedel saw the problem as sometimes lying with Faulkner's loss of control, he also conceded that 'many a complicated Faulkner sentence, when stripped of its adjuncts and excrescences, needs only to be punctuated conventionally to reveal a basically sound framework' (465). Later came studies by Leaver (1958), on Faulkner's virtuosity with words, Zoellner (1959), on the way in which frequent ambiguity of noun-phrase reference fosters an ambience of non-hierarchized impressions, and Ohmann (1964), on the generative derivation of the surface sentences of one short passage from 'The Bear', section IV (also discussed in chapter 9).

Ohmann argues that the kernel (deep-structure) sentences of the passage are related to the surface form by a small number of favoured transformations (e.g. the relative-clause transformation and various 'self-embedding' and optional deletion transformations, such as the 'Wh' transformation, the conjunctive transformation, and the comparative transformation). Ohmann has always regarded a writer's style as in some sense indicative of a preferred way of organizing experience, but here he hardly ventures beyond intimating that Faulkner's style – and world-view – are 'additive'. In partial confirmation of Ohmann, Meyer (1971) finds that conjunction, right-positioned embedding, and parallel embedding are the major means of expansion of underlying simple matrix sentences in her brief sample passages. Relativization is by far the commonest type of transformation noted. She concludes that these features give Faulkner's sentence structure a continual quality, a smoothness, and an impression of blurring sentence boundaries.

Radomski (1974) also focuses on embedding transformations in a corpus of seven 1,000-word samples taken from two novels, and he makes some interesting comparisons within the Faulknerian *œuvre*, and with Hemingway. But his samples are somewhat heterogeneous: besides being from two different novels, most are pure narrative, while one is a two-participant dialogue and another is a character monologue. With that degree of variation of mode of discourse – not to mention variation of dialect – syntactic differences are almost inevitable. In fact there are so many variables involved that convincing isolation of differences is nearly impossible (nor is it attempted by Radomski). Like others, Radomski notes a Faulknerian reliance on participial constructions, nominalizations, and relativizations, and makes the related claim that Faulkner's style is a right-branching one, fairly easily comprehended, in contrast to a Jamesian 'nested' style with central embeddings, which is much more difficult to construe. But actual interpretative evaluation of the style as analysed, with linguistically based hypotheses of the literary functions of distinct features, is rare; and indeed it is clear that the analysis would need to be much more discriminating – sensitive, for example, to types of relativization, and differences of context and co-text – for such interpretation to move beyond the unhelpfully general observation.

Yet such interpretation (which is in part more a coming clean about interpretative orientations already in place) is crucial if the analysis is not to remain a mere typology (that is, continue to masquerade as a value-free naming of parts). Ohmann wrote long ago that 'The move from formal descriptions of styles to critical and semantic interpretation should be the ultimate goal of stylistics' (1964: 434). It would be truer to recognize, as Saussure did during the crucial formative years of modern language study, that 'formal descriptions' are always and inescapably permeated by socially ratified value-systems, and that in linguistics (and, by analogy, so also in stylistics and criticism) it is the perspective of the enquirer that delineates the perceived object of study.

What seems to emerge from most of the earliest style commentaries is considerable resistance to, or distrust of, complexity of style. The rhetoric may be marvellous on occasion – 'thunderous' – but it is 'rhetoric' none the less (where the term 'rhetoric' connotes inflation of treatment, contrivance, a baroque and overwritten style). And it is really rather perverse of Mr Faulkner, a fine storyteller who has depicted many poignant situations, to express his material in this way. Thus the prevailing attitude to his style among the early critics is that of style as authorial expression, as primarily a reflex of the author's apprehension of the world, human relations, and so on. However, even as early as Zink's (1954) essay, that 'psychobiographical' emphasis has given way to descriptivist and textualist tendencies. The descriptivist tendency is most clear in essays that note linguistic patterns or frequencies with a minimum of explanation (whether in terms of authorial motivation, thematic motivation, or some other basis). The textualist tendency is evident in those discussions which interpret linguistic trends in terms of textual and thematic effects (and thereby justify the extended attention to linguistic details that this entails).

Yet this textualism has often failed to go broadly or deeply enough. Thus critics often argue that a particular style reflects or evokes a character or theme, as though the language used 'encoded' a previously determined content: a deeper textualism must treat the language of the text as *constitutive* of character, theme, evaluation, and so on. Moreover, textualist style commentaries have often lacked breadth by confining their attention to brief passages from much larger wholes (especially the opening paragraphs of novels). Studies that undertake a more comprehensive survey, that look for pervasive patterns, stylistic shifts and developments in the course of a long text, and argue in inspectable detail for the discourse-constitutive properties of the patterns they isolate, have been rare. One consequence of this, in relation to Faulkner, is the view of most Faulknerians that stylisticians have not begun to do justice to the rich complexity of his craft.

A LITERARY-LINGUISTIC APPROACH: PROBLEMS AND DISSOLUTIONS

In this section I review some of the major difficulties encountered in taking a literary-linguistic approach to a novel, before discussing the chief procedures adopted here. I also give the reasons for focusing this study particularly on progressive verbs, pronouns, and causal connectives, and I conclude with some observations on the validity of literary linguistics as an analytical procedure.

Faulkner's prose is undoubtedly distinctive, often as rich and characteristic as that of Dickens or James, though in quite different ways. What is also clear on closer reading of a number of his works is that, contrary to the impression given by parodies of bad Faulkner, Faulknerian prose is highly variable, a supple instrument capable not only of what Zink (1954) has called full and terse or graphic styles, but also of a Hemingwayan tough-talk style, a naïve-experiential style, a lyric-romantic style, an opaque ratiocinative style, and so on. This is clear from as early a work as *The Sound and the Fury*. A reader would have to be very insensitive to fail to discern the contrasting styles of the sections of that novel, expressing the different narrating persona of each section.

One of the stylistician's problems thus becomes that of adequately distinguishing and characterizing these separate styles or voices that contribute to the polyphony of a Faulknerian novel. And as the analyst proceeds to delineate both these styles and the verbal structuring of the novel in its entirety (if not its 'unity') there may be some language features that particularly require examination, features that most distinctively and crucially contribute to the literary effect. This would be only analogous to the perception of distinctive voices or accents in everyday speech: what is constitutive of an individual accent or voice is not wholesale difference from other, juxtaposed voices, but specific significant differences. The practical possibility of being able to focus in on the significant linguistic differences is a fundamental assumption of stylistics.

The question that immediately arises, if it is granted that a Faulkner novel is highly distinctive stylistically, concerns how one is to identify these significantly distinct features. How can they be ordered, evaluated, made more than an inventory of subjectively and intuitively attested features? (This was, in part, the question addressed by Riffaterre (1960).) What counts as adequate stylistic description and explanation?

In proceeding to a detailed analysis of the linguistic form of a Faulkner novel the analyst is obliged to be selective, on account of the sheer volume of potentially describable and discussable data. And the selectivity can appear to be a disabling distortion, since it highlights the (inescapable) orientedness of all reading or analysis. In stylistics this selectivity of attention is simply more overt, and more consistently maintained, than elsewhere. However, since all analysis entails recasting matter or phenomena that are in a sense free-standing (*Go Down, Moses* does exist regardless of whether I or anyone else analyses it), a recasting in terms which are exorbitant to the phenomenon itself, selective re-presentation is an inherent feature of all such activity. Whether the selective re-presentation of a stylistician or a new-historicist critic or a Lacanian amounts to misrepresentation and distortion is very much a matter for rational argument rather than a priori presumption; and the rational argument should proceed with all parties mindful that no analysis can offer flawless representation, a rendering entirely free of slant.

Certainly one of the greatest risks of stylistics is that of radically decontextualized discussion of language and effects. But this too is a danger no more inherent in stylistics than in any other mode of analysis. The worst problems arise only when the analyst forgets or ignores the decontextualization that the analysis entails. The understanding of context is, however, still at an early stage. It was as recently as 1976 that Halliday and Hasan published a seminal treatment of intersentential linkage, the context provided by surrounding text, and since then there has been a considerably enlarged attention to contextual factors from pragmaticists, discourse analysts, and systemic linguists. The immense difficulties in generalizing from contextual variation have not, however, caused linguists to revise the view of context in any foundational way. But such a revision is long overdue, a recasting in which the distinction between text and context is seen as an analytical fiction of limited value, since it attempts to impose a separation of verbal behaviour from nonverbal behaviour, as a criterial demarcation, in a way that is quite alien to the integrationalist perspective that language-users actually adopt and linguists should investigate (Harris 1981, 1987).

These issues are as pressing in literary linguistics as in any other branch of linguistics (as I argue elsewhere: see Toolan (forthcoming)) but by no means easy to resolve. Nevertheless the traditional text –context dichotomy must be abandoned (among literary theorists, Culler (1983) is representative of the many who have demonstrated that meaning is context-bound, but context is boundless). These very difficulties in specifying context can, however, constitute an argument for focus on formal units within a text, where explicit discussion and evaluation of a feature's effect in relation to surrounding linguistic material can be, as it were, controlled. But no text is framed or closed off, in terms of interpretation, by its own physical limits: these things are done variously by various readers, the only true contextualizers. So literary linguistics proceeds in resolutely text-oriented fashion, but must increasingly articulate the contextualizations through which it reads a text.

One such contextualization involves no radical shift in mode of analysis or subject-matter: intertextual comparison. Even when we allow for qualifications and exceptions, we can often reach a clearer view of the distinctiveness of a feature's frequency of occurrence by comparison with extratextual norms. Here the nature of the texts used in such comparisons (their context of situation) is crucially relevant. However, there is probably more discriminating information to be gained from comparing local frequencies of a particular feature within a text with that text's general norms of occurrence. When attributing particular meanings or effects to particular forms or patterns, we inevitably assume a determinate context within which that meaning can arise. In the case of extended prose fiction, the text constitutes a world, an economy, and a major contextual frame, within which the meaningfulness of particular patterns is constituted. Beyond the contextualizing discourse of the novel itself, its words and structures make appeal to larger, less determinate contexts: the intertextuality of the literary canon, genres, conventions, and so on, and the infinitely varied uses of the language in other historical or contemporary contexts. But it remains the case that there is in the novel a depth of intratextual context framing and constituting any formal effect perceived, to a degree which has no analogy in shorter literary forms. The 'covers of a book' are indicative of a distinct enclosing of the novel-text and novel-world. In addition, a novel may be viewed as a communication event lasting intermittently for anything from one day to several weeks. It is a critical commonplace to speak of a novel creating an alternative world to the familiar everyday one inhabited by the reader (a heterocosm in which, in the view of Searle (1979), there is no requirement that the words should match the way things are in the everyday world). The sheer extent and ideological elaborateness of a novel facilitate its tendency to impose expectancies – its own norms – on the reader; and sustained local violations of those norms therefore have a significance not typically matched in the more exonormative situation of shorter texts.

Ultimately, the problems of analysing long novels or short lyrics are the same: in both cases the claims of comprehensivity in achieving total description are vacuous and question-begging; in both cases there must be judgemental marshalling and selection from the data. There are always yet more ways of looking at a blackbird than were ever dreamed of in Horatio's philosophy. But the kinds of selectivity of attention and systematicity of sampling adopted in stylistics are, it should be stressed, part of a rational way of proceeding (still not a method). For this reason it is a mistake, and self-defeating, for stylisticians to concede too readily that their enquiries begin with an intuitive hunch. 'Begin' alone is a word currently and understandably problematic in all areas of theory and analysis, while the mere mention of intuition in the context of stylistics has encouraged detractors to draw the false conclusion that 'all is intuitive' in stylistic analysis. The word 'intuition' itself has sharply differing connotations to different audiences: stylisticians intend it to refer to 'unreflected-upon judgement and knowledge', as in native speakers' intuitions about the grammaticality of sentences; but in some literary circles 'intuitive' has come to be a derogatory euphemism for 'that's just your opinion'. Intuition, as a trigger of close linguistic analysis, is evident, and defended, in a range of recent stylistic studies. However, as Crystal and Davy point out, such intuition is – at the risk of tautology – of an informed nature:

> The stylistician [approaching a text] is aware of the kind of structure language has, and thus the kind of feature which might be expected to be of stylistic significance; he is aware of the kind of social variation which linguistic features tend to be identified with; and he has a technique of putting these features down on paper in a systematic way in order to display their internal patterning to maximal effect. (Crystal and Davy 1969: 12)

If anything, this account is insufficiently assertive. The fact is that, thanks to the labours of generations of grammarians and linguists, a stylistician approaches a text with an extensive body of non-intuitive knowledge of the workings of the language – in general, and in relation to various genres of language use. (Nor is there an intrinsic limit to this knowledge: linguists' attention to narrative structure over the past twenty years means that today's stylisticians have potential access to better knowledge of the workings of language in narrative than did their counterparts at the time when Crystal and Davy were writing.) This knowledge of the language is then integrated with other pragmatic and cultural systems of assessment, of the kind that all readers invoke, as the stylistician reads (processes, makes sense of) the text. If he or she is then struck by some unexpected pattern of use in the discourse of some part of the language system, that 'intuition' is based on informed judgement, experience with text structures, and rational inference; it is also only a starting-point, simply the material from which to formulate corrigible hypotheses about the discourse function of a feature of the language.

There are, however, different strategies of selectivity, and it is here that differences of judgement and assumptions, worthy of debate, most clearly emerge. It is easy to see why stylistic analysis of a novel must be unlike either the Jakobsonian 'total' analysis of structural patterns, oppositions, affinities, and so on, in, say, a sonnet; or the more delimited procedures advocated by Riffaterre (1960), whose interest seems to have remained more at the lexical level than at the syntactic. Analysing fictional styles involves turning attention away from numerous language features – certainly through lack of time and space in which to pursue such analysis, but primarily since many linguistic features of a text are discoursally and even aesthetically insignificant. For example, in the absence of local textual evidence to the contrary, general grammatical observation predicts that the preposition and complementizer *to* is used as unremarkably in one author as in the next. *To* is an interesting enough particle from a purely linguistic viewpoint; but it is typically a lower-order contributor to discoursal distinctiveness. By contrast, transitivity choices, patterns of clausal subordination, progressivization, and so on, do vary noticeably from author to author, from text to text, and even intratextually. They are a higher-order component of stylistic uniqueness, salient and shaping features of a text's effect.

Among the possible strategies of selectivity, two have been most commonly adopted. One is to select a small number of passages (randomly, or at points in the text intuitively felt to be of particular importance); the other is to identify (almost invariably on the basis of some interpretative rationale) a small number of linguistic features, and to chart their occurrence throughout the text. Both techniques are, in a sense, comprehensive in their consideration of their chosen textual domains; both are also evidently incomplete and partial as characterizations of surface form. More positively, however, both may prompt further consideration of the interpretative implications of distinctive frequencies revealed in the analyses: they may highlight

64

data which can become the grounds for improved hypotheses about textual functions and effects.

As suggested above, this involvement of description with interpretation is necessary and inescapable. But the nature of the involvement that is proposed is critical for the adequacy or success of the stylistic enterprise: it is at the places where description and interpretation meet that the analyst must be most wary and alert to the excesses of subjective judgements. Literary linguistics combats impressionistic interpretation by introducing and applying, wherever possible and plausible, statistical evidence and linguists' descriptions of the semantic function of the forms or structures under discussion. By comparison with the expression of response in much traditional style criticism, through a largely unshared and unshareable vocabulary and subjective affect, here lies a strength of this orientation. But an undeniable weakness remains: the often limited adequacy of linguistic accounts of many aspects of our language behaviour, of what goes on in the writing and reading of texts. Whitehall's warning that 'no criticism can go beyond its linguistics', when taken as addressed to stylistics and its reliance on whatever insight linguistics affords, continues to be germane (Whitehall 1956). If the inadequacies of semantic or functional linguistic descriptions are a stumbling-block to stylistics, there are dangers too in overly-fashionable linguistics. Carson (1972) notes how the work of Hill, Levin, and Ohmann has suffered from a built-in obsolescence, owing to their commitment to theoretical linguistic descriptions which have not survived critical scrutiny.

The literary linguistics I espouse uses linguistics at two interrelated points in the procedure: first a particular grammatical description will be adopted in assigning features of the text to various grammatical categories; subsequently particular claims concerning the function of members of a particular category, in the discourse, are invoked in the elaboration of the interpretation. At the first stage, that of general grammatical description, what is needed is a descriptive grammar that can categorize the actually occurring ('surface') features and structures in a text with some discrimination but without being over-fussy. A grammar that is workable, and applicable to voluminous data fairly mechanically, is highly desirable. If that grammar is relatively traditional in its approach and terminology, this is all to the good, given the diversity of background of a stylistician's potential audience. Such a grammar is inevitably also interpretative in its commentary on forms and structures, so that the plausibility of these assessments also informs a stylistician's selection of a descriptive model.

Taking all the above criteria into consideration, I have used Quirk, Greenbaum, Leech, and Svartvik (1985) as my model for basic grammatical description. It is the most comprehensive description of English, based on usage, that is currently available. As the authors would be the first to concede, it is not definitive; one must turn to the flood of specialist treatments (of pronouns, aspect, adverbial clauses, etc. etc.) to view the endeavours of those in pursuit of the definitive account of localized topics. The more specialist studies are often drawn upon in the functionalist-interpretative sections of chapters on particular language features that follow. But Quirk *et al.* (1985) is justly regarded as authoritative, not least for the guarded reticence of its interpretative commentary: its descriptions maintain a high level of adequacy while avoiding the built-in obsolescence risked by ambitious 'definitive' explanations.

To turn from general grammatical description to the more speculative studies of particular grammatical features is clearly to narrow the analytical field; the discussions are more narrowed yet, since they are often a selective report from a much more extensive preliminary examination of, for example, contemporary linguistic literature on anaphora. Furthermore, while often acknowledging the existence of multiple potential functions of a language feature, my treatment will emphasize the presence of those functions which are perceived as instrumental in the reader's reception of the novel, that is in ways which have a particular bearing on critical interpretation of the text. Again, there is no question of 'stylistics first, then interpretation': the two are elaborated in tandem and ideally should be mutually justifying. Nevertheless they are distinct, and this is reflected in the remainder of this chapter: first comes a predominantly stylistic discussion concerning the kinds of features chosen as focus of the analysis; subsequently I present my critical interpretation of *Go Down, Moses*, to which the analysis is linked.

THE SELECTION OF FEATURES FOR ANALYSIS

It may be worth noting that my study of particular language features had already begun before I found evidence pointing towards a more general explanation in terms of variable narratorial alignment. The

analysis was commenced in the belief that features such as progressives and pronouns are frequently expressive of subtle textual
strategies and emphases. However, the more that the analysis led
towards an interpretation in terms of narratorial alignments, the
more my attention to linguistic discussions of the features involved
focused on their use in the expression of viewpoint.

The features I consider all operate as options in systems of potential
expressions at important positions in the flow of text, and in different
functional components. Most finite progressive verbs are a marked
option in a system where the non-progressive is the more common
selection; the pronoun *he*, in extended texts, is frequently an alternative option to the name of a participant, or a definite description of
him; causal connectives, more complexly, may be ellipted between
clauses where a causal relation is clear, or their presence may claim a
causal relation where pragmatic or contextual information renders
the claim implausible. The workings of causal connectives are only a
clearer demonstration of the principle which also applies to the
workings of pronouns and progressives: all are possible options in
systems of choice in which there are, regularly, important (conscious
or unconscious) motivations for foregrounding particular formal
options. That choices between lexicogrammatical forms entail
choices between distinct potential meanings is a central assumption of
literary linguistics.

While this study is chiefly directed to the narrative portion of the
novel, the passages of dialogue are not entirely neglected. The
direct-speech rendering of characters' idiolects and sociolects is
discussed, but still in a spirit of stylistic interpretation rather than
dialectology. Gricean principles of conversational co-operation
and implicature, conversational-analytic notions of preference and
recipient design, and the ideal of mutual knowledge are applied
towards that same goal. But the narrative text occupies the forefront
of attention on the judgement that it is the medium, too often
neglected in stylistic studies, of particularly subtle treatment of the
experiences and consciousnesses of individuals, and is quite as 'interactional' as the explicitly multi-voiced text, direct speech. Similarly, the interpretative interest in narrative characterizations could
have led to a more detailed study of the lexical descriptions of the
various characters and their experiences (chapter 8 illustrates one
way of conducting lexical stylistics, with specific reference to the
'Pantaloon in Black' chapter of the novel). But I have worked on the

assumption that the syntax of the narrative may be as central to the nature of the narrative presentations, and in some ways more powerful in its effect, and more in need of stylistic study, since its workings are processed less reflectively by the reader, as if syntax were a transparent enabling medium that did not promote certain meanings and perspectives at the expense of others.

The major syntactic features or systems that might attract an analyst's attention may be familiar from practical and theoretical linguistic studies, and are reflected in the 'checklists' that some stylisticians have devised (Leech and Short 1981: 75ff.; Fowler 1981: 40ff.). They include: personal pronouns; demonstrative pronouns; varieties of naming of participants; complexity of sentences (co-ordination and subordination); sentence adverbials (disjuncts); modal verbs and other expressions of modality; finiteness and non-finiteness; tense; mood; voice (especially passivization); aspect; clausal conjunction; non-pronominal anaphora; transitivity; animacy and agency in clause subjects and objects; nominalization; and so on. Clearly these features and systems operate on a range of levels, but they nevertheless interconnect. The challenge to the stylistician is to identify and study just those features that contribute most crucially to the distinctiveness and effectiveness of the discourse – preferably features which are distinct from each other linguistically, but which operate in an evidently integrated way discoursally.

A first reason for focusing here on progressive aspect, third-person and demonstrative pronouns, and causal connectives is that all three features are sufficiently common characteristics of all extended texts to be regarded as major elements in their construction. That frequency of occurrence greatly reduces the danger of merely mannered or non-generalizable use of these features by the author (cf. a study of the use of subjunctive mood, or complex prepositions, or pseudo-cleft sentences, in a single text). A second attraction is that, while most stylistic effects in literary texts are 'processed' by readers without conscious registering of them, there are advantages in considering linguistic elements with quite distinct surface forms – *he*, *that*, *he was running*, *because*, and so on. Discussing such clearly identifiable forms (cf. the difficulties for the reader in recognizing and categorizing pseudo-transitive clauses, or instances of conflation) is a reaffirming of both the need for such analysis to be relatable to the less developed grammatical formulations of readers, and the influence on interpretation of overt surface forms. Any linguist or stylistician who builds an elaborate account or explanation on the basis of the posited presence (or traces) of layers of submerged structuration is always in danger of exposure as not merely an admirer but the tailor of the emperor's new clothes.

A third and more positive reason for selective attention to pronouns, progressives, and causal connectives is that all three contribute, at a relatively high level of functionality, to the construction and conveying of ideas, judgements, and perspectives in all texts. Thus pronouns are extremely common as a means of effecting textual cohesion, potentially occurring in the subject position of every finite clause. They promote economy in repeated reference to a particular entity, and foster author/reader familiarity with any entity so denoted, but more problematically also draw attention away from the named particularity of individuals or things. They may also be the basis of accidental or deliberate confusion.

The three selected features also display 'language-functional spread'. That is to say, if one considers texts in terms of Halliday's three macro-functions of language, pronouns contribute greatly to the realization of both the interpersonal and the textual functions. The progressivization of verbs, in which the speaker adopts a particular evaluation of the state or process designated – as one which is or was actually perceived, with temporal duration and indefinite points of initial and terminal validity relative to textually adjacent non-progressive verbs – is primarily reflective of the speaker's apperception and evaluation of events and states. It thus contributes to the ideational function of language. So too do causal connectives, with their explicit claims concerning the logical relations between clauses, although they are equally an exponent of the textual function (the conjunctive part of 'theme').

Furthermore, the chosen features operate at contrasting positions in the syntax of the sentence: in terms of Quirk et al.'s (1985) identification of five basic functional elements in clauses (subject, verb, object, complement, and adverbial), progressives are always, in the first instance, components of V, while pronouns realize S, O, or C, and causal connectives are either part of A or outside the clause-analytical system altogether. The fact that this enables a study based on them to scrutinize technique at a range of positions in narrative sentences has been a strong argument in their favour. They interact with many of the other features cited above in important ways: a consideration of each of these features involves attention to those interconnections, and this study introduces relevant commentary at numerous stages. Thus in my study of progressive verbs I consider not only those verbs not ordinarily amenable to progressivization (*I was knowing) but also the interrelated category of tense. Similarly, concern with personal and demonstrative pronouns leads to consideration of indefinite pronouns and some discussion of relative pronouns. It also leads to observation of other means of denoting participants (proper names and definite descriptions) and to consideration of demonstrative adverbs (especially *here*, *there*, *now* and *then*) and that most versatile of items, *it*. Subordinating causal connectives, in turn, compel some consideration of a number of topics: co-ordinate and subordinate clauses; non-finite subordinate clauses; varieties of subordinator (e.g. temporal, concessive, conditional, and spatial connectives); and the latent causal implications sometimes arising with the use of *and*.

In all these cases I have deliberately curtailed my textual study of these adjacent features in order to conduct a more thorough examination of the three features which have been my special concern. Too often studies of particular features have been rendered less compelling by the analyst's decision not to relate those uses of the feature felt to be important to all other 'uninteresting' uses of the same feature. The same partiality has often meant that, while readers are made newly aware of the dynamics of certain striking passages, no sense is gained of the varied and developing functions of a feature through an entire text. By contrast, it is hoped that a text-wide survey of a feature's use makes it more possible to see that use as part of a directed and unfolding process, rather than simply as vivid instantiations of the texture of the work as an omnipresent object. But this remains a hope rather than a certainty: a sense of a text as a continuing process is still in danger of eclipse in intensive feature-based studies such as this. The danger may be lessened, however, by frequent consideration of the extent of use of each feature throughout the narrative, and by the attendant opportunities to chart changes in a feature's use as the novel proceeds. Additionally, I include studies of passages as a companion to feature-based surveys – for example, the comparative study of three extended passages of reflective narrative oriented towards Lucas, Roth, and Ike respectively, presented in chapter 11.

In the act of reading a novel, a literary linguist begins to register various tendencies and distinctive characteristics of the linguistic form. These may even be in the nature of omissions or silences:

consider, for example, a novel containing no proper names, or personal pronouns, or finite progressive verbs. In Spitzerian circular fashion, analysts may wish to see whether the apparent distinctive distribution of a feature is confirmed by a more thorough and organized study, and such study may refine their sense of the precise feature or features they need to consider. This is not quite the Spitzerian circle, in so far as that was geared to identifying the psychological etymon or 'soul' of an author; it is more accurately a dialectical progress from thesis to (always) provisional confirmation, hence less a circular journey than a spiral one. (See also Smit (1988: 24) on legitimate versus disreputable circularity in stylistic argumentation.)

This progress in turn depends crucially on what counts as a 'distinctive' or 'significant' pattern, among all the perceptible language patternings. I have suggested above, in passing, that 'significance' has to be argued for in each particular case: certainly, mere statistical significance will not necessarily persuade the reader of any thematic significance. Thus there is no single answer, in stylistics, for what counts as a 'significant' pattern or trend: each case has to be made separately and judged separately. Nevertheless, unexpectedly high or low frequencies of occurrence of a feature or some atypical tendency of co-occurrence are, in their very unexpectedness or atypicality, noteworthy. Elaborate statistical computations are unlikely to be illuminating in these matters of subtle textual effect. However, as Halliday notes, we should expect 'some quantitative turbulence' when a particular feature is felt to be prominently used, and 'a few figures may be very suggestive'. Halliday also quotes Ullmann (1965: 22), who strikes the appropriate note: 'a rough indication of frequencies would often be helpful'. When detailed frequencies are presented in following chapters, this is often so that such rough indications can be derived.

INTERPRETING *GO DOWN, MOSES*

Ever since Malcolm Cowley's critical resuscitation of Faulkner's reputation in 1946 it has been fairly common practice to emphasize the continuity in the *œuvre*, and to note the way in which, over a writing career of more than thirty years, Faulkner constructed and peopled a definite sociocultural milieu, specifically located in space and time – a vivid Southern region with a familiar history and familiar inhabitants: Yoknapatawpha County. Faulkner himself frequently acknowledged that both major and minor characters in his fictions, inhabiting 'this little postage stamp of native soil', had lived in his consciousness and even developed over the years he had 'known' them. This seems to have been the spirit in which he apprehended Jason and Quentin Compson, Ike McCaslin, Gavin Stevens, the Sartorises, and the Snopeses. It is a spirit which informs their presentation in the novels. One of the goals of this stylistic study is to clarify and substantiate such literary-critical impressions (that the narrative renders uniquely *animated* character portrayals), using the tools of literary linguistics.

From his earliest works to his latest, Faulkner showed a passionate concern with the individual. He was equally concerned with how the irreducible uniqueness of the self is socially situated, and delimited by physical, material, and spatio-temporal constraints. As a consequence Faulkner regarded, as a major human activity, the resolution (or mediation, or mitigation) of the conflicting demands of individual freedom, personal authority, personal power, and the interests, rights, and demands of others, the community. (His own complex set of interests, which drove him to work in Hollywood as a migrant worker trading time and skills for the money which permitted him – simultaneously, as it were – to sustain in Oxford, Mississippi, the role of Southern gentlemanly patron to which he had become imaginatively accustomed, is as eloquent an example as any of the tensions between the individual and the world.) This conflict between personal rights and obligations to the community, from the Declaration of Independence and the Constitution, through the Civil War, the westward expansion, and the various amendments to the Constitution, has been dramatized and given attention to a peculiar degree in American culture.

In *Go Down, Moses* that concern is reflected by means of a shadowy narrator, defying positive identification, who presides over the narrative while adopting, at appropriate points, the viewpoints of the chief protagonists – Ike, Lucas, Roth Edmonds, and others. Various strategies are available to the novelist to effect this narratorial expression of a character's mental and physical response to events, varying from the rather 'external' effect of summarized comment and indirect report to the convention of using an 'abbreviated' syntax (with few cohesive devices or hypotactic structures) to convey a

72

version of the disordered mental impressions of a character, known as stream-of-consciousness technique.

I shall argue that by far the most widespread narrative strategy used to convey character viewpoint in *Go Down, Moses* is a fluid version of free indirect discourse (henceforth FID) – a version that is not always signalled here by its 'canonical' lexicogrammatical markers. It is used not so much in order that readers may 'enter the mind' of any particular character but rather so that they can understand that mind or consciousness in its own terms. Through these extended but temporary narratorial alignments with major characters, the particular values and viewpoints of those characters, their prejudices, blindnesses, romanticisms, arrogance, and vulnerability are all vividly revealed by means of a technique which, unlike stream-of-consciousness (or the rare passages of direct interior monologue), does not rupture the conventional surface of the narrative. There is in this an impression, at least, of significant openness in the narrator's preparedness to subordinate his report of events to the specific viewpoints of particular characters; the decorum of avoiding presumptive narratorial intrusion is combined with vivid immediacy of expression of characters' thoughts and reactions. The character-orientedness of this expression means that, in the act of reading such discourse, the reader participates in a sharing of individuals' private motives and reactions.

This realization of thematic concerns (the concern with free individuals, existing and understood on and in their own terms) through elements of technique is discussed more fully in the following section. Suffice it to say here that my assumption in proceeding has been that the general technique or rhetoric of narratorial alignment with characters is realized to an important degree by the distinctive local deployment of particular features of the language. That view has long been held concerning the workings of deictics, modal and sentential adverbs, and so on, in the realization of standard FID. But the technique I am examining here is much more widespread in the narrative than FID in the conventional sense; and the language features examined are other than those traditionally associated with FID. It is undoubtedly the case, however, that this wider and subtler effect emerges as a possibility only as a result of the conditions fostered by the establishment of FID; and, since the essential nature of FID remains controversial, some further discussion of its workings may be appropriate.

FREE INDIRECT DISCOURSE AND SPEAKERLESS NARRATIVE

The teller of the narrative parts of *Go Down, Moses* is at most a shadowy extra-diegetic voice (not that of a participant in the story it relates), invisible and impersonal, what Chatman (1978) calls a covert narrator. Its presentation often includes the disclosure of the hidden contents of characters' minds – their memories, prejudices, plans, and emotions. But these mind-and-soul portraits are not removed, analytical descriptions of states, as if from the outside. Rather they are often a vivid contrivance of entering into those minds and souls, so that the minds themselves appear to share to a substantial degree in the articulation of their own states and processes. In the terms made current by Genette (1980) and Bal (1985), the narrative discourse is typically a focalization through one of a handful of privileged characters, and the focalization is often directed inward, so that it is consciousness-disclosing. In place of external and static description we often witness an intense, internal, and developing rendering, all the more mimetic of an individual's potential for continual perceiving and conceiving anew.

The narrationally framed mimetic rendering of a character's private words or thoughts, signalled by distinctive formal indices, has been discussed widely by critics and theorists. Defined primarily conceptually, such reporting is regularly labelled as indirect interior monologue or narrated monologue; defined more formally it is commonly termed *style indirecte libre*, *erlebte Rede*, or free indirect style (see e.g. Pascal 1977; McHale 1978; Ginsberg 1982). The designation adopted here is free indirect discourse (FID).

As is widely recognized, FID has formal characteristics which seem to locate it somewhere between direct and indirect speech: it retains the back-shifted tenses and third-person pronouns of indirect speech, but 'freely' dispenses with any framing introductory clause (such as *he thought, she said*). FID reveals its closeness to direct discourse in its propensity for directly expressed questions, exclamations, repetitions, and modal adverbials (*surely, probably*), and deictically proximate expressions (i.e. *now, here, this, yesterday*, rather than those more natural in indirect speech: *then, there, that*, and *the day before*). However, it is often disablingly restrictive, and counter to actual literary findings, to think of FID as simply an intermediate variant between direct and indirect speech. For FID is often quite unlike either of these: it is often not speech at all but thoughts or feelings. Furthermore, in the non-ironic mode which characterizes its use in *Go Down, Moses*, FID involves not quite the silence but the restrained self-effacement of the narrator. In this novel it is a crucial narratorial gesture repudiating (problematically, it should be noted) the tools of taming, enslavement, and authoritarian control.

In this respect it is important to recognize that direct discourse and indirect discourse depend upon the presence of certain framing mechanisms supplied by the narrator:

He said '. . .'.
He said that . . .

These frames differ from any FID counterpart in the degree to which the former carry overt disclaiming of narratorial responsibility or authority for the reported utterance. Even in ironic FID there is only a covert disclaimer of narratorial respect; in non-ironic FID there is no such disclaimer at all, for there is no narratorial assertion of superiority of judgement or knowledge. This makes the attribution of remarks and evaluations in FID passages (either to the narrator or to the character), to put it mildly, a great deal less cut-and-dried than in the other modes. Less mildly, it often means that sentences read as if torn or divided between representing a narrator and a character (on the *invraisemblances* of FID, its inherent dialogism – beyond conventional mimesis or diegesis – see Jefferson (1980)). But in all cases the distinct voice of the character inhabits text that nominally emanates from the narrator, often resulting in a jarring co-telling. All FID, it can be argued, reveals this duality of voice or accent.

Some critics, however, have challenged this 'dual voice' reading of FID – most notably Banfield (1982). Indeed, it is Banfield's radical thesis that there is no textual narrator at all in either FID (which she terms 'represented speech and thought') or conventional narrative, because, 'in narrative, subjectivity or the expressive function of language emerges free of communication' (Banfield 1982: 19). How Banfield comes to this conclusion requires a brief rehearsal of some of her views, but this may be useful in any case, as a reminder of the perils of decontextualized formalism.

The first stage of Banfield's argument is relatively uncontroversial: comparative examination of the grammar of direct and indirect speech presentation is useful, since the grammatical indices of what is subjective in language emerge in such a comparison. At the outset the implausibility of transformationally deriving direct speech from indirect speech – or vice versa – is noted. It is proposed instead that the initial PS-rule node for such sentences should be E (expression), which may then be expanded by a variety of non-sentential 'expressive elements' and/or S (S in turn rewriting as Comp-S). Since the expression node can only be recursive through co-ordination, these 'expressive elements' (e.g. exclamations, incomplete sentences, and other features of the immediacy of direct speech) cannot be embedded under S, but are always a property of the E node. These proposals seem to answer to what is or is not acceptable in direct and indirect speech, for, while the quoted clause of the former is an E (and can thus present expressive elements), that of the latter is merely an S (only the quoting clause of indirect speech can present expressive elements; the quoted clause allegedly presents only expressionless propositional content). The larger implications of this analysis is that 'one cannot indirectly quote another speaker's expression' (where 'expression' denotes 'subjectivity'), one can only indirectly quote another's communication.

These bold claims are supported by copious reference to (sometimes problematic) example sentences and universalizable principles. The first of the latter is that 'for every expression (E), there is a unique referent of I (the SPEAKER), to whom all expressive elements are attributed, and a unique referent of *you* (the ADDRESSEE/HEARER)' (Banfield 1982: 57). In addition, for every expression there is a unique referent of the present tense (PRESENT), which is cotemporal with present-time deictics (NOW). In fact Expression is not the largest textual unit: TEXT has that status, and the above-mentioned principles of concordance of tense and person must then be applied to TEXT:

1 TEXT / 1 SPEAKER / 1 PRESENT

Direct speech escapes the concordance restriction, since the quoted Expression of direct speech embodies a shift to a new TEXT.

In this scheme, then, there is only one subjectivity or point of view in any instance of FID, that of the Expression's SELF – there is no simultaneous covert narration:

> Rather than being narrated, consciousness in this style is represented unmediated by any judging point of view. No one speaks in represented E[xpression]s, although in them speech may be represented. (Banfield 1982: 97)

Thus FID is neither a framed and evaluated report of speech nor a direct representation of speech:

> Instead, the speech or thought of the SELF represented retains all its expressivity without suggesting that its grammatical form was that uttered by an original speaker, whether aloud or silently. (108)

Thus Banfield's theory of the 'speakerlessness' of narrative and FID is a suggestive and extensively argued alternative to the 'dual-voice' characterization of FID. The reaction to the theory, however, from many students of narrative mixes respect for the intellectual vigour and detail of argumentation with scepticism concerning the project's groundings and conclusions. Thus in the course of a penetrating critique McHale writes:

> Operating with a pragmatics-free grammar of English, she aims to establish the *essence* of various types of narrative sentences, what they *are* in isolation from any real or constructed context of occurrence and use. From this essence, in turn, she derives her definition of what a narrative text is; of what fiction is; of what literature is. Nowhere does the theory make contact with the facts of context, whether textual or historical. (McHale 1983: 43)

If one word looms particularly large in Banfield's thesis it is the word 'sentence'. From the title of the book itself (*Unspeakable Sentences*), through the opening chapter's efforts to give a generative analysis of the command relations in direct and indirect speech, Banfield's orientation is inflexibly towards regularities at the level of sentence. One upshot of this is that, in her dispute with dual-voice theorists, the argument appears to founder on cross-purposes. It is perhaps best, therefore, to emphasize the attractions of an effort at reformulation from both camps. Below I suggest some revisions of each perspective that may be useful.

In asserting that there is no speaker in narration or FID, Banfield expounds a belief I simply cannot share. I would claim that when confronted with seemingly coherent intended text we always make conjectures about the (undeclared) author or speaker. All language, and not merely communicative language, always by definition entails a speaker who, in the absence of others, becomes the addressee also. I find the notion of speakerless narration a theoretical misdirection, more a riddle than an explanation. Equally, Banfield's preoccupation with sentence-level analysis is both a practical and a theoretical

77

misdirection. While it is true that many literary texts conveniently switch modes of narration and presentation of speech and thought at sentence (or clause) boundaries, it is more important to recognize that many others – often the most challenging and narrationally complex texts – do not. This latter observation, crucial to the dual-voice case, is one that Banfield's grammar simply disallows and cannot comprehend: hence the arguing at cross-purposes. Regardless of what Banfield's grammar permits, expressivity and subjectivity are slipped into, and out of, with remarkable subtlety, within clauses and even within phrases. The very strength of FID, as Ginsberg (1982) has recently reiterated, is its resistance to determinate specification on innumerable occasions in the greater writers (James is pre-eminent in a long list). Banfield's entire enterprise suppresses this central fact, in a failed attempt at taming.

Having registered these objections to the 'speakerless narrative' theory, I now wish to note also what seem to me difficulties in the dual-voice model. For I sympathize with Banfield's underlying assumption that an utterance cannot emerge from two distinct subjectivities at once. Accordingly, in the version of dual-voice description I adopt, the emphasis is on the interweaving of the narrator's and character's voices and perspectives: the *impression* of duality or merging comes from the scarcely perceptible slipping or modulation from one subjectivity to the other, even in the course of a single phrase. The duality of voices thus emerges in the text's linearity, within the developing reading experience; it is not a property perceptible statically or at any *point* in the text or sentence. Individual words, then, are not, in my view, double-voiced. In making this claim I may be at variance with some dual-voice theorists, and certainly with the tenor of argument concerning 'the double-accented word' in Bakhtin (1973), but a renewed emphasis on (free indirect) discourse-processing as developmental and sequential is perhaps overdue in narrative theory.

MERGED VOICES IN *GO DOWN, MOSES*

In *Go Down, Moses*, I have claimed, the covert impersonal narrator rarely intervenes or judges. The major and memorable occasions when he does so are in 'Was', section I, a couple of brief passages in section IV of 'The Bear', and perhaps the first two pages of 'Go Down, Moses'. Only in the above passages (and in brief glimpses of ironical portraiture) can it be said that the narrative carries any suggestion of privileged knowledge beyond the awareness of the characters depicted. Instead the emphasis is firmly on the characters and their experiences, which are almost constantly presented from a narratorial perspective which is close to, if not simply expressive of, the judgements of the characters themselves.

If the narratorial point of view is nearly always close to that of one of the characters, the narrative voice – in terms of the lexicogrammatical form of the narrative – is often quite distinct from characters' voices as evidenced in the direct-speech reports. This is the case even in passages of FID (where there is definitionally, for any dual-voice theorist of FID, a combination of perspectives; in *Go Down, Moses* the combination regularly comprises narratorial voice and characterological point of view).

Narratorial adoption of the phraseology or idiolect of a character, although rare, does occasionally occur, particularly in the least serious story, 'Was'. For example, one report of Mr Hubert's opinions uses some of his own words:

> Mr Hubert said he not only wouldn't buy Tomey's Turl, he wouldn't have *that damn white half-McCaslin* on his place even as a gift. (p. 6; my emphasis)

Similarly, Cass's confirmatory expression is adopted when the narrative reports:

> So when they came out on the long flat about three miles from Mr Hubert's, *sure enough*, there was Tomey's Turl on the Jake mule about a mile ahead. (p. 8; my emphasis)

Moreover, humorous effects arise from the narrative's reporting (while still closely aligned to Cass's innocent viewpoint) of the actual words of the manoeuvring adults – Miss Sophonsiba as the object of Uncle Buck's reluctant affection – in the same story:

> and Miss Sophonsiba said how *seriously now neighbors just a half day's ride apart ought not to go so long as* Uncle Buck did, and Uncle Buck said *Yessum*, and Miss Sophonsiba said Uncle Buck was *just a confirmed roving bachelor from the cradle born* and this time Uncle Buck even quit chewing and looked and said, *Yes, ma'am*, he *sure* was, *and born too late at it ever to change now but at least* he could *thank God no lady would ever have to suffer the misery of living with* him. (pp. 11–12; my emphases)

The density of the interweaving of narrative voice and character voice in such passages argues against preoccupation with just those sentences revealing strict or 'well-formed' FID. More widespread and significant are those which are not strict FID yet which convey, through their distinctive formal choices, a temporary narratorial alignment with a particular character. In strict FID, the voice rendered is predominantly that of the character – the narrator simply supplies the structural frame for the content, asserting his presence through back-shifted tenses and third-person pronouns. By these means the mind of the character is unobtrusively disclosed and, if the presentation is not ironic or critical, respect for that mind and voice is also implied.

However, irony and criticism of a character are often effected, even when the narrator adopts the stance of respectful conveyor, through FID, of a character's seemingly valued thought and speech. The evident narratorial involvement in rendering FID at first suggests to the reader that the narrator values the speech or thought as highly as the character does. But when those freely rendered opinions are seen (by readers) to be questionable – motivated by the character's jealousy, pride, self-interest, vanity, prejudice, or whatever – we see that the narrator has subtly stylized a particular character's voice or viewpoint in order to expose and mock its source.

Accordingly FID is indeed often ironical, as Pascal has noted (1977: 41). But when FID and temporary narratorial alignment are empathetic, and characters' attitudes are presented without discernible mockery of those attitudes (it is left to the attentive reader to see whatever flaws there may be in the characters' attitudes), then we have non-ironic use of FID, arguably a necessary condition for a fully subject-oriented presentation of independent characters or consciousnesses. There may remain the irony of contrasts between characters' expectations and actual reported outcomes (situational rather than narratorial irony); but that is an irony based in the circumstances, the *histoire*, and is not stylistically encoded in the *discours* by an intruding, gently mocking, and judging narrator.

Irony does operate in this novel, but not presentationally through FID or temporary narratorial alignment. Incidental ironies surface in 'Was', 'The Fire and the Hearth', and 'The Bear', section IV, while implicitly critical FID passages relating to Ike are common in 'Delta Autumn' – there operating to expose the sombre extent of his failure of heart, courage, and fraternity. We may also note FID or narratorially aligned passages in 'Go Down, Moses' exposing Gavin Stevens's ineradicable prolixity, his leaden intellectualizing, and his sense of oppressive constriction during his visit to the grieving Worshams.

The narrator, then, is sometimes implicitly critical of characters (most clearly in 'Delta Autumn'), but he is rarely so by using conventional FID means of exposing a character's follies via that character's own words. As Chatman has commented:

> Disparity between the character's point of view and the narrator's expression of it need not entail ironic opposition. The narrator may verbalize neutrally or even sympathetically what (for reasons of youth, lack of education or intelligence, and so on) the character cannot articulate. This is the whole structural principle of James's *What Maisie Knew*. (Chatman 1978: 156)

The ironies of *Go Down, Moses* are a function of the gulf between the evaluations of situations by characters and by the reader: there is (after 'Was', section I) scarcely any ironical gulf, such as would be reflected in phraseology, between characters and narrators. The fact that narratorial alignment with characters and expression of their viewpoints as they would wish them expressed may not preclude a reader's distaste for and condemnation of those characters is most acutely apparent in 'Pantaloon in Black', section II.

A RHETORIC OF FREE CHARACTERS

The term rhetoric seems appropriate to describe Faulkner's adoption of this mobile narratorial perspective I have discussed, in which there is movement towards and entering of the minds of characters, then a withdrawal from them. That rhetoric is consistent with a major theme of the novel: the difficulty, given the oppression and injustices within any sociohistorical context, of achieving a true communal, egalitarian brotherhood built on honour, pride, humility, courage, the truth of the heart, and so on – but the continuing and desperate need to attempt such an achievement.

The importance of the freedom of the individual, both as a central element in Faulkner's world-view and as a recurring theme in his fiction, can hardly be over-emphasized. It is prominent also in the non-fictional reflections on society, collected in his *Essays, Speeches and Public Letters* (1967). Of particular note are the essays 'On privacy' (1955) and 'On fear' (1956), the only completed parts of a planned book on the American dream. In 'On privacy' Faulkner laments the fading of that ideal according to which every individual could be free 'within a fabric of individual courage and honorable work and mutual responsibility' (1967: 62). That ideal was, Faulkner argues, not an idea but a condition; it was also a rejection of hierarchy and subjection, and a celebration of the individual (63). However, he regrets, the lived dream has been lost by recent generations who have allowed themselves to be 'owned and possessed' by the dream itself without striving to maintain its essential components: individualism, privacy, work, and mutual responsibility.

It has also already been remarked that Faulkner seems to have treated his major characters as if they were living individuals. He once declared:

> Those characters to me are quite real and quite constant. They are in my mind all the time. I don't have any trouble at all going back to pick one up. I forget what they did, but the character I don't forget, and when the book is finished, that character is not done, he still is going on at some new devilment that sooner or later I will find out about and write about. (Gwynn and Blotner 1959: 78)

This does not mean that Faulkner was an uncritical enthusiast for his own characters, as is clear from his recorded comments on Ike McCaslin (Gwynn and Blotner 1959: 246; see also Jeliffe 1956). Rather it means that, as Vickery put it thirty years ago,

> Faulkner's interest in form and technique cannot be divorced from his interest in character. . . . The anonymous Voice so often detected in his fiction is the author seeing himself distanced as one more perspective on the scene, one more legitimate but not conclusive point of view. . . . Throughout, his aim is to avoid limiting the freedom of character, reader, or author. (Vickery 1959: 298–9)

These deep personal and aesthetic convictions, of the primacy of characters and individuality, are the life-force of theme and technique in *Go Down, Moses*.

ISAAC MCCASLIN

While a number of characters are drawn in the novel, Isaac McCaslin remains the major figure. Any assessment of Ike must consider his several failures. The position in which Ike finds himself at the age of

21, in 'The Bear', section IV, is framed by a complex grouping of personal preferences and social responsibilities. The young man we have seen developing into a submissive and idealistic disciple of the wilderness is here confronted with the accumulated outrages and guilts of his family, his class, his race, and indeed the whole of the South. As readers we can see increasingly clearly that there can be no simple reconciliation of those personal impulses and social demands. If Ike's 'communal anonymous brotherhood' (my emphases) and his recorded compassion for the blacks are to mean anything, he must make choices, intervene, and engage with the forces that maintain the oppression of these individuals. In the course of the story Ike does, indeed, make choices; but they are either choices with insufficient impact, not sustained, or they are 'choices' which are simply explicit decisions to withdraw or disengage.

Ike's tendency to relinquish active involvement is powerfully portrayed through the first three sections of 'The Bear'. There he is shown seduced by the mystical, ritual, and atmospheric qualities of the wilderness and the hunt. He passively surrenders to the wilderness in section I, as he will passively surrender to his wife at the end of section IV. The submission as it is depicted in section I – experiencing the entry into the wilderness as a profound rebirth, discarding the instruments of manipulative civilization in order to encounter the bear – is arguably defensible and fitting in an adolescent novice. It cannot continue to be as Ike becomes a mature young man with other responsibilities – the inheritance of the tainted land and the injustice to the black McCaslins, and the personal commitment to a marriage partner.

As the elaborate incantatory sentences at the opening of section I reflect, Ike is also seduced by the talking associated with hunting. But he never attends critically to the destructive and exploitative side of hunting, the possibility of wanton killing, the appalling 'impersonal malignance' of Lion and the evidently limited sensibilities of Boon. Although Sam welcomes the presence of Lion, Sam's condition is very different from Ike's: the former is an old man, apparently trapped and shamed by the fact that his blood mingles that of Indian chiefs and a negro slave; all his life he has 'had to be a negro', submitting to forces beyond his control.

For Sam, Lion is the messenger of death in a quite personal sense, and is accepted by him as such. But Lion cannot have that function for the young Ike. What Lion should be for Ike is a reminder of the elements of brutality and mortality which are a fact of the wilderness as of society. (It is a lesson he appears to learn in encountering the ageing, death-carrying snake in section V; but his knowledge remains chiefly a mental phenomenon reflected in verbal rhetoric, not a knowledge reflected in resultant action.) Repeatedly, Ike pays lip-service to forces much more powerful than words, and one is drawn to agree with Michael Millgate that, 'Although it is obviously an over-simplification, there is a sense in which it is true of Ike that what he says is *right*, but what he does is *wrong*' (Millgate 1966: 210). He persists in responding to the wilderness and the community as a romantic naïf, although he has encountered much that demonstrates that romanticism and relinquishment are insufficient.

The final lines of section II of 'The Bear', with their romanticized treatment of the situation as an intense drama, express Ike's damaging pre-judging of his own future experiences, so that these experiences might contain those idealized qualities that the true son of the wilderness is supposed to have. Those qualities include humility, pride, and courage. Here Ike's resolves – 'He would be humble and proud that he had been found worthy to be a part of it too or even just to see it too' (p. 172) – are rendered in a FID sentence which emphasizes the submissive enthusiasm for, and lack of active criticism of, what requires a careful assessment in terms of the conflicting values and interests it exposes.

Ike's failure to be at least a critical witness in section II foreshadows his failure to act constructively in the course of section IV. There the insidious narcotic of talking is seen as Ike's psychological substitute for action. All Ike's discussions in section IV point to his strong sense that acts have consequences, that personal and social history are explicable and must be explained. Yet he ignores the consequences of his own acts or failures to act. His work as a carpenter makes him an instrument of the wilderness's destruction, for example. More significant, though, is his passive submission to seduction by his wife at the close of the section, in which she trades sex for Ike's promise (counter to his resolve to relinquish the land) to reoccupy the farm. Equally passive is his apparent acceptance of the subsequent attenuation of his marriage, when Ike breaks that promise.

OTHER CHARACTERS

Go Down, Moses is, however, as much about the characters that are juxtaposed to Ike as about Ike himself. Ike's responses to the questions of the relations between white and black; to the demands of personal, familial, and regional historical context; to the conflict he perceives between his initiation into the wilderness and the principles of ownership for control and profit that seem to shape life on the farm and in the town: these are all compared and contrasted with the experiences and values of Lucas, Roth, Cass, and others.

Lucas's behaviour contrasts with that of Ike in several important ways. He claims an independence of judgement and strength of will similar to that of Ike, but is paradoxically very proud of his McCaslin inheritance, while Ike is chiefly ashamed of his. Their respective inheritances are seen by these two heirs in quite different terms: for Ike, his grandfather engendered to him shame, corruption, ruthless exploitation of land and people; for Lucas, his inheritance from old Carothers is one of pride, determination, and arrogance. That latter inheritance is not wholly admirable: coupled with a presumably unfounded suspicion of his wife's fidelity, it leads Lucas to attempt to kill the alleged adulterer, Zack. Nor is Lucas without flaws – at first arrogantly and unfeelingly planning the exposure and imprisonment of his prospective son-in-law, George Wilkins; subsequently careless of how his obsession with treasure-hunting is wrecking his marriage. But there is a clear contrast between Lucas's handling of the crises in his marriage and Ike's responses to the crises in his life (when confronted by his family inheritance of shame, the material inheritance of the land, the demands of his wife, and the expectations of his distant black relation in 'Delta Autumn').

At the close of the long Lucas-oriented recollection in 'The Fire and the Hearth', chapter 1, section II (pp. 45–7), Lucas is seen just managing to restrain himself from extinguishing the fire on his hearth, the steady burning of which symbolizes his enduring marriage. His stopping short here is indicative of his commitment to his marriage and is reported as a parenthesis within the record of his adoption of an alternative and much more positive mode of action: confrontation of Zack. Such comparisons of the actual responses of Ike and Lucas to their different circumstances should remind us that, if an ideal of individual freedom is examined within the novel, any assessment of the degree of freedom achieved by the various characters has to be considered within the context of the possibilities of freedom of action which their different conditions permit.

Sam, for example, the son of Doom and caged all his life by his own mixed blood (p. 167), who 'for seventy years now had had to be a negro' (p. 215), who 'quits' (p. 248) at the death of Ben and Lion, 'childless, kinless, peopleless – motionless' (p. 246), and is finally ritually buried in the woods in the old Indian fashion, 'the way he wanted it' (p. 255), has had little opportunity for freedom outside the wilderness environment of his Indian forefathers. It would seem that Lucas, the chief black McCaslin in the book, has much greater freedom to live as he pleases. We may note that some of those options, as expressed from the viewpoints of Ike and Roth, entail accepting monetary compensation for his ancestors' violation by Carothers, and using that money to leave the McCaslin farm. But Lucas never considers that repudiation of his McCaslin roots – although he is canny and worldly enough to take his share of the money inheritance when he is eligible! Lucas's accommodation with circumstances, living in the cottage given to him by Cass, farming the fields he 'neither owned . . . nor wanted to nor even needed to' (p. 35), refusing all advice on cultivation 'yet drawing supplies from the commissary as if he farmed, and at an outrageous and incredible profit, a thousand acres' (p. 117), with no intention of ever paying that account, and quietly trading his moonshine whisky, leaves him proud and independent in his old age. At the end of the story, when Lucas relinquishes and repudiates the treasure-hunting machine, he explains to Roth:

'Man has got three score and ten years on this earth, the Book says. He can want a heap in that time and a heap of what he can want is due to come to him, if he just starts in soon enough. . . . That money's there. . . . But I am near to the end of my three score and ten, and I reckon to find that money aint for me.' (p. 131)

Thus runs the final verdict of a man who all along has been a compound of stubbornness, determination, and tolerance, a man whose limited aspirations are consistently supported by his actions.

The other major character in *Go Down, Moses* besides Ike and Lucas is Roth Edmonds, who pragmatically carries on the management of the farm and is portrayed living out an alternative response to the white McCaslin inheritance. In 'The Fire and the Hearth', chapter 3, section I, we witness Roth's vivid memories of his unwitting entry into a heritage of racial estrangement, when he repudiates his black cousin Henry as brother or equal, and later recognizes and begins to understand the cold antagonism between his father and Lucas. That estrangement is poignantly shown to be felt by Roth as an acute loss, made more so by the fact that Lucas's wife, Molly, has been the only mother he has ever known – raising him, feeding him, and teaching him. The portrait of him that emerges from this story is of a rather innocent solitary bachelor, fond of directing others and hence all the more choleric when his orders are thwarted. A rich extension of that portrait, sharpened by the explicit contrasts with the values of Ike as an old man, is presented in 'Delta Autumn', to which I now turn.

In 'Delta Autumn', where the narrative returns to the present time of narration (1941–2), we see the endpoint of the versions of individual freedom and responsibility adopted by Ike and Roth. Both options are seen to be deeply flawed. The major focus is on Ike, the old man, and we witness a development within the story: at first we see him as possessing a natural and humane authority over horses and men. (This authority is rejected by Roth Edmonds alone: the other men linger at the dinner table 'apparently held there yet by his [Ike's] quiet and peaceful voice as the heads of the swimming horses had been held above the water by his weightless hand' (p. 348).) Later, however, the reader recognizes anew that Ike is also a man of limited vision, motivated by a romantic rhetoric of withdrawal rather than the commitment of human love. We can also see that his wisdom as a child of the wilderness promotes in him a calm that is in fact often complacent; it is a calm radically disrupted by the appearance of his young black relative.

'Delta Autumn' also provides us with a fuller impression of the darker side of Roth Edmonds. His responses here constitute a series of bitter and anguished repudiations: he repudiates any claimed sanctity in the hunt; he repudiates his own society, and the essential goodness of man; he rejects his lover and their child; and he repudiates Ike and any wisdom he may have acquired. Indeed, so starkly drawn are the lines demarcating the limits of the humanity and compassion of Roth and Ike in 'Delta Autumn' that reading this story in its position in the novel after the millennial rhetoric of 'The Bear' is a chastening experience. Now, the passivity, the failures, the impotence, and the degeneration are all on the surface, and narratorially emphasized. Thus the fact that Ike has passively submitted to burial alive for the last fifty years is hinted at in the recurring references to his adoption of a mummified position in the tent, lying on his cot with his hands crossed on his breast, his eyes closed. Similarly, Ike's eyes, 'blurred and irisless and apparently pupilless' (p. 359), are symptomatic of his more general loss or failure of vision.

FAILURES OF INSUFFICIENCY IN IKE AND ROTH

All his life Ike has claimed to have relinquished power and withdrawn from any involvement in the injustices of his society. But even here at the end of his life, as an apparently passive intermediary between Roth and his lover, Ike is shown as not being able to live without perpetuating old and palpably insufficient gestures of restitution and compensation. Thus here he proceeds with his appointed task of conveying a money reparation to Roth's lover, even after he (unlike Roth) knows that she is a Beauchamp/McCaslin. With regard to that money he says to her, almost hysterically, 'Take it. . . . Take it out of my tent' (p. 362), half concealing the fact that he is actively giving the conscience money to her.

Ike's latent racism and paranoia concerning the mixing of the races shows horrifyingly clearly in the contrasts between his rhetorical eulogies and his actual thoughts and deeds. On p. 348 he declares:

> I think that every man and woman, at the instant when it dont even matter whether they marry or not, I think that whether they marry then or afterward or dont never, at that instant the two of them together were God.

This halting declaration of the divinity of human love at its purest is rapidly contrasted with the narrowness of Ike's insight when confronted by the young black woman. Ike discovers her to be the granddaughter of James Beauchamp (older brother of Lucas McCaslin, both being sons of Tomey's Turl and Tennie Beauchamp, Turl being the son conceived in Carothers McCaslin's rape of Tomey, Tomey being the daughter conceived in Carothers McCaslin's rape of Eunice). He proceeds to announce to her that there is nothing they can do for her; he even surmises that she became involved with Roth for 'revenge'. The love she evidently feels for Roth is the very feature of the situation that Ike cannot begin to understand. As his outpouring on p. 364 indicates, interracial love is not possible in his scheme of things; he can only see it as bestial breeding and spawning, a definitive nightmare of social degeneration and ecological destruction.

As many critics (including Faulkner himself) have said of Ike, his failure is that, having been granted induction into the wilderness, his subsequent gestures are insufficient, 'not enough' (a quantifying phrase which has a special resonance in this novel, as I attempt to show in chapter 8). Burdened by the sins of earlier generations, he –

largely unwittingly – contributes to the burdens and travails of future generations by his sins of omission. (In the final story, 'Go Down, Moses', we see a future generation still living along lines of racial and social division, with the fertile woods ruined and one black McCaslin having degenerated into crime and murder.)

The Roth of 'Delta Autumn', with his multiple repudiations of influences and obligations, is the victim of his own nihilism. But that nihilism may in turn be the fruit of an excessive indulgence, as is suggested in James Beauchamp's granddaughter's claim that Roth was spoiled by them all (p. 360). (In chapter 11 I show how patterns of relative clauses reflect Roth's *seeking out* of pity and special treatment, which he certainly seems to have received from Molly.) In a similar way, it is possible for the characters in a novel, however they are rendered, to be over-indulged by an author, especially if there is no direct criticism of their most glaring defects by the narrator or other characters. I believe the narrator of *Go Down, Moses* negotiates a path in which characters' experiences and viewpoints are substantially released from narratorial control, while the characterological fallibilities and prejudices thereby incidentally exposed are never narratorially indulged. The narrative frame around the various alignments with characters and the expressions from their viewpoints is always in place; close study of the narrative language shows that the narrator who respects and expresses characters' viewpoints can also adopt the resources of the language to be firmly but unironically critical of those untamed characters.

TOLERANCE AND CONTROL

There is great restraint on the part of the narrator in entering the minds of characters. Such restraint reflects the fact that Faulkner is often nearer Flaubert than Virginia Woolf in technique. He is not much concerned, after *The Sound and the Fury*, with using chance occasions or accidental triggers to initiate the rendering of processes of consciousness. He is more willing to edit and select reflections. While he remains concerned with individuals, he increasingly sees a need to relate individuals to sociohistorical contexts, so as to draw them forth from their mental cocoons. In Guerard's view (1976: 223), truncated or stream-of-consciousness interior monologue is rare in Faulkner after *As I Lay Dying*, since he found it an uncongenial technique in which his imagination was not 'energized'. More positively, however, I believe that Faulkner discarded such forms of presentation because he moved away, in his aesthetics and in his personal world-view, from the presumption of being able to present an exhaustive, intimate disclosure of the thoughts and impulses of characters. The argument is in part about claimed authorial omniscience (on the imprecision of this term, see Kuroda (1973)). The more reticent and 'respectful' disclosures of minds and values in *Absalom, Absalom!* and subsequent novels are correspondingly less forced and more plausible.

The book's compositional history, too, supports a treatment of the novel as an interplay of characters' perspectives without an overtly controlling or authoritative one. For behind the various chapters are the separate styles and voices of such stories as 'Almost', 'A Point of Law', 'Gold is not Always', 'Lion', and 'The Bear' (stories that were substantially recast when used in the novel). And there is a noteworthy correlation of theme and technique underlying the opposition of white proprietors and Negro slaves, of the civilized town or plantation and the wilderness, and of the hunter and the hunted, all of which dramatize the problematic activities – and states – of taming and being tamed.

When Major de Spain sees the recently captured dog, Lion, ceaselessly crashing against the walls of the hut which cages him, de Spain warns Sam that he will never tame Lion, who is apparently an embodiment of brute force.

'I dont want him tame,' Sam said; again the boy watched his nostrils and the fierce milky light in his eyes. 'But I almost rather he be tame than scared, of me or any man or any thing. But he wont be either, of nothing.' (p. 217)

Soon afterwards Ike similarly tells McCaslin, 'We dont want him tame. We want him like he is' (p. 219), asserting this despite his evident knowledge that an untamed Lion spells doom and destruction for Ben and, by extension, for the whole wilderness. A little later, at the opening of 'The Bear', section IV, there is explicit reference to 'the tamed land' (p. 254), tamed – or at least believed to have been tamed – by old Carothers McCaslin. And the concordance to *Go Down, Moses* confirms other significant uses of the words *tame* and *tamed* (Capps 1977).

Faulkner too, like Sam and Ike with respect to Lion, did not want his main characters 'tame'. They are presented with such attention to all the forces that may have shaped them, and (thematically and rhetorically) with such a strong sense that they are responsible individuals capable of intervening to adjust their fates, that it seems clear that Faulkner primarily wishes them to be understood (as individuals), not judged (as 'cases'). In these important respects, although I will not elaborate the case here, the novel is exemplary of Bakhtin's theory of the polyphonic, dialogical novel (Bakhtin 1973; Volosinov 1973; Bakhtin 1985).

If Faulkner's individualist ethic does indeed shape his poetics, it should also be acknowledged that such an approach involves a relinquishing of control over characters, analogous to Ike's relinquishment of control over the plantation. And it may be as problematic; for it raises all the perennial ethical problems of freedom – how tolerance of and respect for others may lead the individual to tolerate and even perpetuate the injustices of others. The acceptance of presented characters as independent subjects may seem laudable avoidance of authorial tyranny and limitation; it may also seem to be a failure in responsibility and protective vigilance, leading to the chaos and bleakness at the novel's end (a din that ought to be repressed, rather than a polyphony that ought to be expressed). Characteristically, the novel refuses to make a definitive choice between these alternative evaluations of its own technique.

Faulkner's concern with free individuals in this book inevitably prompts the reader to consider the ethical implications of authoritarianism and its extreme corollary, slavery; and of their opposites, freedom, 'untamedness', the tolerance of others as complex and unpredictable individuals. That consideration should embrace the book's technique as well as its overt content. Thus Ike may be judged to have failed through not doing enough, relinquishing control in a way which entailed withdrawing from important personal relationships: Ike's gestures involve repudiating his wife, the black McCaslins, and the community. Yet in other respects Ike remains an attractive and admirable figure, in his love and knowledge of the wilderness, his revulsion from exploitation of the blacks and the land, his rejection of acquisitive materialism, and in his simple optimism. Such mixed critical judgement of Ike is facilitated by the manner of narration, which encourages detached appraisal (within a framework of compassion) of its characters – even while, paradoxically, the narrative itself refrains from occupying that privileged position of judgement.

91

Possession, property, and control are not only central thematic concerns in this collective novel about various strategies for eluding control, various experiences of the power of that control, and various bids by individuals to be independent and answerable only to themselves; they are also central concerns of stylistic technique. Many critics before Wayne Booth registered their unease at the prospect of the author (and narrator, in third-person novels) withdrawing into a position of claimed impartiality, allowing the morally weak or reprobate to flourish without overt censure. The particular trend recognized by such critics as Booth is that certain Jamesian and post-Jamesian authors not only adopt those goals, but have also refined the ideal literary mode – non-ironic FID and narratorial alignment – for its presentation. In doing so, as Flaubert remarked, these authors adopt a godlike stance towards their creations.

God too has been criticized for allowing the forces of evil the freedom and independence which make it possible for their evil to spread. There is a direct analogy with the narrator in non-ironic FID – an analogy of which Faulkner was perhaps aware. Indeed, he seems to have been sufficiently aware of it to introduce an altercation between Ike and Cass in section IV of 'The Bear' which concerns not merely Ike's view of God, or Ike's view of his own act of withdrawal. The debate is, by analogy, a characterization and defence of the godly self-effacing narrator, who refuses to intervene to condemn the characters he presents as free and independent equals.

On p. 258 of section IV Cass provocatively suggests to Ike that the latter's God, who could allow the shame of slavery and its continuation on land seized by Carothers McCaslin, must have been either 'perverse, impotent or blind'. Ike breaks into the flow of Cass's invective to argue that God was none of these things but that he was chiefly dispossessed. Ike says God 'ordered and watched it', but did not intervene to rectify the evils or reverse the dispossession: that had to be effected, if at all, by man himself as free individual.

The God–narrator–Ike analogy continues: on p. 282 of section IV, resuming the record of the discussion after Ike's sixteen-page recollection of the ledger revelations, Ike explains God's continued nonintervention in these terms:

Because He had already worried with them [men] so long: worried with them so long because He had seen how in individual cases they were capable of anything any height or depth remembered in mazed incomprehension out of heaven where hell was created too and so He must admit them or else admit His equal somewhere and so be no longer God and therefore must accept responsibility for what He himself had done *in order to live with Himself* in his lonely and paramount heaven. (my emphasis)

This is Ike's analysis of God, but it is also a version of Ike's own rationale: six pages later he reminds Cass that he is doing all this talking in order to explain things to himself 'because I have got myself to have to live with for the rest of my life'. Similarly, while Ike has seen God's home as 'lonely and paramount', such adjectives might well describe Ike's final years. And there is also Ike's confused and unconvincing comparison of his own chosen trade of carpentering with the similar choice made by 'the Nazarene' (p. 309).

It should suffice to acknowledge how this God–narrator–Ike analogizing is unflattering to Ike, highlighting his inflated self-image. With an arrogance as deep as his grandfather's, Ike claims godlike detachment from the world, adopting the role of the voluntarily dispossessed, watching, waiting, grieving, but declining to intervene. In asserting this divinity Ike flees from his humanity, and reminds us again of the inevitable difference between human and divine compassion. Faulkner himself often emphasized that it was human compassion which he wished to evoke. He once declared:

What the writer's asking is compassion, understanding, that change must alter, must happen. . . . It's to have compassion for the anguish that the wilderness itself may have felt [being destroyed for petty profit]. . . . It's not to choose sides at all – just to compassionate the good splendid things. (Gwynn and Blotner 1959: 277)

A full response to both the themes and techniques of this novel requires of the reader a commensurate human 'compassionating'.

4

PROGRESSIVE VERBAL FORMS IN THE NARRATIVE

PROGRESSIVES AS, AND IN, 'HEIGHTENED WITNESSING'

The final paragraphs of section 2 of 'The Old People' constitute one of the passages in *Go Down, Moses* where the role of progressive verbs is particularly crucial. The passage is part of an intense evocation of the young Ike's induction into the wilderness as a mystical environment (and follows his earlier, more conventional initiation into it as the domain of noble hunting). The passage is immediately preceded by a hunting sequence (completed by the familiar 'flat single clap of Walter Ewell's rifle which never missed') in which, the boy imagines, he has suffered a 'missed opportunity, the missed luck'. The text continues:

> And he would remember how Sam was standing. Sam had not moved. He was not tall, squat rather and broad, and the boy had been growing fast for the past year or so and there was not much difference between them in height, yet Sam was looking over the boy's head and up the ridge toward the sound of the horn and the boy knew that Sam did not even see him; that Sam knew he was still there beside him but he did not see the boy. Then the boy saw the buck. It was coming down the ridge, as if it were walking out of the very sound of the horn which related its death. It was not running, it was walking, tremendous, unhurried, slanting and tilting its head to pass the antlers through the undergrowth, and the boy standing with Sam beside him now instead of behind him as Sam always stood, and the gun still partly aimed and one of the hammers still cocked.
>
> Then it saw them. And still it did not begin to run. It just stopped for an instant, taller than any man, looking at them; then its

muscles suppled, gathered. It did not even alter its course, not fleeing, not running, just moving with that winged and effortless ease with which deer move, passing within twenty feet of them, its head high and the eye not proud and not haughty but just full and wild and unafraid, and Sam standing beside the boy now, his right arm raised at full length, palm-outward, speaking in that tongue which the boy had learned from listening to him and Joe Baker in the blacksmith shop, while up the ridge Walter Ewell's horn was still blowing them in to a dead buck.

'Oleh, Chief,' Sam said. 'Grandfather.' (pp. 183–4)

In this evocation of a transcendent epiphany, Faulkner employs a range of stylistic resources to convey the intensity of the experience which Ike shares with Sam. What is depicted is the necessary supervised encounter with the mystery of the wilderness, prior to Ike's similar but independent and solitary encounter with the bear at the close of 'The Bear', section I. The whole passage is a record of a temporary heightened awareness in Ike, in which the majestic buck not only dominates the scene but seems almost to choreograph it. The very qualities ascribed to the buck – 'walking, tremendous, unhurried', 'just moving' – seem to be mimed in part in the text's distinctive lexicogrammatical characteristics.

Chief among these are the type and aspect of the finite verbs, and the options in transitivity which they realize. Of the twenty-seven finite verbs here, eight are in progressive aspect. Of the nineteen non-progressive verbs a very high number are 'mental process' verbs of perception or cognition (*remember*, *know* (twice), *see* (four times), *relate*, *learn*) or the copula verb *be* (three), and few of them accept progressivization. Of the mere seven verbs which we may expect to operate in 'material process' clauses, all but one (*alter*, which itself is used in a negative statement – *It did not even alter its course*) are used as intransitive verbs in middle-voice, one-participant clauses. (On the typology of mental, material, and relational process clauses, see Halliday (1985a).)

The explanation for these trends in clause and verb type lies in the subtle narratorial depiction of the nature of the activity presented. There is action in this scene, but it is of a very particular kind: it is neither goal-directed nor the explicit operating of one participant on another. Nor is there any direct contact between the humans and the buck. What is reported is a profound witnessing, culminating in

Sam's salute. In that witnessing, the emphasis is on how events are perceived from Ike's viewpoint. That it is Ike's viewpoint that is expressed is evident from the very opening, where Ike has turned to face Sam only to find him looking up the ridge over the boy's head, and is confirmed by the report that Sam stands beside him; it is reflected also in the psychological viewpoint implicit in 'he would remember' and 'the boy knew'. Temporally, too, we are presented with the event as Ike experienced it, as the informality of such temporal qualifiers as *still* and the use of both the proximate and the non-proximate deictics, *now* and *then*, would suggest.

Among other features worth noting here is the alternation of very short simple sentences with much longer ones containing series of post-positioned non-finite relative clauses (part of what Ohmann (1964) has described as the additive tendency in Faulkner's style). There is also a high degree of negation in the passage (*not* occurs twelve times). As is often the case in describing mystical or paranormal experience, the narrator (aligned with Ike) attempts to convey the uncanny nature of the event by indicating those things which it was not. In the encounter, both the buck and Sam repeatedly defy Ike's conventional expectations of their behaviour. Thus the buck is not running, is unhurried, does not even alter its course, and so on, while Sam 'had not moved', is beside the boy 'instead of behind him as Sam always stood'.

But perhaps no single language feature contributes so powerfully to the impression of an intense experience in which, as it is put on p. 183, 'the solitude held its breath', as the many finite progressive verbs. They reflect an intense concentration, on the part of the witnessing narrator, on the abnormal duration of the viewing of the buck, whose every action is 'unhurried'. The progressives promote a sense of the unhurried walking of the buck as an activity perceived by the witnesses in its every detail, with the buck 'slanting and tilting its head to pass the antlers through the undergrowth'. With such implicit speaker involvement with (or, in the terms of Allen (1966) speaker intrusion in) the continuing processes denoted by the verbs, it comes as no surprise to find those verbs regularly modified by adverbial phrases or clauses, mainly of time or place.

I have claimed that the progressives here – as, I shall argue, elsewhere in the narrative – are to be regarded as particularly expressive of the viewpoint of a character with whom the narrator is aligned. They do not express any 'neutral' facts about a situation, but reflect the character's (and narrator's) intense involvement and subjective perspective on the situation. This would seem to be confirmed by the contexts of finite progressives in the passage: all occur in contexts where the reader is strongly aware of the mental-processing activities of Ike and Sam (looking, knowing, seeing).

For most of the first paragraph, in which all but one of the progressives occur, the emphasis is on what the man and boy perceive. Towards the close of that paragraph, and most clearly in the first lines of the second paragraph, the topic of the discourse has shifted quite sharply away from the humans and towards the buck. Repeatedly, the sentential subject and theme is *It*, the buck, while the men are relegated to the position of sentential object and part of the rheme (*them*), if they are mentioned at all. With the new topic of the buck itself, rather than its subjective perception by the men, no finite progressives occur, the frequency of action (material-process) clauses increases sharply, while that of mental-process clauses decreases. Reflecting the active power of the buck (a power sufficient to alter the style of the narrative reporting), a nonce-word is introduced as verb: *then its muscles suppled.*

The site of this important shift of narrative focus (from the humans to the buck), with its concomitant stylistic adjustments, is fore-shadowed in the revelatory sentence which closes the first paragraph quoted. This extended sentence is worthy of detailed examination. For convenience, I reproduce it below:

> It was not running, it was walking, tremendous, unhurried, slant-ing and tilting its head to pass the antlers through the undergrowth, and the boy standing with Sam beside him now instead of behind him as Sam always stood, and the gun still partly aimed and one of the hammers still cocked.

To begin with, it should arguably comprise five co-ordinate main clauses, which I list below:

> It was not running:
> it was walking;
> the boy was standing;
> the gun was still partly aimed;
> one of the hammers was still cocked.

However, after two finite progressive verbs referring to the buck, the subsequent three clauses referring to Ike and his gun lack the crucial disambiguating and tense-carrying element, *was*. This syntactic disruption reinforces the reader's impression that the power of controlling the situation has left Ike and Sam who are implicitly reduced to the status of passive witnesses within the scene. In fact one way of processing the sentence leads the reader to treat these three clauses as adverbial, with Ike, Sam, and the gun being material as inert as the undergrowth, all of which the buck passes his antlers through (on readers' trial-and-error processing of textual syntax, see Dillon (1978)).

A similar sense of the men as powerless choreographed witnesses, conveyed by a clause with deleted finite particle, occurs in the second paragraph: 'and Sam standing beside the boy now'. In the latter case note that the run of the sentence, with its series of post-modifying descriptions of the deer – 'not fleeing . . . just moving . . . passing . . . its head high' – initially induces the reader to interpret 'and Sam standing' etc. as simply further post-modificatory description of the deer. In an important sense, that 'misunderstanding' represents the true situation: mention of Sam here does not usher in a fully independent, Sam-oriented, co-ordinate clause: the whole sentence is built around the thematic subject, the deer, just as the man and boy are here ordered and compelled by a profound (non-verbal) authority. In both cases, the disrupted syntax promotes reader recognition of the extraordinary 'tied-ness' or interrelatedness of the buck, Sam, and the boy – mutual and mutually defining, profoundly interdependent, an intimation of natural order and significance.

In this brief discussion of Ike's and Sam's encounter with the buck I have sought to identify the significant role played (in promoting alignment between narrator and character, and in expressing the intensity and mystical strangeness of the experience for Ike) by a number of language features: abundance of mental-process clauses, paucity of two-participant material-process clauses contrasted with the many intransitive verbs, frequency of adverbial qualification and negative particles, ellipsis of the finite element in verb phrases, and switching of discourse topic away from the humans and their perception of events and to the behaviour of the buck itself. All these features appear to have clustered in this passage, and they work together to achieve the noted literary effects; but none of them seems as vital to the effects as the deployment of finite progressive verbs.

THE FUNCTION OF PROGRESSIVE ASPECT

I turn now to a more general consideration of progressives and their function throughout the narrative, prefaced by a brief discussion of the functions of progressives in English, and by some general statistical information on their distribution here, in order to ensure some degree of comprehensiveness.

Several recent studies of English progressive-form function are of interest to the stylistician – notably Twaddell (1960), Ota (1963), Joos (1964), Scheffer (1975), Ljung (1980), Nehls (1978), Comrie (1976), Huddleston (1984: 153–8), Dry (1981), Quirk *et al.* (1985: 198ff.), Edgren (1985), Brinton (1985), and Ehrlich (1987). Best of the earlier studies, perhaps, is Allen (1966), who emphasizes the now standard view that expansion (i.e. progressivization) must be discussed in terms of entire predications rather than simply the verbs involved. Along lines largely consonant with Comrie's later treatment (Comrie 1976), Allen treats tense as a basic two-way system of time reference (past and present), which is supplemented by subsystems of time relationship. Progressive aspect is one such subsystem (the other major one being so-called perfective aspect). Neither of these subsystems of time relationship serves to specify, in relation to the speaker, the time at which it is asserted the reported event took place or the reported state was the case. That task, however problematically, is undertaken by the primary system of tense. Rather the aspectual subsystems, while still very much to do with temporal information, may be said to offer temporal characterizations rather than temporal orientation: tense is deictic, aspect is not. For Allen, progressives are used so as to characterize a process as viewed intrusively and non-inclusively. Predicates with inclusive reference treat the processes they denote 'from outside' and at a distance, while intrusive reference treats material non-inclusively, intimately, 'from inside'.

Some of this terminology is more metaphorical than would be ideal, but it does point to the now generally accepted idea that the aspects in English promote distinctive ways of viewing the event or state expressed in the lexical verb. The progressive primarily signals that the activity described was or is still in progress at the time specified by accompanying indicators (tense inflections, time adverbials). The perfective primarily signals that the activity described continued or has continued over a span of time, from some past time to a more recent past time or up to and even including the present time of speaking. A perfective-aspect verb phrase typically conveys that something that began to be the case at a time prior to the current reference time continues to be the case up to and possibly beyond that current reference-time progressive, and is therefore particularly relevant to other events or states that obtain or obtained simply at that current reference time.

None of this is to deny that there are important differences in usage between the aspects in present- and past-tense verb phrases. Thus the progressive (rather than the non-progressive or simple) is the marked choice in past-tense verb phrases, typically used only in the sketching in of the 'ongoing' background, otherwise suggesting an excessive attention to the protractedness of activities which are in any event, from the speaker's present perspective, over. But the simple present tense is the marked choice for the descriptions of activities in present-tense verb phrases, conveying a variety of specific implications: timeless/generic truth; habitual activity; the historic present of some oral narrative and much contemporary fiction; and the 'glossing' function of running commentary accompanying sports broadcasting and cookery and 'how to' demonstrations. Progressive-aspect present tense is the unmarked option, to report current activities, precisely because the 'ongoingness' of those activities, as still in progress, is the natural assumption. To answer the question 'Where's Miriam?' with 'She sleeps in the other room' will sound either oddly Shakespearian or an inappropriate reporting of habitual behaviour when Miriam's current behaviour was the questioner's concern.

In summary, to progressivize a verb phrase is to treat the activity that is denoted as in process and, where the verb phrase is also past tense rather than present, as perceived in process. Dowty (1986) similarly emphasizes the perceptibility of the ongoing event as a crucial effect associated with progressivized rendering. It is because the stative verbs (such as *know*, *realize*) and copula-type relational verbs (such as *seem*) denote processes that are not ordinarily amenable to inspection as they develop that they are heavily resistant to progressivization. Some sense of the overt perceptibility of the action or state denoted by the predicate seems normally to be a prerequisite for expansion. Where that requirement holds, switching from simple past tense to past progressive emphasizes the ongoingness/incompleteness, and 'condition of being perceived going on, by the speaker', of the predicate. This is not to suggest that non-progressive forms invariably lack connotations of ongoingness –

From March to September he walked the length of the Cascades.

– or that they never give the impression of describing a perceived process –

> Tugging and jerking against its inert weight, he dragged the body from his car to the water's edge.

Comparatively, however, these emphases are more marked and, by implication, attended to in progressivized forms. In fact the connotational tendencies that we attribute to the progressive are evidently interrelated and, to a degree, mutually entailing. Thus the most general impression of imperfective state, or incompleteness, naturally gives rise to an emphasis on ongoingness: that which is not completed, we assume, is still in progress. And the fact of having especially reported on the incompleteness of an activity, we again assume, implies that the reporter has been particularly struck (has observed with the vividness of the intrusive perspective) by the ongoingness of the activity. That intrusive perspective, and the greater immersion in the scene described that it entails, means that progressives give an attenuated sense of the temporal limits of activities: in remarking upon the internal progress of an activity, they necessarily neglect to convey a sense of its terminal points, its understood points of onset and termination. This lack of distinct temporal boundaries, in progressivized predicates, means that when progressive constructions are used alongside other constructions (simple or progressive) there are strong impressions that the activities rendered in the progressive temporally overlap all adjacent others. (Allen (1966) actually claims that overlapping is the chief function of expanded forms, being a device for indicating that a significant and more-than-usual interrelation exists between one event and another.) The emphases I attribute here to past progressives – on ongoingness, on the implicit intrusive view, on events as perceived and developing – differ somewhat from the more general characteristics attributed to progressives in Quirk *et al.* (1985: 198ff.). Quirk *et al.* emphasize temporariness (limited duration) as the distinct quality of progressivized predicates. But it is clear that many non-progressive predicates can express limited duration – particularly in the past tense. In fact it is probable that the pastness expressed by the use of past tense in narratives is itself sufficient expression of limited duration: past-tense reports of past-time events are thereby reported as of limited duration (not 'now' the case). Accordingly, other functions than limited duration come to the fore in progressivization of past-tense predicates.

The views offered here are largely consonant with a number of literary discussions of the topic. Writing on Faulkner's progressives, Hogan (1981) suggests that they evoke immediacy, immersion in the flux of the moment, and suspension within a single moment of time. However, while he emphasizes the 'dreamlike quality' of that reader involvement, it should be noted that the effect of Faulkner's progressives is often not at all 'dreamlike', but disturbing – a kind of assault on the reader's expectations. The immersion may thus be dynamic, not static. R. C. Taylor (1979) argues that progressive constructions are a major element of what he identifies as Blake's most prominent style, an aspectual mode which he justly labels 'endless process'. Of progressives in general Taylor suggests: 'The construction obligatorily signifies process; even if the lexical root of the verb represents a definite change, an event, this event is necessarily understood to be incomplete and continuous' (1979: 37-8). Hatcher (1951), writing somewhat earlier, notes that, in present-tense instances with verbs where the unexpanded form is the norm of usage, replacement of the simple form by the progressive means 'an exceptional emphasis either on overt activity . . . or on developing activity' (1951: 279).

One of the few studies of progressivization in literary texts is Raybould (1957), an examination of progressive verbs in Jane Austen. Raybould concludes that such forms are used in Austen as a substitute for subjunctives or modal auxiliaries, expressing 'a point of view or an emotional inclination that is not sure of realization' (1957: 183); and she suspects that such progressives have an affinity with *erlebte Rede* (free indirect discourse) – a speculation amply supported in the analyses below. Before turning to those analyses it may be worth reiterating the need, if we are to get an adequate view of progressives and their use, to relate them to their entire sentential settings. Progressivization is not something that happens merely to the item filling the lexical verb slot. The nature of the temporal adverbial specification with progressive verbs, for example, may reveal important tendencies of co-occurrence. And the frequency of accompanying temporal adverbials should not be neglected: Crystal (1966) found that 25 per cent of expanded clauses had temporal specification in the immediate context (same clause or subordinate clause), while I have found that 60 per cent of main-clause progressives in the narrative of *Go Down, Moses* have immediate-context temporal specifiers.

My working assumptions concerning the progressive will be that the form usually indicates that the action or event described is perceived by the speaker as occurring not as a unified and clearly bounded particle, but as a multi-phase wave of activity without sharply defined points of origin and termination. In this way an action that otherwise might have been expressed non-progressively has its incomplete perceptible ongoingness highlighted, and is implicitly endowed with an internal shape or progression. The endowment is implicit rather than explicit: the shape is not specified, and instead the speaker's attention seems often to be on a portion of that implied whole. And this discriminating attention entails adoption of a partial, intrusive, non-inclusive perspective. Considered in relation to co-text, it becomes apparent that progressive verbal forms imply disruption of the conventional linear succession of events – of the kind that a sequence of clauses reporting actions in simple past tense would suggest. Because of a progressive's indefinite boundaries of application, it is likely to overlap, temporally, one or more of the non-expanded verbs adjacent to it in a text. For Quirk *et al.* (1985: 209) the relation between a past progressive and a simple past predicate in the same sentence is one of time inclusion rather than the relation of time sequence typically understood between two adjacent simple past forms. This is the essential reason for Labov's exclusion of progressivized verb phrases from his canonical narrative clause, in which superordinate clauses in simple past tense, exhibiting clear sequence and juncture, are the norm (Labov 1972; see also Toolan 1988, ch. 5). Progressivized verbs, in Labov's oral narratives, are commonest in the 'orientation' and 'evaluation' sections of the telling (among story-internal evaluation devices, they are a type of correlative, often conveying simultaneity of occurrence of distinct actions). More generally, we can observe that in all narratives they enhance the temporal density of the reported actions, through implied event-overlap and non-instantaneousness. But the most striking claim a speaker can make, in switching from simple past to past progressive, is that the process designated is not merely perceptible but actually was perceived, in progress, by the reporting speaker. In such cases, as I shall demonstrate, the assumption that progressivized material is circumstantial background (Hopper 1979; 1982) is quite inappropriate; such clauses are rather in the characterological and so narrative foreground (see also Ehrlich (1987), in support of this view). The very fact that predicates that might routinely have been 'left' in non-progressive form are cast in the marked progressivized form draws the reader's attention to material that would otherwise have remained unremarkable.

PROGRESSIVES IN THE NARRATIVE

Numbers of main verbs in the narrative parts of the seven chapters or stories of *Go Down, Moses* (further divided into their main sections) are set out in table 1, which also lists the percentage of main-verb progressives in each story. The percentage of the latter in the narrative as a whole tallies fairly closely with the frequencies found by Allen (1966) (4.3 per cent), Scheffer (1975) (4.6 per cent), and Ota (1963) (6 per cent in a mixed corpus, 2.3 per cent in a corpus of written material).

Frequency of progressives fluctuates considerably throughout the narrative: it is high in 'Was', section II (7.3 per cent), low in chapter 2 of 'The Fire and the Hearth', particularly high in section 2 and the brief section 3 of 'The Old People', while there is only one main-verb progressive in the admittedly atypical section IV of 'The Bear'.

Table 1   Frequencies of types of narrative main verbs

	Total	Simple	Perfec.	Prog.	% Prog.
'Was' I	2	2	0	0	0
'Was' II	286	237	28	21	7.3
'Was' III	185	176	6	3	1.6
'Was' IV	8	8	0	0	0
'Fire/Hearth' 1	606	502	86	18	3.0
'Fire/Hearth' 2	317	298	16	3	0.9
'Fire/Hearth' 3	493	433	40	20	4.1
'Pantaloon'	272	224	31	17	6.3
'Old People' 1	174	116	54	4	2.3
'Old People' 2	141	112	18	11	7.8
'Old People' 3	28	23	2	3	10.7
'The Bear' I	218	181	29	8	3.7
'The Bear' II	309	258	43	8	2.6
'The Bear' III	484	416	55	23	4.8
'The Bear' IV	121	100	20	1	0.8
'The Bear' V	132	101	28	3	2.3
'Delta Autumn'	374	324	37	13	3.5
'God Down, Moses'	205	170	27	8	3.9
Totals	4355	3681	520	164	3.8

If we adapt Quirk *et al.*'s (1985) classification of verbs into eleven sub-classes, a continuum from the most dynamic (eight sub-classes) to the most stative (three sub-classes), all but two of the 'Was' progressives are from dynamic, activity-verb classes. Since activity verbs are those which most naturally accept expansion, only verbs not falling within such classes can be said to be to any degree marked in being progressivized. The two exceptions are *were just coming* (a transitional-event verb) and the interesting case of *He had been hearing her all the time*, where a stative verb is, against expectations, progressivized. The immediate context of this option is:

> They listened a minute [to Miss Sophonsiba screaming]. He had been hearing her all the time. She was nowhere near as loud as at first; she was just steady. (p. 22)

The unexpected progressive captures the tension in the situation: Buck is in the process of being framed, married off against his will, and fittingly the verb *hear*, conventionally recording inert perception, is overlaid with a progressive meaning of protracted enactment, still not completed – the continuousness of the manipulation of Buck by Sophonsiba's screams. Someone who is reluctant even to hear is being compelled to listen. A more conventional description in place of the progressive would have been 'He heard her (now) – and had heard her all the time', but this rather wooden version is displaced by a past-perfective progressive which with comic effect telescopes all past occasions of hearing the screams (each of which occasions is, logically, a point-action) and the immediate point-action occasion of hearing (this last would normally be expressed, in a past-time narrative, by the simple past: *he heard*) into one continuous process – not a stative but an active perception.

Progressives are often used in 'Was' and other chapters not simply to assert a temporary process or action but to assert a temporary state. Here the concepts of incompletion and overlapping of adjacent events seem particularly germane to explanation of their effect. Notable examples include the following:

> Only, for a while Tomey's Turl didn't seem to be at Mr Hubert's either. The boy *was still sitting* on the gatepost, blowing the horn. . . . Mr Hubert *was sitting* in the spring-house with his boots off and his feet in the water, drinking a toddy. (p. 9; my emphases)

105

The first thing he [Cass] saw was Tomey's Turl's head slipping along above the lane fence. But when he cut across the yard to turn him, Tomey's Turl *wasn't even running*. He *was squatting* behind a bush, watching the house. (p. 13)

he [Uncle Buck] had forgotten when even a little child should have known: not ever to stand right in front of or right behind a nigger when you scare him; but always to stand to one side of him. Uncle Buck forgot that. He *was standing* facing the front door and right in front of it . . . he said the first he knew was when the fyce gave a shriek and whirled and Tomey's Turl was right behind it. (p. 19)

The four stative progressives and one dynamic one (*wasn't even running*) noted do not particularly emphasize duration, if compared with their unexpanded counterparts. But some of them are incomplete, imperfective, in a special sense. Sitting, for example, as an activity, is completed once the transition to the state of being seated has been effected. Thereafter, *be sitting* is a perfected activity but an imperfective state (the same account holds for *squat* and *stand*). The four stative examples, then, show the progressive used apparently gratuitously to reiterate the ongoingness of an inherently imperfective state. And in the first example duration is emphasized by the temporal adverbial *still*. In short, these progressives are not here for the purposes of disambiguation or descriptive accuracy in any routine sense, and one is accordingly drawn to consider other purposes. The purpose they do seem consistently to serve is that of representing the scene as it was focalized (Bal 1985) by the young Cass, the participant-observer from whose perspective of innocent fascination this narrative is related. Thus, in the first example, it is likely that we are being presented with Cass's envious awareness of his black contemporary's prolonged sounding of the dinner horn.

The concept of overlapping and the appropriacy of progressives in denoting events or states which have already commenced before they are encountered or reported by the speaker are both relevant to interpretation of the first three of these four stative progressives. In the second, for example, the progressive is preferable, since it emphasizes that Hubert is *discovered* in the spring-house by Buck and Cass, that Hubert is already in the process of relaxing and imbibing. The question whether Mr Hubert has been sitting and drinking long enough to cause intoxication must remain open, although the (Cass-oriented) report of Hubert's initial confusion points discreetly in that direction: 'for a time it looked like Mr Hubert couldn't even place who Uncle Buck was talking about' (p. 14).

In 'The Fire and the Hearth' we encounter a vivid example of the progressive used to emphasize that the narration is being constructed as if from Lucas's viewpoint – an involved participant actually going through these experiences. It occurs on p. 52:

> He was waiting for daylight. He could not have said why.

As the following free indirect presentation of Lucas's mental judgement confirms, this comment is presented as if coming from Lucas himself at the time of the experience. There could have been narratorial adoption of the character's viewpoint even with the more conventional form: 'He waited for daylight.' However, the progressive implies that there is nothing particularly ratiocinative in Lucas's act of waiting: it is something instinctive which he finds himself in the process of doing, perhaps a compulsion to which he submits.

The other most interesting main-clause progressives are those occurring on pp. 111 and 113. All three relate to Roth's recollections of his traumatic childhood entry into that part of his cultural inheritance which involves him in treating all blacks, even black McCaslins, as alien and inferior. What triggers the surfacing in the young Roth of 'the old curse' is, quite plausibly, not specified. All we witness is his sudden announcement, on impulse, when at the home of his black kin, 'I'm going home' – a declaration which breaches the custom according to which he and his black foster-brother Henry, having eaten supper together, would be sent to bed together by Molly:

> They had finished supper at Henry's house and Molly was just sending them to bed in the room across the hall where they slept when there, when suddenly he said, 'I'm going home.'
>
> 'Les stay here,' Henry said. 'I thought we was going to get up when pappy did and go hunting.'
>
> 'You can,' he said. He was already moving toward the door. 'I'm going home.' (p. 111)

Roth's assertion of difference is strengthened by his refusal to discuss his decision with Henry, or to be concerned at all with Henry's views. Roth is not merely declining to consult Henry, he positively wishes to convey to him that he is not consulting him. And the progressive verb at this point underlines Roth's new self-image as different and superior: 'He was already moving towards the door.' For only the progressive here can stress that Roth's moving had begun, was in process, and does not cease even with his reiterated 'I'm going home'. The non-progressive past perfect form – *He had already moved towards the door* – would imply that Roth had come to a halt by the door, that his resolute and hostile behaviour was being temporarily disrupted by Henry's interjection; while in the simple past form – *He moved towards the door* – the important impression that the process of moving had already begun would be utterly lost, and the temporal particle *already* could not be used.

In the immediate sequel to Roth's almost instinctive withdrawal from community with the black McCaslins, we find a progressive used at the close of a long sentence describing the cool hospitality Roth subsequently experiences from Molly, Lucas, and Henry (even after he believes he has redeemed himself, made things 'all right'):

> The table was set in the kitchen where it always was and Molly stood at the stove drawing the biscuit out as she always stood, but Lucas was not there and there was just one chair, one plate, his glass of milk beside it, the platter heaped with untouched chicken, and even as he sprang back, gasping, for an instant blind as the room rushed and swam, Henry was turning toward the door to go out of it. (p. 113)

Particularly striking here are the poignant impact of Roth's progression in observations from the impersonal accoutrements – 'one chair, one plate' – to the deliberately personalized ones – '*his* glass of milk' (my emphasis) – and the way in which the repeated *always* conveys Roth's wished-for reintegration within that secure cycle of familiar activity and experience that distinguishes the black McCaslins. The sentence proceeds in a series of brief and precise co-ordinate clauses (with uncomplicated subordination), until the final clausal co-ordinator introduces, against expectations, not another S V (C) (A) sentence but a long and involved temporal adverbial clause, in which is embedded a non-finite relative clause and a further finite temporal clause introduced by *as*. Thus the final main clause with its progressive-form verb is foregrounded by an extended contextualizing which conveys the shock (to Roth) of the rebuff by portraying a bewildering simultaneity of perceptions.

The density of temporal qualifiers here – *even as, for an instant, as* – confirms the emphasis on temporal particularity; and in this moment of anagnorisis Roth, Henry, and the room itself have all become animate agents in motion. Indeed, not only is Roth in motion, springing back, he is also gasping and momentarily blind; and *the room* is the agentive subject of verbs which normally require an animate subject – 'the room rushed and swam'. The sentence culminates in an expanded predicate ('Henry was turning toward the door') whose connotation of an action of some extension in time, perceived in detail as it progresses, attests to the empathetic narratorial alignment with Roth's active involvement in this scene. One may note that this answering snub of Roth by Henry is all the more effective since it involves, just as did the one on p. 111, the rejected party observing the rejector turning away and moving towards the door.

In 'Pantaloon in Black' the four main-verb progressives of pp. 151–2 are noteworthy, having a similar function to that identified in relation to Lucas's waiting, on p. 52:

> And then it was all right. He was moving again. But he was not moving, he was drinking, the liquid cold and swift and tasteless and requiring no swallowing, so that he could not tell if it were going down inside or outside. But it was all right. And now he was moving . . .

Rider is the agonized victim of inconsolable grief at the death of his young wife, and the story charts his desperate attempts both to retain Mannie's ghostly presence and to keep his own body in motion. The progressives of pp. 151–2 suggest that, as was claimed of the expanded-verb description of Lucas on p. 52, Rider has little control over his own actions. Instead, he finds himself *already engaged* in actions, apparently responsive to instincts and subconscious compulsions.

In a similar vein, the opening progressives of 'The Old People' are used to convey the incomplete recollections of a participant who has been so involved in an experience that he cannot recall the particulars or causal sequence of the episode. The sequence of events is indicated merely by the vague temporal *then*:

> The boy did not remember that shot at all. . . . He didn't even remember what he did with the gun afterwards. He was running. Then he was standing over the buck where it lay. (p. 156)

In the final two stories, 'Delta Autumn' and 'Go Down, Moses', there is an interesting expansion of verbs of active perception, where the report is the free indirect one of the perceived, powerless individual (*not* the 'controlling' perceiver). During old Ike's traumatic meeting with James Beauchamp's granddaughter in 'Delta Autumn', Ike notes on several occasions the woman's look, a fixed regard of 'immersed contemplation, . . . bottomless and intent candor, of a child' (p. 357), a look that makes her seem both remote and powerful. On p. 361, as Ike rejects her even as he adopts a curiously black idiom – 'Cant nobody do nothing for you!' – the narrative reports:

She moved; she was not looking at him again, toward the entrance.

The disrupted syntax of this sentence, as well as the distinctive combination of progressive + negation + iterative temporal qualifier, presents the scene from Ike's viewpoint. He seems to be undermined and rendered inert by the impact of her gaze, and is accordingly only able to assert himself when she looks away. The young black woman's mesmeric power is akin to that of Ike's wife in the seduction scene at the end of 'The Bear', section IV, although the latter woman does not even need to look at him (pp. 313–14) and continues not to do so.

In the final chapter, 'Go Down, Moses', three of the eight main-clause progressives occur with the verb *look*, while a fourth occurs with *watch*. All of these confirm the narratorial adoption of Gavin Stevens's viewpoint, since all four are observations as to whether or not the two old women with whom he has discussions – Miss Worsham and Molly Beauchamp – are regarding him (or even simply aware of him). These women too can use their gaze to control men. Not yet apprised of his mission, Gavin Stevens suggests to Miss Worsham:

'And then maybe in about two or three months I could go out there and tell her [Molly] he [Samuel Beauchamp] is dead and buried somewhere in the North . . .' this time she was watching him with such an expression that he ceased talking; she sat there, erect on the hard chair, watching him until he had ceased.

'She will want to take him back home with her,' she said. (p. 376)

SUBSTITUTIONARY PERCEPTION

The phrase 'substitutionary perception' is proposed in a richly suggestive early article on free indirect speech (Fehr 1938); it is Fehr's characterization of the process of free indirect reporting of characters' perceptions. Translating *erlebte Rede* strictly and narrowly as 'substitutionary speech' (henceforth SS), in which the speeches of an actor

110

and a reporter are blended, Fehr posits a closely related free indirect speech category, 'substitutionary perception' (henceforth SP). While SS is the domain of merged speeches, SP is the domain of merged perceptions, 'the reporter running in on the actor's vision and . . . the actor lending his sight to the articulate reporter'; it is 'vision by proxy' (Fehr 1938: 98). The topic Fehr broaches is later treated, in somewhat different ways, by Uspensky (1973) on the one hand, and Genette (1980) and Bal (1985) on the other; but Fehr's observations are of interest, since they particularly focus on formal description, including the role of progressives.

One major component of SP, Fehr argues, is a 'perception indi- cator' – an introductory signal that a character is in the act of perceiving (e.g. an exclamation such as *Look!* or *Listen!*, or reports such as *He looked up, He listened*). A second component is the progress- ive form. Fehr explains the functional presence of progressives in SP passages in terms reminiscent of Allen's characterization of them (Allen 1966) as 'intrusive':

> A window is opened abruptly into a scene where things are going on for the eye to see, for the ear to hear. Now the chances are that perception will break right into the midst of one or more of those many processes in course of being at the moment the window is thrown open. (Fehr 1938: 101)

The distinction between SP and SS is, for Fehr, quite clear:

> The latter is an attempt at a verbal rendering of the stream of reflections in the actor's [character's] mind. With Substitutionary Perception, however, we are under the illusion of receiving a direct verbal replica of visions and auditions not yet affected by the stream of reflections. (101–2)

Progressive forms are a necessary element in Fehr's 'substitu- tionary perception' mode of discourse, for they regularly imply that the states or actions denoted are perceived processes. That this is so has been amply demonstrated in the many examples from the narra- tive discussed so far. The use of the progressive form in almost every case conveys the character's and/or narrator's distinct sense that the reported activity is one that is extended in time and not yet complete (possibly overlapping surrounding events rendered in non- progressive forms), and is reported as though in the process of being experienced, as a directly observed phenomenon.

111

This narratorial responsiveness to the self-oriented perceptions of a character is a major tool of narrated monologue. The rendering of character-oriented perceptions in SP passages often amounts to a specific sub-variety of free indirect discourse, in which a character's sense-impressions are registered, prior to any elaborate interpretational processing by that character. SP passages with functional progressive forms are a major means of effecting temporary narratorial alignment with a character, in which that character's viewpoint is promoted while the narrator's viewpoint is muted. As one commentator has put it:

> By locating descriptive details within the perceptual apparatus of a character, the reader makes them serve no longer simply as residual signs of the 'real', but as marks and measures of human consciousness. The notion of 'substitutionary perception', in other words, is a principal strategy for organizing a text according to limited points of view. (McHale 1978: 278)

In search of confirmation of these claims concerning progressives as a signal of SP and temporary narratorial alignment, a re-examination of the 'Was' main-clause progressives was made (reported briefly below). This showed that those progressives do regularly occur in passages of such alignment with a character. In 'Was' that character is always Cass. But it should be noted that the narratorial alignment, while usually perception by proxy, is sometimes 'cognition by proxy' – a direct verbal rendering, within the narrative, of a character's thoughts and reactions. As a result I propose adding a third type of proxy discourse to Fehr's SS and SP, namely 'substitutionary cognition' or SC. In practice the boundaries between SS and SP and SC are often rather blurred, with SS and SC particularly closely interrelated.

SP is a highly plausible interpretation of the context of the first progressive in 'Was' –

> and Uncle Buddy [was] bellowing like a steamboat blowing

– since earlier in the same sentence, in the first main clause, we have encountered what for Fehr would amount to a perception indicator:

> they [he and Uncle Buck] heard Uncle Buddy cursing and bellowing.

The second 'Was' progressive, by contrast, is not part of SP but substitutionary thought or cognition, as the preceding context makes clear:

Because they knew exactly where Tomey's Turl had gone. . . . He was heading for Mr Hubert Beauchamp's place. (p. 5)

The third progressive is neither SP nor SC, but clearly the SS type of free indirect speech, in which the boyish vehemence of Cass's voice – 'ride him down in two minutes' – dominates the narratorial voice:

Uncle Buck was riding Black John, because if they could just catch sight of Tomey's Turl at least one mile from Mr Hubert's gate, Black John would ride him down in two minutes. (p. 8)

The next two progressives also occur in a FID passage, perhaps classifiable as SP in terms of being reflective of a delayed self-awareness:

[The horse came running out of the trees] with Uncle Buck right up behind his ears now and yelling . . . and he was running too; the mare went out before he even knew she was ready, and he was yelling too. (pp. 8–9)

In summary, the analysis suggests that twenty-one of the twenty-four 'Was' finite progressives occur in FID contexts, and more than half function in strategies of substitutionary perception (thirteen are SP, eight are SS or SC). Sample analyses of other stories in the novel suggest that, throughout the narrative, progressives regularly occur in FID passages, within which they regularly contribute to the presentation of substitutionary perception.

TEMPORAL QUALIFICATION OF PROGRESSIVES

A particular focus of attention in studies of the progressive, as already noted, has been the type and extent of adverbial qualification of such verbs. In this narrative there is a great density of adverbial qualification: the vast majority of progressives (125 of 164) are so qualified, often with more than one adjunct. Most frequent are time adverbials, especially of specific points in time (sixty-four such clauses) or of time relationship (twenty-three instances). But nearly a third of all the progressives are qualified in terms of place.

An easily discernible result of this heavy qualification is that progressives are not swiftly passed over in the process of reading the text. The co-occurring adjuncts help to retain the reader's attention, elaborating upon those predicates and their implications, and diverting the reader yet further from the linear sequence of events ordinarily signalled by a succession of non-expanded predicates in simple past tense. As noted earlier, the past progressive is unmarked for, or leaves unanswered questions concerning, the precise terminal points of the activity designated. Counterbalancing this relative uncertainty, however, there is (in the cases where there is adverbial qualification) a relative precision and elaboration of temporal and locative commentary.

One of the curious things about this temporal qualification is that much of it is strictly speaking redundant. We have repeatedly seen that progressives imply extended attention at a specific point of time, that *he was approaching* always means that the activity of 'approaching' was in progress at an identified past time and that it overlaps that time. In such cases it is not necessary to state that *he was approaching then*, and yet this occurs over and over again with the progressives in *Go Down, Moses*. Arguably one effect of this is to emphasize that, while progressives are durative, that duration is limited (i.e. to a specific designated time: then or now). But we have also seen that these qualificatory adverbials (projecting a spatial or temporal immediacy of events despite the prevailing past tense of narration) contribute, along with the progressive verbal forms, to the construction of FID passages of temporary character–narrator alignment. Seen in this light, both the progressives and the adjuncts in clauses such as *he was coming now, he was coming here, he was coming today* function in the furtherance of FID.

It is therefore possible and perhaps important to distinguish between the (seemingly) redundant 'now'/'then' adverbials and more clearly information-bearing qualifiers of that time-when type, such as clauses: *even as he sprang back, When they were out of the office*, etc. Such adverbials as *now, then, this time, still, just, again, already*, and so on, seem to be used here not so as to contribute to a specific contextualization of the event, but simply to convey the temporal sequence (and cancel any mistaken assumptions of simultaneity of events). By their frequent implicit reflection of a character's viewpoint, they regularly contribute to temporary alignment of a narrator and character. More substantial temporal information comes from temporal phrases and clauses or is inferred from the narrative context. Absence of temporal specification with progressives is often very effective in conveying the sense of a character being swept along by events, as happens to Cass during the initial pursuit of Tomey's Turl:

> Uncle Buck whooped once from the woods, running on sight, then Black John came out of the trees, driving . . . with Uncle Buck right

up behind his ears now and yelling . . . over the ditch and across the next field, and he was running too; the mare went out before he even knew she was ready, and he was yelling too. (pp. 8–9)

SUBORDINATE AND NON-FINITE PROGRESSIVES

Two further topics are worthy of brief discussion. These are : (1) finite progressives in subordinate clauses and (2) non-finite progressives in main and subordinate clauses. Primary analysis does not invite any particularly broad interpretative deduction. One can simply note trends, such as the high frequency of nominal *that* clauses (26 per cent of all the dependent progressive clauses), and the high frequency of adverbial clauses of manner in the three stories centred on Ike and his development ('The Old People', 'The Bear', and 'Delta Autumn'), in relation to their occurrence in the other stories. Sixteen of the narrative's eighteen clauses of the latter type occur in these three stories. These tend to be either clauses introduced by *as* in past perfect tense, emphasizing the recurrence of a familiar experience or condition –

Then Sam Fathers, standing just behind the boy as he had been standing when the boy shot his first running rabbit with his first gun (p. 163)

– or clauses introduced by *as if* and conveying a hypothetical claim concerning an entity, and often reflecting the young Ike's awed and bewildered attempts to interpret or at least describe his own impressions:

Sam said nothing now . . . inscrutable, as if he were just waiting for them to stop talking so he could go home.

From time to time the great blue dog would open his eyes, not as if he were listening to them but as though to look at the woods for a moment before closing his eyes again . . . (p. 248)

She regarded him . . . as though she were not only not looking at anything, she was not even speaking to anyone but herself. (pp. 359–60)

PROGRESSIVES IN 'PANTALOON IN BLACK'

A particular stylistic characteristic merits further comment here: the markedly high frequency of dependent progressives occurring in

'Pantaloon in Black'. This story has an average of 6.7 dependent progressives per page, much in contrast with the averages for all the other stories, which range from only 3.3 to 5.0 and thus are all much closer to the overall average of 4.1. Furthermore, this abnormally high figure for 'Pantaloon in Black' is not at all due to a high frequency of finite progressives in dependent clauses; in fact, with only four in twenty-four pages, this story has the lowest frequency of these.

'Pantaloon in Black' is a story which falls into two clearly defined sections: one of nineteen pages recording Rider's frenzied and desperate grief over his wife's death, ending in a killing in self-defence; and a second one of six pages, mainly direct speech, recording the deputy's view of subsequent proceedings. It is not surprising, then, since progressives in direct speech are excluded from this analysis, that nearly all the many narrative non-finite dependent progressives in the story occur in the first section (159 of 163). This leaves us with the exceptional frequency, for the first section, of 8.4 dependent progressives per page. In addition, these progressives are not spread evenly through the sentences of the section. Rather they occur in clusters, in a small number of multi-clause sentences. In fact, all 159 dependent progressives occur in a mere sixty-one sentences, forty-one of which have multiple occurrence of dependent progressives. Multi-clause sentences are far from rare in *Go Down, Moses*, but in no other part of this book are complex sentences with several non-finite progressive dependent clauses anything like as common.

Before I attempt to characterize their special effect it may be valuable to quote a few examples from 'Pantaloon' of the sort of non-finite progressive clustering I have in mind:

He released one hand in midstroke and flung it backward, *striking* the other across the chest, *jolting* him back a step, and restored the hand to the moving shovel, *flinging* the dirt with that effortless fury so that the mound seemed *to be rising* of its own volition, not built up from above but *thrusting* visibly upward out of the earth itself, until . . . (p. 135; my emphases)

himself, his own prints, *setting* the period now as he strode on, *moving* almost as fast as a smaller man could have trotted, his body *breasting* the air her body had vacated, his eyes *touching* the objects – post and tree and field and house and hill – her eyes had lost. (p. 137)

a big dog, a hound . . . *coming* out from beneath the gallery and *approaching*, not *running* but *seeming* rather to drift across the dusk until it stood lightly against his leg, its head raised until the tips of his fingers just touched it, *facing* the house and *making* no sound . . . (p. 139)

Now he was kneeling too, the other six dollars of his last week's pay on the floor before him, *blinking*, still *smiling* at the face of the white man opposite, then, still *smiling*, he watched the dice pass from hand to hand around the circle as the white man covered the bets, *watching* the soiled and palm-worn money in front of the white man gradually and steadily increase, *watching* the white man cast and win two doubled bets in succession then lose one for twenty-five cents, the dice *coming* to him at last, the cupped snug clicking of them in his fist. (pp. 152–3)

The non-finite progressives in the passages above appear to possess several of the semantic implications of finite progressives, but with distinct differences also. The first passage, for example, is endowed, via its progressives, with a strong sense of a variety of actions occurring almost simultaneously, and definitely with overlap and interrelation between the events. The narrator only vouches for the serial progression of the most banal, least interesting events in the sentence: 'He released one hand in midstroke and flung it backward . . . and restored the hand to the moving shovel'. It is in the clauses of qualification appended to this narrative statement that the sense of multiple (synchronous) actions (implying a powerful source of all this energy) is promoted.

There are distinct differences of semantic implication between finite and non-finite progressives. One of these (perhaps the chief) derives from the general absence of conjuncts in non-finite clauses. This absence of conjuncts (and other introducers) leads to an attenuation of explicit causal, temporal, purposive, or other relations between the non-finite clauses and those on which they depend. Other relations are also weakened – for example, not requiring an explicit subject, the non-finite clause allows ambiguities over the subject of the non-finite verb (see Quirk *et al.* 1985: 1,123–7). It should perhaps be noted that by a non-finite progressive I mean any verbal form ending with *-ing* whose function is verbal rather than nominal or adjectival. Thus the *-ing* form in *He heard the hounds crying* is progressive, while that in *He heard the crying children* is not.

The question whether non-finite progressives can carry full progressive meaning remains controversial. Comrie argues:

Although the -*ing* form is an essential ingredient of the English Progressive, in nonfinite constructions without the auxiliary *be* the -*ing* form does not necessarily have progressive meaning; in fact, in such constructions it typically indicates only simultaneity (relative present time reference) with the situation of the main verb. (Comrie 1976: 39)

He cites the example 'Knowing he was away, I burgled his house', which may be treated as equivalent not to a finite progressive form but to a non-progressive one: 'As I knew [not "was knowing"] he was away, I burgled his house.' It may be significant, however, that in the four cited passages from 'Pantaloon in Black' the only forms to fail Comrie's 'progressiveness' test (in this specific context) are *was striking*, *was jolting*, and *was seeming*.

Few of the present participles in 'Pantaloon in Black' are directly preceded, without an intervening comma, by their subjects. It is for this reason that uncertainty arises as to the implicit relations between such non-finite clauses and adjacent clauses. These relations may be relative, causal, temporal, resultative, or some other. And such problems of interpretation are compounded by the previously noted difficulties of selecting or identifying which of the nearby nominals *is* the clause's subject. In many texts, the difficulty is insignificant: in this story I believe the difficulty is deliberately posed and interpretatively significant.

A rereading of the first example passage from 'Pantaloon in Black' supplied above suggests that here, although it is easiest simply to treat *He* (i.e. Rider) as the subject of verbs such as *striking*, *jolting*, and *flinging*, a counter-argument may be proposed. This is that the first two of these take *one hand*, and not *He*, as their subject, while *flinging*, again supplanting *He*, takes *the moving shovel* as subject. The suggestion is that agency is ascribed not solely to Rider but also to conventionally inanimate parts of his body and the shovel in his hands. There is a peculiar appropriateness in this strategy, since the sentence proceeds explicitly to acknowledge the apparent independent agency of the mound 'thrusting visibly upward out of the earth itself'. The foregoing putative transferrals of agency prepare for this more thoroughgoing and overt declaration. An interesting subsidiary effect derives from the inexplicit reference of the word *itself* here. It may simply qualify the nominal *the earth*, hence paraphrasable by *the very earth* or some such phrase. What is also possible, and perhaps more interesting, is that, headed by a deleted *by*, it could qualify the participle *thrusting*, so that the clause might be recast thus:

[It was] thrusting by itself visibly upward out of the earth.

Such an interpretation clearly emphasizes the independent agency attributed to the mound.

This discussion of the possible changing of subject in a series of two or more non-finite clauses relates also to another kind of versatility shown by these clauses. As is well known, non-finite clauses are consonant with a variety of time references (relative to the time of speaking). Their lack of tense entails lack of 'grounding' relative to the present time of the speaker. Thus the same non-finite progressive clause can co-occur with various finite verb phrases:

We leave tomorrow, taking the 9 a.m. train.
We had already left, taking the 9 a.m. train.
We left yesterday, taking the 9 a.m. train.

Here the non-finite clauses involve a reduction, respectively, of predicates referring to a future intention, the distant past, and a recent past. Context, as so often, is crucial in interpreting such temporal relations. But the point of chief interest is that such non-finite clauses are not truly devoid of temporal reference: the orientation is simply implicit rather than explicit and grammaticized. Thus there can be no uncertainty, under normal circumstances, about the fact that in all three sentences above the boarding of the 9 a.m. train precedes or initiates the act of leaving: these two narrative events are an ordered sequence. The same principle holds in many other cases where non-finite clauses are used in narratives, cases where it would be fundamentally mistaken to assume that the activity in the non-finite clause was outside the strictly ordered sequence of narrative actions, was a clause of background material that could be 'freely' moved elsewhere in the sequence, or invariably caused a 'suspension' from the drive of surrounding finite narrative clauses.

The present participles in 'Pantaloon in Black' and in other chapters, for example, carrying implicit past-time reference, often record important developments in the action of the story, non-random sequences of events, in a way more akin to finite verbs that are non-progressive rather than progressive. They are less a contextualization of previous finite-clause-encoded material than the carriers of new and subsequent events. Contrary to the popular

119

impression that Faulkner's fiction progresses by way of series of frozen tableaux (a view perhaps first propounded in 1941 by Beck (Beck 1976), these non-finite verbs often propel the narrative onward with alacrity:

> Then he straightened up and with one hand flung the shovel quivering upright in the mound like a javelin and turned and began to walk away, walking on even when an old woman came out . . . and grasped his forearm. (pp. 135–6)

> Then . . . the log seemed to leap suddenly backward over his head of its own volition, spinning, crashing and thundering down the incline. (p. 146)

REPRISE

A count of the relative frequencies of lexical verbs in the progressive, despite the small corpus, shows some unusual details: the commonest main-verb progressives are *look* and *wait* (thirteen occurrences), *go* (ten), *run* and *sit* (nine), *move* and *stand* (eight), *watch* (five), and *pant* and *speak* (four). Of these, *look, go, sit, move*, and *stand* are recorded as common progressives by Ota (1963) and/or Scheffer (1975). But *wait* (in thirteen main verbs, and also three dependent ones), although noted by Ota as a commonly progressive verb, seems unusually frequent in *Go Down, Moses*.

Duration is clearly part of the verb's meaning. The particular effect of the progressive-form use here of *wait* seems to be to place the reader abruptly *in medias res*, as if the speaker were unable to view the limits of the period of waiting and could only recognize that the waiting had already begun. This *in medias res* effect, often noted, is not easily defined. But in *Go Down, Moses* it regularly has to do with the implied temporary alignment of the narrator (and hence the reader) and some character, which I have already discussed at length. If a text runs

> Ike rose early and went to his stand. Sam was waiting for him there.

rather than

> Ike rose early and went to his stand. Sam waited for him there.

version one, arguably, is one level closer to an immediate report (by Ike) in one distinct way. If Ike himself had reported these events, he might have said:

I rose early and [then] I went to my stand. Sam was waiting for me there.

It is highly improbable that Ike would comment, 'Sam waited for me there'. It is arguable, then, that in the mediation of the report by a narrator most 'direct commentary' progressives are replaced by verbs converted to their non-expanded forms. In a few cases this stage of distancing from the actual experience is not enacted, and the reader can more immediately recognize the direct record of events. These suggestions, it must be stressed, are only a tentative observation on the *in medias res* effect of some progressives, and may apply only in cases where a single clearly identified character in the text is the 'reflector' of events, the perspective from which the report is understood to be cast.

However, in fact on numerous occasions the narrative has sentences of the structure

When x, y.

where x is: the salesman drove up that evening
      or: Ike reached his stand
      or: they arrived by the foal's carcass
and y is: Lucas was already waiting
      or: Sam was (already) waiting

The complex sentence with preposed temporal clause is perhaps typically used in stories to conjoin non-reversible narrative clauses (in the sense of Labov (1972)). The syntactic clauses can be reordered of course, but the narrative contents cannot, without change of story content. Cf.:

When he realized he was lost, he made a backtrack.

and

He made a backtrack. Then he realized he was lost.

A major attraction of fronting the subordinate time clause is that this maintains iconicity with the experiential order of events, as these are experienced by the agent or processor in the fronted temporal clause.

None of these features applies in the structures noted above, however – as the progressive-aspect main verbs make clear. The 'when x, then y' expectation is flouted, because we find that, even before x, y was already the case. It is too simple to say that Lucas and Sam act, while the white men react, but there is a trend along such lines. Nor are Lucas and Sam waiting simply because they are punctual and the others are late. Rather it is because, while the others are acting at a certain time, such men as Lucas and Sam choose to be at certain places, to do certain things, on grounds other than those of the compulsions of the clock, safety, or conventional logic. It may be no accident that, when time does elapse in the narrative, the new temporal orientation of events is supplied when characters such as Lucas and Sam are not the focus of attention.

This chapter has been built around detailed examination of the functioning of narrative progressive-form verbs as they are fore-grounded at specific points in the novel – the close of section 2 of 'The Old People', the rejection of Roth by Henry in 'The Fire and the Hearth', the frenzied, anguished dynamism of Rider in 'Pantaloon in Black', and so on. But those points of foregrounding stand out, independently of any interpretative considerations, by virtue of their marked frequencies of progressive-form usage relative to textual norms. A different general trend that has been noted is the density of adverbial qualification of clauses with progressive verbs. That trend confirms the view that progressives in narratives give depth to an otherwise potentially monotonously linear succession of events recorded in simple past tense. If a progressive lexical verb in isolation promotes lack of temporal precision, these adjuncts set such progressives in a rich context of designated times and places.

At the same time, while finite progressives do often retard the narrative thrust, 'stretching' points of time, foiling our expectations that one recorded event will succeed the previous one, we have seen that the book's non-finite progressives may encode rapid sequences of actions – ones which do not even overlap each other, but rather displace each other quite abruptly. Noting the numerous non-finite verb forms in Faulkner's novels, Kaluza has commented: 'The high frequency of nonfinite verbal forms blurs the outline of the presented actions, while conveying them as just happening (particularly by means of the -*ing* form) and thus making the reader participate in them more directly' (Kaluza 1964: 16).

In support of my broader interpretative proposals, then, I hope to have shown that there is considerable evidence of progressive verbal forms in the narrative occurring in passages of FID or temporary narratorial alignment with specific characters. Ehrlich has suggested that a similar function is attributable to many of the progressives in the narrative of Woolf's *To the Lighthouse* and *Mrs Dalloway* (Ehrlich

1987), but suggests: 'It is precisely when events in progressive aspect overlap with predicates of speech or thought that they are interpreted as part of a character's inner speech or thought' (1987: 370). The evidence I have presented suggests that this is too restrictive a characterization: character-oriented use of progressives can emerge even without adjacent predicates of speech or thought, or canonical indices of FID. A subtler technique of narratorial alignment is at work. Main-clause finite progressives are frequently seen sustaining presentation of a character's thought or – especially – perception by proxy. Their use in narrative foregrounding of characters' experience is felt to be particularly appropriate in view of earlier characterization of the progressive form as regularly implying that the speaker treats the state or action denoted as a perceived process.

MEANINGFUL SYNTAX

Perhaps the most fundamental assumption of this chapter has been that syntactic options in a language, such as that between progressive and non-progressive aspect with dynamic verbs, carry important choices between different meaning options; in short, that some syntax is meaning-bearing. Suspicion of this principle is always at least latent in non-stylistic circles. Recently, in Barry (1984) – a critical response to a stylistic essay by F. Austin (1982) on V + *ing* forms in Eliot's *Four Quartets* – there has been a vigorous attack on any such assumption of 'semantic syntax':

> I suspect that semantic syntax is another variant of what I have elsewhere called the enactment fallacy . . . the tendency to attribute meaning to every aspect of the 'physical' properties of words and phrases in an attempt to show that good literature acts out as well as states its meanings. Though the notion is attractive the evidence usually turns out, in the end, to be unconvincing. (Barry 1984: 36)

Barry argues against a literal-minded assumption that the conventional names of verb forms (present, continuous, etc.) express inherent semantic values of verb tokens of those types. Whether all this is fair criticism of Austin's paper is debatable: as her response emphasizes (F. Austin 1985), she is neither literal nor unquestioning in her descriptions of the present participle. Where Austin is perhaps more vulnerable, in a way not quite confronted by Barry's literalism argument, is in heavy reliance on interpretative leaps of the kind to which stylisticians are prone. Thus she recasts an unexceptionable claim, that non-finite forms lack temporal reference, in a tendentious way: 'The ambiguity of "past or present time" *leads naturally* to "out of time", which is *the* effect of the non-finite forms' (F. Austin 1985: 167; my emphases).

But the Barry–Austin dispute seems conducted on the wrong grounds. Without adopting Austin's interpretative claims, one might still make the following points in relation to the passage from Barry quoted above.

1. Focusing on just -*ing* forms seems the very reverse of attempting to extract meaning from 'every aspect of the "physical" properties of words and phrases'; it is the inescapable analytical and interpretative move to selective attention.

2. Discussion of -*ing* forms hardly constitutes a discussion of the 'physical' properties of words. The effect of rhythmic and phonic repetition in the physical articulation and audition of the -*ing* forms, for example, is not part of Austin's argument.

3. Barry asserts a sharp division between semantics and syntax, and between acting out meaning versus stating meanings, in order to question Austin's alleged efforts to demonstrate the motivated workings of syntax in the service of a particular semantics. But quite where Barry stands on the question of the possibilities of correlation across this division is unclear. The conclusion of his note implies that attention to the sense of syntax is irrelevant: literature (as distinct from all other text?) simply states its meanings, he declares, as if no interpretative work is ever necessary or appropriate. Yet much of his argument rests on an appeal to that expressivity or sense in syntax: Austin is said to be wrong because she has got the typical functions of the present participle wrong (functions which Barry knows and specifies). Barry's own paper thus shifts between treating -*ing*-form meanings as either purely arbitrary and subjective or in the public domain and corrigible.

The escape from an unprofitable *dialogue des sourds* in this area must begin with a recognition that stylisticians never discuss syntactic forms except in so far as they convey particular effects, are marked or unmarked ways of presenting information, evaluation, and so on. Always finally use-oriented rather than form-oriented, stylistics is equally invariably semantic.

5

PRONOUNS AND NAMING

PRONOUNS, DEIXIS, AND ANAPHORA

In *The Philosophy of Grammar* (1929) Jespersen offers a fairly orthodox definition of the role of the pronoun: 'A pronoun is a substitute for a noun and is used partly for the sake of brevity, partly to avoid the necessity of definite statement' (1929: 82). But he immediately notes exceptions: 'No one doubts that *nobody* and the interrogative *who* are pronouns, but it is not easy to see what nouns they can be said to be substitutes for.' Such exceptions force us to qualify – or elaborate – the assumption that pronouns are substitutes for full forms, with a definite referential tie as rendered explicitly by that full form. Jespersen also refers to the claim that pronouns are characterized 'by their signification being variable and essentially contained in a reference to some circumstance which is found outside of the linguistic expression itself and is determined by the whole of the situation' (82). He finds such a classification too indiscriminate. However, one of the ironies that may emerge from the following overview is that, as far as interpretation of actual text is concerned (rather than interpretation of decontextualized system sentences), attention to 'the whole of the situation' is often important.

Traditionally, pronouns are examined in relation to nouns. In *Language*, Bloomfield expounds the notion of grammatical substitution in which, among other cases, a pronoun is treated as a substituted form for a previously stated or understood expression (Bloomfield 1935: 249). This implies that pronouns substitute for nouns, or what Bloomfield calls the class of substantives. But he, like Jespersen, recognizes exceptions: 'We usually find some independent uses of substitutes that are ordinarily independent as, for instance, the independent use of *it* in *it's raining*' (249). (Bloomfield also states the cardinal tenet of deixis: demonstrative pronouns express relative nearness to the speaker or hearer.)

It may be useful to clarify, at the outset, the way in which the term 'reference' is to be used in this chapter. I adopt the widely held view that reference is an abstract construction of ties or relations between linguistic forms and real-world objects (or referents). The tie between a linguistic form (or 'referring expression', the term preferred by Lyons (1977: 24)) and a referent, such that the former denotes or designates the latter, is made by an addresser or addressee. Referring expressions may have a multiplicity of different referents in different situations. The expression *my hat* may refer to a potentially infinite number of different hats, depending on who the speaker is – or none at all, if it is used as an exclamation of surprise or disdain. The potential, in or through natural languages, to refer to now one, now another, referent or object has long been recognized as one of the sources of the creative complexity of a language, when compared with other sign systems. (This principle of 'shifting reference' is celebrated, for example, in Cassirer (1953).) But in particular sentences, especially where sentences form a coherent text bound together by subject-matter, situation, and so on, the range of possible referents of particular expressions is likely to be quite restricted. One concern of this chapter is to consider the means – grammatical or discoursal-pragmatic – by which reference becomes less arbitrary, more determined, and more predictable in coherent text, and how these means are exploited in *Go Down, Moses*.

The standard resources of pro-form reference are deixis and anaphora:

> By deixis is meant the location and identification of persons, objects, events, processes and activities being talked about, or referred to, in relation to the spatiotemporal context created and sustained by the act of utterance and the participation in it, typically, of a single speaker and at least one addressee. (Lyons 1977: 637)

It is often said that deixis is the function, in language, of pointing; but as much could be said of anaphora. The important feature of deictic pointing is that it not only cites referents but gestures towards locating them – in relation to a speaker and a hearer. To that extent it is more closely tied to the specific act of speech, in a context of situation, than anaphora. In English, deixis is traditionally thought to be expressed by personal and demonstrative pronouns, demonstrative adverbs, and tense; but other features may well be involved too, particularly if, following Levinson (1983) and Lyons (1977), we speak of five types of deixis: social and discoursal, as well as of person, place, and time. Crucial to deixis is the notion of the egocentricity of the speaker in any language act: a speaker situates referents, both temporally and spatially, in relation to him- or herself, speaking 'here and now'.

Jespersen argued for a rather broad category of deictics or 'shifters' as they have often been called (see Jespersen 1922; Cassirer 1953; Russell 1948; Jakobson 1957), and he included such expressions as *mother*, *father*, *enemy*, and *home*. Cassirer focused more narrowly on demonstratives and personal pronouns, as key expressions of the tension between subjects and objects, and hence an essential base of language – a theme that has been pursued, via the influential contributions of Benveniste (1966) and Barthes, into modern literary-critical theory of the subject. Russell, as Crymes has noted (1968: 20), disputed the indispensability of shifters, or what he called 'egocentric particulars' (Russell 1948: 108–15). Treating of words 'of which the denotation is relative to the speaker' – *I*, *this*, *now* – he believed that they 'are not needed in any part of the description of the world, whether physical or psychological'. One consequence of adopting such a language without egocentricity, however, would be literal disorientation and detachment. To dispense with deictics would be to attempt to disregard the fact that they, and the principle of egocentricity, are simply a reflection of the way in which any natural language is centrally to do with expression and constitution of self (and other): self-expression, -protection, -identification, and -orientation.

Deixis is defined by Crymes as 'any pointing that locates either a real-world referent or a linguistic referent in terms of its orientation to the speaker spatially, temporally, discriminately, or affectively' (Crymes 1968: 63, n.64). As she notes, deixis and anaphora may be signalled simultaneously by the same pointing word, as in:

Take a look at this book. *This* is the best book I've read in a long time. (my emphasis)

Following Benveniste, she categorizes pronouns and other deictics into those with subjective referents – in French, the *je–ici–maintenant* system – and those with more objective referents – the *il–là–alors* system. Because the 'objective' deictics are often used in a non-contrastive (and so non-orientational) way, some commentators (including Crymes) have excluded them from their class of shifters. It is certainly the case that *now* and *then* are often seemingly interchangeable or non-contrastive, that selection between them is 'stylistic' (Crymes 1968: 78, n.47): in such cases any deictic force they may have is severely attenuated. Nevertheless, on countless other occasions, use of items like *there* and *that* are contrastive, to be understood in relation to their counterparts (*here*, *this*, *the*) in closed systems of spatio-temporal orientation. In a well-formed utterance with two participants, an addressee interpreting the comment *Take a look at that girl!* will expect that the referent of the demonstrative is non-proximate to the speaker and, most likely, non-proximate to the addressee, just as surely as one's expectations about the nature (specifically the gender) of the referent would contrast when hearing the injunctions *Take a look at him* rather than *Take a look at her*. These last examples also show how third-person pronouns, in offering a gender description of their referents and not merely an identification, come to be termed 'impure deixis' (Lyons 1977). It should be noted that I have written above of the 'expectations' that use of demonstrative *that* triggers, rather than of a meaning that it could be said to guarantee. As in the case of progressivization, this linguistic option carries a shared, expected value, rather than a fixed value or invariant sense. Accordingly, non-canonical uses of demonstrative *that* are not so much exceptions to a fixed rule of use but creative departures from the norm, the force of which we 'calculate' by making reference to the normal usage (cf. the 'calculation' of conversational implicature, as in Grice (1975), mentioned in chapter 12). Thus, to return to the two-participant exchange described above, it is perfectly possible for the speaker of *Take a look at that girl!* to use this utterance as a kind of appreciative greeting of an attractive female addressee, with no other individual present or intended as referent of *that girl*. Clearly the canonical use of *that*, distancing and objectivizing, does not apply here literally; but both parties know this canonical literal application, and so the addressee infers that a figurative or rhetorical objectivizing of the addressee is intended here, a kind of putting on record that the addresser sees and treats the addressee as new and set apart in some way. (Cf. 'Wow, look at you!') Essentially the deictic opposition is one between proximate and non-proximate:

proximate : non-proximate : neutral

I	you	
		she/he/it
this	that	the
here	there	
now	then	

The second fundamental mode of reference in pronouns is anaphora. This is the coreferential tie or relation between a pronoun (the anaphor) and a – usually preceding – phrase or clause (the antecedent). The simplest kind of anaphora ties a personal pronoun to a preceding full noun phrase (NP):

> When Edmonds glanced up from the ledger and saw the old woman coming up the road, he did not recognize her. He returned to the ledger and it was not until he heard her toiling up the steps and saw her enter the commissary itself, that he knew who it was. Because for something like four or five years now he had never seen her outside her own gate. He would pass the house on his mare while riding his crops and see her . . . (p. 99)

In this example, from the very beginning of chapter 3 of 'The Fire and the Hearth', there is a coreferential tie between the NP *Edmonds* (the antecedent) and *he* (the anaphor). Interestingly, the definite description *the old woman* is anaphorically tied to a series of pronouns (*she* and *her*) that follow. Many lines later, at the foot of this page, coreference continues through new definite descriptions – *the negro woman, the only mother he ever knew*. Only by inference can we deduce the woman's name – Molly Beauchamp – aided by various ironizing cues. Thus on the next page Edmonds asks Molly, 'What are you doing over here? Why didn't you send Lucas?', and yet at the tumultuous close of the previous chapter he had dismissed her husband Lucas with the words 'Dont ever come back. . . . When you need supplies, send Aunt Molly after them.' In this fuller context, the varied means adopted in the text to denote Molly – *the old woman, she, the negro woman, Aunt Molly*, and so on – can be seen to be not merely referential but also descriptive and informative, revealing evaluations of the woman by the narrator or speaker. The switch from the use of *her* to *Molly* is potentially as significant as the *tu/vous* alternation in French, entailing assessments of speaker's and referent's power, solidarity, affiliation, and so on. A major interest of this chapter will be the interplay, in use of pronouns,

names, and definite descriptions to denote characters, between maintaining textual coherence (adequate cross-referencing) and achieving
important descriptive and evaluative effects.

Anaphora involves positing a common referent for two or more
contiguous referring expressions. Some linguists (e.g. Halliday and
Hasan 1976) have introduced the term 'cataphora' for the less
normal, anticipatory, or forward-looking anaphora, where anaphor
precedes antecedent. In the generativist literature this is termed
'backwards anaphora' (*sic*), since in the process of interpretation of
such an anaphor the processor must 'bring back' a following full
expression. Huddleston (1984: 298) has an excellent note on this
terminological tangle, and makes the straightforward distinction
between unmarked- and marked-order anaphora (anaphora and
cataphora, respectively). Some such distinction does have to be made
between the two types of anaphora, for there are different constraints
on backward- and forward-looking anaphora respectively. Forward-
looking anaphora, for example, is rarely possible in English across
co-ordinate clauses (subscript indices mark intended coreference):

*They$_i$ came home and the boys$_i$ went to bed.

However, there are exceptions to this constraint, particularly with the
co-ordinator *but*, as noted by Mittwoch (1983) and discussed below.

Contemporary linguistic discussion of anaphora was largely initiated by chapter 15 of Bloomfield's *Language* (1935), on substitution.
There he refers to anaphoric pronouns as anaphoric or dependent
substitutes. This proposal seems the point of departure for the
analyses of Allen (1961) and Crymes (1968). Allen begins by correct-
ing Bloomfield's mistaken concentration on substitute nouns, arguing
that entire nominal constructions are substituted. He then distinguishes the constructional feature, substitution, from the semantic
one of reference. In

There is a clock. It is an alarm clock.

he notes that the pronoun *it* corefers with *a clock* but does not
substitute for *a clock*. Rather it substitutes for a replaced identified
nominal:

There is a clock. It [the clock there] is an alarm clock.

Allen observes that 'the primary function of a substitute word is to
replace that particular kind of form-class or construction-class which

is its domain' (1961: 12). However, while 'replacing' may be the primary syntactic function of substitutes, no account is given here of their semantic function. The point to stress is that pronouns are not merely different from their antecedents in form-class terms. They also differ, very often, in their intended sense. Brown and Yule (1983: 201–2) explore the use of pronouns in cooking recipes in particular, and descriptions involving change of state in general, where what is no longer quite the same onion, or no longer an onion at all, continues to be denoted by the 'same' pronoun. Thus substitutes or pro-forms frequently signal specific meanings not signalled by their antecedents. In

> It would not be Boon. He had never hit anything bigger than a squirrel. (p. 235)

the closed system of third-person subject pronouns, from which the speaker has chosen, yields information – about the +/− human status of Boon and, being human, the gender – not grammaticalized by the proper name. (The third-person pronouns are not, however, invariably reliable guides to, for example, animacy: cars, boats, animals, and human babies regularly take *it*. For a discussion of the domains of *who* and *what* and how they overlap in application, see Jacobsson (1970).)

COHESION AND DISCOURSE ANAPHORA

Perhaps the fullest text-oriented treatment of anaphora to date is Halliday and Hasan (1976), whose overriding concern is the variety of sources of verbally encoded inter-sentential linkage in a text, phenomena which they group together under the term 'cohesion'. Five major sources are identified: reference, substitution, ellipsis, conjunction, and lexical cohesion. Only the first two, involving pronouns, concern us here (conjunction is addressed in the course of chapters 9–11, lexical cohesion in chapter 8). Referential cohesion subsumes use of personal, demonstrative, and comparative pronouns, which all involve pronominal coreference of one kind or another; while the indefinite pronoun *one(s)* and the pro-forms *do* and *so* are exemplars of substitutionary cohesion. The latter category involves what might be called 'parallel reference' but not usually coreference or strict identity. Thus when the substitute *one* is used in the drinks order, 'He'll have a Budweiser and I'll have one too', it signals identity of sense (same type of entity as that just mentioned) but not identity of reference (not the same single Budweiser). For some linguists, it should be noted (e.g. Huddleston 1984: 278), neither of the noun phrases under scrutiny in the above sentence is strictly a referring expression, since *a Budweiser* lacks the defining definite article; but this is a semantic distinction that should not obscure the fact that some process of referring is still involved. As Brown and Yule remark of the typical use of indefinite NPs in discourse,

> We can say that the speaker intends the hearer to recognise that there is an individual entity referred to by the expression used. It does not seem to be a necessary condition of this type of introductory reference that the hearer should be able to 'identify uniquely', in any strict sense, the individual referred to. (Brown and Yule 1983: 208)

As has been noted, the widespread assumption that pronouns are replacements of adjacent NPs, denoting the same referents as their antecedents, is not supported by many cases where the anaphor must be understood as referring to an entity that has undergone modification. Brown and Yule give the example:

> Wash and core six cooking apples. Put them into a fireproof dish. (Brown and Yule 1983: 201)

The example is simple but its implications are major. We must doubt any picture of anaphoric chains that assumes a static reinstatement of a previously given entity. In its place we must see such chains as part of a developing and changing presentation of particular (developing, changing) referents. We do not interpret *them* in the example simply by 'scanning back' to *six cooking apples*. More complexly, the *them* is interpreted in the light of the entire process of washing and coring predicated of the apples.

Early in their study, Halliday and Hasan distinguish between *I/you* and *he*, along lines similar to those of Crymes (1968) and Lyons (1977):

> Only the third person is inherently cohesive, in that a third person form typically refers anaphorically to a preceding item in the text. First and second person forms do not normally refer to the text at all; their referents are defined by the speech roles of speaker and hearer, and hence they are normally interpreted exophorically, by reference to the situation. (Halliday and Hasan 1976: 48)

The distinction they propose between situational (exophoric) and textual (endophoric) reference should not, however, obscure the principle that the referents of all pro-forms (save code-focused or textually deictic forms such as *that* in ' "It's the Ashmolean." "How do you spell that?" ') are entities outside the text. That they may be alluded to, by anaphoric or deictic means, within the text, is a separate issue. Halliday and Hasan go on to note cumulative anaphoricity, in long texts where, for example, a named man is the antecedent of a series of *he* pronouns:

> This phenomenon contributes very markedly to the internal co-hesion of a text, since it creates a kind of network of lines of reference, each occurrence being linked to all its predecessors up to and including the initial reference. The number and density of such networks is one of the factors which gives to any text its particular flavour or texture. (52)

A clear example of the phenomenon is provided by the opening lines of chapter 3 of 'The Fire and the Hearth' (p. 99), quoted earlier in this chapter. Halliday and Hasan also note how *it*, *this*, and *that* may refer, beyond a person or object, through extended reference and text reference. Extended reference occurs where *it* is related to a whole process:

> After it was over – it didn't take long; they found the prisoner on the following day, hanging from the bell-rope in a negro schoolhouse about two miles from the sawmill, and the coroner had pronounced his verdict of death at the hands of a person or persons unknown and surrendered the body to its next of kin all within five minutes – the sheriff's deputy who had been officially in charge of the business was telling his wife about it. (p. 154)

Text reference occurs where *it*, *this*, etc., are related to a fact reported in the text:

> 'They're taking a nap now,' he said. 'But never mind that;' (p. 13)

Concerning *this* and *that* Halliday and Hasan make the interesting claim that 'Extended reference probably accounts for the majority of all instances of demonstratives in all except a few specialized varieties of English' (1976: 66).

Halliday and Hasan also look briefly at the problematic area of how we disambiguate referring items across sentences, when it is not immediately clear which of several antecedents an anaphoric item is tied to. That they dwell on this important topic so briefly perhaps reflects the systemicists' preoccupation with the encoder in language and the repertoire of networks available for realizing meanings. There is now much attention directed both to the frequent problems, for decoders, of anaphor interpretation and to possible procedures by which we resolve such problems. But many of the issues, it is acknowledged, remain ill understood (see Kantor *et al.* 1982; Clark and Marshall 1981; McKay and Fulkerson 1979; Chastain 1975; Nunberg 1978).

A vivid example of the antecedent-identification dilemma in *Go Down, Moses* presents itself to the reader at the very opening of 'The Bear':

> He was sixteen. For six years now he had been a man's hunter. For six years now he had heard the best of all talking. It was of the wilderness, the big woods, bigger and older than any recorded document: – of white man fatuous enough to believe he had bought any fragment of it, of Indian ruthless enough to pretend that any fragment of it had been his to convey; bigger than Major de Spain and the scrap he pretended to, knowing better; older than old Thomas Sutpen of whom Major de Spain had had it and who knew better; older even than old Ikkemotubbe, the Chickasaw chief, of whom old Sutpen had had it and who knew better in his turn. It was of the men, not white nor black nor red but men, hunters, with the will and hardihood to endure and the humility and skill to survive, and the dogs and the bear and deer juxtaposed and reliefed against it, ordered and compelled by and within the wilderness in the ancient and unremitting context according to the ancient and immitigable rules which voided all regrets and brooked no quarter; – the best game of all, the best of all breathing and forever the best of all listening. (pp. 191–2)

Here it is as if it is the 'game' of *telling* that is celebrated, even as it is played. For the entity denoted by the *it* pronoun switches unpredictably from 'the talking' to 'the wilderness' to 'a scrap of wilderness' and back (presumably) to 'the talking' ('It was of the men . . .'); then (perhaps) to 'the wilderness' again (are the men and dogs reliefed against the wilderness or the talking?), so that the reader becomes quite uncertain whether 'the best of all breathing and . . . listening' describes talking or hunting. (To the surprise of many, subsequent text leans towards attributing the description to the former activity, the talking.) The dexterous use of the ambiguous *it* pronoun and the referent hunt on which it sends the reader off contribute to the impression that the text is struggling to remain 'about' hunting while all its dynamics reveal that the hunting is chiefly a pretext for the talking.

Concluding their discussion of the topic of identifying antecedents, Halliday and Hasan doubt the value of grammatical rather than semantic criteria. But they add: 'OTHER THINGS BEING EQUAL, it seems that the most probable target of a cohesive reference item is the Theme of the preceding sentence' (1976: 312). A similar argument to this one has been developed by Clark in his notion of 'bridging', but this has also received some criticism (see e.g. Brown and Yule 1983: 218–19). Halliday and Hasan's conclusion is suitably tentative:

> Given the range of POSSIBLE targets in a connected passage, it is unlikely that any purely grammatical principles could suffice for resolving the issue, and the semantic principle of 'making most sense', difficult as it may be to make explicit, is the only one that could really be expected to apply. (1976: 312)

If Allen, Crymes, and Halliday and Hasan represent various non-transformational developments of Jespersen and Bloomfield in the analysis of pro-forms, the transformational-generativist accounts are far more extensive. Little purpose would be served, however, by charting the numerous revisions in the generativist treatments of pronouns and anaphora, from Lees and Klima (1963), Chomsky (1965), McCawley (1968, 1970), Lakoff (1968), J. R. Ross (1969), and Postal (1969), to Langacker (1969), Hankamer and Sag (1976), Williams (1977), Reinhart (1983), and Lust (1986) – to mention only a representative selection. As generativists themselves are eager to acknowledge, their interest is in an optimally simple characterization and explanation of the well-formed grammatical options unconsciously available to a native speaker of a language (and, ideally, some account of the universal conditions or constraints assumed to underlie this language and others). This is a quite different interest, in their view, from that of studying the actual exercise of those options in particular texts. Accordingly generativist-oriented studies are theoretical and abstract, and geared to correct use of pronouns at the level of individual sentences rather than extended discourse. They are drawn on in studies of natural language processing, psycholinguistics, and language acquisition, but their relevance to the study of patterns of pronoun use in long texts remains tenuous. Furthermore, despite their immense analytical sophistication, problems accrue to generativist accounts of anaphora because of their tacit adoption of the bi-planar telementational account of linguistic communication – an account which, following Harris (1981, 1987), I regard as fundamentally mistaken.

Much the same objection to Banfield (1982) that was raised in chapter 3 in the section on 'Free indirect discourse and speakerless narrative' applies to generative studies of pronominalization: a sentence-grammar approach is inadequate to the unpredictabilities and creative individualist considerations shaping contextualized discourses. As studies such as Bolinger (1977) confirm, pronoun occurrence in English repeatedly defies capture by syntactic rules and constraints, and instead pronominalization can often be accounted for only in terms of contextual pragmatic considerations, the encoder's desire to topicalize certain subjects, and so on. This seems to have been conceded in the mid-1970s by leading generativist theorists, who began to postulate 'pronouns of laziness' (Partee 1975), 'pragmatically controlled anaphora' (a terminological paradox), and 'impure textual deixis' (see Lyons 1977: 670 ff.).

However, the remoteness of these generativist accounts from the variabilities of pronoun usage in extended texts remains the most immediate stumbling-block to applying them. Stylisticians (perhaps here conducting one of the central tasks of linguists) are concerned with how pronouns work in full texts or discourses; but generativists have typically confined themselves to the principles for pronoun generation in sentences. There are plenty of reasons for doubting that a grammar postulating pronoun-generating ties between items in decontextualized constructed example sentences relates at all directly to the patterning of pronoun use in contextualized discourse. In response to this aporia, a new subdiscipline has emerged in very recent years – discourse anaphora – whose findings are intended to be relevant to various interests that have traditionally drawn on linguistic insights – artificial intelligence, cognitive science, and machine translation, among the 'algorithmic' disciplines – and relevant to linguists interested in universals of narrative structuring (e.g. patterns of foregrounded and backgrounded story elements). On discourse anaphora, see Hinds (1977), Grimes (1978), Linde (1979), Clancy (1980), Givon (1983), and Fox (1987). One of the fundamental questions that has exercised many in this field may be

formulated as follows: when do storytellers pronominalize a previously mentioned story entity, and when do they not, and why? Tentative answers to this question have invoked as criteria the distance in
clauses between current and previous mention; potential ambiguity
due to the presence of other possible referents; whether the entity to be
pronominalized is discourse topic or thematic in previous sentences
(cf. Halliday and Hasan 1976); and whether or not the coreferential
tie crosses a major discourse boundary or not (e.g. a new episode, a
shift in mode of presentation). Other analysts have suggested, as Fox
reports, that

> Certain anaphors are associated with central characters under
> certain conditions, while other anaphors are associated with minor
> characters, where the centrality of the character is defined either
> within the entire narrative or within some subpart of the narrative
> (e.g., an Episode). (Fox 1987: 160)

While Fox suggests such an approach does not transfer well to the
popular written English narratives she examines, a version of some
such discriminatory anaphorizing does seem to operate quite visibly
in some episodes of *Go Down, Moses*. And Fox's more general objection
to purely quantitative approaches to the question of 'anaphorisabil-
ity', approaches that focus purely on clausal distance and a rather
mechanical identification of potential ambiguity, seems well founded:
'Other factors having to do with the functional, hierarchical structure
of narratives [seem] to be much more influential' (162). On the basis
of her own study of anaphora patterns in four contemporary popular
English novels, Fox hypothesizes:

> A referent is pronominalizable until another character's goals and
> actions are introduced, unless those goals and actions are inter-
> active with the first character's, that is . . . there is some confronta-
> tion or active interaction between the two characters [in such
> narrated interaction, both characters may be pronominalized].
> (162)

According to this hypothesis, 'when a second character is introduced
that is not interacting directly with the first, pronominalization seems
to be blocked' (165). But when two characters of the same gender are
involved in the same action then the character denoted by the
grammatical subject of the clause may be pronominalized in the next
mention, while that character denoted by the non-subject NP will not

be so pronominalized. Over and above this pattern, however, 'there tends to be an association between the beginning of a narrative unit (typically the first slot of a development structure) and the use of a full NP' (170).

These are illuminating characterizations of a discourse 'maxim', for the use and interpretation of pronouns, that may be ordinarily followed in simple narratives. But it does have to be noted that the narratives Fox studies are indeed simple (e.g. Alan Dean's *Alien* and James Kahn's *Return of the Jedi*), without claims to literariness or narrative complexity. One index of their simplicity is the ease with which a single major event-line can be identified in each narrative. Identifying the major event-line (a notion Fox adopts from Hopper and Thompson (1980)) is important, since off-event-line asides and recollections, concerning other individuals, are said not to count as introduction of another character's goals or actions (and so do not 'trigger' full NP next mention of the character in the immediately prior event-line material). Again, these may be important general trends, but they do not transfer to *Go Down, Moses* in an unproblematic way, partly, no doubt, because this is a literary narrative with multiple interconnected event-lines. One of the first things one suspects, when turning from discourse anaphora to literary-discourse anaphora, is that writers have long been aware of the everyday conventions concerning the 'blocking', 'warranting', 'inducing', and 'triggering' of pronouns. They are sufficiently aware of the conventions that they may choose, in their more than conventional artistry, to block what is ordinarily warranted in matters of anaphora, so as to induce particular thematically motivated interpretations.

BACKWARDS ANAPHORA

Despite the general inappropriacy of sentence-oriented discussions of pronominalization in the context of discourse-anaphora patterns, some treatments that branch out from the sentential-syntactic view towards a larger discoursal-pragmatic one are worthy of attention. One example is recent discussion of backwards anaphora – or cataphora, or marked-order anaphora – (henceforth BA). At first glance BA seems to be perfectly acceptable in preposed subordinate clauses, but unacceptable across co-ordinate clauses. Cf. sentences 1 and 2 below:

1 Because he$_i$ was tired, John$_i$ went to bed.

2   *He$_i$ was very tired, but John$_i$ refused to go to bed.

But on closer scrutiny it transpires that, while BA is rare in co-ordinated sentences, it is by no means impossible, particularly in sentences co-ordinated with *but* –

3   I haven't seen him$_i$ yet but John$_i$ is back.

– and in sentences containing a postposed subordinate adverbial clause:

4   We were all talking about him$_i$ when John$_i$ walked in the room.

I shall chiefly consider below sentences like 3. However, it is interesting to note that sentences of just the kind exemplified by 4, narrative sentences with a *when* clause and a progressivized main verb, are ones in which the *when* clause has a marked, non-backgrounded interpretation (see the discussion in chapter 9, 'The functions of clausal subordination'). Also, there seem to be clear constraints on when sentences like 4 may be used. Sentence 4 is improbable in discourse-initial position, but much more likely to occur at the close of one section (or 'episode') of a narrative and the commencement of the next – for example, as a transition between 'orientation' and 'development'. If these judgements are correct, they show BA contributing to the patterns of alternation between full NPs and pronouns proposed by Fox (1987).

Examining a series of sentences of the type exemplified above by 3, Mittwoch (1983) has noted the overt or implicated negativity of the first clause of the co-ordination, and the tendency for there to be past-time reference. She suggests that the marked ordering is adopted for pragmatic purposes: a discourse strategy of downgrading the first clause and foregrounding the second clause (even if it is syntactically subordinate) as 'the speaker's main point' (Mittwoch 1983: 133). On the basis of examples such as 'Don't tell John Ø but *I've scratched his car*', Mittwoch arges:

> The first conjunct serves to neutralize . . . possible obstacles to the proper 'uptake' of the message; and the appearance in it of an as yet uninterpretable anaphoric device signals to H[earer] that the main point is to follow. (137)

Macleod (1984) claims *but*-co-ordinated BA as a distinctive journalistic style, particularly exploited by the news magazines *Time* and

Newsweek. It is perhaps more broadly a stock attention-getting technique in rhetorical writing, the unidentified pronoun serving to 'hook'
the reader on the text at least as far as the delayed disambiguating
antecedent. Macleod also argues that in this form of BA a useful
separation is achieved of the tasks of existential assertion (done by the
preceding pronoun) and informative naming or denomination:

> *They* cover Peking and Paris and most points in between. But last
> week, *the staff of the prestigious, employee-operated newspaper Le Monde*
> *was making news instead of reporting it.*

(Notice, incidentally, how this rearrangement mitigates if it does not
resolve the difficulties of number agreement in the sentence). Alternatively it could be argued that the technique achieves existential
assertion in two stages rather than all at once, as the reverse structure
would do, so that BA is a particular kind of staging of discoursal
assertion. First you get a highly provisional and incomplete existential assertion ('There is a *they*'), then you get a proper and semantically heavy fleshing out of this. The structure is like getting a wrapped
gift instead of an unwrapped one: the pronoun is a wrapping promis-
ing you that some entity is inside, but requiring you to proceed
beyond the wrapping to see quite what you have been given.

If the types and constraints on BA are to be better understood, it
may be important to distinguish different orders of BA, even within,
for example, Mittwoch's initial set of fifteen examples with *but*
co-ordination. Thus cases with a NP antecedent are structurally
rather different from those with a clausal antecedent. Among the
latter, replacement tests seem to suggest significant differences in
behaviour between antecedents comprising the entire clause following the *but* conjunction, and those embedded within the second clause
– for example, sentences 5 and 7 respectively:

5   Don't tell John $\emptyset$, but *I've crashed his car.*

6   Don't tell John I've crashed his car.

7   I don't believe *it* but John$_i$ swears *he$_i$'s become a Moony.*

8   I don't believe John$_i$'s become a Moony, but he$_i$ swears [he has].

The syntactic difference is that the former type, under unmarked
antecedent placement, reduces to a single complex clause, as in
sentence 6, while the latter type remains significantly compound-
clausal, as in sentence 8. Semantically the consequences are many,

but at the very least we can say that the second pair are roughly synonymous, while the first pair emphatically are not. According to Carden (1982), we should also distinguish a very general intra-sentential BA phenomenon from the particular business and stylistic effect of employing a 'withheld antecedent' across two or more sentences, which seems to appear only in texts 'with some literary pretensions', such as fiction, feature-story journalism, and advertisements.

By way of conclusion to this discussion, certain very general principles involved in deictic and anaphoric reference may be noted. One of these is that, whatever and wherever its source, we normally seek to establish a coreferential relation between a pronoun and an antecedent. Personal pronouns in texts are usually substitutes – or at least alternative forms – for known or named participants. Alongside this compulsion to identify co-textual links (a 'rage for cohesion'), there is an equal concern among readers to get our spatio-temporal bearings (a 'rage for orientation'). As a result, egocentricity and contrast of spatio-temporal nearness and distance are crucially important in interpretation of personal pronouns and demonstratives. Perhaps most basically this is because fictional narrative, like any other discourse, must have a speaker addressing an addressee, and must have the speaker exploiting deixis in orienting the text. A text like *Go Down, Moses* complicates the picture by effecting subtle shifts in the deictic orientation, so that it is often not a neutral teller who is at the deictic centre but a character. The implications of such shifts extend far beyond traditional literary stylistics, since they involve a recognition that understanding and evaluating utterances cannot be divorced from a knowledge of who is doing the uttering to whom, when, and where.

As Brown and Yule (1983: 222) stress, a simple substitutionary view of pronouns in discourse fails to explain very many actual cases where no substitutable antecedent is available:

9 There's two ladies go up to the whist and both have a wig and *they*'re most natural. (Brown and Yule 1983: 222)

10 I had my first divorce case today. The husband said *she* was always nagging him and the wife said he never talks to her. (constructed example)

In example 10 it seems we have to draw on our general knowledge that divorce cases involve married couples in order to understand that the

141

she in the second sentence denotes the wife. This is a particular instance of the general operation of what Brown and Yule treat as a sense-making interaction of background knowledge of the world with a foregrounded 'discourse representation' (1983: 206–7). The interpretative procedure here differs only in degree from the 'bridging' technique of implicature-constructing (Clark 1977) which we use to postulate an intended referent for the underlined phrases in the sentences below, such that coherence will be maintained:

11 I met two people yesterday. *The woman* told me a good story.

12 I went shopping today. *The walk* did me good.

Particular attention also needs to be paid to the referential ambiguity of the various pronouns. For while the pronouns *I, you,* and *he* are usually referentially determinate for the speaker (or, here, the narrator) they may not be so for the hearer/reader. Furthermore, words like *this, that, they,* and *it* may not be referentially determinate and unambiguous even for the speaker/narrator, let alone the reader. Yet in a written text, by contrast with face-to-face verbal interaction, the encoder/narrator has much greater control over the information and disambiguation made available to the reader. More specifically, in accordance with my interpretative judgement that the novel's narrative involves an interplay of character's viewpoints, I will tend to look for significant fluctuations in the manipulation of referential determinacy or ambiguity of pronouns. And a most important reflector of shifting narratorial alignment with a character in this novel (greater or lesser adoption of that experiencing character's perspective) will be seen to be the shifts in preferred means of designating particular individuals – from the pronominal option, to the proper name, to definite description.

The foundational interpretative task remains that of assigning reference, i.e. moving from text to (an imagined) world. Both anaphors and deictics, like all other means of referring, are thus alike at a more general level. The only difference is that with the non-deictic pronouns there is the possibility of attending to an intermediate layer of coreferring co-textual items, in the course of the reader's ascription of reference. Thus it is important to bear in mind that co-text in general (not merely the patterns of cohesive ties but also the broader cumulative sense of the propositions of the discourse, as the reader understands and interrelates them) will constrain and shape interpretation. Yet here too contradictions may emerge; for example, there may be an awkward mismatch between co-textual emphases and a reader's 'pre-textual' interpretative conventions and strategies. When Brown and Yule declare that 'The more co-text there is, the more secure the interpretation is. Text creates its own context' (1983: 50), one needs to add the proviso that new text can function to *un*ravel the sense woven by preceding text. Rather than saying text creates context we should see that readers choose to use text as part of an interpretative context. And in making sense of texts we look for coherence and cohesion, rather than their opposites: it is one of our most deeply rooted interpretative conventions. Nevertheless, there are no grounded guarantees that different readers will make quite the same sense of a text. Moreover, since we lack, in fiction, further feedback from the encoder, just what counts as an adequate interpretation of a particular text, even at the humdrum level of pronouns, may vary from case to case and from one addressee to the next. Multiple meanings, irony, ambiguity, and so on, may be actively sought, even insisted upon, by some interpreters but not others.

PERSONAL PRONOUN AMBIGUITIES AT CHAPTER OPENINGS

> While I am sure that prose fiction may make great demands on our attention, it ought not to make these demands arbitrarily, and there is no reason why Mr Faulkner cannot settle to whom the pronoun 'he' refers.

Thus was Faulkner rebuked by Lionel Trilling (1942: 632) when the latter reviewed *Go Down, Moses* in the year of its publication. Trilling was exercised by the referential uncertainties that are most likely to tax the reader at the beginning of a story or section. The *in medias res* pronominal designation of characters, as if they were already familiar to the reader and so needed no more explicit designation, is a stock device of fiction. Its prominent use in *Go Down, Moses* was unsympathetically received by Trilling; but, taking issue with that view, this section suggests that there are significant reasons, in terms of narratorial motivation, for the recurring pronominal ambiguities at chapter openings.

No such ambiguities attend the novel's opening, however, whatever subsequent practice may be. The one-page section I of 'Was' introduces Ike in elaborate fashion. The very first words of the text are

143

'Isaac McCaslin, "Uncle Ike"'. In fact most of 'Was', section I, constitutes a single richly qualified NP, a single elaborated referring expression describing Ike. This opening gambit is all the more exceptional since it introduces a character who is not involved (even as a spectator) in the story that follows. The principle whereby we assume the persistence of immediately preceding patterns of reference is violated. Only on the basis of information obliquely conveyed in section I, and cumulative information during section II, can we grasp that the *he* pronoun at the opening of section II denotes a different individual from that which it denotes at the close of section I.

From the world of Cass, Buck, and Buddy at the close of 'Was', the reader must make similarly rapid adjustment in order to comprehend the very different world of 'The Fire and the Hearth', chapter 1, which opens thus:

> First in order to take care of George Wilkins once and for all he had to hide his own still. (p. 33)

On a first reading the reader is likely to consider the following as possible referents of this *he* pronoun, in this order of probability: (1) Ike, (2) Cass, (3) someone else (Buck or Buddy?). Cass has been the *he* of 'Was', but 'Was', section I, goes to some trouble to emphasize that the story is atypical of the novel in this respect, so that we expect subsequent stories to have Ike as the chief participant or witness. One immediate clue towards disambiguation is the information that the referent owns a still. This fact tends to exclude both Cass and Ike, chiefly on grounds of class. It is gradually revealed that this *he* is an old black man with close ties to the McCaslin family, a man who was born on the land. But it is only seven pages into the story, on p. 39, that he is named – 'He, Lucas Beauchamp, the oldest living McCaslin' – during a passage of character-aligned exuberant self-promotion. By contrast, chapters 2 and 3 of 'The Fire and the Hearth' make quite clear who is denoted by their initial *he*: an antecedent is supplied:

> About a hundred yards before they reached the commissary, Lucas spoke over his shoulder without stopping. 'You wait here,' he said. (p. 78)

> When Edmonds glanced up from the ledger and saw the old woman coming up the road, he did not recognize her. (p. 99)

At the opening of 'Pantaloon in Black' the reader is again put at a disadvantage:

He stood in the worn, faded clean overalls which Mannie herself had washed only a week ago . . . (p. 135)

It emerges that the man is black, called Rider, young and strong, attending the funeral of his wife Mannie.

In each of these three stories, then, the reader is thrust into a new social milieu. In each milieu in turn, the narrative treats the reader as familiar with the central participants. Accordingly the participants may be specified by name, or a pronoun may suffice, but in any case the narrative action is immediately embarked upon; in none of these stories is there any section of orientational preliminaries, in which the characters are introduced, their attributes and history rehearsed, prior to immersion in the reported complex of events. (The one stark exception to this, as already noted, is the profile of Ike in 'Was', section I.) This way of proceeding is possibly intended to imply that the stories' various milieux do in fact interrelate, or comprise the facets of a single community. Such a narratorial assertion of community would itself give grounds for assuming that the reader of any one of these stories is already somewhat familiar with the members of that community.

It is only in 'The Old People' that Ike reappears, after 'Was', section I. Yet even here the story embarks on an account of the experiences of a boy who is Sam's protégé, without disclosing that this boy is Ike. Instead he is called *the boy* or *he*. The act of naming (a process so valued by the narrator in relation to various characters in the text: Lucas, Sam, Ben, and Lion) must be enacted independently by the reader. The reader is obliged to consider all the information put at his or her disposal in the opening pages of 'The Old People' (e.g. that the boy would live to be 80, that his father had a twin brother, that McCaslin Edmonds was sixteen years his senior and more his father than his cousin, etc.), in arriving at the tentative conclusion that the individual presented here is indeed the same Ike as was introduced in 'Was', section I. In fact, in 'The Old People', Ike is called by name only once, and that by Cass in a passage of direct speech (p. 173).

Identifying participants at the opening of 'The Bear', section I, presents no difficulty: as noted earlier, the problem lies rather in identifying the topic. In fact there is repeated naming of protagonists – Sam, Boon, Old Ben, and Lion, three of whom are new to the reader – but, as before, with a marked absence of clarificatory description. The procedure is thus different from that at the opening of 'The Fire and the Hearth': here there is naming. But in both cases, whether names or pronouns are used, these appear without description or introduction; they are merely a labelling of individuals. No attempt is made at this stage of 'The Bear' to flesh out these labelled individuals. Rather the second paragraph opens with attention directed to an adolescent whom we may presume, following 'The Old People', to be Ike: 'He was sixteen. For six years now he had been a man's hunter.' Subsequent sections of 'The Bear' open with an unnamed *he*, but the story has been so much to do with Ike that few doubts arise as to the pronoun's referent. Similarly the opening commentary in 'Delta Autumn', on a sensation familiar to 'him' each November for fifty years, strongly suggests Ike as referent of *he/him*.

The opening of the final chapter, 'Go Down, Moses', breaks with the two contrasting strategies of earlier chapters, the naming or pronominalizing, as familiars, of members of an (assumed to be known) community. Here is a flat, journalistic, visual description, impressionistic without being interpretative. The narrative style is as antipathetic to the prisoner as is the latter's contrived alienation from his Southern black roots. The use of *he/his* is minimalized. The opening runs:

> The face was black, smooth, impenetrable; the eyes had seen too much. The negroid hair had been treated so that it covered the skull like a cap, in a single neat-ridged sweep, with the appearance of having been lacquered, the part trimmed out with a razor, so that the head resembled a bronze head, imperishable and enduring. He wore one of those sports costumes called ensembles in the men's shop advertisements, shirt and trousers matching and cut from the same fawn-colored flannel . . . (p. 369)

The neutral, even dehumanizing, definite article is repeatedly selected here, in place of the more predictable possessive pronoun – 'His face . . . his eyes . . .', and so on. In the next sentence, the use of the distal deictic *those*, and the indirect introduction of the term *ensembles*, again suggests narratorial alienation from the described individual; cf. 'He wore an ensemble of . . .'. The description asserts the character's recognizability at every turn, but denies his familiarity: this character is emphatically categorized, via the lack of narratorial naming or pronominalization, as outside the known community. The fact that the man's name is actually disclosed in the action of the scene – amidst the census-taker's annotations – only highlights his narratorial unnameability. (It would be unthinkable,

146

for example, that the narrative begun in the style evident from the above extract could start to refer to the prisoner as *James*, or even just *Beauchamp*.) And in the dialogue with the census-taker that follows, although the latter is referred to as *the census-taker*, Beauchamp does not correspondingly become *he*, but *the other*, and is thus further removed from narratorial empathy, as if even the census-taker is more acceptable to the narrator than Beauchamp is.

After that stark and hostile portrait, the final section of the book, 'Go Down, Moses', section 2, introduces and names Gavin Stevens, describing his profession, his face, his degrees, his hobby, in a manner of innocent frankness that mirrors Stevens's own innocent frankness. The style is conversational and leisurely:

> It [the wind] fluttered among the country-attorney business on the desk and blew in the wild shock of prematurely white hair of the man who sat behind it – a thin, intelligent, unstable face, a rumpled linen suit from whose lapel a Phi Beta Kappa key dangled on a watch-chain – Gavin Stevens, Phi Beta Kappa, Harvard, Ph. D., Heidelberg, whose office was his hobby, although it made his living for him, and whose serious vocation was a twenty-two-year-old unfinished translation of the Old Testament into classic Greek. (pp. 370–1)

The rhetorical design of this orientational sentence, with its parabola-shaped information structure (the secondary facts about the wind and the classic Greek occupying sentence-initial and sentence-final positions, the primary description and naming of the character placed medially), deserves a study to itself. And Faulkner surely intended comparison to be made with the portrait of Samuel Beauchamp given at the opening of the first section of 'Go Down, Moses'. Syntactically the sentences have much in common, particularly in their pattern of loose or right-branching structure. But the effect of that structure is quite different in each case, owing to the acute contrasts in character presentation. Beauchamp's sculpted negroid hair contrasts with Stevens's 'wild shock of prematurely white hair'; the flashy flannel ensemble contrasts with the rumpled linen suit; and Beauchamp's declared occupation – 'Getting rich too fast' (p. 370) – contrasts with Stevens's 'hobby' and 'vocation'. Most apparently, the unnameability of Beauchamp can be set beside the many names of the lawyer: 'Gavin Stevens, Phi Beta Kappa, Harvard, Ph. D., Heidelberg'. Granted, this is naming by institutional affiliation, and Stevens is not an intimate of the farm-based McCaslin circle (Stevens is more a 'pillar' of the community than a mere member of it); none the less his nameability reflects the fact that he is *of* the community in a way that Samuel Beauchamp and the white salesman in 'The Fire and the Hearth' (as we shall see) are not.

PRONOUN DISTRIBUTION IN THE NARRATIVE

Table 2 shows totals of pronominal occurrence in the narrative, with each story (where appropriate) analysed according to its sections. The category of pronouns is itself subdivided into the four traditional classes:

1 Central pronouns (i.e. personal, possessive, reflexive).
2 Relatives (*that, who(m), which*).
3 Demonstratives (*this, that, these, those*, and demonstrative use of *so* and *such*). Note that this category comprises demonstratives in both their pronominal (e.g. *this* as NP head, 'standing alone') and their determiner (e.g. *this* in *this time*, modifying some other headword) functions, and so is not a purely pronominal category: syntactic class (pronoun versus determiner) was judged to be far less important than discourse function (all the demonstratives are deictic or anaphoric).
4 Indefinites (a large group of forms, fuzzily bounded).

The table notes the page length of the sections and stories. More importantly, it also shows the number of narrative pages in each story. The focus of enquiry is pronominalization in the narrative; it is therefore necessary to quantify (in pages) the extent of (a) narrative and (b) direct speech in each story section.

In general, the data of table 2 are too aggregated to reveal the contrasts and significant deviations which a stylistic enquiry requires in order to be adequately motivated. However, on the basis of the totals of occurrence we can calculate average frequencies of each pronoun class per page, and thereby note distinct divergences from these textual norms. The norm, per narrative page, is 31 central pronouns, 3.6 relatives, 2.4 demonstratives, and 4.8 indefinites. The following story sections reveal exceptions to such norms (the norm-based predicted quantity is given in parentheses after the actual number):

Abnormal frequencies of pronouns

Centrals

mean: 31.11 per page

standard deviation: 3.95 (27.16 → 35.06)

'The Fire and the Hearth', chapter 3 (high), 736 (608), 38.0 per page

'Pantaloon in Black' (high), 572 (483), 36.9 per page

'The Bear', section IV (low), 929 (1,117), 25.9 per page

'The Bear', section V (low), 302 (387), 24.4 per page

'Go Down, Moses' (high), 233 (197), 37.0 per page

Relatives

mean: 3.65 per page

standard deviation: 1.28 (2.37 → 4.93)

'Was', section I (high), 12 (5), 9.2 per page

'Was', section II (low), 17 (45), 1.37 per page

'Was', section III (low), 5 (18), 1.0 per page

'The Bear', section II (low), 23 (46), 1.79 per page

'The Bear', section IV (high), 192 (131), 5.35 per page

Table 2   Distribution of narrative pronouns in *Go Down, Moses*

	Central	Rel.	Demon.	Indef.	Pages	Narr. pp.
'Was' I	44	12	4	9	1.3	1.3
'Was' II	391	17	19	66	16.5	12.4
'Was' III	185	5	4	17	8.5	5.0
'Was' IV	12	0	2	2	0.5	0.4
Total	632	34	29	94	26.8	19.1
'Fire/Hearth' 1	963	107	67	121	45.0	32.9
'Fire/Hearth' 2	284	23	6	38	19.0	8.7
'Fire/Hearth' 3	736	86	36	87	33.0	19.4
Total	1,983	216	109	246	97.0	61.0
'Pantaloon'	572	48	31	69	25.0	15.5
'Old People'	554	89	60	89	24.0	18.4
'The Bear' I	499	80	36	72	19.5	17.0
'The Bear' II	406	23	41	79	16.5	12.8
'The Bear' III	671	55	34	86	27.5	21.4
'The Bear' IV	929	192	118	200	60.0	35.9
'The Bear' V	302	41	36	60	16.0	12.4
Total	2,807	391	265	497	139.5	99.5
'Delta Autumn'	614	59	57	123	30.0	17.9
'Go Down, Moses'	233	30	13	21	15.0	6.3
Totals	7,395	867	546	1,139	357.3	237.7

Demonstratives
    mean: 2.37 per page
    standard deviation: 0.78 (1.59 → 3.15)
'Was', section II (low), 19 (30), 1.53 per page
'Was', section III (low), 4 (12), 0.8 per page
'Was', section IV (high), 2 (1), 5.0 per page
'The Fire and the Hearth', chapter 2 (low), 6 (21), 0.69 per page
'The Old People' (high), 60 (44), 3.26 per page
'The Bear', section II (high), 41 (31), 3.2 per page
'The Bear', section III (low), 34 (51), 1.59 per page
'The Bear', section IV (high), 118 (85), 3.28 per page
'Delta Autumn' (high), 57 (43), 3.35 per page

Indefinites
    mean: 4.79 per page
    standard deviation: 0.95 (3.84 → 5.74)
'Was', section I (high), 9 (6), 6.9 per page
'Was', section III (low), 17 (24), 3.4 per page
'The Fire and the Hearth', chapter 1 (low), 121 (158), 3.68 per page
'The Bear', section II (high), 79 (61), 6.17 per page
'Delta Autumn' (high), 123 (86), 6.87 per page
'Go Down, Moses' (low), 21 (30), 3.3 per page

(Identification of sections as exhibiting a marked divergence of frequency from the norm is limited to those cases where the frequency is beyond one standard deviation from the norm for the entire narrative.)

Of the twenty-five judgements of abnormal frequency noted here, only five concern central pronouns, the most cohesive of the four populations, with a standard deviation that is 13 per cent of the mean (the least cohesive population, the relative pronouns, has a standard deviation that is 35 per cent of the mean: a rather flat bell curve). As a class the centrals are by far the most numerous group of pronouns (about 7,500, or 75 per cent of the 10,000 or so pronouns in the narrative). These figures in turn emphasize how common a category pronouns are: on an estimation that the narrative part of *Go Down, Moses* totals about 70,000 words, pronouns comprise approximately 15 per cent of the narrative text.

In the light of the relatively large sample of central pronouns, and the class's apparent resistance to abnormal frequency of occurrence, we may tentatively hypothesize that, in those cases where abnormal frequency does occur among centrals, the deviation is all the more discoursally significant. In the following paragraphs I consider further those five noted cases.

I begin by noting an apparent irony. The reader's intuition is very strongly to the effect that across the novel in its entirety the 'he' is Isaac McCaslin, the character dwelt upon at by far the greatest length. Yet, in two of the sections dominated by his thoughts and reactions, central pronouns such as 'he' are strikingly rare. Conversely, three of the novel sections which have nothing to do with Ike, sections dominated by 'supporting' characters rather than Ike or Lucas – Roth Edmonds, Rider, and Gavin Stevens – use of central pronouns is abnormally extensive.

The reasons why these five sections are so distinct, in pronominal usage, seem to involve a complex interaction of factors. If we first consider the most 'extreme' cases, 'The Fire and the Hearth', chapter 3, and 'The Bear', section V, it appears that the degree to which these sections are structured around dialogue, rather than narrative report, is an important determinant of the frequency of personal pronouns. Thus section V of 'The Bear' contains some of the novel's most extended passages of narrative reflection, removed rather than interwoven with dialogue. If we set aside the exceptional case of 'Was', section I (very brief, and purely narrative), 'The Bear', section V, is one of the most narrative-weighted sections of the novel (12.4 of its 16 pages are narrative rather than dialogue: 78 per cent against a novel norm of 67 per cent). Other narrative-weighty sections include 'The Bear', sections I and II.

It seems reasonable to hypothesize that frequency of personal pronouns (especially *he*, *him*, etc.) will be lower in stories where there is relatively more dialogue, since this entails the co-presence of two or more participants (in this novel, almost invariably male) to whom turns of direct speech need to be allocated without needless ambiguity. The narrator is unlikely, without good cause, to report the successive utterances of Boon, Sam, and Ike, for example, by 'he said . . . then he said . . . then he said'. Accordingly, we should expect lower frequencies of centrals in heavily dialogized sections.

The novel's norm for degree of dialogue per section or story is 33 per cent (119 of 357 pages). The most heavily dialogized sections – calculated on the basis of the figures in the final two columns of table 2 – include 'The Fire and the Hearth', chapter 2 (54 per cent dialogue), 'Go Down, Moses' (58 per cent), 'The Fire and the Hearth', chapter 3

(41 per cent) 'Delta Autumn' (40 per cent), 'The Bear', section IV (40 per cent), and 'Pantaloon in Black' (38 per cent). These are the sections where we have hypothesized that a lower frequency of personal pronouns is to be expected; but certain sections stand out here for departing from that expectation, in some cases rather sharply. The sections that stand out most sharply include the two that are most distinctively dialogized. Thus 'The Fire and the Hearth', chapter 2, despite being largely direct speech, has a slightly higher than average frequency of central pronouns; and 'Go Down, Moses', a shorter but even more dialogical story, has a markedly high frequency of them. Emphatically supporting our prediction, the relatively dialogue-oriented section IV of 'The Bear' has a significantly low frequency of central pronouns, and also requires further consideration. Of the other two sections from among the five noted above as abnormal in narrative pronominalization frequency, both 'The Fire and the Hearth', chapter 3, and 'Pantaloon in Black' use central pronouns in the narrative significantly highly, despite being relatively dialogue-oriented.

In the preceding paragraphs I have invoked two quantitative instruments – first, numerical frequency of narrative pronouns relative to a narrative norm; then preponderance of dialogue within sections, presumed to inhibit recourse to narrative central pronouns – so as to highlight sections of the novel where abnormally high or low frequencies of central pronouns occur, and where this cannot be explained simply by reference to that same gross structural feature, namely, that the particular sections are respectively narrative-heavy or dialogue-heavy. In the process of setting the factor of 'dialogue-heaviness' against the basic statistical deviations extrapolated from table 2, one story section not on the original list of five has emerged as noteworthy in its frequent use of central pronouns ('The Fire and the Hearth', chapter 2), and four others from the original list have been confirmed, as it were, in their pronominal atypicality: 'Go Down, Moses'; 'The Bear', section IV; 'The Fire and the Hearth', chapter 3; and 'Pantaloon in Black'. There are thus good statistical grounds for pursuing the question whether and in what ways there are thematic motivations in these five stories for the numerical pronominal prominence they each display. A first requirement in pursuit of these issues is to operate with a clearer sense of just which central pronouns are frequent or infrequent in these stories. Accordingly the frequencies of central pronouns in the narrative are analysed by their various forms in table 3 (table 4 presents a similar analysis of the distribution of the demonstratives in the narrative).

The two most widespread and discoursally significant pronouns treated in table 3 are *he* and *it*. The latter will be discussed at length in chapter 6. Frequencies of the former help to pinpoint the sources of the abnormal counts for central pronouns as a class, noted above. Thus with a mean of 10.5 instances of *he* per narrative page, sections I, III and IV of 'Was', chapters 2 and 3 of 'The Fire and the Hearth', and section IV of 'The Bear' are again the sections to emerge as distinctive in use. The sections of 'Was' noted are all so short as to discourage complex stylistic explanation: 'Was', section I, is, as already noted, essentially introductory, 'Was', Section IV, is clearly a lighthearted coda rather than part of the narrative action. ('Was', section III, will, however, be examined further in chapter 7.) But in the other cases we are again drawn to pay particular analytical attention to 'The Fire and the Hearth', chapters 2 and 3, and 'The Bear', section IV. Only two of these sections – 'The Fire and the Hearth', chapter 2, and 'The Bear', section IV – are treated at length in the following chapter.

An explanation of why no extended consideration was undertaken of 'The Fire and the Hearth', chapter 3, and other sections with markedly divergent frequencies of central pronouns ('Pantaloon in Black' and 'Go Down, Moses') is in order. Part of the justification is that just those two sections singled out, among the five, focus on the novel's two main characters, Ike and Lucas. Additionally, as has already been implicitly noted in the previous section in this chapter, there are relatively transparent grounds for the scarcity of personal pronouns in 'Go Down, Moses' (Beauchamp is 'pronominally un-nameable', Stevens is nameable but not an intimate part of the extended McCaslin community). 'The Fire and the Hearth', chapter 3, by contrast, shows extensive narratorial alignment with Roth Edmonds and is, in essence, his version of events. It includes, in the long opening narrative-weighted section, reflections on Lucas and on Roth's own childhood rejection of Henry. Both of these are discussed elsewhere in this study (chapter 11 and chapter 4, 'Progressives in the narrative', respectively). Central pronouns are, as predicted, much less common in the shorter, dialogue-weighted sections II and III. Finally, prominence of personal pronouns in 'Pantaloon in Black' is clearly attributable to the narratorial alignment with Rider through-out the first section; additionally, much of this section is a one-

Table 3 Frequencies of central pronouns in the narrative

	he	his	him	she	her	it	its	they	them	[other]
'Was' I	7	19	3	1	6	3	0	0	1	4
'Was' II	107	52	40	20	7	55	1	82	17	10
'Was' III	84	39	10	2	2	25	0	14	7	2
'Was' IV	3	1	1	0	0	3	0	3	1	0
'Fire/Hearth' 1	364	163	64	36	52	170	9	38	24	43
'Fire/Hearth' 2	128	42	27	1	1	36	6	25	7	7
'Fire/Hearth' 3	259	136	56	40	51	112	7	29	18	28
'Pantaloon'	192	161	37	24	13	67	5	16	16	23
'Old People'	158	109	53	0	1	93	8	42	45	45
'The Bear' I	193	68	44	0	1	120	5	29	19	20
'The Bear' II	123	41	27	11	3	100	23	42	24	12
'The Bear' III	235	108	65	1	0	112	10	88	41	11
'The Bear' IV	254	186	68	33	40	179	12	44	33	80
'The Bear' V	106	32	23	0	1	79	14	19	9	19
'Delta Autumn'	207	105	44	39	12	99	9	36	12	34
'Go Down, Moses'	78	26	26	35	19	26	2	10	4	7
Totals	2,498	1,288	588	243	209	1,279	111	517	278	345

Table 4 Frequencies of demonstratives in the narrative

	this	*that*	*these*	*those*	*so/such*
'Was' I	2	1	1		
'Was' II	5	14			
'Was' III	1	3			
'Was' IV	1	1			
'Fire/Hearth' 1	9	52	1	4	1
'Fire/Hearth' 2	2	3	1		
'Fire/Hearth' 3	5	26		2	3
'Pantaloon'	11	17	1	2	
'Old People'	4	50		5	1
'The Bear' I	12	20		2	2
'The Bear' II	7	33		1	
'The Bear' III	8	25		1	
'The Bear' IV	23	85		8	2
'The Bear' V	8	25	1	1	1
'Delta Autumn'	15	33	3	4	2
'Go Down, Moses'	2	9		2	
Totals	115	397	8	32	12

participant narrative, where pronominalization is to be expected. The story was discussed extensively in relation to its patterns of progressivization, and is also the focus of chapter 8. In conclusion, further analysis of central pronouns focuses on sections not yet the subject of extended scrutiny, in which no straightforward circumstantial explanation of the foregrounding is apparent.

Besides distinctive deployment of central pronouns, trends in the demonstratives class may be the most interesting and significant: the demonstratives are a closed class of four items, and have distinct deictic core meanings affecting their use. Closer scrutiny is accordingly undertaken, in chapter 7, of some of these sections with marked frequencies of demonstratives: section III of 'Was', chapter 2 of 'The Fire and the Hearth', and section II of 'The Bear'.

In the pursuit of stylistically significant pronoun usage it is assumed here that use of the personal pronouns, *it*, and the demonstratives may be of interest, but that relative and indefinite pronouns do not merit further attention, and cannot be viewed as a standard stylistic resource. Compared with the central and demonstrative pronouns, variations of frequency among relatives and indefinites are less likely to yield evidence of significant trends. Relative pronouns are essentially introducers of relative clauses that postmodify nominal headwords. They rarely operate independently to realize the key nominal sentential roles of subject and object (beyond special cases such as 'Who dares, wins'), but typically must be a secondary substitutionary and connective element functioning within a complex nominal group. Whether introducing non-restrictive or restrictive clauses, relative pronouns operate within strict constraints, and their referents are usually immediately evident from preceding linguistic co-text. Embedded within noun phrases, they supply intraphrasal linkage but have little to do with text-building links across sentences; in Halliday and Hasan's terms (1976) they are a structural device, not a cohesive one. But their marginal relevance to a study of discourse anaphora and narrative cohesion does not mean that relative pronouns and relative clauses are stylistically insignificant in other respects: on the contrary, relativization is a distinct way of presenting material, and will enter into the discussion of subordination and syntactic styles in chapters 9 and 11.

The class of indefinite pronouns is something of a ragbag of items, including what Quirk *et al.* (1985) call the universals (*each, all, every-*), the assertives (*any-, either*), and the negatives (*no-, neither*). It seems most unlikely that variations in frequency of such a heterogeneity of indefinite pronouns will show correlations with specific literary strategies such as empathetic alignment. The functioning of the assertive *enough*, however, is so prominently used as to compel closer examination, and this is offered in chapter 8.

6

PRONOMINAL FOREGROUNDING IN *GO DOWN, MOSES*

NAMING AND DECEPTION IN 'THE FIRE AND THE HEARTH', CHAPTER 2

Chapter 2 of 'The Fire and the Hearth' relates the elaborate steps Lucas takes in order to dupe and outmanoeuvre both the salesman and Edmonds, in an obsessional hunt for gold coins. I shall argue below that these simple facts of content, and additionally Faulkner's concern to tell these facts in a deceptively reticent way, are by no means unrelated to the prominent use of central pronouns, most notably the pronoun *he*, in an essentially multi-participant, dialogue-oriented section. As I hope to have shown, the extended examination that follows is prompted by a simple but detailed frequency analysis. But it would not be true to say either that the imputed use of the *he* pronoun here is an overt foregrounding that stares every observer in the face, or that what limited linguistic commentary I bring to bear on the chapter predicts or predetermines the interpretation that evolves. Analysis and interpretation develop in tandem.

It was noted earlier that a standard way of identifying participants in a text is by means of phrases such as *he said, the other (one) replied*, and so on. However this option is not adopted in 'The Fire and the Hearth', chapter 2:

> Edmonds sat at a roll-top desk beside the front window, writing in a ledger. Lucas stood quietly looking at the back of Edmonds's neck until the other turned. 'He's come,' Lucas said. (p. 78)

This has much to do with the nature of the participants here, and the particular narrative perspective adopted in the section.

To understand this we need briefly to consider how the *he* pronoun is generally used in this novel. In fact, *he* is a form used in the narrative under certain restrictions (see the last section of this chapter). It tends to be used, wherever possible, to refer only to Ike, and tends not to be used, even where it would be grammatically unexceptional or discoursally unambiguous, to refer to other individuals. It is true that other animate males – including the dog Lion – are denoted by *he* in the text: there are no absolute exclusions (although the bear is always referred to in the narrative by *it*, never *he*). But there are still marked trends in the use of *he*. Millgate has noted, in his introduction to the West Point concordance to the novel, that while Lucas's name appears 319 times in the book (i.e. in both the narrative and the dialogue) *Isaac* and *Ike* occur a mere 60 times altogether (Capps 1977). He adds:

> The principal explanation of this phenomenon is to be found in the extraordinary total of 3012 occurrences of the pronoun 'he' (as against 334 occurrences of 'she' and 633 of 'they') and in the realization that throughout 'The Old People', 'The Bear', and 'Delta Autumn' Ike's speeches are identified exlusively by the potentially ambiguous 'he', never by Isaac or Ike. The question of what Faulkner intended or achieved by this clearly deliberate device might well provide part of the subject matter of the kind of detailed study of Faulkner's stylistic habits – among them the exploitation of an extraordinary range of minor typographical devices – which we so sorely need. . . . It seems clear, however, that one effect of the repeated 'he' is to emphasize Ike's centrality to the novel, his role as moral vehicle or battleground; it also provides some evidence – especially in conjunction with the paragraphs prefaced to 'Was' – to support the technical argument that Ike serves as the book's pervasive point of view. (Capps 1977: x)

Millgate's suggestive observations are a reminder of the stimulus a good concordance can be, although it is arguable that he overemphasizes the importance of Ike's viewpoint by contrast with those of other characters with whom the narrator is, for periods, aligned. There are also some important patterns in the designating of Ike as speaker which Millgate does not mention: the fact that in 'Delta Autumn', for example, Ike as speaker and participant is repeatedly referred to as *the old man*, while in 'The Old People' he is almost invariably, as noted earlier, *the boy*. These patterns will be examined later.

Returning to the patterns of use of the *he/his* pronouns in 'The Fire

Table 5   Discourse references of *he/him/his* narrative pronouns in 'The Fire and the Hearth', chapter 2

	he	him	himself	his
Section I				
Lucas	20	1	0	3
the salesman	8	1	0	3
George	0	1	0	2
Edmonds	2	3	0	0
Total	30	6	0	8
Section II				
Lucas	9	3	1	2
the salesman	32	4	0	17
George	3	1	0	1
Edmonds	43	9	2	13
Total	87	17	3	33
Section III				
Lucas	4	2	1	3
Edmonds	7	0	1	3
Total	11	2	2	6
Totals	128	25	5	47

and the Hearth', chapter 2, table 5 gives information about the discourse referents of these and other forms in the chapter's three sections. This more detailed analysis seems necessary if the frequency of these forms is to be accurately related to numbers of participants and narrative perspective. Too often quantitative stylistics operates with such gross numbers and distinctions that a plausible elucidation of the detail of narrative discourse simply is not possible. Even here, however, the table conceals the fact that in sections I and II there is variation in numbers of narrative participants, and that only briefly are all four characters copresent, as the following annotation reflects:

'The Fire and the Hearth', chapter 2, section I

Lucas + salesman
Lucas + Edmonds
Lucas + salesman + George

'The Fire and the Hearth', chapter 2, section II

Edmonds (+ Dan & Oscar)
Edmonds + Lucas + George + salesman (1.5 pages)
Lucas + George + salesman
Lucas + George

Lucas + George + salesman
Lucas + George

'The Fire and the Hearth', chapter 2, section III
Lucas + Edmonds

At this point it may be useful to chart the variations in the narrative's perspective informally. The chapter opens with a rather detached authorial point of view, aloof but not omniscient, well suited to a story whose themes include the inscrutability of Lucas. The narrative assumes a perspective as impartial and resistant to seekers of concealed empathy as does its chief concern, the impenetrable Lucas. This is confirmed, for example, by the use of proper names and definite descriptions even in dialogues (where one participant could easily be denoted by *he*). Impartiality is sustained by sequences of dialogue framed by such comments as *Edmonds said. . . . Lucas said . . .* , and *Lucas said . . . the salesman said. . . .*

The second section opens with its focus on Edmonds, and intermittently adopts his viewpoint. If it did not do so, it would have been difficult to convey both his 'mental turmoil and physical effort' and his innocence: the ease with which he forgets the image of himself he is presenting when, like an upset child, he gets excited and enraged by events. The narrative perspective is blandly aligned with Edmonds only to expose, all the more mockingly and ironically, both his inflated sense of self-importance and his variability of mood. The text appears to be a neutral recording of Edmonds's actual feelings as he tracks the 'mule-thieves':

> It was hot, and there was an eagerness upon him, a kind of vindictive exultation as he plunged on, heedless of underbrush or log, the flashlight in his left hand and the pistol in his right, gaining rapidly on the torch . . . (p. 85)

But in effect the narrative is setting him up all the more ruthlessly for ridicule when he discovers (and is disclosed discovering) the true situation: the mule-thieves are his own farmhands, who have borrowed the mule for their gold-hunt. (A matrix of narrative techniques here is examined in a comparison of the 'mental turmoil and physical effort' of Lucas and Roth Edmonds, as reflected in their portrayal on pp. 40–1 and 85–6 respectively, in the section on 'Turmoil and effort in Lucas and Roth' in chapter 9.)

Later in section II of chapter 2, after Edmonds has departed, the narrative point of view is more aloof again, as in section I. This section spans most of two nights of the reported treasure-hunt. It is in the morning after the first night that the major but unhighlighted narrative development occurs: Lucas dispatches George to town to buy silver dollars, and the two men begin colluding so as to dupe the salesman and recoup their losses. Accordingly, as the section progresses, and notwithstanding the appropriacy of continuing to depict Lucas as detached and impenetrable, the narrative's point of view does edge towards alignment with that of Lucas. There is, for instance, little sympathy with the salesman, despite his being misled by Lucas at the outset over the ownership of the mule. Rather he is seen as a flashy outsider, whose crude manoeuvre in not having legally sold the machine to Lucas is vulgar in comparison with the far more subtle and effective subsequent deception perpetrated by Lucas and George. In section III, after some neutral commentary, Lucas's point of view is juxtaposed to that of Edmond's, so that we come to see the sense in Lucas's attitude, while vividly understanding why Edmonds is infuriated by him, filled with impotent rage as he learns of Lucas's latest brazen perversity of behaviour. The switching of perspectival alignment is particularly felicitous here, with the sudden jumps to Edmonds's perspective mirroring the man's angry but frustrated attempts to bring pressure to bear on Lucas. First we get passages of alignment with the calm and complacent Lucas –

He let himself go easily back against the edge of the counter. He took from his vest pocket a small tin of snuff and uncapped it and filled the cap carefully and exactly with snuff and drew his lip outwards . . . and tilted the snuff into it and capped the tin and put it back in his vest pocket.

– where Lucas's ordered and leisurely proceedings are cast in a series of simple paratactic clauses, and material-process transitive verbs with Lucas as agentive subject. Into this atmosphere of unshakeable contentment Edmonds struggles to insert his questions and criticisms, although the narrative attention turns away from him to convey an elaborate visual impression of Lucas. When Lucas resumes speaking, explaining (not insisting) that there is still treasure down by the creek, Edmonds's anger can no longer be controlled, and he attempts to repel Lucas by rising and shouting. The text vividly conveys his difficulties: for, even as he rises and walks towards Lucas, the latter continues explaining his maddening and incontrovertible

161

plans, while the narrative designation of both men by their proper names signals, as surely as does his 'shout' issuing as a whisper, Roth's lost battle to impose his will:

> Now Edmonds got himself out of the chair and on to his feet. He drew a long breath and began to walk steadily towards Lucas. 'And now we done got shut of him, me and George Wilkins –' Walking steadily towards him, Edmonds expelled his breath. He had believed it would be a shout but it was not much more than a whisper.
> 'Get out of here,' he said. 'Go home. And dont come back. Dont ever come back. . . .' (p. 98)

Stylistic pointers on perspective include such sentences as 'Lucas stood quietly looking at the back of Edmonds's neck until the other turned' (p. 78). Here the use of *the other* instead of a more neutral *Edmonds* or *he* implicitly positions Lucas as proximal, 'the one', while Edmonds is non-proximate, *the other*. A major turning-point of chapter 2, section II, is the moment when Lucas and George (and the reader) witness the salesman taken in by the 'find' of fifty silver dollars (buried there earlier that day by Lucas), and so falling prey to their deception. Recognizing the salesman's interest in continuing the search, Lucas can risk confrontation in his renegotiation of the terms on which they hunt. He refuses to proceed with the search unless the salesman gives him a legitimate bill of sale for the machine immediately:

> 'I want half [of what is found],' Lucas said. . . . 'And that mule paper back, and another paper saying that that machine is mine.' . . .
> 'Tomorrow,' the salesman said.
> 'Now,' Lucas said.
> 'Tomorrow.'
> 'Now,' Lucas said. The invisible face stared at his own invisible face. Both he and George seemed to feel the windless summer air moving to the white man's trembling. (pp. 94–5)

Here, although all three faces are invisible, so that the referent of *The invisible face* could be any of them, it is the salesman's face that is picked out (by the definite but deictically neutral modifier *the*), and juxtaposed to Lucas's face, denoted by the less deictically neutral NP, *his own invisible face*. And in the next sentence the narrative effects a rare intrusion behind the masks of surface appearances projected by

Lucas and George, to report an impression of theirs, of 'the windless summer air moving'. This implies some special and unverifiable insight into their feelings, while the salesman is further removed from sympathetic identification by being designated as we may imagine Lucas and George might themselves designate him, as *the white man*.

It seems possible to posit, for chapter 2, section II, of 'The Fire and the Hearth', an inverse correlation between narrative empathy or alignment with a participant's point of view and frequency of personal pronouns denoting that participant. This paradoxical suggestion is prompted by the fact that in the second half of section II – i.e. after Lucas has resolved to extricate himself from his self-generated difficulties by resorting to deception (p. 89) – the narrative persistently (and, arguably, increasingly) designates Lucas by proper name rather than by a referential pronoun. And this occurs while the salesman is frequently referred to by personal pronouns. If this section II has a generally detached perspective, we may yet maintain that the view is one of detached sympathy for Lucas and detached mockery of the salesman, and that the contrasting frequency of pronominal reference to these characters is one index of the operation of this irony.

There are three broad ways of denoting a specific character in English:

1 by definite description via a proper name: *Lucas, George*, etc.;
2 by pronominal reference: *he, her*, etc.;
3 by definite description: *the old woman, the salesman, the others*, etc.

Some difficulty arises here because the salesman is never named, so that *the salesman* appears to operate as a substitute for a proper name; in any event, the very fact that this man is not accorded the status of a personal name (like the nameless swamp-dwellers in 'The Bear', section I, p. 193, unlike the animals Ben and Lion) is one reflection of his diminution from the narrator's perspective. Accordingly, table 6 collates, into groups, all the proper-name references, all the singular pronominal references, and all the other definite descriptions of each participant, in 'The Fire and the Hearth', chapter 2.

These figures are immediately interesting for showing that, in terms of absolute numbers of occasions of reference to participants, the salesman is referred to over 200 times in section II, while Lucas is referred to fewer than 100 times. Why should this be, in a section where, many readers will feel, it is Lucas more than anyone else who is

Table 6 Frequencies of various forms of reference in 'The Fire and the Hearth', chapter 2

	he/his/himself	proper name	definite description
Section I			
Lucas	24	27	3
the salesman	12	0	4
George	3	7	0
Edmonds	5	8	0
Section II			
Lucas	15	61	6
the salesman	53	0	148
			(*the salesman* = 138)
George	5	25	0
Edmonds	67	15	1
Section III			
Lucas	10	6	1
Edmonds	11	7	0
Totals	205	156	163

at the centre of the story? An initial response might be that this tendency fosters an image of Lucas as detached, reticent, and impenetrable, while the salesman and Edmonds (in his short appearance in this section) appear excessively involved and engaged – even, by implication, transparent and readily comprehensible in their motivations and acts. Pronominal reference seems here to imply transparency rather than, as elsewhere, genuine narratorial sympathy. As for the frequent reference to the salesman, overwhelmingly by means of the definite NP describing his occupation, this seems to serve to dismiss the salesman as unworthy of the narratorial recognition that a proper name might entail.

But table 6 prompts other questions also. Why should the narrator have chosen to designate the salesman, on 138 or 70 per cent of occasions, by the specific definite description *the salesman* rather than a proper name or a pronoun, even while he chose to designate Lucas most of the time by the proper name *Lucas*, and only 15 times by a singular personal pronoun? In section II, Lucas is designated by *he/his* etc. 15 times, by *Lucas* 61 times; Edmonds is denoted by *he/his* etc. 67 times, by *Edmonds* only 15 times.

Partial explanation of these figures may lie in the fact that Edmonds appears and is discussed mainly at the opening of the section, where he appears virtually alone (with Dan and Oscar only subordinate participants) and thus – particularly since his internal views and responses are being recorded – may tend to be denoted by *he* rather than the proper name. By contrast, Lucas appears predominantly in the company of others (especially the salesman), where the pronoun might often be too ambiguous to substitute for the name. But this can account for only a very few instances; the tendency is too dominant to be so easily explained.

Nor, as the table shows, are the tendencies uniform throughout this chapter. Certain short passages reveal more conventional patterns of reference to participants. Consider, for example, the confrontation between Edmonds and Lucas on pp. 86–8, where Lucas is caught having borrowed the mule without Edmonds's consent. In that passage there are 21 references to Edmonds, of which 12 are pronominal, and 9 are by name (while Lucas is denoted 10 times, 5 pronominal and 5 nominal). The prominent contrasting usage does not occur here, then, but must figure elsewhere in the section. There are ample pragmatic reasons for the breach, in these two pages, of the trend in this chapter of 'The Fire and the Hearth', towards low pronominal reference and high proper-name reference to Lucas, the character with whom the narrator is frequently tacitly aligned (as evident from other FID indicators). For in pp. 86–8, as in the opening two pages of the section, it is Edmonds who is temporarily at the centre of the action. He is the intervener, the man of power and property (such as the mule) who can dictate to others. Interestingly, in the confrontation on pp. 86–8, while his quarrel is obviously chiefly with Lucas, Edmonds's altercations are almost wholly with George and the salesman. That is a further reason for variant referential trends in these pages: in those situations, as here, where Lucas is clearly in the wrong or in a weak position, he always adopts a discreetly low profile.

It would seem that, in at least section II of 'The Fire and the Hearth', chapter 2, a relatively low frequency of reference by name is a signal of an underlying contempt, on the part of the narrator, for the person so denoted. Such a conclusion seems supported by the following frequencies, for means of specifying the participants, in that section:

	names	pronouns	definite	NPs
Lucas	61	15	6	= respect
Edmonds	15	67	1	= mild contempt
the salesman	0	53	148	= contempt
George	25	5	0	= ?mild contempt

In the abundant reference to Edmonds by *he*, and reticence over naming him as *Edmonds*, the narrative appears to adopt Lucas's own habits of referring to his 'betters':

> even as a child the boy [Roth Edmonds] remarked how Lucas always referred to his father as Mr Edmonds, never as Mister Zack, as the other negroes did, and how with a cold and deliberate calculation he evaded having to address the white man by any name whatever when speaking to him. (p. 104)

> the old negro who in his case did not even bother to remember not to call him mister, who called him Mr Edmonds and Mister Carothers or Carothers or Roth or son or spoke to him in a group of younger negroes, lumping them all together, as 'you boys'. (p. 116)

There seems to be a three-way system of contrasts in evaluation operating in the section analysed, such that proper naming reflects narratorial respect, definite description reflects narratorial contempt, and pronominal reference denotes an intermediate narratorial evaluation of mild dismissal. These patterns, intriguingly, run counter to our expectations that more intimate perspectival alignment with an individual correlates with predominantly pronominal reference, and that more distantly viewed characters are generally denoted by proper name (cf. Burelbach 1986). This local misdirection of the reader skilfully reflects the deception of the salesman, while luring us into becoming fellow victims of his mistaken assessment of Lucas.

'IT' IN THE NARRATIVE

It was noted above, in the discussion of marked pronominal frequencies highlighted in tables 2 and 3, that 'The Fire and the Hearth', chapter 2, has a normal frequency for central pronouns as a set and a markedly high frequency of the *he* pronoun (both of which are counter to expectations for a dialogue-heavy section). A closer look at table 3 shows that this chapter fails to emerge as pronominally foregrounded in table 2 itself solely because of the scarcity of its use of the *it* pronoun. The narrative mean is 5.37 *it* pronouns per page (standard deviation: 0.96), but this chapter has only 36 instances across its 8.7 narrative pages, a frequency per page of 4.1. If we exclude 'Was', Section I, this is the lowest frequency for *it* in the entire novel, shared only by 'Go Down, Moses'.

Of the 36 instances of *it* in 'The Fire and the Hearth', chapter 2, fully 32 seem to be tied to specific previously mentioned NPs which, with the exception of *the whole situation*, refer to material entities. Of the other four, three are anticipatory (such as the *it* in *It took them almost an hour to find where the tracks had disappeared* (p. 148)), and only one involves the sort of extended textual reference that was noted as a special property of *it* by Halliday and Hasan (1976):

> But Lucas merely looked at him. It was not stubbornness but an infinite, almost Jehovah-like patience, as if he were contemplating the antics of a lunatic child. (p. 80)

Here the *It* must refer not merely to 'the look' Lucas gives Edmonds but to Lucas's entire attitude to Edmonds – an attitude which outrageously reverses a 'normal' evaluation of behaviour. For, despite the fact that it is Lucas's intentions that are fanciful and naïve, while Edmonds is the stern realist father-figure, here it is Edmonds's behaviour which Lucas is said to regard as 'the antics of a lunatic child'. Comparison of *it* frequency here and elsewhere in the text can be made by reference to table 3. Interesting contrasts include 'Go Down, Moses', with its equally low frequency of *it* (4.12 per narrative page) and 'The Bear', sections I and II, with their high frequencies (7.05 and 7.81 per narrative page, respectively).

In 'Go Down, Moses', *it* is used in reference to a relatively small number of material entities – hair, the wind, the desk, the hearse – plus two instances as an empty pronoun in a cleft sentence, and two adjacent occurrences of more interest, at the point where Stevens has visited the mourning Worshams and becomes almost literally stifled through lack of air as, in various other situations, Rider, Lucas, and Ike have been before him:

> He descended the stairs, almost running. It was not far now; he could smell and feel it: the breathing and simple dark, and now he could manner himself to pause and wait . . . (p. 381; cf. pp. 48, 183, and 225)

The first *It* initially appears to refer to some vague idea such as 'the exit' or 'outside'. But the second *it* incontrovertibly refers to the same entity as that denoted in the post-colonic NP, 'the breathing and simple dark'; and, since this second *it* follows the first so closely, it may well be that both refer to this 'breathing dark'. These two uses of *it* are perhaps the only ones noted so far which depend on subsequent text for disambiguation (backwards anaphora). In these two cases – and perhaps in many others too – such preposing of the substitute *it* implies both a sense of haste-induced disorder (anaphor preceding antecedent despite their co-occurrence in surface structure in the same sentence) and a sense of empathy and perspectival alignment with Stevens, the participant not only doing the smelling and feeling and moving but also clearly concerned to reach the breathing dark. The alignment is suggested by the iconicity: intimations of 'the breathing dark', urgently sensed, come first in the sentence order as in the character's experience; the dark itself, syntactically and experientially, is noticeably delayed. A further indicator that this is free indirect discourse is the Stevens-oriented temporal deictic *now*, used twice.

In 'The Bear', section I (as in section II also, although most of the following examples are taken from section I), the first thing of note concerning use of *it* is the greater variety of its referents. In particular, there are far more instances of ambiguous or partially ambiguous reference. By contrast, in 'The Fire and the Hearth', chapter 2, and in 'Go Down, Moses', it is as if all situations where *it* is at all open to uncertainty in interpretation have been disambiguated by the simple expedient of avoiding the pronoun and using some other more specific form. There is at least one other crucial difference in 'The Bear', section I: the form *it* is used to refer to both an animate participant, the bear, and an inanimate but semi-agentive entity, the wilderness. (In section II, in addition to these two entities, the pronoun also designates Lion.) Such factors alone would yield a fairly high frequency of the form in these sections. But the number of ambiguous uses of *it* here, particularly in section I, suggests a deliberate strategy. There will inevitably be dispute over such figures, but I find that at least 14 of the 120 uses here are at least partly ambiguous, or require a more than routine effort of interpretation. Again, perhaps significantly, the most notable of these seem to occur in passages at the opening and close of the section. Typically polysemous instances include the following:

> It seemed to him that at the age of ten he was witnessing his own birth. *It* was not even strange to him. He had experienced *it* all before, and not merely in dreams. He saw the camp – a paintless six-room bungalow. (pp. 195–6; my emphases)

> *It*: his birth? / the camp?
> *it*: his birth? / the camp?

The pronoun is also used semi-agentively to refer to the wilderness:

> The wilderness closed behind his entrance as *it* had opened momentarily to accept him, opening before his advancement as *it* closed behind his progress. (p. 203; my emphases)

Besides exploitation of the pronoun in the passages at the section's opening and close, discussed elsewhere, the most striking use is in the suggestion of a temporary dehumanization of Sam, under the influence of the bear's unseen presence:

> The boy no longer heard anything at all, yet still Sam's head continued to turn gradually and steadily until the back of it_1 was toward him. Then it_2 turned back and looked down at him – the same face, grave, familiar, expressionless until it_3 smiled ... (p. 198; my emphases and subscripts)

Here, substitution of *it* for reference to Sam (and his head) by name seems to constitute a local shift, from treatment of Sam as gendered individual to presenting him as mere head or face. We may list the reference options for the three uses of *it* in the passage as follows:

it_1: Sam's head
it_2: Sam's head/Sam's face (the *head* turns back, but it is the *face* – or eyes – that look(s) down)
it_3: Sam's face

The following example, from section II, involves more than routine anaphoric linkage (the *its* and *it* denote rather more than just the crooked print), while not being too complex once the reader has grasped that the passage is focalized from the viewpoint of the young Ike and his preoccupations with the bear:

> He could find the crooked print now whenever he wished, ten miles or five miles or sometimes closer than that, to the camp. Twice while on stand during the next three years he heard the dogs strike *its* trail and once even jump *it* by chance, the voices high, abject, almost human in their hysteria. (pp. 210–11; my emphases)

A review of the arguments in this and the preceding section may be in order. There are clear divergences of frequency of certain central pronouns in different parts of the book. This is only partly attributable to easily verified contrasts in numbers of participants involved in the reported scenes. A major and separate motivation is taken to be narrative perspective on participants. The evidence from chapter 2 of 'The Fire and the Hearth' suggests that frequency of central pronouns as a proportion of the total number of expressions referring to a particular character, and in particular by contrast with frequency of use of the proper name, is a complex, contextually conditioned index of narratorial empathy or antipathy towards that character. Ironically, and for the purposes of concealing narratorial sympathy even as an ingenious scheme of deception by concealment is reported, Lucas is denoted by distancing proper name, Edmonds and the salesman otherwise. In the case of *it* frequency, we have also seen marked contrasts in the range of uses, and especially (at one end of the scale) in frequency of ambiguous and troubling reference to ill-defined animate (or agentive) forces.

The argument here is all to do with degree. Ambiguity is present in all natural language. What is claimed here is a fluctuating tendency for the *it* pronoun to be used prominently where reference is ambiguous or difficult in some other way. There are ambiguities in 'The Fire and the Hearth', chapter 2, despite its few instances of ambiguous *it*. But they are realized differently from, and relate to less important issues than, those in 'The Bear', sections I and II. If the form *it* in the analysed FID or narratorially aligned passages of these chapters is representative, the ambiguities in 'The Fire and the Hearth' and 'Go Down, Moses' are not expressed formally to anything like the degree that they are in (particularly) 'The Bear', section I. On the basis of the analysis of *it* occurrences, it seems both metaphorically and grammatically true that much confusion, uncertainty, ignorance, and even fear are on the surface in the latter chapter, but not so in the other two.

That section I of 'The Bear' is partly about 'not knowing', about a child's development from fear and misunderstanding towards courage and understanding, is thus frankly acknowledged by the narrator. That this process is incomplete, that the character-aligned narrator himself is not omniscient, but confused and perplexed by the events he relates, may also be hypothesized. The pronominal ambiguities are an indication of the seriousness with which this section needs to be taken. In 'The Fire and the Hearth', chapter 2, by and large the ambiguities are not encoded in the surface structure. The confusions lie in interpretation – on one level, of 'fortuitous' events such as the retrieval of the fifty gold dollars, so ill interpreted by the salesman. On another level, there are our difficulties with understanding Lucas's obsession with the business of hunting treasure, his credulousness. But the linguistic form of the discourse is not noticeably ambiguous. We have few doubts, and can ascribe few doubts to the narrator, concerning what has actually happened; our questions are chiefly concerned with what is meant by what has happened. All this contrasts, especially, with the opening section of 'The Bear', as the use of the pronoun *it* reflects: here we hazard judgements as to what is meant even as we grapple with an occasionally mysterious representation of 'what has happened'. These trends invite the conclusion that, just as narratorial linguistic strategies – and subsequent critical interpretations – are more rich and complex in 'The Fire and the Hearth' than they were in 'Was', 'The Bear' continues the progression by being the site of still more complex linguistic practices and interpretative responses.

'HE' IN 'THE BEAR', SECTION IV

The second of the two sections we have determined to have the most significantly atypical frequency of central pronouns is the extraordinary section IV of 'The Bear' (929 occurrences, against a norm of 1,117). Interestingly, the section also has markedly low frequencies of relative pronouns and demonstratives. If the section is 'underpronominalized' in relation to patterns in the novel as a whole, it is so even in relation to other sections of 'The Bear'. Adopting norms for key central pronouns in 'The Bear' as a whole (100 narrative pages), we may expect, on average, 9 instances of *he*, 4 instances of *his*, and 6 instances of *it*, per narrative page. For 'The Bear', section IV (35.9 narrative pages), we may then project norms to be compared with actual occurrences:

	he	*his*	*it*
'The Bear'-based norm:	323	144	215
'The Bear' IV actual:	254	186	179

The frequency of *his* is slightly high against the norm for 'The Bear', that of *it* is slightly lower, and *he* occurs with 79 per cent of this local frequency. Relative to the frequencies of these narrative pronouns for the entire novel, *he* occurs at only 66 per cent of the mean frequency per page, while *his* and *it* at 94 and 92 per cent of the norms respectively are entirely unexceptional. All this suggests that it is a question not of less prominent male participation in the narrative, but

171

of a marked shift away from pronoun use towards, presumably, proper names. As in other sections, the particular situation must be partly responsible for these figures. 'The Bear', section IV, is often thought of as dominated by dialogue for much of its length, and there are certainly passages which are virtually entirely dialogue (pp. 256–61 and 282–8). Yet there remains a substantial amount of narration in the section: it is not in fact one of the most dialogue-weighted of sections.

There seem to be a number of reasons for the low frequency of *he* pronouns on particular pages of 'The Bear', section IV. First we may note the tendency, in the narrative, to use long hypotactic sentences with increasing detail of description as the embedding develops. These expository sentences inform the reader of the richly detailed past which is an important backcloth to the present time of the narrative (Ike's 21st birthday) and are part of the focus of the section. Inevitably, this recorded past is about other people – especially Carothers and his children and grandchildren (both black and white) – rather than Ike. And often these other characters must be referred to by name in order for the text to be comprehensible. Once such a character has been named, and so given a distinct identity, it is perfectly normal to use the possessive, *his*, where appropriate. This may be the key to the maintenance of normal narrative frequency of this pronoun, despite the drop in use of *he*.

He, then, is used infrequently of characters other than Ike, since comprehensibility generally requires use of their proper names. But of Ike too its use is restricted: it is almost always used in the attribution to him of his preceding or following direct speech (in 'The Bear', section IV, *he said* almost invariably substitutes for *Ike said*, never *McCaslin said*). But *he* rarely occurs, with reference to Ike, in less mechanical allocatory functions. This may be because the narrative itself is so closely aligned to Ike's consciousness. The vast majority of impressions and memories and judgements forming the texture of the narrative passages – including the pauses (some only of milliseconds of chronological time) between and during the alternate turns at talk taken by Ike and Cass and later by Ike and his wife – are all Ike's. In Genette's terms (Genette 1980), the section is intensely scenic, with duration so extended as to approach the zero point of null narrative advance. Throughout the section, furthermore, Ike is present and proximate in the scenes depicted; he is the reflective chronicler whose version of events is indirectly transcribed. The narrative records Ike's

172

thoughts with too close an alignment to the character for *He thought* and *He imagined* to be appropriate or necessary framing clauses: here the narrator–character alignment which I have argued operates in many parts of the book is most like fully fledged free indirect discourse and even, 'beyond' FID, sometimes resembles stream-of-consciousness.

Frequency of narrative *he* in 'The Bear', section IV, contrasts with that in 'The Bear', section I, where it appears relatively commonly. Section I is a thematically and stylistically homogenous text, in which Ike learns through active participation in events; section IV is thematically and stylistically heterogeneous, shifting from the spoken confrontation of the 21-year-old Ike and Cass in the commissary to the almost wordless physical confrontation of an older Ike and his wife in their rented room. In section IV, Ike learns chiefly through imaginative reconstruction and interpretation (i.e. through indirect rather than direct experience). Of course this section is as much to do with Ike as was section I, but here he is understood, and understands himself, in relation to his familial and sociohistorical context. The distribution of the few linguistic forms noted reflects a more general characteristic: section IV is a much more complex and many-sided text, while section I is firmly focused on Ike as direct experiencer.

The complexity of section IV is reflected in the fact that, despite the general avoidance of the *he* pronoun here, there are a few pages where it appears uncommonly frequently (so setting the general avoidance into sharper relief): pp. 268, 276, 313, and 314. While certain of these high frequencies are attributable to transient participants (e.g. the black stranger on p. 276), there is a correlation, on at least three of these pages, between high frequency of *he* and high frequency of *he* reference to Ike (i.e. pp. 268, 313, and 314). In particular, it seems more than coincidental that the two highest frequencies (pp. 268 and 313, with 20 and 17 occurrences respectively – even the latter being more than two standard deviations above the novel's mean number of 10.5 per page) are on pages variously reporting Ike's two most crucial anagnorises in the section. What seems to be involved is a slight shift away from the 'inwardness' of narratorial alignment, which approaches stream-of-consciousness and can dispense with pronominal references to the thinking character, noted above. The shift is towards a narrator–character alignment more formally akin to canonical FID: the density of pronominal reference on such pages contributes to the effecting of empathetic narratorial alignment with

Ike as experiencer, even while helping to convey his reactions (the latter reportorial activity can be achieved only by inferences, and with difficulty, in stream-of-consciousness).

Page 268 records Ike's naïve earliest expectations of the ledgers, the use of *he* being almost an index of the child's egocentricity:

> As a child . . . when he had learned to read, he would look up at the scarred and cracked backs and ends but with no particular desire to open them, and though he intended to examine them some day because he realized that they probably contained a chronological and much more comprehensive though doubtless tedious record than he would ever get from any other source . . . it would only be on some idle day when he was old and perhaps even bored a little . . .

The page also records his rapid putting on of knowledge, as a prescient adolescent:

> Then he was sixteen. He knew what he was going to find before he found it . . . thinking. . . . Why did Uncle Buddy think she had drowned herself? finding, beginning to find on the next succeeding page what he knew he would find, only this was still not it because he already knew this . . .

On p. 313 is the heart of Ike's ecstatic but fearful sexual and emotional discovery of his wife:

> He heard the bed and turned and he had never seen her naked before, he had asked her to once, and why: that he wanted to see her naked because he loved her and he wanted to see her looking at him naked because he loved her but after that he never mentioned it again . . .

Very rarely are the majority of references of *he*, even locally, diverted away from Ike in 'The Bear', section IV. As was suggested above, a good number of them are 'tags' on sentences of direct speech, with the implicit verb (*said*) sometimes ellipted. In fact 36 of the 199 instances of *he* referring to Ike in section IV are of this kind. Of the other 163 a remarkable number are subjects of verbs of cognition or perception, i.e. mental activity. Here, for example, are the lexical verbs (with frequencies) occurring with *he* as subject and referring to Ike, on pp. 254–75 inclusive:

be (8); think (6); see (5); find, look (3); get, learn, recognize (2); say (non-dialogue), cry, remember, intend, realize, seem, need (1).

On pp. 276–7, where Ike's active search for Fonsiba is described, a few dynamic verbs appear among the statives: *carry, travel, ride,* and *shove*. But on the 'deviant' pages 268 and 313 the collocating verbs are:

   p. 268: find (4); be, know (3); learn, get (2); take, remember, look, intend, realize, believe (1).
   p. 313: hear (3); want, love, pause (2); understand, do, move, know, ask, mention, think, see, remember, stand, lean, turn (1).

With very few exceptions these are verbs which occur in what Halliday (1985a) terms mental-process clauses, rather than ones of, for example, relation, behaviour, or material process. The 'actor–goal' analysis of participants in material-process clauses cannot apply here, where Ike's ineradicable tendency to witness, experience, and 'respond' passively is expressed in a syntax devoid of transitive verbs or transactive, causative clauses.

As all this evidence might suggest, and further scrutiny of the text confirms, pp. 268, 276, and 313–14 are three loci in the narrative of 'The Bear', section IV, where FID-like narratorial alignment with the character is most emphatic and most exploited. These passages of alignment, it has been stressed, are not in fact the places in this section where the most 'inward' or character-oriented presentations occur: they do not amount to a displacement of the narrator by the character, as in stream-of-consciousness – where it would be entirely inappropriate to the adopted perspective to narrate, of the character, 'he' 'thought'/'saw'/'want'. Rather, in the three passages noted, the narrator's voice is merged with the intensely experiencing consciousness of Ike, and this merging is reflected in the occurrence of other indices of FID such as use of the present-time adverbial *now*. With regard to the topic of a later chapter, it is interesting to note in these passages the distinctively high frequencies of subordinate clauses purporting to supply reasons for actions and events. The stylistic foregrounding is thus on various levels.

These final remarks must constitute part of a defence of what some may feel now seriously needs defending: the tendency to proceed rhizomatically in pursuit of stylistically significant linguistic frequencies and patterns. In this and later chapters it is evident that the focusing upon particular textual phenomena for detailed examination is determined by 'forking-path' procedures. The procedures are informed by a set of judgements concerning the functions of, for example, personal pronouns *vis-à-vis* definite descriptions (and all other linguistic forms), but nothing more fixed or mechanical than that. Functional descriptions cannot be fixed, since the language itself is not a fixed phenomenon; but, on the other hand, these conditions should not give rise to dismissal of the analyses as 'subjective' or 'arbitrary' (in my opening chapters I have suggested that applications of the term *arbitrary*, in linguistics and elsewhere, have often been inappropriate and pernicious). I have attempted to defend the interrelated judgements and decisions I have made in the course of exploring, rhizomatically, the roots of certain stylistic effects. But it is clear that the data overwhelm the analysis – in the sense that the sheer complexity of the meshing of motivated textual choices, in extended artistic prose such as Faulkner's, cannot even be annotated in a study of normal length. And yet there are no better alternatives, in stylistics, to this procedure, which combines established multi-contextual grammatical description, attention to discriminating frequency counts of particular forms in the text in its entirety and in particular sections, and informed judgements as to where stylistic technique is likely to be involved. There is one negative alternative, of course: that of sharing the tacit understanding of many stylisticians that their methods just cannot work very well on long texts such as novels. Resisting this pessimism, in the next chapter I pursue the patterns and effects of deixis in the narrative.

7

DEICTIC PATTERNINGS

DEMONSTRATIVES IN 'THE FIRE AND THE HEARTH', CHAPTER 2

This chapter explores some of the implications of marked variations of frequency of demonstrative pronouns and determiners in particular sections of the narrative. I begin with chapter 2 of 'The Fire and the Hearth', where only six demonstratives occur, by contrast with the narrative norm, for such a length of text, of twenty-one. These are presented below in their contexts:

1 'No!' Edmonds said. Lucas looked at him for a good minute *this* time. He did not sigh. (p. 80; my emphasis here and subsequently)

2 Edmonds found the mule was missing as soon as the lotmen, Dan and Oscar, brought the drove in from pasture *that* evening. (p. 83)

3 Then, cursing aloud now and leaping quickly again to avoid the invisible second mule which would be somewhere on *that* side, he realized . . . (p. 84)

4 The two arrested figures gaped at him – the one carrying before him what Edmonds might have taken for a receptacle containing feed except that he now knew neither of *these* had taken time to feed Alice . . . (p. 86)

5 But he wore now a pair of cotton khaki pants still bearing the creases where they had lain folded on the store's shelf when it opened for business *that* morning. (p. 90)

6 'What about them fifty dollars . . . ?' *This* time the salesman merely stood laughing at them . . . (p. 95)

These demonstratives are united in functioning deictically, expressing spatial or temporal orientations from an experiencer's position. But the experiencer here, from whose deictic centre the spatio-temporal 'pointing' is undertaken, is not always properly the narrator. In examples 3 and 4, it seems clear, there is a deictic transference from the narrator to the position of Edmonds.

With regard to the core proximal/non-proximal opposition articulated by deictics, the phrase *this time* is akin to *now*, while *that time* is akin to *then*, or at least *not now*. This is evident if we contrast *I'll do it this week* (which generally refers to what is for the speaker the coming, proximate week, and can hardly refer to the week three weeks ahead) and *I'll do it that week* (which cannot refer to the current or coming week, but may refer to any subsequent week). In 'The Fire and the Hearth', chapter 2, the narrator uses *this time* on the two noted occasions, since its deictic force connotes 'now' – i.e. that the events recorded are located proximate to him, the engaged and witnessing narrator. *That time* or *then* would have sharply reduced such implied involvement, and increased the implicit detachment.

But any adoption of proximal deictics has to be reconciled with the use of the narrative tense, the preterite, for which temporals like *then* are more normal; and with such distancing (although particularizing) time specifiers as the two noted above: *that evening, that morning*. A first reaction is that there is inconsistency here – a reaction I believe to be well founded. But the inconsistency is grounded not on compositional weakness but on strength. Through fluctuation of spatio-temporal location of the narrator in relation to the events recorded, the degree of intensity, subjectivity, and character–narrator empathy can be adjusted to suit varying circumstances.

Every deictic expression in a novel such as *Go Down, Moses* may be viewed by the reader as a marked choice, deliberately preferred in the narration to some other more neutral expression. Certainly, in the six cases quoted above, the reader may wonder why the noticeable departure from normal usage has occurred. These departures, it should be acknowledged, are of varying distinctiveness. Thus, of the six examples above, *that evening* and *that morning*, though slightly more noticeable than the neutral *in the evening* and *in the morning*, need not delay us, being part of the repertoire of standard storytelling focusing techniques. But we also have *this time*, in place of *then* or *now*; *that side*, in place of the far more neutral *the other side*; and *these* where *them* might have been expected (examples 1, 3, 4 and 6 above).

Although there are few temporal adverbials in chapter 2 of 'The Fire and the Hearth' prior to the use of *this time* on p. 80, a firm context of pastness and completedness, of non-immediate events detachedly recorded, has already been established by means of the past tense. The noticeable effect of *this time* here is to emphasize that the look Lucas gives Edmonds is one in a series (the fourth, following those on pp. 78, 79, and earlier on p. 80, l. 9). If the phrase partly suggests 'nowness', it also suggests 'on this particular occasion among the occasions': both immediacy and cyclicity are expressed.

The enhanced narratorial immediacy at this point (p. 80, l. 22) is apparent also in the use of *now* in the narrative description just a few lines further on, where no temporal specifier is in fact necessary. (Among important studies of time, tense, and deictics, see Hamburger (1973), Weinrich (1964), Banfield (1982), and Bache (1985, 1986).) Lucas sees that the formerly aloof and urbanized salesman 'now squatted [i.e. revealing his country boy origins] in the shade of a tree'.

That evening (p. 83) and *that morning* (p. 90) are temporals which almost obligatorily adopt the non-proximal demonstrative. Disentangling the reasons for these expectations in the reader is not easy. One may point to the fact that they locate events in relation to Edmonds and the salesman respectively, the two participants with whom the narrator has little evident empathy. However, even if Lucas and George were discussed here, the non-proximal demonstrative might have been felt to be necessary, as the oddity of the rewritten version with proximal deictic suggests:

?This evening Lucas and George led the mule and the salesman into the creek bottom.

Two reasons for this are involved. The first is that the deictic accompanies report of overt narrative action, and so has nothing to do with a character-centred orientation of thoughts, reflections, or private assessment. The second reason concerns the narrator's wish to signal a time-lapse between the story's sections I and II – that is, between the morning and the evening. To make the scenic jump clear, using a form such as *evening*, the non-proximal is obligatory to indicate that the events of the following scene are not temporally proximate to the narrator who has just reported the previous scene.

Over and above these grounds, based in narrative logic, for adopting the non-proximal deictic to situate Edmonds and the salesman in various scenes, it also has to be noted that forms such as *that morning* are never used in direct relation to Lucas and George, even where they would be discoursally unproblematic. Only the more subjective forms (such as *this time*) are used in such a way, while all three instances of *that* in 'The Fire and the Hearth', chapter 2, operate in sentences about characters other than Lucas and George.

Such patterns of use support the interpretation that characters such as Lucas (and Sam) live within time in a way quite different from the control of time attempted by such 'aliens' as Edmonds and Major de Spain. Lucas and Sam are presented as neither the masters nor the slaves of time, but having a healthy respect for it, while rarely acting in accordance with any mechanical, chronologically predictable pattern. This characteristic enhances their inscrutability and the distinctiveness of their motivations.

As for *This time* (p. 95), we may well wish to treat this, like the occurrence on p. 80, as partly denoting 'now' and partly denoting 'the last (or most recent) in the series'. If this is the case, a crucial question that arises is: who else – besides the narrator and the reader – perceives that there is a series here? It may be suspected that Lucas also is assumed to be aware of a sequence here; for he is its instigator and orchestrator, while the salesman is the unwitting instrument enacting the sequence –

'What about them fifty dollars we done already found then?' he [Lucas] said. 'Dont I get half of them?' This time the salesman merely stood laughing at him . . .

– blithely unaware that he is being manipulated. It is Lucas who not only forms the overarching strategy of deception but also choreographs each stage of its enactment:

'Well, I done found this much of it anyhow,' Lucas said. The salesman, one hand spread upon the scattered coins, made a slashing blow with the other as if Lucas had reached for the money. . . .
   '*You* found? This machine dont belong to you, old man. . . .'
   'I give you a billy sale for it [the mule],' Lucas said.
   'Which never was worth a damn,' the salesman said. 'It's in my car yonder. Go and get it whenever you want to. It was so worthless I never even bothered to tear it up.' (p. 93)

Turning to the fourth noted demonstrative, the occurrence of *these* to denote Lucas and George on p. 86, perhaps a first reaction is surprise that it should occur at all: *neither of them* would seem to be the more conventional option, which the narrator has chosen to forgo in favour of a more distinctive choice. The context makes clear that the proximal demonstrative is not here serving to express the experiencer's empathy with or closeness to the referents. On the contrary, given that the denoted individuals are human beings, the switch from a personal pronoun (*them*) to a demonstrative (*these*) is a clear marker of distance and antipathy. The marked choice sets up an implicit contrast between the two pairs of 'arrested' figures, suggesting that the current sentence is concerned with *these* arrested figures, while earlier sentences have discussed other figures (*those*). For Edmonds in hot pursuit of his 'stolen' mule, the *those* implied in the use of *these* to denote Lucas and George must be Dan and Oscar. Dan and Oscar are the hands who have led Edmonds to the treasure-hunters, but who have been as infuriatingly reticent as Lucas himself. They have neglected to tell Edmonds that it was indeed Lucas who had taken the mule and, during the nocturnal pursuit, have failed to warn Edmonds before stopping dead in their tracks just ahead of him, with the result that he barely escapes maiming by the mules. On p. 86 Edmonds is depicted in the not unfamiliar role of outraged patriarch, a self-appointed figure of authority reduced to apoplexy by the conduct of the 'family' of blacks that surrounds him. His bitterness is in part aimed at his own ineffectualness, in a world seen in terms not of them versus us but of me versus everyone else, and in some respects it parallels that of Jason Compson in the third section of *The Sound and the Fury*.

DEMONSTRATIVES ELSEWHERE IN THE NARRATIVE

I have examined, in the previous section, the particular effects of the few demonstratives in 'The Fire and the Hearth', chapter 2; this section considers marked frequency of demonstratives elsewhere in the narrative – specifically in 'Was', section III, and 'The Bear', section II. The general conclusion that emerges is that in all three cases these demonstratives are a subtle expression of either neutral or empathetic narratorial alignment with a prominent character whose general viewpoint is adopted. In 'The Fire and the Hearth', chapter 2, as we have seen, the alignment with Edmonds is of a neutral kind, entailing no particular sympathy with this character. We shall find much the same pattern in 'Was', section III; and in both these cases the recurring demonstrative used within these character-aligned passages is the distal deictic, *that*. In 'The Bear', section II, by contrast, the narratorial alignment is implicitly empathetic with Ike, and the recurring demonstrative here is the proximal one, *this*.

In 'Was', section III, there is a remarkably low frequency of demonstratives, with just four in all:

1 'Yes, sir,' he said, telling *that* too: how Uncle Buck waked him at daylight and he climbed out a window and got the pony and left . . . (p. 25; my emphasis here and subsequently)

2 And *that* was about all. (p. 25)

3 looking at Uncle Buddy, who was . . . all one grey colour, like an old grey rock or a stump with grey moss on it, *that* still . . . (p. 26)

4 'Hah,' Mr Hubert said, only it wasn't loud at all *this* time, nor even short. (p. 28)

The last of these operates in the temporal adverbial by now familiar to the reader – *this time* – while the third has comparative force and points backwards to other NPs postmodifying the head *Uncle Buddy* for fuller explication. In this latter case, the deictic comparative *that (still)* points back to images initially introduced for another purpose, namely to describe the greyness of Uncle Buddy. With the appended comment *that still*, the reader must switch from imagining the greyness of a rock or stump to considering also its stillness.

Of the two demonstratives functioning as syntactic head (pronouns), one (example 2) denotes the full briefing which Cass has given to Buddy prior to the latter's arrival at Warwick as troubleshooter. In addition, as it occurs with *about*, it can be treated as part of Cass's fairly casual memory of the story, recast by the narrator. There is little doubt that free indirect discourse is also used earlier in this section, for example, at its opening, indirectly recording Cass's version of events:

> When he reached home . . . he was just about worn out. . . . In fact, he must have gone to sleep while he was telling Uncle Buddy, because the next thing he knew it was late afternoon and he was lying on some hay. . . . They must have come fast, because they were not more than two miles from Mr Hubert's . . . (p. 21)

Perhaps the most interesting of the four demonstratives, however, is example 1, since, like the form in example 4 in 'The Fire and the Hearth', chapter 2, it sets up an opposition not apparently required in the context. Just as the unmarked option in the latter case was *them*, the unmarked option here is *this*. This is so notwithstanding the general principle that *that* is the unmarked and *this* the marked term in the system. *This* is the more expected form here simply because it is the usual choice of demonstrative for forwards reference, with *that* the norm for backwards reference. As a result, rather than being a neutral signal, *that* here indicates narratorial distance and detachment from the facts and events reported. Forwards reference (or backwards anaphora) is clearly involved, with the information-heavy, extended-text antecedent appearing after the demonstrative. (The example is thus, like many of the other demonstratives I have discussed, anaphoric as well as deictic: anaphoric in its linkage to co-text, deictic in its implying a contextual orientation.) The chief reason for using *that* and so suggesting narratorial detachment from the events denoted is that the observing participant here is not Ike but Cass; and Cass has no special status in the narrator's pantheon.

That is to say, as argued in chapter 3, a certain character's subjective view of events may be portrayed through FID without the narrator being committed to empathy with that character. It was therefore most appropriate for Pascal (1977) to emphasize the 'dual voice' nature of FID: FID is an amalgam of a character's voice and a narrator's voice, and both may be 'audible' (i.e. accessible to characterization on the basis of the linguistic forms used). Here in 'Was', section III, Cass's account is frequently transcribed using what must be taken to be his own words, but the narrator shows no particular empathy with Cass. The prediction here is that if Ike, by contrast, had been the spectator of the events of 'Was', the narrative alignment would have been more clearly empathetic; and example 1 would have run thus:

'Yes, sir,' he said, telling *this* too: how Uncle Buck waked him at daylight and he climbed out a window . . .

By contrast with 'Was', section II, and 'The Fire and the Hearth', chapter 2, 'The Bear', section II, has a rather high frequency of demonstratives (41, against a norm of 30). Two instances where *this* occurs may be offered as support for the argument concerning contrast between empathetic and neutral FID presentation (as of Ike and Cass respectively). In 'The Bear', section II, we encounter the following passages:

1 They [Ike and the fyce] were so close that it [the bear] turned at bay

although he realized later *this* might have been from surprise and amazement at the shrill and frantic uproar of the fyce. (p. 211; my emphasis)

2 Sprawling, he looked up where it loomed and towered over him like a thunderclap. It was quite familiar, until he remembered: *this* was the way he had used to dream about it. (p. 211)

What the narrator records as something Ike 'realized later', and what the narrator records as something Ike 'remembered', are not different in any essential way from what the narrator records on p. 25 as something Cass 'told'. Yet there is a contrast in the selection of demonstratives. Here in 'The Bear', section II, the deictic suggesting proximity to the reported facts or spectacle is used. And the narrator uses *this*, even though, in this case as in the one in 'Was', *it* would have been an acceptable and less foregrounded option. By contrasting *this*, *that*, and *it* in the sentence from 'The Bear' we can see the enhanced narratorial involvement intimated by the chosen form, the perspectival alignment of the narrator and Ike:

> They were so close that it turned at bay although he
>   {this}
> realized later {that} might have been from surprise and
>   {it}
> amazement . . .

There seem to be good literary critical reasons for very delicate and discriminating use of language in such passages as this one. Here, after all, is one of the key epiphanies in the book, an experience in which Ike learns much concerning courage, power, the appropriacy or otherwise of the hunter's urge to kill, and the truth of the heart. By using proximal deictics the narrator suggests that his perspective is not one of disinterested detachment with regard to the values that Ike is striving to recognize and understand.

A further characteristic of the two pronominal uses of *this* in 'The Bear', section II, and of five of the other demonstrative pronouns there, is the fact that they involve what Halliday and Hasan (1976) call extended textual reference. They require, for interpretation, that the reader refer (usually backwards) to some fairly lengthy portion of nearby text. A minority of demonstrative pronouns in the section are of a more easily processed kind, substituting for some fairly clearly defined NP:

He could find the crooked print . . . ten miles or five miles or sometimes closer than *that*, to the camp. (p. 210)

They read the tracks . . . the long tracks of dead and terrified running and *those* of the beast . . . (p. 214)

However, where extended textual reference is involved, interpretation of demonstratives may well be less straightforward, and more inferencing may be necessary. Page 220, for example, records Lion's ruthless disdain for the other hounds, and then Boon's veneration of the dog:

Boon said, 'Jesus. Jesus – Will he let me touch him?'
'You can touch him,' Sam said. 'He dont care. He dont care about nothing or nobody.'
The boy watched *that* too. He watched it for the next two years from that moment when Boon touched Lion's head and then knelt beside him, feeling the bones and muscles, the power.

It is not obvious what *that* refers to here; the referent must be inferred from passages of preceding and following text. Even on such a basis we may construe a composite of possible referents: (a) the 'not-caringness' of Lion, alluded to by Sam; (b) the quasi-marital attachment of Boon to Lion – and the latter's toleration of it.

A little further on, on p. 222, the young Ike is reported questioning the apparent usurpation of Sam's place by Boon, in the day-to-day care of Lion. The text runs:

I wonder what Sam thinks. He could have Lion with him, even if Boon is a white man. . . . And more than that. It was Sam's hand that touched Lion first and Lion knows it. Then he became a man and he knew *that* too. It had been all right. *That* was the way it should have been . . . (first three sentences italicized as in the original, my emphasis of the two demonstratives)

Here, too, the referents of *that* (especially the first one) are not self-evident but need to be reconstructed from the surrounding co-text. Some possibilities can be rapidly discarded. We would not paraphrase the text as 'Then he became a man and knew that he had become a man too'. Nor would there be much to recommend a version interpreting the preceding sentences as referent: 'Then he became a man and he knew that it was Sam's hand that touched Lion first and Lion knows it too.' Rather we must assume that behind the formulation *I wonder what Sam thinks* Ike is really asking, 'What is the explanation for this state of affairs?' The *that* of p. 222 can be satisfactorily interpreted only as a gesturing towards an explanation for the situation witnessed to in the preceding sentences, an explanation partially sketched in the following sentences but never fully articulated.

'THIS' AND 'THAT' IN TEMPORAL ADVERBIAL EXPRESSIONS

Among the 30 demonstratives functioning as determiners in 'The Bear', section II, as many as 22 are in temporal adverbial expressions. Of these temporals, 17 use *that* while only 5 use *this*. These latter five may reward closer scrutiny:

1 Then on the third morning Sam was waiting again, *this* time until they had finished breakfast . . . (p. 216)

There are important motivations for the linguistic foregrounding here – the proximal deictic and the progressivized main verb. Information is relayed here not for its face value (although, as a narrative often recording an adolescent's views, the question of whether or not breakfast was taken may assume greater importance than it would for an adult; cf. p. 214), but for its inferential value. As suggested earlier the waiting of men like Lucas and Sam is not passive or gratuitous (see chapter 4 above), even if it sometimes appears so. Their form of waiting is a positive act, probably undertaken consciously. The inference here is that Sam waited (or rather 'was waiting') because he chose to, and that the others had breakfast because Sam chose to let them: he exerts a barely perceptible negative control. The control is reflected in the sentences that follow:

He said, 'Come.' He led them to his house . . .

And it is confirmed by the subsequent narrative revelation that Sam has trapped and caged Lion, that he does indeed hold power, controlling the only dog powerful enough to threaten Ben with destruction.

All four other occurrences of *this* in temporal adverbials (all are of the form *this time*) appear towards the end of this section, and have a common function. They are part of the description of the second and final occasion in section II on which Lion gets near to trapping the bear:

This time Lion jumped Old Ben more than five miles from the river and bayed and held him and this time the hounds went in, in a sort of desperate emulation. (p. 224)

It is for Ike an occasion of intense excitement and fear, rendered by multiple non-finite progressives – 'he was running now; panting, stumbling, his lungs bursting' – and almost demands the imaginative narratorial alignment and subjective empathy involved in the use of deictics signalling relative spatio-temporal nearness.

Such expressions as *this time* are somewhere about the middle along a continuum of temporal relationship, with *then* and *now* as endpoints. A speaker who speaks of an event as happening *then* is probably conceiving of it as a past and distant event (although it is possible to use *then* while wishing to denote presentness and immediacy). The probabilities are reversed with *now*, as the following diagram seeks to show:

```
                    recorder
                   /        \
            probable         possible
               /                  \
*then*     event                  event
          _____
              past           present


                    recorder
                   /        \
         less likely         more likely
              /                    \
*this time* event                  event
          _____
              past           present


                    recorder
                   /       \
          possible         probable
             /                 \
*now*    event                 event
         _____
             past           present
```

187

In contrast with the temporal flexibility of *this time, that time* cannot be used to record copresent events (or with any present perfect tense forms: *this time/*that time he has gone too far*), but conveys implicit temporal disjunction of recorder and event.

It may also be possible to posit the following more delicate opposition:

that time + past tense verb: periods of greater duration
this time + past tense verb: periods of lesser duration

This suggestion is prompted by what appears to be a contrast, in the text of 'The Bear', section II, between the majority of temporal adverbials with *that* and past tense, denoting a weakly specified and fairly extensive period of time, a more generalized specification; and the recorded minority of cases with *this*, denoting a much more specific instant or occasion. The one clear exception to this trend is

He watched it for the next two years from that moment when Boon touched Lion's head. (p. 220)

REVERENTIAL DISTANCING

While use of the proximal deictics (*here, this, now*, etc.) and such temporals as *today* and *yesterday* often expresses narratorial alignment with a character's perspective on facts and events, we have seen that the non-proximal deictics often contribute to a narratorial perspective of neutral detachment. Given a context of intermittent FID, however, this remoteness or detachment may be in the relation not merely between events and the narrator but also between events and a character. If, within a FID passage, the text suddenly adopts non-proximal deictics, before reverting to FID (i.e. with continued focalization from a single character's viewpoint), the distinctive local linguistic selections may not merely signal a reversion to the more objective or neutral perspective of the narrator (as is the conventional opinion). It may instead be a subtle way of intimating that what is denoted is remote, unassimilatable, even awe-inspiring, for the subjective FID-rendered character.

This might account for the fact that, among the six occurrences of *that* as determiner not yet discussed (all in non-locative, non-temporal adverbials), five introduce NPs whose reference, while often fairly specific, frequently remains incompletely defined. The vagueness and remoteness of these denotations may reflect their special status for the character Ike himself. All five referents are qualities or values which Ike respects, even if he does not embrace them:

1 He had a . . . fyce . . . possessing *that* sort of courage which had long since stopped being bravery and had become foolhardiness. (p. 211)

2 They read the tracks where the frantic mare had circled and at last rushed in with *that* same ultimate desperation with which she had whirled on Sam Fathers yesterday evening . . . (p. 214)

3 the Indian face [of Sam] in which he had never seen anything until it smiled, except *that* faint arching of the nostrils on that first morning when the hounds had found Old Ben. (p. 216)

4 'It's a dog,' Sam said, his nostrils arching and collapsing faintly and steadily and *that* faint, fierce milkiness in his eyes again as on that first morning . . . (p. 217)

5 It [Lion] stood . . . with cold yellow eyes and a tremendous chest and over all *that* strange color like a blue gun-barrel. (p. 218)

The phenomena introduced by these distancing demonstratives are strange but intensely memorable to Ike. The difficulty for whomever reports here, it might be supposed, lies in the rendering of the phenomena, putting them into words. For recording narrator or experiencing character these qualities are highly valued but ill understood, sometimes even mystical. In the record of Ike's encounter with the buck (p. 184), discussed at the opening of chapter 4, relatedly, the deer moves with '*that* winged and effortless ease' and Sam responds 'in *that* tongue which the boy had learned from listening to him and Joe Baker in the blacksmith shop' (my emphases). In a conventional narrative passage of indirect speech one might accept that using *that* to introduce such phenomena merely serves to imply that the narrator is removed from or uninvolved with the phenomena so denoted. In a passage aligned with Ike's perspective the situation is different.

In such passages, then, the distal deictic domonstratives, when tied to qualities or features respected and even revered by Ike, are used to suggest that Ike *himself* knows that the qualities are ones he does not consciously share or fully understand. In all five quoted sentences, depicting completed past events, *that* is a marked alternative to the other possible determiners here, *a* and *the*. By contrast with them, *that* endows the referent designated by the noun phrase with qualities of uniqueness, and that accolade is one conferred from Ike's view of the world. The narratorial version of Ike's experiences confirms that these phenomena and their sources – Sam, the fyce, and Lion – are respected and honoured by Ike even as he recognizes his difference from them. In my discussion of Ike in chapter 3, I referred at length to his failures of heart and action, his confused and, finally, limited commitment to wilderness or town. The phenomena introduced by the instances of *that* noted here are centrally expressive of the qualities and commitment Ike lacks, or thinks he lacks: uncalculating courage and fearless resolution; desperate protective love for another; and total commitment to the untamed freedom of the woods, as a place to live in and a code to live by.

8

LEXICAL STYLISTICS: THE 'BREATHING' MOTIF IN 'PANTALOON IN BLACK' AND *NOT ENOUGH*

LEXICAL PATTERNING

If *Go Down, Moses* is not to be characterized as a hastily assembled patchwork of independent stories, but rather as a collective novel, where lies its unity? In particular, can the claim that this book is a single coherent fiction also locate the seemingly maverick chapter, 'Pantaloon in Black', within such a unificatory treatment? The numerous contributors to this debate include Brooks (1963), Vickery (1959), Tick (1962), Stoneback (1976), and Thornton (1975). Perhaps the most recent assessment, and certainly one of the most ambitious, is Limon's (1986), which argues that the various failed rites within the story dramatize the blindness of belief in any rite of interpretative integration. The 'novel' thus dramatizes its own failed integration, and Faulkner sees what Stanley Fish and Martin Luther King (Limon's instances) failed to see: 'What Faulkner says to Fish is that the American belief in the power of interpretive communities is akin to an idealist's dream of an integrated South' (Limon 1986: 423). By contrast, this chapter has a rather modest but text-based thesis concerning one aspect of textual integratedness: I argue that the careful analysis of the deployment of single foregrounded lexical items (and semantically related words) demonstrates an underlying integrative purpose in the narrative of 'Pantaloon in Black' and the novel as a whole.

In *Go Down, Moses* thematic unity is a matter of preponderance: the chapters preponderantly involve some form of hunt, are preponderantly about the McCaslin family, and preponderantly deal with black–white relations. These preponderances overlap from chapter to chapter, forming many unexpected connections between disparate

191

elements. But at no level is such unforeseeable bonding more pervasive, effective, and unifying than at the level of recurring motifs. Through the network of motifs and verbal or situational echoes, the reader constructs, through the course of the novel, a community of shared experiences, constraints, and possibilities. That community shapes and is shaped by the circumstances and events and participants depicted, and the latter may be of dissimilar race, social position, occupation, and historical period. The community and commonality are thus very much the construction of the reader, suitably cued by the text. Part of this sensed community is achieved by the great density of verbal echoes and scenic parallels running through the chapters, which sets up reverberations in the reader's imaginative apprehension of the novel, akin to the sympathetic harmonies of the Coleridgean Aeolian harp. Moreover, just as the harmonies of the harp are no incidental by-product of a pre-existing melody, so too is this verbal and scenic patterning an integral constituent of the literary message and effect.

However, while integration via motifs suggests a degree of community of experience, it does not exclude radical disruptions of that community. Indeed, it is those disruptions which are immediately registered in a first reading of the novel. I include, among these disruptions, the several minor tragedies that follow from contrasts in the inheritances of various characters: the serious threats to the marriage of Lucas and Molly, the genetic entrapment of Sam, the collapse of the wilderness, the manipulation of the black McCaslins, the diminishment of Ike's marriage, Ike's denial of his young black relative in 'Delta Autumn', and of course the death of young Samuel Beauchamp in 'Go Down, Moses'.

A recurring motif may, in a broad sense, be understood as a distinct and frequently occurring characterizing detail, appearing in a range of narrative situations and related to a range of protagonists. Like any literary work, but more richly than most, *Go Down, Moses* contains a number of themes and motifs. While the many thematic interpretations of the book are abstractions, relatively remote from its surface linguistic form, much more immediately relatable to the surface text are motifs – the distinctive recurrent details through which the writer has chosen to articulate his themes. They are a major means of effecting Faulkner's narratorial strategies at the lexical level, often comprising brief and idiosyncratic descriptive phrases dispersed through the text. Such brief phrases are distinctive enough for the

192

reader to register, consciously or unconsciously, the similarities and dissimilarities between their varied contexts of use. Parallel claims to these can be found in Thornton (1975), who argues for Faulkner's achievement of a distinct kind of novelistic unity, in *Go Down, Moses* and elsewhere, through a technique of 'latent juxtaposition'. Thornton notes that 'The juxtaposition may be suggested by the repetition of some concrete object, or a phrase or motif' (1975: 75). Both Thornton's procedure and that adopted here apply fundamental structuralist principles: the identification of similarity and difference, repetition, association, and combination.

Among the major motifs constituting and unifying *Go Down, Moses* are: having to be a negro; the power of the heart; blood; types of housing; and bringing, coming, or going home. Some idea of the distribution of these motifs through the entire novel can be gained from using the invaluable concordance to the novel. Here, because of space constraints, attention will be directed to just two motifs. The first is of pre-eminent importance in interpretation of 'Pantaloon in Black', and of considerable importance in several of the other chapters, and yet has been largely ignored in the extant criticism. The motif may be generically labelled one of 'breathing', since the com-

Table 7 Occurrences of the 'breathing' motif in *Go Down, Moses*

	pant(s) panted panting	yawn yawned yawning	gasping	inhalations inhaling	breath(s) breathe breathed breathless
'Was'					2
'Fire/Hearth' 1	2	1	1	1	11
'Fire/Hearth' 2		1			4
'Fire/Hearth' 3	1		1		1
'Pantaloon'	8	1		1	9
'Old People'	1				10
'The Bear' I	1			1	2
'The Bear' II	2	2			2
'The Bear' III	1				5
'The Bear' IV	1				5
'The Bear' V					2
'Delta Autumn'	2				4
'Go Down, Moses'					3
Totals	19	5	2	3	60

mon underlying concern of all its occurrences is with breath, its presence or absence. It has derived specific realizations such as not-breathing, panting, and shortness of breath, while instances of yawning comprise a related set of instances. The occurrences and distribution of this breathing motif are noted in table 7.

RIDER'S BREATHING HUMAN PASSION

In 'Pantaloon in Black' the motif first occurs on p. 140, with three distinct but interrelated citations. The first of these introduces the dilemma that persists throughout the story. Rider and his dog enter his house, and the dusk-filled room 'where all those six months were now crammed and crowded into one instant of time until there was no space left for air to breathe'. The implication here is that memories have physical extension, displacing air to the extent that breathing is difficult. A rather conventional metaphorical assertion that a grief-stricken individual may be 'choked' by poignant memories is vividly recast as an actual physical menace. Paradoxically, Rider's breathing appears undisturbed – there continues 'the deep steady arch and collapse of his chest'. But this situation does not last long. Almost immediately Rider sees Mannie: 'He didn't breathe nor speak until he knew his voice would be all right.' But when Rider relaxes (and, we infer, breathes again) Mannie begins to fade, so 'He stopped at once, not breathing again, motionless, willing his eyes to see that she had stopped too' (p. 140).

Even this early in the story, we may suspect that the breathing motif exemplifies the broader Faulknerian theme of the contrast between motion and stasis, and the folly and transience of stasis set beside the inevitability of motion and change. Faulkner himself, in his fiction, has often been interpreted as celebrating 'frozen moments' of time, and as constructing his mammoth sentences out of a related impulse, to halt the flux of time at some idyllic moment when there is wilderness, bear to hunt, Southern chivalry and pride, and so on. But that is a distortion of the books; those impossible romantic dreams are treated as such. Here in 'Pantaloon in Black', for example, Faulkner recognizes breathing as a form of movement, as the unceasing respiratory cycle which man must live with and through, and as an individualized process shared by man and animal alike. Rider, seeing Mannie, talking to her, not-breathing, is struggling to repudiate the inexorable facts of death, grief, loss, and flux; but he is doomed to fail.

It is with the same doomed conviction that he attempts to compel himself to eat:

> looking down at his plate, breathing the strong, deep pants, his chest arching and collapsing until he stopped it presently and held himself motionless for perhaps a half minute, and raised a spoonful of the cold and glutinous peas to his mouth. (p. 141)

His body rejects the food. Breathing is one (fundamental) indicator to Rider of the tragic way in which the mere motion of existence is moving him inexorably away from Mannie. It is the archetypal way in which his own body denies his struggle for stasis. Rightly focusing on the centrality of possession (or articulation) and loss in the novel, Matthews makes much of Rider's name and reputation as a rider of logs and women, and asserts: 'Riding becomes the story's metaphor for the coincidence of possession and loss' (Matthews 1982: 240). Breathing, however, is much more frequently invoked in the text, and equally vividly captures the poignant simultaneity of possession and loss.

It is Rider's own physicality that haunts and hounds him. And his breathing is the immediate cause of his display of outrageous strength in handling the log:

> Then the trucks were rolling again. Then he could stop needing to invent to himself reasons for his breathing, until after a while he began to believe he had forgot [*sic*] about breathing since now he could not hear it himself above the steady thunder of the rolling logs; whereupon as soon as he found himself believing he had forgotten it, he knew that he had not, so that [he raised a log single-handed, and hurled it]. (p. 145)

At odds with the dismissive contempt of the story's title, and the subhuman comments of the deputy, Rider is in several respects close to the type of the grief-stricken lover, the tragically young and innocent, with Romeo Montague a closer ancestor than Pantalone. He is torn by conflicting impulses: his desire to retain Mannie, to deny the loss, impels him to be motionless, unbreathing. Yet his very attempts in such a direction provoke a mental and physical reaction: being alive, young, and strong, he is also impelled to act and move. Out of control, he seeks mental and physical stasis, but cannot stop breathing, walking, drinking, thinking – or even laughing (p. 159).

195

Fleeing from rooms that stifle him is no release: he moves rapidly through the canestalks, but even they 'possessed something of that oppression, that lack of room to breathe in, which the walls of his house had had' (p. 147).

Thus caught, Rider can find only temporary relief in the 'snake pizen' of alcohol, but is always aware that whisky is ultimately more a hindrance than a help to him. At first when he drinks he pauses, 'gulping the silver air into his throat until he could breathe again' (p. 148). The alcohol in his body is like oil in a machine; it flows 'past then enveloping the strong steady panting of his lungs until they too ran suddenly free as his moving body ran in the silver solid wall of air he breasted' (p. 148). As the image of the 'silver solid wall of air' suggests, Rider is still struggling to reconcile elements which appear to be flowing and easy-moving with others which appear solid and unmoving. He has accepted an illusion of peace and resolution when he believes in 'the deep strong panting of his chest running free as air now because he was all right' (p. 148). But that illusion is shattered when his body begins rejecting the alcohol, indeed rejecting it not as a malleable fluid but as a solid column of matter.

> He drank again. Again his throat merely filled solidly until two icy rills ran from his mouth-corners; again the intact column sprang silvering, glinting, shivering, while he panted the chill of air into his throat . . . (p. 149)

Once again, as in the truly substantial memories choking Rider in his home, a menacing material transformation, in which a liquid becomes a solid, undermines him. All this can be compared with the use of the breathing motif in 'Go Down, Moses', where it articulates Gavin Stevens's choking nausea in the Worshams' home:

> He rose quickly. . . . *Soon I will be outside*, he thought. *Then there will be air, space, breath.* . . . It was not far now; now he could smell and feel it: the breathing and simple dark. (pp. 380–1; emphases in original)

In the 'Pantaloon in Black' story, just one realization of the breathing motif using the word *yawn* occurs, in a context of poignant contrasts. Elsewhere in *Go Down, Moses*, *yawn* and its cognates are almost entirely employed in descriptions of Lion, and serve to confirm the dog's haughty, fearless, insouciant spirit; the dog's breathing is so untroubled as to be barely breathing – just yawning. Lion is one of a small set of participants in Faulkner's fictional universe that yawn because they are fearless, foreknowing, or impenetrable; others are the wilderness, and women such as Eula Varner. Here the tormented Rider, paralysed as it were by movement and breathing, walks through the pasture, 'passing the black-and-silver yawn of the sandy ditch where he had played as a boy' (p. 149). A fleeting juxtaposition is effected of Rider's simple and carefree past and his restless, self-destructive present existence. Once more back in that agonized present he speaks to his aunt, 'speaking quietly out of the tremendous panting of his chest which in a moment now would begin to strain at the walls of this room too' (p. 150).

THE BREATHING NETWORK: FROM STORY TO NOVEL

There is space here to note only the more crucial occurrences of the breathing motif elsewhere in *Go Down, Moses* and to suggest how they relate to those in 'Pantaloon in Black'. Not surprisingly, they are most commonly related to Ike. In the extended preliminaries of pp. 182 and 183 of 'The Old People', prior to the appearance of the majestic buck, the recorded fluctuations in breathing are a key signal of intense attentiveness, not merely in Ike and Sam, but in the entire setting. At first the man and boy 'stood motionless, breathing deep and quiet and steady'. Then

> There was a condensing . . . of what he had thought was the gray and unchanging light until he realized suddenly that it was his own breathing, his heart, his blood . . . and that Sam Fathers had marked him. . . . He stopped breathing then; there was only his heart, his blood, and in the following silence the wilderness ceased to breathe also, leaning, stooping overhead with its breath held, tremendous and impartial and waiting. (p. 182)

Soon, however, Ike believes the moment has passed, and only Sam and the unbreathing woods seem not to confirm his judgement:

> Then it had passed. . . . The solitude did not breathe again yet . . . and the boy knew as well as if he had seen him that the buck had come to the edge of the cane and had either seen or scented them and faded back into it. But the solitude did not breathe again. It should have suspired again then but it did not . . . rigid, not breathing himself, he thought, cried *No! No!* (p. 183; original emphases)

197

Ike assumes the buck has already gone, but is held in place by Sam's instruction – 'Wait' – using the verb we have already found foregrounded in numerous ways. Utterly confused, the astonished boy now witnesses the passing of the mystical buck (discussed in the first section of chapter 4).

Records of breathing and not-breathing are thus prominent in major experiences of Rider and the young Ike: breath as a component and symbol of life, passion, and transience (the long sequence of expirations) is a foregrounded means of reporting their comparable passionate trials.

On the other hand, uses of the breathing motif in 'Was' are rare, and comic in tone (e.g. in descriptions of Uncle Buck on p. 23, and on p. 38 when he collides with Tomey's Turl and is winded). In 'The Fire and the Hearth' the motif is sometimes comic, as in 'Was', sometimes intensely serious, as in later chapters. At first it helps dramatize Lucas's desperate encounter with Zack Edmonds, whose suspected adultery with Molly threatens to destroy the Beauchamps' marriage. Here, as in relation to Rider and Ike, it serves to show the major character experiencing barely tolerable strain, reflected in the impression of nearness to physical collapse. Later, in a quite different vein, the audible breathing of George Wilkins, the unsubtle dissembler 'who drew his breath with a faint hissing sound' (p. 82), is repeatedly remarked upon. That comic tone reappears later in 'The Fire and the Hearth' when Roth Edmonds's steady breath strives to conceal his exasperation with Lucas's subtle deceits.

The motif is instrumental again in chapter 3 of 'The Fire and the Hearth', in Roth's moving recollection of that moment in his childhood when he irrevocably restated the racial divide between himself and his black cousin, Henry. Roth's insistence that he and Henry sleep separately reaps terrible consequences: an immediate sense of shame, so that 'the boy didn't sleep, long after Henry's quiet and untroubled breathing had begun', and a subsequent appalling confirmation, by Molly, Lucas, and Henry, of the segregation Roth had earlier sought:

> The table was set in the kitchen . . . and there was just one chair, one plate . . . and even as he sprang back, gasping, for an instant blind as the room rushed and swam, Henry was turning toward the door to go out of it. (p. 113)

In the second paragraph of 'The Bear', section I, hunting is called 'the best game of all, *the best of all breathing* and forever the best of all listening' (my emphasis). By hunting is understood not merely the successful kill, but also the many unsuccessful chases, the very experience of taking part in the ancient contest, and the innumerable memories and stories relating to that contest. It is appropriate, therefore, that one form of the best of all breathing should be recorded later in the section when Ike and Sam merely sense the distant presence of the bear:

> He could hear Sam breathing at his shoulder. He saw the arched curve of the old man's inhaling nostrils.
> 'It's Old Ben!' he cried, whispering. (p. 197)

But in section II of 'The Bear' we are reminded that excited breathing may be as much that of the pursued as of the pursuer. On p. 225 Ike's laboured breathing reflects his identification with the hunted animal. Indeed, he is winded and bayed, as Old Ben temporarily has been:

> He saw the blood from General Compson's shots, but he could go no further. He stopped, leaning against a tree for his breathing to ease and his heart to slow, hearing the sound of the dogs . . .

In contrast to this strain, when Sam approaches death in section III, 'his breathing was so quiet, so peaceful that they could hardly see that he breathed '(p. 247). Yet when Ike wishes to stay with the dying Sam but is being overruled by McCaslin he again feels trapped and, like Rider, starved of air:

> He could feel his breath coming shorter and shorter and shallower and shallower, as if there were not enough air in the kitchen for that many to breathe. (p. 250)

Interestingly, the breathing motif scarcely appears at all in the long fourth section of 'The Bear', but surfaces in section V when Ike moves within the myriad life of the woods, 'breathing and binding and immobile' (p. 238), and encounters the aged snake:

> Immobile, one foot just taking his weight, the toe of the other just lifted behind him, not breathing, feeling again and as always the sharp shocking inrush from when Isaac McCaslin long yet was not. (p. 239)

There are several reasons for regarding 'Delta Autumn' as the climax of the novel, in which we see some of the consequences of the choices made by Ike, his black McCaslin cousins, and other members

of the community such as Major de Spain and General Compson.
Here Ike is in his old age, and the breathing motif strikingly shadows
his degeneration, in the story, from initial portrayal as a man of
natural authority over horses and men (Edmonds rejects that authority at dinner on the first night in camp, but the others linger
'apparently held there yet by his quiet and peaceful voice as the heads
of the swimming horses had been held above the water by his
weightless hand' (p. 348)), to the final characterization as one of
narrow vision and limited compassion, moved by a romantic rhetoric
of withdrawal rather than the commitment of love. We see that his
wisdom as a child of the wilderness promotes in him a calm which,
when attained, is often complacent. But it is a calm that is radically
disrupted by the intrusion of his young black relation.

The night before her appearance, Ike 'lay on his back, his eyes
closed, his breathing quiet and peaceful as a child's' (p. 353). The
next morning that calm persists when, as usual on the first day, he
keeps to bed while the other men go off to hunt: 'He lay with his eyes
closed, his breathing gentle and peaceful' (p. 353. However, this
peace is broken when Roth appoints him go-between, and withdraws
from the tent seemingly only moments before the woman herself
arrives – a swiftness rendered through the breathing motif:

> The tent flap falling on the same out-waft of faint and rain-filled
> light like the suspiration and expiration of the same breath and then
> in the next second lifted again. (p. 356)

The effect on Ike of the encounter with Tennie's Jim's granddaughter
is, clearly, devastating. The meeting starkly and conclusively exposes
the inadequacies of the stand Ike has taken in his life, a stand which
cannot conceal radical failures of compassion. The reader cries out
'Yes!' when the black woman rhetorically asks: '"Old man . . . have
you lived so long and forgotten so much that you dont remember
anything you ever knew or felt or even heard about love?"' (p. 363).
Fittingly, this devastating exposure is followed by a final use of the
breathing motif, through the item *panting*, so consistently applied in
this novel to individuals who have lost control, are cornered and
desperate: 'Lying back once more, trembling, panting, the blanket
huddled to his chin and his hands crossed on his breast' (p. 363).

Why is the phenomenon of breathing so emphasized in this work?
We might note that breath and life are equated in the first book of the
Old Testament, perhaps the richest cultural source for Faulkner:

And the Lord God formed man of the dust of the ground, and breathed into his nostrils the breath of life; and man became a living soul. (Genesis 1:7)

Faulkner was also much attached to the work of Keats. Blotner (1964) confirms Faulkner's frequently stated love of the poetry, revealing that the novelist had three sets of Keats's poems in his possession at the time of his death. *Endymion*, almost certainly familiar to him, begins by celebrating the beautiful as a promoter of quiet breathing:

A thing of beauty is a joy for ever;
Its loveliness increases; it will never
Pass into nothingness; but still will keep
A bower of quiet for us, and a sleep
Full of sweet dreams, and health, and quiet breathing.

More conclusively, there are pertinent lines in 'Ode on a Grecian Urn', a poem which figures directly in *Go Down, Moses*. The third stanza depicts the lovers on the urn, arrested in the mental and physical attitude of commencing to love, not tainted or disappointed by the human experience of satiety and change:

More happy love! more happy, happy love!
For ever warm and still to be enjoy'd,
For ever panting, and for ever young;
All breathing human passion far above,
That leaves a heart high-sorrowful and cloy'd . . .

Here, in effect, is one way of expressing Rider's impossibly romantic and idealist impulse to freeze life, reduce it to a scene on an urn, and so retain the ever-fleeing past he cherishes. One interpretation of this ode might claim that, having witnessed this celebration of the urn with all its connotations, the reader is or should be teased 'out of thought': one of Rider's problems, however, is that, like the Quentin of *The Sound and the Fury*, he is never free from destructive introspection – ' "Hit look lack Ah just cant quit thinking" ' (p. 159).

Quite basic patterns in human psychology and physiology may also have shaped Faulkner's use of the breathing motif. A standard textbook of psychiatry, for example, notes:

The respiratory system is involved in the earliest significant relationships that the individual has with other people and provides one of the earliest means of expressing emotional reactions and needs. One of the most common complaints of anxious patients is difficulty in breathing. Patients often demonstrate this by deep sighs or state that they cannot get enough air. The respiratory concomitants of anxiety are primarily ventilatory in nature and may vary from deep sighs or hyperventilation to breathholding. (Freedman and Kaplan 1967: 1,068)

More specifically, the detail of Rider's fluctuating breathing pattern is startlingly similar to the condition known as periodic breathing, or the Cheyne–Stokes phenomenon, which may occur to an individual suffering shock. Periodic breathing is described thus in Butterworth's *Medical Dictionary*:

Rhythmical waxing and waning of respiration, consisting of alternating periods of hyperpnoea (increased depth and rate of respiration), and apnoea (cessation of respiration). Respiration steadily increases in depth, then wanes, until finally it ceases entirely. After a few moments the cycle is repeated.

Motifs such as that of breathing are important bonds holding *Go Down, Moses* together. For it is clear that several more conventional structuring devices of the novel are not adopted here. Chronological sequence, for example, is not paramount; rather it is freely violated (there are causes and effects, but no simple progressions). And major themes, such as the burdens of inheritance, do not appear in every section (inheritance has little significance in 'Pantaloon in Black'). This might seem a flaw in a conventional novel. But *Go Down, Moses* is not such a work; rather it generates a milieu occupied and articulated by themes and motifs (see also Cleman 1977), and the fictional unity of this novel lies in its verbal texture. The many motifs form associative networks in similar or contrasting semantic contexts. They are a major exponent of intratextuality, the various means by which a work of art is fashioned into a single, integrated text; and in a highly wrought novel such as this they may be at least as influential, in the reader's reception of the work, as intertextual factors. The motif networks and the visual images they project bind the separate narratives within *Go Down, Moses* by their implication of characterological and experiential commonality.

'NOT ENOUGH'

The lexical and motif patterning that I take to be so important in the larger design of this collective-novel is not restricted, however, to items that are lexical in the narrower linguistic sense. Even items from relatively closed grammatical classes are a possible resource for exploitation in subtle effects of echo, iteration with difference, ironic repetition, and so on. I shall briefly discuss one of the most interesting examples of this, the recurrent use of the quantifying expressions 'enough' and, especially, 'not enough'.

Chapter 3 argued at length that Ike's actions and interventions are insufficient. I suggest that this evaluation of Ike is also carried by the narrative itself: at the content level of plot, of course; and at the syntactic level chiefly concentrated upon in this book; but even on occasion at word level. Most directly at this last level, the theme and judgement are underlined by the use of the quantifying determiner *enough*, which the standard concordance (Capps 1977) reveals occurs over 100 times in the novel, 64 times within the narrative.

That high frequency of *enough* in the narrative reflects a striving, on the part of Lucas and Ike in particular, for the achievement of *adequacy* in their experiencing and judgement of the world. Only very occasionally here does the item *enough* occur in colloquial expressions such as *sure enough* and *curiously enough*, where it is an empty phatic emphasizer. Far more often it is used in quantitative judgements, from the point of view of a particular participant, passing verdict on the sufficiency or otherwise of a particular element in the situation under scrutiny. Furthermore, these quantitative judgements commonly concern intangible qualities that are not strictly measurable ('enough courage'), rather than mundane concrete particulars ('enough money').

Early in 'The Fire and the Hearth', chapter 1, for example, the narrative reports Lucas's reflections on the need to find a hiding-place for his whisky still which is 'far enough away and secret enough to escape any subsequent disturbances' (p. 33). Soon after, mulling over what he regards as a power-struggle for the land among the white McCaslins, he judges that Cass Edmonds, by contrast with Ike, had 'enough of old Carothers McCaslin in his veins to take the land', was 'strong enough, ruthless enough, old Carothers McCaslin enough' (p. 44). For Lucas, then, in the field of major actions in his life as in the less serious area of protecting his (illegal) avocation, a quantitative or materialist principle is invoked in evaluating actions. We see this poignantly confirmed at a more intimate level when he estimates that his daughter Nat – even when fortified by the new stove, back porch, and well that he has promised to give her – is too frail for all the trials of marriage:

> Lucas could see her trembling. She looked small, thin as a lath, young; she was their youngest and last. . . . She was too young to be married and face all the troubles married people had to get through in order to become old and find out for themselves the taste and savor of peace. Just a stove and a new back porch and a well were not enough. (p. 73)

It is Ike, however, who reveals the most widespread compulsion to measure the effectiveness of an action or the impact of a condition by the postulated quantitative sufficiency of the elements involved. And these judgements of sufficiency, within Ike-aligned narrative, become increasingly controversial as the novel proceeds.

Thirteen of the narrative occurrences of *enough* are implicitly Lucas's judgements, but as many as twenty-eight, in 'The Bear' and 'Delta Autumn', are Ike's. Ike judges that the white man had once been 'fatuous enough' to think he could own the wilderness (p. 191); and that in order to be a true hunter one needed to be 'humble enough and enduring enough' (p. 192). Seeking the bear unarmed, he finds 'that had not been enough, the leaving of the gun was not enough' (p. 208), and so relinquishes watch and compass. Later, when he and Boon, the only ones to understand Sam's wish for an Indian death and burial, are harassed over this by the other men, their breath comes shallower and shallower 'as if there were not enough air in the kitchen for that many to breathe' (pp. 250, 253: note the interconnection here with the 'breathing' pattern). More sombrely, Ike reflects in 'The Bear', section IV (p. 293), that 'two hundred years had not been enough to complete and another hundred would not be enough to discharge' the shameful record of slavery and racial exploitation.

The preoccupation is far from confined to the narrative. Within the multiply embedded conversations of 'The Bear', section IV, when Cass is driven to anger by the aloof declarations of the black clergyman stranger who comes to him to announce his intention of marrying Fonsiba, the text runs:

> 'That's enough, I said,' McCaslin said. 'Be off this place by full dark. Go.'

The emphasis on 'enough' is neatly picked up and turned to his own advantage by the stranger:

'Yes,' he said. 'After all, this is your house. And in your fashion you have . . . But no matter. You are right. This is enough.' (p. 276)

A few pages later, when Ike and Cass's own conversation is resumed, Cass reminds Ike of the efforts of the preceding generation to rectify, however fumblingly, the injustices of slavery and exploitation. Ike's immediate retort is that those gestures were inadequate: '"But not enough. Not enough of even Father and Uncle Buddy to fumble-heed in even three generations"' (p. 282). It is precisely the inadequacy of white attempts at reform, in Ike's view, that prompted God to intervene by means of the cataclysmic Civil War:

'Until one day He said what you told Fonsiba's husband that afternoon here in this room: *This will do. This is enough*: not in exasperation or rage or even just sick to death as you were sick that day: just *This is enough. . . .*' (p. 283)

However – and this is why such verbal repetitions are so effective – the emphasis on *enough* is not maintained without change of context and values, even changes which confirm a depressing narrowing of sympathies on Ike's part. Thus at the end of his life, in 'Delta Autumn', Ike is revealed commonly using his yardstick of sufficiency on an old man's petty discomforts: his mattress is not soft enough, the blankets are less and less warm enough, and the bed itself is 'not wide enough nor soft enough nor even warm enough' (p. 352). To such trivial considerations has Ike retreated. The degeneration is fore-shadowed in the complacency of his reflection, towards the close of 'The Bear', section IV, when he uncritically acknowledges that his own ends,

although simple enough in their apparent motivation, were and would be always incomprehensible to him, and his life, invincible enough in its needs, if he could have helped himself, not being the Nazarene, he would not have chosen it. (pp. 309–10)

For the reader who has struggled through the tortuous philosophizing of section IV, the claim here that Ike's ends are 'simple enough' takes a bit of swallowing. The claim is part of a descent into obscurantist self-justification.

The degree to which self-interest dominates Ike in the final story he appears in, a self-interest that amounts to a more subtle version of the covetous possession that Ike elsewhere deplores, is evident in the final narratorial occurrence of *enough* in the book. This comes towards the close of Ike's final recorded reverie, and shows the use of both causal connectives and the *enough* particle in a blatant example of double-think. Ike has been reflecting on the primeval wilderness. The narrative continues:

> He could almost see it [the myriad silence of the woods]. . . . Because it was his land, although he had never owned a foot of it. He had never wanted to, not even after he saw plain its ultimate doom, watching it retreat year by year before the onslaught of axe and saw and log-lines and then dynamite and tractor plows, because it belonged to no man. It belonged to all; they had only to use it well, humbly and with pride. Then suddenly he knew why he had never wanted to own any of it. . . . It was because there was just exactly enough of it. He seemed to see the two of them – himself and the wilderness – as coevals . . . the two spans running out together . . . (p. 354)

The frequency of causal connectives here at suspect stages in the reflection should alert us to the sophistry to which Ike is prone (the causal connectives are a hallmark of Ike's strained and self-justificatory excursuses, and are a direct concern of chapters 10 and 11). The sophistry serves extraordinarily selfish ends: there is just enough wilderness for Ike's purposes, and when he dies it will die with him, and they will both endure in a world beyond time and space, for ever fixed and adjacent, like the figures on Keats's Grecian urn, or the tracks of a railway. Ike has long ago lost his wife and the son he never had (p. 351); now he definitively abandons both land and people to whatever fate or revenge comes their way – as wanton an abandonment as that of his grandfather.

A final point in support of the view taken here, that the recurrent use of *enough* in Go Down, Moses is a prominent and deliberate strategy furthering oblique themes, textual coherence, and subtle character evaluations, concerns its late emergence in the compositional history of these stories. I have compared the novel text with those of the magazine-published stories from which the novel was fashioned, the story versions typically having been written long before the novel version. In the vast majority of cases, these descriptions involving mention of *enough* are noticeably absent from the earlier magazine versions of this material. The patterning is thus, quite explicitly, a deliberately added feature in the novel's design.

9

SUBORDINATION AND NARRATIVE

THE FUNCTIONS OF CLAUSAL SUBORDINATION

This chapter considers some of the effects of clause subordination in narratives, and in doing so reviews some recent linguistic discussions and stylistic commentaries on the subject. This general discussion then makes way for a contextualized analysis, quantitatively based, of subordination patterns at the opening of each subsection of *Go Down, Moses*. The next chapter focuses more narrowly yet, and in more detail, on just one type of subordination: causal clauses.

Patterns and principles in English causal subordination have received relatively little attention from contemporary linguists, so that the stylistician in search of analytical commentary on such phenomena is often better served by the discussions in the standard descriptive grammars. There have been various efforts towards writing a supra-sentential grammar of text, specifying rules governing the chaining of sequences of sentences (see e.g. van Dijk 1977; de Beaugrande and Dressler 1981). But these text grammars remain programmatic and theoretically suspect (Levinson 1983), a weak foundation on which to base a stylistic analysis. For the stylistician, the first concern here is with interclausal relations; but these the text grammarians have tended to neglect, directing their attention to the imputed macro-structures of paragraphs and texts. However, while the amount of attention to English subordination and its subtypes has been relatively slight, several commentaries are noteworthy for their revision of traditional assumptions.

In his *Parataxis and Hypotaxis as a Criterion of Syntax and Style* (1952) Rynell challenges the assumption that principal matter regularly belongs in principal clauses and subordinate matter in subordinate clauses – a view which he shows has been based on both objective

207

logical grounds and subjective psychological ones. His reminder that superordinate content is not always carried in superordinate clauses remains germane; it could be invoked, for example, in critique of Labov's model of oral narratives of personal experience (Labov 1972), where only main clauses are assumed to be possible narrative ones.

Notwithstanding Rynell's reservations, it remains the case that one elementary difference between main and subordinate clauses lies in the fact that all the latter may be deleted from a text and yet, frequently, well-formed sentences will be preserved (however inadequate they may be as coherent text). No such well-formedness-preserving operation may ever be applied successfully to main clauses. Relatedly, a reader may skim through a text, attending only to the main clauses, and identify a body of comprehensible information in a way that is virtually impossible in the case of a text from which all main clauses have been excised. Any text in which all the main information (however defined) appears located in subordinate clauses by that very fact gives grounds for suspicion that this circumstance is not merely fortuitous but strategic.

However, as one delves into the patterns of co-ordination and subordination in a passage, it is important to keep in mind the obvious point that they are not, as far as effective discourse is concerned, two radically distinct modes, but rather two facets of a single mode of structuration, mutually dependent and mutually supportive:

> It is the flexible use of both [co-ordination and subordination] that endows a text with a variety of expression on the one hand and with a well-ordered presentation on the other. The combination also enables one to achieve a high degree of complexity within a single, unified whole. (Quirk *et al*. 1985: 1,474)

A more recent variant of the traditional assessment that Rynell challenges is the view that subordination has a backgrounding effect, that material in subordinate clauses is treated as background information relative to the highlighted or foregrounded material in the main clause. The syntactic basis for contrasting main and subordinate clauses, however characterized, still serves, in many cases, as the grounds for such informativity distinctions. Thus Thompson and Longacre (1985) cast main and subordinate clauses as sentence 'nuclei' and 'margins' respectively, and this syntactically based distinction is then extended to semantic-discoursal commentary.

Tomlin (1985) also effectively reinstates the traditional picture in an analysis of story retellings in which he found that foreground and pivotal information was encoded in independent clauses, while dependent clauses coded background information. Tomlin's study can be interpreted as applying only to spoken discourse, and in particular to story recapitulation (and its conventions) rather than to storytelling proper; but it still suggests that there is normally a congruence between informational prominence and syntactic prominence.

A related area of possible misunderstanding concerns the variation in the use of the terms 'subordinate', 'dependent', and 'embedded'. Some linguists find the label 'subordinate', in particularly, hopelessly indiscriminate. Thus Thompson would be happy to give up the term 'subordinate clause' altogether, and suggests that subordination is 'at best a negative term which lumps together all deviations from some "main clause", which means that it treats as unified a set of facts which . . . is not a single phenomenon' (Thompson 1984: 86). Many writers (but not all) refer to nominal (or complement) and restrictive relative clauses, but not adverbial clauses and non-restrictive relative clauses, as embedded and dependent. Nominal clauses, in particular, are integrated into main-clause structure, performing the function of, for example, a subject or object noun phrase, in a way that is not the case with adverbial clauses. And restrictive relative clauses, while as freely deletable as adverbial clauses without rendering the residue a syntactic fragment, are dominated by noun-phrase heads which are integral elements in main-clause structure. This greater 'boundedness' of nominal and (restrictive) relative clauses means that they both quite naturally restate or paraphrase recently given or background or presupposed information. But the 'non-boundedness' of adverbial clauses (finite or non-finite), by the same token, means that these are not so designed necessarily to convey background information. The distinction I am proposing here, between bounded and unbounded subordinate clauses, is reflected in systemic-linguistic description in the distinction between embedding (= bounded) and hypotaxis (= unbounded).

In place of the characterization of subordinate-clause content as 'backgrounded and Given (retrievable from preceding discourse)' we may do well to substitute the characterization 'not foregrounded, not Topic-introducing or -carrying, but not necessarily Given'. This formulation encapsulates several of Dillon's conclusions on subordinate-clause content (Dillon 1981); its negative cast is perhaps eloquent confirmation of Thompson's judgement, reported above, that 'subordination' itself is a negative term. Such a characterization, however, describes the pervasive tendency rather than the invariant rule. There are various instances to the contrary, such as the syntactically subordinate clause in the following constructed snippet of 'performed narrative':

I'm just putting the dishes into the washing-up bowl when this policeman comes rushing in.

It is hard to maintain that the (chiefly orientational) main clause is either more important or more in the foreground than the following subordinate clause. Such cases suggest a need to proceed to a more discriminating analysis, where, for example, not all '*when* clauses' are treated identically. Semantically, a *when* clause may report an event wholly prior to the event reported in the superordinate clause, or the two clauses may be partially or wholly overlapping in time reference; while in performed narratives (as above) and news bulletins, with a progressive-aspect main verb, a sequential 'and then' sense emerges. Notice also that in the latter case the *when* clause cannot felicitously be preposed:

?When this policeman comes rushing in, I'm just putting the dishes into the washing-up bowl.

'The Agamemnon' was returning to port in Cyprus, when it was hit by rocket fire.
?When 'The Agamemnon' was hit by rocket fire, it was returning to port in Cyprus.

The 'movability' typically ascribed to adverbial subordinate material seems not to apply in these cases, and this leads to several distinct observations. The first is that this type of *when* clause is not particularly subordinate; the second, looking at these facts from a different standpoint, is that initial and final adverbial clauses are not always communicatively equivalent; a third point to note is that the combination of main-clause progressive aspect and subordinate-clause non-progressive aspect is crucial to the acceptability of the 'reportorial' use of the *when* clauses in the examples above. Thus *when* clauses with non-progressive main clauses, while unexceptionable, are typically assumed to be carrying old or background information:

'The Agamemnon' returned to port in Cyprus(,) when it was hit by rocket fire.

When 'The Agamemnon' was hit by rocket fire, it returned to port in Cyprus.

Interestingly, when the main clause contains perfective aspect and an 'aspect-like' particle such as *just* (or even *begun to*), the 'salient new information' interpretation of the postposed *when* clause applies, just as in the case of a progressivized main clause:

'The Agamemnon' had just returned to port in Cyprus, when it was hit by rocket fire.

As so often in this study, we see here that detailed commentary on a grammatical feature requires that careful attention be paid to its complex interaction with other features; here, temporal subordination cannot be considered apart from aspect, linear ordering, and tense (the 'new information' reportorial *when* clauses arise only with past tense).

The informativity of postposed reportorial *when* clauses, it should be noted, is somewhat at odds with the findings of most discussions concerning the non-equivalence of initial and final subordinate clauses (the more general topic which has recently attracted the attention of linguists). In most discussion it has been suggested that it is the initial subordinate clauses, not the final ones, that are more interesting and important; and in the majority of uses this seems to be the case. Dillon (1981), following Bolinger (1977) and Lanin (1977), suggests that initial temporal adverbial clauses, by contrast with their sentence-final counterparts, often imply a 'more than contingent' association with the main-clause material that follows. Such initial adverbials are often used to convey the salient setting or conditions for what follows, while final adverbials are often more 'afterthoughtive', to use Bolinger's term. In the case of *because* clauses, we might tentatively suggest that, while those that are preposed express causes, those that are postposed merely express explanations. Cf.

Because the train was cancelled he was late for work.

and

He was late for work because the train was cancelled.

In a similar vein, Ramsey (1987) has applied a number of criteria of discourse-connectedness in the empirical analysis of preposed and postposed *if* and *when* clauses in a mystery novel. The hypotheses she finds supported are that *if* and *when* clauses have a broader scope when preposed, being thematically associated to the preceding discourse as well as the following main clause, while such clauses when postposed have a 'localized' scope, namely just the preceding main clause. And in the specific case of preposed *when* clauses she suggests that these 'form an integral part of the narrative in that they help to sequence the temporal contour of the main line of the narrative', while postposed *when* clauses 'only function as added comments to the main clause' (Ramsey 1987: 385). Clearly, some of my example sentences cited earlier are exceptions to Ramsey's latter generalization. A further distinction that may be relevant here is whether the adverbial clause, preposed or postposed, is part of the same informational unit as its main-clause partner (for example, in written text, not separated off by a comma). For Chafe (1984: 444) it is only the 'free' preposed adverbials (i.e. comprising a separate informational unit) that are properly 'guideposts' and orientational 'for the information in the upcoming main clause'. Judgements on these matters vary considerably, and again we may have to conclude that there are many different kinds of subordination, performing different functions, available to the language-user.

A linguist whose work has most forcibly demonstrated that the options within types of co-ordination and subordination comprise a repertoire that speakers and writers can draw upon is Halliday. In the process, he has been one of several to challenge the received notion that clausal subordination is particularly a feature of written text while spoken language is predominantly paratactic. In Halliday's view written language is marked more by its lexical density and complexity than by syntactic complexity; this lexical density reflects the static nature of written text. Spoken language, on the other hand, is distinguished by its dynamic complexity at the level of clause conjunction and by its 'intricacy of movement' (Halliday 1985b: 87). (These are more adventurous claims than Chafe's (1982) contrast of the 'integrated' nature of written discourse with the 'fragmented' nature of spoken language). Analysis of extracts in Halliday (1985b), and the findings of Beaman (1984), who worked with a more controlled corpus of spoken and written narratives, both show surprising reversals of the trends that have usually been assumed to hold:

> The nominal subordinate clause is, overall, the most frequent type of subordinate clause in both modalities [spoken and written

narrative samples]. Whereas the nonfinite nominals and adverbial subordinate clauses are more frequent in written narrative, finite nominals and adjectival subordinate clauses are more common in spoken. (Beaman 1984: 78)

Beaman's findings have been questioned (Chaika 1987); but they are in part confirmed by a more limited study of subordination in formal and informal discourse by Thompson (1984). Thompson first excludes from consideration those dependent clauses which are 'in constituency with' some preceding noun, verb, or preposition (i.e. restrictive relative clauses, and nominal clauses that complement verbs or prepositions, such as 'I don't believe in *giving money to charity*'). This set of clause types excluded from consideration are very largely those characterized above as 'bounded' and integrated within the superordinate clause. The 'unbounded' subordinate clauses Thompson does consider, in samples of formal and informal written text and of informal spoken text, are finite and non-finite adverbials and non-restrictive relatives. She finds that, as a group, these unbounded subordinates are scarcer in informal discourse (both spoken and written) than in formal written discourse; and within the group the non-finite verb forms and non-restrictive relatives seem to occur primarily in, and thus are associated with, writing.

The distinction proposed here between 'bounded' and 'unbounded' subordinate clauses may be an important basis for a parallel distinction, in discourse-structuring, between prominent and non-prominent informativeness. Thus the 'not new, not topical' characteristics mentioned above may apply particularly to 'bounded' subordination, while 'unbounded' subordination, intermediate between 'bounded' subordination and free main clauses, has greater possibilities of going against the functional grain and conveying new information or introducing a topic. However, when such subordinate structures – the arena of the background, as it were – do carry such prominent information, the effect will still be jarring and so, paradoxically, a kind of foregrounding. Yet again we see that a norm of use becomes a resource to be exploited in both the observance and the breach, and that what is of particular importance is that we have as accurate a sense as possible of the norm(s) involved.

Also of direct application to the present study will be Halliday's treatment of clause transitivity, and the role he ascribes to subordinate clauses in that account. I will not rehearse the basic elements of Hallidayan transitivity here: chapter 5 of Halliday (1985a) is the authoritative guide, while brief sketches and stylistic applications of the system can be found in Kennedy (1982), Burton (1982), Fowler (1986), and Toolan (1988). One point to emphasize is that Halli-dayan transitivity is more a semantic than a syntactic analysis, with many of the characteristics of a case grammar. A sentence is parsed in terms of the semantic process (material, mental, relational, and so on) expressed by the verb; the essential participants to that process are categorized in terms of a delimited set of possible roles (actor, goal, recipient, senser, carrier, and so on); and the reported circumstances surrounding or associated with the process, adverbial material speci-fying its extent, location, manner, cause, etc., are noted. Thus a Hallidayan transitivity analysis of a sentence identifies three fun-damental constituents: a process, the participants, and the more peripheral circumstances. And this in practice means that, in any complex sentence containing an adverbial clause, that entire sub-ordinate clause (which itself comprises a configuration of process, participants, and optional circumstances) is at a first level of analysis a single peripheral circumstance attending the process represented in the dominant clause.

A similar assumption is evident in chapter 7 of Halliday (1985a), where the nature of tactic and logico-semantic relations between the clauses in complex sentences is explored. The primary logico-semantic contrast is between 'expansion' and 'projection'. The types of projection are essentially the variant means of reporting speech or thought; examples include a first co-ordinate clause that 'projects' a second co-ordinate clause of direct speech (*He said 'I'm tired'*), and a first main clause that projects a second subordinate clause of indirect thought (*Mary thought John was tired*). The complexities of projection, and especially the ambiguous projections of free indirect discourse, are a recurrent theme of this study. However, as far as subordination is concerned, it is the logico-semantic relation of expansion that is of most relevance. Expansion can be of one of three kinds: elaboration, extension, and enhancement. Expansion by enhancement, hypotacti-cally related to a dominating clause, is the Hallidayan category for what are traditionally called adverbial subordinate clauses. Of such expansion by enhancement Halliday writes: 'One clause expands another by embellishing it: qualifying it with some circumstantial feature of time, place, cause or condition' (1985: 197).

Thus this grammatical account of the semantics of subordination is making appeal to its most general properties – its function of enhancement, embellishment, or circumstantial qualification. Much, however, remains to be explored concerning the specific impact of types of subordination as they are used in discourse. A substantial beginning is made by Thompson and Longacre, who argue that adverbial clauses, especially of time, function to 'maintain discourse perspective' (Thompson and Longacre 1985: 206). A travel guidebook they examine is dotted with clauses such as the following: 'As you walk through the huge chambers decorated with the great icy-looking columns . . .'. The 'huge chambers' and 'icy-looking columns' have been introduced in prior text; what is more noticeable is the assumption that you are walking or will walk through the chambers. A situation and a perspective are presupposed for readers; in effect, they are also imposed upon them.

Before closing this section, I wish to acknowledge the delimited nature of the analyses that follow, and how in chapter 10 so much less than a comprehensive study of all causal relations in the novel is attempted. The rejection of fixed-code bi-planarity (see chapters 1 and 2) forces the recognition that any expression has the potential, in principle, of conveying a causal relation. But in practice, in literary texts, familiar standard devices predominate and deserve to be the focus of attention. Indeed, the variety of secondary devices implying causality is so syntactically diverse, and productive of so much controversy when classifications are attempted, that they will have to be left largely unconsidered in this study. As Spitzer (1948) emphasized, stylistics must always proceed from the analysable to the seemingly unanalysable, from the patent to the latent. For this reason, most attention will be directed to the explicit co-ordinators and subordinators. Some note will also be made of those instances where there seems clear evidence of, for example, an implicit causal relation, where the character or narrator appears to have contrived to play down a causal explanation. These judgements may well involve what Dik (1968: 269) has termed 'interpretational probability', interpreting a particular sequence of expressions in the context of the entire section, or chapter, or novel. An instance of the difficulties of such analysis may be useful. The following extract shows how an overt resultative connection may often be replaced by the polysemantic connective *and*:

[the dogs which were supposed to hunt out Tomey's Turl knew him so well that] they greeted him instead with affection until even Tomey's Turl slowed down and he and the dogs all went into the woods together, walking, like they were going home from a rabbit hunt. *And* when they caught up with Uncle Buck in the woods, there was no Tomey's Turl and no dogs either . . . (p. 14; my emphasis)

A resultative relation is overtly expressed in the *until* that introduces the first reported consequence of the dogs' familiarity with Turl. But there is little question that Turl's good relationship with the dogs is also the cause of their subsequent absence from Uncle Buck's planned ambush in the woods. This second resultative relation must be inferred, being partially concealed by the use of *And*.

Another item which we may regard as occasionally substituting for a causal connective is the adverbial conjunct *now*. This is used to good effect in a tense three-sided confrontation between Edmonds, Lucas, and the salesman over who is the true owner of the mule Lucas has sold to the salesman:

[Edmonds told Lucas] 'That mule is going to be in her stall in my stable at sunup. Do you hear?' Now the salesman appeared suddenly at Lucas's elbow. Edmonds had forgotten about him.

'What mule is that?' he said. Edmonds turned the light on him for a moment. (p. 86)

We infer that the *Now* conveys not merely temporal sequence and narratorial 'proximity', but an additional sense that Edmonds's words were the cause of the salesman's sudden appearance. The salesman is responding to Edmonds's demand, of Lucas, that he return a mule which he (the salesman) believes himself to own. A little later Edmonds reiterates his instructions:

'Do you hear me?'

'I hear you,' Lucas said sullenly. Now the salesman spoke again. (p. 87)

Again, *Now* partly conceals a resultative connection. Immediately after, it is the salesman whose threatening remarks provoke a response from Edmonds. Once more, the resultative relation is partly concealed through the use of a temporal adjunct:

'All right, big boy. . . . If that mule is moved . . . I'm going to telephone the sheriff. Do you hear that too?' This time Edmonds jumped, flung, the light beam at the salesman's face.

'Were you talking to me, sir?' he said.

'No,' the salesman said. 'I'm talking to him. And he heard me.'
For a moment longer Edmonds held the beam on the other.

STYLISTICIANS ON SUBORDINATION

Stylistic studies of subordination in prose fiction begin, in the modern period, with Spitzer's study of a seeming compulsion to attribute causes in the narrative of C.-L. Philippe's *Bubu de Montparnasse*. This compulsion Spitzer relates directly to his sense of the writer's *Weltanschauung*. Although Spitzer's preoccupation with the 'psychological etymon' of the author – style as authorial expression – has found some favour with subsequent style critics (Ohmann 1964; Freeman 1975), my own study will assume that explanations of such effects must first be in terms of textual strategy and aesthetic effect.

More recently, Hayes (1969) has offered a statistical and transformational approach to style in his analysis of the contrasting complexities of sentences in Gibbon and Hemingway. But Hayes makes an imaginative leap from notation of statistically significant syntactic contrasts between the two writers' styles to the declaration that:

> The table [of statistics] indicates what we already knew intuitively, that the styles of Gibbon and Hemingway are different – that the style of Gibbon is 'grand', 'majestic', 'complex', and that the style of Hemingway in comparison is 'simple'. (Hayes 1969: 88)

In fact, Hayes's statistics cannot in themselves make any such declarations about the style. Rather they quantify solely syntactic differences between the selected passages – and these are typically not foreknown. In his use of the word 'complex' in the quoted sentence, he commits the familiar fault of blithely importing the syntactic sense into the literary description-cum-evaluation. Smit (1988: 23) notes the same tendency in other stylisticians, and correctly describes it as taking a grammatical description and applying it thematically.

The strategy of comparing two passages in order to perceive stylistic distinctiveness is also adopted by Gibson (1969) in his more informal analysis of a passage from Howells's *A Modern Instance* and the opening of Hemingway's *A Farewell to Arms*. The former is said to blend causal co-ordination and subordination, while the latter consists almost wholly of co-ordinated clauses. The absence of subordination in the Hemingway passage, in Gibson's opinion, assists it in its promotion of a stance of familiarity with the reader. He argues that Hemingway's lack of subordination reflects a deepseated reticence: a lack of subordinates involves absence of extended (i.e. finite-verb-structured) nominal, relative, or adverbial clause information. That is to say, it involves an absence of extended identification of subjects and objects (or agents, beneficiaries, and goals, and their spatial, temporal, and causal contexts). Regrettably, Gibson conducted no analysis of the relative degrees of non-finite qualification in the passages, an important alternative means of providing contextualization in texts.

Gibson's conclusion concerning Frederic Henry, the narrator of *A Farewell to Arms*, is that he is a 'tough talker' who conceals his vulnerability by claiming only limited knowledge of the story he tells, and who narrates via a limited rhetoric, involving short sentences, verbal repetition, and the colloquial speech of an assumed speaker–listener familiarity. He adds: 'He lets his reader make logical and other connections. . . . He prefers naming things to describing them, and avoids modification, especially when suggestive of value' (Gibson 1969: 235). Reasonable as these views may appear, from a stylistician's point of view they require greater substantiation and greater investigation. Gibson's two samples of text, for example, are perilously brief, and no comprehensive statistics concerning any syntactic feature are presented. In long texts internal stylistic variation, development within the narrative as it proceeds, must be a focus of the analyst's attention. It would be interesting to know if Henry is as 'tough', and tough in the same way, at the end as at the beginning of the novel.

Hemingway is also treated in the work of Wells (1969), who offers statistical comparison of his style with that of Hemingway and Fitzgerald. In her choice of writers for study, clearly, she avoids some of the criticisms (in terms of incompatibility of genre, culture, or period) that might be levelled at Hayes. And her work can be usefully related to Gibson's. Thus she suggests that, although Frederic Henry may have been a tough talker, later Hemingway narrators are more eloquent: 'The progression from the style of *In Our Time* to the style of *For Whom the Bell Tolls* was a progression toward more complexity and variety in all matters except diction' (Wells 1969: 48). Furthermore, aspects of Well's methodology seem sensible adjustments to conditions: she analyses quite lengthy stretches of prose from Fitzgerald's 'The Rich Boy' and Hemingway's 'Big Two-Hearted River', and confines herself to narrative passages. Too often earlier stylistic analyses had lumped together prose and dialogue, disregarding the intuitive conviction of most readers that the language of the narrator and what counts as the direct speech of characters are often two distinct styles (and that each character may have his or her own distinct style of speech).

Wells finds that the early Hemingway's sentences are, on average, half the length of Fitzgerald's (12 words and 24 words, respectively, and that 73 per cent of Fitzgerald's sentences are complex or compound-complex, while only 25 per cent of Hemingway's are. All this relates to early Hemingway: in the later work, these stylistic contrasts between the two writers are attenuated. Her conclusion, however – that Hemingway's early monoclausal writing is 'child-like', while his later style is more mature – is far too sweeping and indiscriminate.

Wells notes, as does Gibson, that Hemingway eschews causal connectives. That this should be the case in a first-person novel such as *A Farewell to Arms*, in which Frederic Henry is both main character and narrator, is not wholly surprising. But it can also occur in non-first-person novels, such as *Go Down, Moses*, where scarcity of causal connectives is overlooked because of the attention given to subsuming technique, that of free indirect discourse (FID). FID is often the verbal rendering of a character 'thinking aloud'; and individuals involved in such an activity do not usually need to furnish themselves with the causal links between their world-interpreting observations. If thought proceeds swifter than the verbal rendering of thought, a vivid stylistic impression of rendered thought may well involve dispensing with such syntactic features as semantically specific clause connectors. Where causal subordinators do persist, in FID passages in *Go Down, Moses*, I shall argue that a quite specific local effect, of strained and compulsive ratiocination or self-justification, is conveyed.

There seems some justification for positing a cline charting the overt semantic relatedness of sentences/clauses in a text. The use of specific subordinators would mark one end of that cline; then, reflecting less specific semantic relations, would come the mono-semantic co-ordinators *but*, *or*, and *for*; next would come use of the polysemantic connective *and*; and finally the least specific formal means of expressing relation, linkage by intra-sentential punctuation. These four steps on the cline are simply the most immediately apparent: there are numerous ways of using clause-internal adverbials, for example, to signal linkage with adjacent text (see Altenberg 1984); and Mann and Thompson (1986) is only one of the most recent studies to demonstrate that in coherent texts there are necessarily inferred relational propositions (of elaboration, solutionhood, motivation, reason, etc.) that hold between distinct sentences, often without any formal indicators. But the four levels of formally signalled interclausal linkage are perhaps the most prominent and uncontroversial. Of the last of these levels of connectivity, that of sentence-internal punctuation, we may predict that it will occur relatively more commonly in texts which purport to transcribe the unedited flow of a particular individual's thoughts, such as passages of stream-of-consciousness in modernist novels. Even a brief glance at the FID and stream-of-consciousness passages of novels by Woolf and Joyce supports such a specific prediction, and the entire hypothesized cline also. At the opposite end from such linguistically a-connective, subjective-expressive prose, we may expect texts with high frequency of connectives (especially subordinating and/or causal ones) to signal detached, objective discourse. If such a cline holds valid in relation to the rendering of various degrees of intimacy of consciousness, it does so, it should be stressed, since it is a reading of a well-developed literary convention. The claim here is thus not about any mental or psychological reality or verisimilitude in the reduced syntax adopted in the presentation of stream-of-consciousness.

Among earlier analysts who discuss subordination and causal clauses specifically in Faulkner, Zoellner (1959) notes the suspension and enclosure of material, within cocoons of more peripheral information, in a manner that runs counter to the reader's expectation of 'secondary' material appearing chiefly in embedded clauses. Similarly Zink (1954: 393) writes of an impression of 'a pervasive syntactical continuousness, a quality of intense suspension'. But neither of these studies draws on detailed linguistic analysis, and both suffer from a debilitating observational generality which Dillon (1978: 175) notes to be a permanent danger of style commentary.

Ohmann's 'Generative grammars and the concept of literary style' (1964) was inspirational for style students with respect to a range of topics, but some of its central assumptions are certainly contentious. Applying an early transformational syntactic grammar to sentences in 'The Bear', Ohmann judges Faulkner's style to be 'additive', on the basis of the high frequency of relative, conjunction, and comparative transformations in the analysed passage. He treats these three 'additive' transformations as preserving the semantic load of underlying sentences. He argues that the two sentences *The threads were impalpable* and *The threads were frail* may be transformed via relativization, conjunction, or comparison thus:

(a) The threads which were impalpable were frail.
(b) The threads were frail and impalpable.
(c) The threads were more frail than impalpable.

There seem good reasons for objecting to the forms of Ohmann's transformed sentences (a) and (c), which arguably should be respectively

The threads, which were impalpable, were frail.

and

The threads were as frail as they were impalpable.

But in any case his argument is more centrally weakened by his claim that the three transforms are 'somewhat similar, both formally and semantically' (Ohmann 1964: 143). The implication is that all three transformations are essentially 'additive', and distinct from each other only in some minor respects. An entirely contrary conclusion could be drawn: the semantic contrasts between these transforms are arguably of significance in their own right, and should be fully explored before proceeding to claims about how 'syntactic preferences correlate with habits of meaning that tell us something about [an author's] mode of conceiving experience' (154).

A final point of orientation will be Radomski's (1974) doctoral thesis, 'Faulkner's style: a stylistic analysis'. Radomski compares frequencies of certain familiar syntactic devices in two passages of 1,000 words taken from Faulkner and Hemingway respectively, and finds a general tendency in the Faulkner passage (from *Intruder in the Dust*) towards considerable nominalization, little passivization, and many infinitival and participial constructions. He suggests that the frequent subordination 'indicates that Faulkner is continually re-evaluating and changing the perspective of the action he is viewing' (Radomski; 1974: 72), a suggestion that makes the large assumptions that it is indeed Faulkner (and not some textual persona) who views and reports on the action in the passage, and that subordination is especially indicative of change of evaluation and change of perspective. He also suggests that reading Faulkner is 're-creative', since 'Faulkner's subordination indicates a tendency on the part of the author to think in "causal chains" dependent on past history or preceding events or ideas, which are often unspecified or revealed only in future narrative – sometimes even in other works' (90). Again two claims stand out here as in need of fuller scrutiny: the claim that a textual pattern is to be treated as a 'tendency on the part of the author' (style as authorial expression – the Spitzer–Ohmann tradition – noted by Smit (1988)); and the claim that subordination invokes causes and contexts without adequately specifying them.

The studies mentioned above are an eloquent reminder of how difficult it is to pinpoint the essential dynamics and effects of Faulkner's writing. Additionally, for all their achievements, these studies also reveal a pervasive tendency to move from concrete but intractable grammatical descriptions and frequencies to abstract and suggestive interpretative verdicts, without benefit of an adequate account of why just these syntactic patterns have just the particular literary effects claimed. By adequacy of account I do not mean some conclusive demonstration or proof that a certain grammatical pattern must carry the claimed effect or value. The very idea of conclusive proofs, in relation to the shifting values and significations of human language, belies subjection to the language myth described in earlier chapters. As was suggested there, adequacy of account of a linguistic description must be a matter of the persuasiveness and appropriacy of the interpretative steps taken in a commentary, including the persuasiveness of the interpretative steps taken at the outset, in the adoption of a particular descriptive grammatical apparatus.

SAMPLING THE SYNTAX

Let me talk now. I'm trying to explain to the head of my family something which I have got to do which I dont quite understand myself, not in justification of it but to explain it if I can. I could say I dont know why I must do it but that I do know that I have got myself to have to live with for the rest of my life and all I want is peace to do it in. (Ike addressing Cass, p. 288)

Ike McCaslin in 'The Bear', section IV, is explicitly concerned with explaining his actions, if he can – even if he 'dont quite understand' them himself. But all through *Go Down, Moses* the reader is concerned to understand the characters and know why it is that Lucas, Roth, and Ike think and act as they do. Ike's attempt to explain things to Cass breaks down in mutual incomprehension (p. 300), and we may feel that Ike does not ever fully understand himself: 'Isaac McCaslin's ends, although simple enough in their apparent motivation, were and would be always incomprehensible to him [i.e. Ike himself]' (pp. 309–10). The reader, however, persists in the attempt to understand and evaluate characters, to 'compassionate' with them, as Faulkner once described the process (Gwynn and Blotner 1959: 277). In doing so he or she is directed in part by the narrator's revealing perspectival alignments with characters, in which patterns of subordination and causal connectivity play an important part.

In order to have some sense of the details of the narrative's sentential structuring at different points in the novel, I have drawn up structural descriptions of the first five sentences of all nineteen major sections of the text (i.e. the four sections of 'Was', the three of 'The Fire and the Hearth', the two of 'Pantaloon in Black', the three of 'The Old People', the five of 'The Bear', and the single main sections of 'Delta Autumn' and 'Go Down, Moses'). Table 8 shows the frequencies, for each section opening, of main clauses, finite and non-finite subordinate clauses, of finite-clause subordinators, and of the three chief types of subordinate clause – nominal, relative, and adverbial.

Many problems of analysis in compiling table 8 have been resolved on a practical basis. How, for example, is one to mark the opening section of 'Was,' or the opening paragraphs of 'The Bear', section IV, in terms of sentential boundaries? Pragmatically, any period punctuation provided by Faulkner is recognized as marking a sentence boundary. But paragraphing too, even where the text lacks a period at the close of one paragraph and an upper-case letter at the opening of the next, is treated as a sentential limiter. Thus in my reading 'Was', section I, contains four sentences, two of which are non-finite.

A second problem relates to the decision to restrict the analysis to narrative sentences. On this basis, sentences of the form 'He said, "I hear you"' are passed over in the identification of the first five wholly narrative sentences of a section. On the more specific level of structural description, many appositive clauses (usually non-finite) have been interpreted as dependent relatives. Thus in

> General Compson and Walter Ewell invented a plan (1) ... –
> an invention doubtless of the somewhat childish old General (2)
> (p. 315; my clause numberings)

while clause 2 is in apposition to 1, it is here described as a non-finite dependent relative clause. In several cases, however, it seems more accurate to describe the additive relation such as that of 4 to 3 in

> He could say it (3), himself and his cousin juxtaposed (4) (p. 254)

as one in which 4 is a non-finite adverbial clause of contingency. As many have recognized, non-finite and reduced clauses typically carry the counterposed qualities of greater versatility of use, on the one hand, but lesser semantic independence and specificity on the other. Dillon remarks:

> There is an almost paradoxical combination of inexplicitness in
> surface marking and tightness of semantic dependence: essentially,
> reduction makes the material even more dependent on the main
> clause, even less capable of making a comment or adding New
> information than the non-reduced clause. (Dillon 1981: 140)

Consequently interpreters processing such clauses must draw more heavily on their powers of inference, rather than simply on powers of decoding, in deriving a possibly intended sense.

A clear difficulty in generalizing from the findings of table 8 lies in the fact that they relate solely to the openings of the nineteen sections. On what basis, if any, can we be confident that the tendencies revealed here are consistent throughout the relevant sections? It is possible that in many cases the trends evident at the openings of sections are not maintained, that the shifting context of the narrative leads to substantial stylistic adjustments. In Labovian terms, many of these opening passages may have Abstract or Orientational characteristics, and no others. At the same time, however, it is widely acknowledged that the opening of a text or subsection of text, at which a tone of general perspective may be established that will be sustained throughout that text, is a particularly salient place to subject to stylistic analysis. And in this collective novel the section openings are themselves 'connectives', placing the ensuing narrative in relation to the just completed section, alerting the reader to the new narrative orientation. In those cases where I do make claims about the persistence, through a section, of prominent features noted in the section's

Table 8 Distribution of connectives and clause types in five-sentence samples from the opening of each novel section

	main cl.	finite sub. cl.	n.-finite sub.cl.	fin.-cl. subords	sub.-cl. type nom.	Rel.	Adv.
'Was' I	2	23	20	19	2	23	18
'Was' II	17	9	8	7	1	6	10
'Was' III	6	11	7	8	0	3	15
'Was' IV	8	10	4	13	0	1	13
'Fire/Hearth' 1	8	6	4	6	0	5	6
'Fire/Hearth' 2	8	2	2	2	0	1	3
'Fire/Hearth' 3	10	7	7	6	1	6	7
'Pantaloon' 1	11	14	7	8	2	13	6
'Pantaloon' 2	11	3	3	3	0	5	1
'Old People' 1	7	7	10	4	0	9	7
'Old People' 2	9	1	1	1	1	1	0
'Old People' 3	7	2	1	2	0	1	2
'The Bear' I	4	4	1	3	0	2	3
'The Bear' II	7	0	2	0	0	0	1
'The Bear' III	7	3	8	1	2	5	3
'The Bear' IV	3	34	23	27	7	28	22
'The Bear' V	6	11	9	8	4	6	10
'Delta Autumn'	5	8	2	4	0	6	4
'Go Down, Moses'	9	4	6	2	1	7	2
Totals	145	159	125	124	21	128	133
Sample norms	8	8	7	7	1	7	7

opening, I shall support the claims by reference to samples of subsequent text in that section.

A first step in analysing table 8 may be taken by concentrating on the first two columns, which record the numbers of main and subordinate clauses within each sample. The variations in frequency here reflect the fluctuating emphasis in the text's syntax, now on co-ordination, now on subordination. The sample norms, for main clauses and subordinate clauses, are 7.6 and 8.4 respectively. But there are many distinct departures from these norms, and these marked frequencies will be the focus of the discussion that follows.

'Was', section I, a sample consisting of only four sentences, shares the distinction of 'The Bear', section IV, of containing two sentences lacking a finite main clause. It is also like 'The Bear', section IV, in its compensating density of subordination. In fact the co-ordination:subordination ratio in 'Was', section I (2:33), is almost identical to that of 'The Bear', section IV (3:34). As this analysis proceeds, the stylistic continuity of these spatially removed sections will become increasingly clear. It is a continuity which, in a sense, is not remarkable, in view of the compositional history of these two sections. Whereas versions of most of the stories were completed and submitted for publication in the late 1930s, 'Was', section I, and 'The Bear', section IV, were both composed rather later (spring and autumn 1941 respectively). They were specifically written for the book, one of their functions being to knit the various stories into a fictional whole (see Blotner 1974: 1,068–95; Creighton 1977). The heavy emphasis on subordination in these two sections may reflect the absence of narrative events here, and their distinct function of discursive contextualization and explanation – purposes more naturally served by nominal material than verbal. Dillon (1981: 126–44), in a discriminating assessment of the nature and functions of subordination, gives qualified support for the view that subordinated material is never foregrounded material, never Topical, though it may be New. Along these lines, the two sections under consideration contain few foregrounded facts – and no foregrounded events – but an elaborate fabric of background information.

The whole of 'Was', section I, can be viewed as a situation-establishing act of identificatory description, effected by means of a single, multiply complex, multiply modified noun phrase. The section is far more an explanation of a situation than a report of events. The narrator describes the essentials of Ike's condition as concisely as possible. Having performed this task, the narrator-as-detached-commentator virtually disappears from view. There is an almost obsessive chaining of relative clauses:

> But Isaac was not one of these – a widower these twenty years, who in all his life had owned but one object more than he could wear and carry in his pockets . . . and this was the narrow iron cot . . . – which he used camping in the woods . . . who owned no property . . . who lived still in the cheap frame bungalow in Jefferson which his wife's father gave them on their marriage and which his wife had willed to him at their death and which he had pretended to accept . . . (p. 3)

The claim that 'Was', section I, is stylistically and compositionally distinct from the rest of 'Was' (in which Ike does not figure at all) is certainly supported with regard to the contrasting syntactic structure of the samples from sections II to IV. Sections III and IV have unremarkable frequencies of main and subordinate clauses, while section II is noteworthy for its density of main clauses, averaging three per sentence. Sections II–IV are told largely (and indirectly) from the perspective of young Cass: the five analysed sentences of section II are the first to come from his perspective. They convey both the chaotic progress of the fox-chase, and Cass's tendency simply to record events, without organization or comment, as though caught up in the simple experiencing of them:

> When he and Uncle Buck ran back to the house from discovering that Tomey's Turl had run again, they heard Uncle Buddy cursing and bellowing in the kitchen, then the fox and the dogs came out of the kitchen and crossed the hall into the dogs' room and they heard them run through the dogs' room into his and Uncle Buck's room, then they saw them cross the hall again into Uncle Buddy's room and heard them run through Uncle Buddy's room into the kitchen and this time . . . (p. 4)

The quite different clausal structuring here from that at the opening of 'Was', section I, then, reflects and contributes to the quite different purposes that the two passages serve.

The next sections that merit further inspection seem to be the two sections of 'Pantaloon in Black'. These have a relatively high number of main clauses (11 each); but, while section 1 has a commensurately high frequency of subordinates, section 2 has very few. The opening of the story is a highly eventful passage, full of description of action rather than explanation of it (thus, both in its syntax as in its content, virtually the converse of 'Was', section I, or 'The Bear', section IV). To that extent, the density of main and subordinate clauses here aptly reflects the entire section's emphasis on constant restless motion, as Rider wrestles with his grief. But section 2's sample may be offered as further evidence of the remarkable fit between patterns in the language of certain narrative passages, and the effecting of temporary perspectival alignment with specific characters.

It was suggested above that there is a congruence between chains of co-ordinated statements recording events as if with breathless excitement, and the perspective or 'mind-style' of the young Cass, in 'Was', section II. Here a congruence is contrived between the syntactic form of the narrative and the 'mind-style' of the deputy. For the narrative's frequency of main clauses and absence of subordination seems wholly compatible with the deputy's response to events, a response which is an excited and disorganized flood of statements (no reflective organization of material into a foreground and a background has been undertaken). The deputy is 'a little hysterical' (p. 154): so too is this opening passage. It articulates his unthinking and compassionless attachment to the status quo. Sentences 1 and 4 are the key ones. In sentence 1, the final procedures of officialdom in relation to Rider are telescoped into a parenthetical series of formulaic statements (quoted here on p. 133). And sentence 4 runs:

> The deputy had been out of bed and in motion ever since the jail delivery shortly before midnight of yesterday and had covered considerable ground since, and he was spent now from lack of sleep and hurried food at hurried and curious hours and, sitting in a chair beside the stove, a little hysterical too. (p. 154)

Rider is not designated by name, but only by such definite descriptions as *the prisoner* or *the body*. In this second section of 'Pantaloon in Black', then, the narrator treats Rider as impersonally as he did the salesman in 'The Fire and the Hearth', chapter 2. But for the reader, of course, the situation is very different in the case of Rider, and another kind of irony is being adopted. Our sense of the narrator appearing to endorse – or at least not challenge – the prejudice and inhumanity of the deputy whose experience is reported only heightens our understanding that Rider is a victim of a complex of hostile forces. As often before, it needs to be stressed that the style here is not mimetic of, for example, dehumanizing dismissal: it constitutes it.

The total absence of finite subordinates at the opening of 'The Bear', section II (the only sample so devoid of them), seems due to this passage's status as the indirect empathetic rendering of Ike's viewpoint. Furthermore, this is not simply the FID rendering of the 13-year-old Ike's viewpoint, as the opening sentences indicate:

> So *he should have* hated and feared Lion. He was thirteen *then*. (p. 159; my emphases)

Such comments are from the perspective of a mature Ike. Other sentences, however, may well be the FID rendering of the young Ike's views:

> By *now* he was a better woodsman than most grown men with more [experience]. (my emphasis)

Such juxtaposed sentences are as clear an indication as any of the important switching of narratorial perspectival alignment that often occurs. In sentences such as 'He should have hated and feared Lion', the modal auxiliary of obligation is used, of responses (hating and fearing) that the young Ike evidently did not have. That this subordinator-less passage should be largely in FID also seems to confirm a hypothesis already touched upon: that character-aligned styles generally tend to curtail subordination in favour of co-ordinated or merely paratactic structures. Accordingly, I take the predominance of simple or compound structures here, together with such indicators of FID as *now* (with past tense) and such conversational particles as *so* and *even*, as cumulative evidence for treating these lines as perspectivally empathetic with Ike, even an articulation of his viewpoint – openly proud of his early maturity and excellence as a hunter and woodsman.

A final distinctive main:subordinate clause ratio among the samples is that for the opening of 'Go Down, Moses'. While there are plentiful main clauses, there are only four subordinate ones. Moreover, although two of the narrative sentences are framed by direct speech, the infrequency of subordinates cannot be due solely to that constraint here, as it may be in chapter 2 of 'The Fire and the Hearth' and section 3 of 'The Old People'. Rather we have a further example of congruence between narratorial style and narratorial topic: a Faulknerian version of the tough-talk manner that Gibson (1969) ascribed to Hemingway's narrator, Frederic Henry. The parallels, in frequency of major syntactic structures, between the opening of 'Go Down, Moses' and an early Hemingway narrative or a Chandler narrative are striking. Of course, the narratorial voice is not Beauchamp's – as the passage's many comments critical of his appearance confirm. But it is the voice of a speaker who wishes to appear tough, like Beauchamp, and slick, worldly-wise, and defiant:

> The face was black, smooth, impenetrable; the eyes had seen too much. . . . He wore one of those sports costumes called ensembles in the men's shop advertisements, shirt and trousers matching and cut from the same fawn-colored flannel and they had cost too much and were draped too much, with too many pleats. (p. 369)

Much of the hostility conjured here inheres in the recurring phrases of excess: the *too much* (three times) and *too many*. This repetition may be set beside the motif of *not enough*, discussed in chapter 8.

TURMOIL AND EFFORT IN LUCAS AND ROTH

Extending the comparison of the experiences and viewpoints of Lucas and Roth, I have analysed two brief passages which show temporary narratorial alignment with each of these characters. The passages chosen are the final two paragraphs of section I of chapter 1 of 'The Fire and the Hearth' (pp. 40–1), narrated from Lucas's viewpoint, and the text that runs from the middle of p. 84 to the middle of p. 86, which is narrated from Roth's viewpoint.

These were selected because of their similarities of theme and content, operating on two quite dissimilar characters. Both passages record incidents in which degrees of 'mental turmoil and physical effort' (p. 84) are experienced by the protagonists, in the arrival at some fairly minor discovery. They also reveal stylistic continuities between the reported behaviour of the two men (e.g. both are reported as 'whirling' and 'leaping' in sudden reaction to surprise) and certain stylistic contrasts also, contrasts which seem to reflect underlying differences in their self-images. In the Lucas passage, pp. 40–1, the old man, tired but excited after a night spent hiding his whisky still and looking for gold, disturbs his spying daughter, whose precipitate flight does not prevent Lucas from identifying her, drawing elaborate inferences to explain her behaviour, and adjusting his plans accordingly. In the passage about Edmonds, the younger man exhausts himself pursuing what he believes to be mule-thieves, only to make the maddening discovery that, as was known to the lotmen all along, the culprits are Lucas and George.

In terms of transitivity (Halliday 1985a), the clauses of the Lucas passage are characteristically ones of material process (23 of 34) rather than mental process (4) or relational (7). Of the material-process clauses, 15 are one-participant, middle-voice clauses, and 8 are two-participant, operative-voice ones; only 6 of them, all one-participant, have Lucas as clause subject (and, since there is a sole participant, 'affected' rather than truly 'agentive'). In general, 'thematic' position and 'agentive' role are reserved for entities, in the scene, of which Lucas takes skilful account – the light, the slide, the fleeing quarry, the situation (*it*), and the prying intruders. Only in one short passage is Lucas the active subject:

> He rose to his feet. But he still could not straighten up completely. With one hand pressed to his back and still bent over a little he began to walk stiffly toward a clump of sapling cottonwoods . . .

when something crashed into flight within or beyond it and rushed on, the sound fading and already beginning to curve away toward the edge of the jungle while he stood for perhaps ten seconds, slackjawed with amazed and incredulous comprehension. . . . Then he whirled and leaped . . . running parallel with it, leaping with incredible agility and speed . . . (p. 40; my ellipses)

Precisely where Lucas needs to respond swiftly and intelligently, he does so; and subsequently we find the FID rendering of his deliberations in a network of self-directed stipulations concerning what, for Lucas, would be desirable future developments, expressed in the recurring modal verb *must*:

So that was that. . . . In a way, it even simplified things. Even if there had been time . . . it would do no good to move his still to another hiding-place. Because when they [i.e. the police] came to the mound to dig they must not only find something, they must find it quick and at once . . . which would cause them to desist and go away. . . . Because . . . George Wilkins must go. He must be on his way before another night had passed. (p. 41)

Despite considerable difficulties (old age, fatigue, stiffness), Lucas is canny enough to track his fleeing observer (he runs not towards the fugitive but parallel with him/her). He does so with a skill and success absent from Roth's strivings on pp. 84–6. As the narrative succinctly expresses it, Lucas responds to the startling turns of events here, as elsewhere, with 'incredulous comprehension' (p. 37). This near-oxymoron indicates that, while he is surprised by events, he still understands them. Roth Edmonds, however, appears to remain both surprised and uncomprehending.

The slightly longer narrative passage on pp. 84–6, aligned with Roth, contains 58 finite clauses. Compared with the Lucas passage, there are proportionately fewer material-process clauses (31) and many more mental-process ones (16). The material-process clauses divide into 18 middle-, 11 operative-, and 2 receptive-voice clauses; and as many as 18 of these have Roth as grammatical subject. Taken together with the many mental-process clauses, all with Roth as subject and processor, they confirm the passage's preoccupation with Roth's thoughts and actions, by contrast with the Lucas passage. It is a preoccupation which, in this context of narrative alignment, highlights Roth's self-pity and the tendency of his egocentricity to disrupt a balanced response and adjustment to unforeseen developments in the course of his personal turmoil and effort. Despite Roth's noted repeated occupation of subject position in the clause, the implication that he is thereby controlling agent of events is repeatedly undercut. In this way the text's syntax conveys Roth's efforts after control and direction, while exposing the emptiness of those claims. The second sentence of the passage runs:

> He expected to find the marks where the mule had been loaded into a waiting truck, whereupon he would return home and telephone to the sheriff in Jefferson and to the Memphis police to watch the horse-and-mule markets tomorrow. (p. 84)

Typically, Roth is here subject and agentive participant in mental-process and material-process clauses. But Roth's expectations and conditional plans are immediately foiled: 'There were no such marks.' Characteristically, Roth is subject in material-process clauses without being fully agentive (often, as here, because his actions are reported in *irrealis* clauses: the finding of marks and telephoning of the authorities are expected developments which do not eventuate). Instead he is the passive experiencer, more an affected participant than an initiator or causer of events.

A fuller example of this occurs where the narrative reports that Roth 'was walking too now', like his lotmen –

> *lest he dash his brains out against a limb*, stumbling and thrashing among briers and undergrowth . . . leading the mare with one hand and fending his face with the other arm and trying to watch his feet, *so that he walked into one of the mules*, instinctively leaping in the right direction as it lashed viciously back at him with one hoof, before he discovered that the negroes had stopped. Then, cursing aloud now and leaping quickly again to avoid the invisible second mule which would be somewhere on that side . . . (p. 84; my emphases)

In both of the italicized material-process clauses Roth is grammatical subject; he is also, in practice, the potential victim in both events (Roth's walking into the mules is an accidental result, not an intentional one, and the act threatens him, not the mules, with injury). The pervasive impression that Roth's problems and injuries are at least in part unwittingly self-inflicted is nicely sustained by the *so that* connective here. Interclausal *so that* can carry both purposive and resultative readings, and while we come to see that the latter must be the sense intended here it is hard completely to expunge the purposive reading (which makes Edmonds seem so ludicrous) we may have briefly considered. For purpose connectives are in evidence elsewhere here: *lest* is introductory of purposely avoided circumstances, and Edmonds proceeds to leap on purpose a second time, 'to avoid the invisible second mule'.

Elsewhere Roth occupies subject position but remains a dependent or submissive subordinate. Thus 'he *followed* the two shadowy mules' and 'He *relinquished* the reins' (my emphases). In addition, both passages have several causal connectives; but while those in the Roth passage relate to relatively minor purposes, or are conditional upon hypothetical events, those in the Lucas passage are much more to do with broad interpretations – by Lucas – of the implications of actual events. At one point in the extract Roth does for once explicitly act independently: 'He went on without waiting'. But his actions are not ratiocinative, as Lucas's are on pp. 40–1; they are merely a response to the stimuli of hot rage and 'eagerness'. His ill-judged excitement seems to be mocked in the literariness of the narrative here: 'It was hot, and there was an eagerness upon him, a kind of vindictive exultation as he plunged on, heedless of underbrush or log'. When Roth is on the very point of coming face to face with his 'thieves', the lotman Dan murmuringly discloses the banal facts of the situation, that the men ahead of them are George and Lucas:

> He [Edmonds] stopped dead in his tracks. He whirled. He was not only about to perceive the whole situation in its complete and instantaneous entirety, as when the photographer's bulb explodes, but he knew now that he had seen it all the while and had refused to believe it purely and simply because he knew that when he did accept it, his brain would burst.

In this elaborate simile, Roth should, strictly speaking, be equated with the photographer, capturing the 'arrested' figures in the scene in their nefarious and abruptly exposed activity. However, the sentence structure, in which the flashbulb is topicalized and the photographer himself is not mentioned, invites us to see Roth (or at least his mental faculties) as more like the bulb, both of them being passive, manipulated, explosive instruments. In this situation, Roth seems to have no more chance of employing his brain without causing it to burst than a photographer has of using a flashbulb without causing it to explode. This long third sentence is also linguistically marked in its nesting of interconnected mental-process clauses. What is really at issue in this passage is not perceptual illumination but its adjunct, cognitional illumination, as the high frequency of verbs of cognition suggests. In contrast with Lucas's startled, incredulous comprehension, his reponse of 'incredible agility', we see Roth's ill-judged eagerness and rage, and his near-apopleptic reaction, in which 'He could neither breathe nor see for a moment'.

SOME GENERAL COMMENTS ON SUBORDINATION IN THE NARRATIVE

As table 8 shows, nominal subordinate clauses are rare in the section-initial passages analysed in the previous section. Nominal clauses, like noun phrases, are normally abstract, referring to events, states, or ideas rather than to objects; and low frequency of nominal clauses may reflect narratorial reluctance to state facts and events overtly when they may be dramatized. (On the possible consequences of nominalized style, see Halliday (1967 and 1985b).) As literary critics such as Beck, Zink, and Aiken have noted, Faulkner's narrators habitually resist and delay the setting down of any facts or judgements that would have the effect of foreclosing the enquiry into grounds and contexts, in favour of a dense contextualization, so that an event as slight as a gesture of the hand may be qualified and explicated by a page or more of text situating that gesture within both the individual's present circumstances and his or her past history. Such strategies of contextualization almost inevitably lead to a relative preponderance, among finite and non-finite subordinate clauses, of relatives and adverbials.

As indicated earlier, it is the clauses of reason that should be of particular interest, as potential syntactic indicators of distinct and shifting narratorial perspective and character empathy. Adverbial subordinators in general seem much more likely to function in this way, since they generally have the most specific semantic force of all the connectives. These semantic compartmentalizations are not watertight, in that certain adverbial connectives may be used for more than one category of clause (e.g. *even if* occurs with clauses of both concession and condition; *as* occurs with ones of manner, comparison, time, and reason). Yet in the majority of cases disambiguation of occurrences in context is almost immediate. This fact, taken together with the sample-based evidence that 75 per cent of finite subordinates have a co-occurring subordinator (124 of 159), is strong support for the belief that there are discernible constraints operating in this area of subordinate adverbial clauses. In most cases, a connective is expected; and in most cases the semantic category of that connective is predetermined by prior informational choices at the level of the clause. Interest may then centre on those instances (presumably a minority of cases) where the narrator appears to have taken pains to resist the unexceptional submission to expectations and predeterminations. In formal terms this resistance to supplying the expected connective may issue in one of a small number of ways:

1 Ellipsis of the subordinator, with or without punctuation to mark clause boundary.
2 Distortion or blurring of the interclausal semantic relation by insertion of, for example, an ambiguous connective like *so* (which may signal purpose or result) or *when*:

He quit his job when he couldn't stand it any longer.
[less temporal than causal]
Why do you say that when you know it's not true?
[less temporal than conditional/concessive]

3 Suppletion of a more specific connective by a more general, all-purpose one such as *and*:

I hadn't been listening to him, *and* he flew into a rage.

The data would suggest that roughly half the narrative's finite subordinate clauses are adverbial, and that the majority of these are either of reason, time, or comparison – in that order of frequency; 46 (62 per cent) of the 76 finite adverbial clauses in the samples are clauses of reason. It is perhaps worth noting in passing that high frequencies of finite clauses of reason are present in the samples from 'Was', sections I and IV, and 'The Bear', section IV (the first and third of which have already received some discussion), but a broader base for interpretative manoeuvres is both desirable and operationally feasible in this well-defined area. Accordingly an analysis was made of all causal connectives in the narrative part of *Go Down, Moses*. An exploration of both the specific and general implications of the careful deployment of these forms in the narrative constitutes the topic of the following chapter.

10

CAUSAL CONNECTIVITY, EXPLANATION, RATIONALIZATION

CAUSAL CLAUSES AND NARRATIVITY

The attraction for literary linguists of causal connectives and the clauses of reason, purpose, and result which they introduce is almost self-explanatory. Such clauses purport to convey the causes, justifications, or motives of the characters, states and events on which they comment, and so are a particularly direct expression of the articulated causes and consequences in a story. In fact causal clauses and causal relations are a core and essential property of narratives. Unlike nominal clauses, relative clauses, and many other adverbial clauses, they inescapably assert a before and after and, further, a consequentially related before and after. (More precisely, such temporality and consequentiality are entailed in causal clauses as standardly used – as giving a cause 'for x' – but not as they are derivatively used – to give a cause 'for claiming x'. This distinction will be returned to.) It is simply impossible to use a causal clause (in the standard way) without fulfilling that essential condition of narrative: the report of consequentially related change. No other type of subordination, by contrast, carries this guarantee of 'inherent narrativity'. The closest contenders only inconsistently articulate narrative dynamism. Thus temporal clauses may express mere simultaneity, or an indefinite but encompassing duration; conditional clauses express mere possible narratives, conjectured and unconfirmed: neither class of clause invariably narrates.

Furthermore, an implicit clause of reason underlies, and should give shape to, the entirety of any storytelling. This is the clause that would encapsulate the 'point' of the narrative. Labov was the first of a host of sociolinguists to remark on the fact that a compelling answer – however implicit – to the addressee's potential challenge, 'Why are

236

you telling me this?', is essential to a successful narrative (Labov 1972).

More generally yet, the perception of causes lies at the heart of the human drive to interpret and make sense. Much human activity is a business of discovering and coping with our own conditions and those of the people in the various communities each of us inhabits. When we manage to construct a version of the world that seems to make sense, and seems to make the world comprehensible or at least tolerable, then we are comforted and feel more secure. Much deconstructionist and new-historicist criticism uncovers the numerous ways in which this can go on in the writing and reading of literary texts (for samples of the work of these schools, see e.g. Culler (1983) and Greenblatt (1987)). It is often apparent, on closer inspection, that our reassuring versions of circumstances entail many irrational leaps and unjustified assumptions. Thus, less flatteringly, our piecing together of true causes, consequences, and certainties may be better seen as an inevitably pro-tem rationalization of contingencies and localized conjunctions – as philosophers have long recognized (see Sosa 1975).

It is therefore doubly apparent that causal clauses are far from being transparent disambiguators of narrative causes and conse-quences. If that were the case, understanding and interpreting a text would be a relatively straightforward business of interpreting all the clauses of reason present. But only in the case of the most delimited and routine of non-literary texts can we entertain such a possibility – and even in such cases there will always be an elaborate background of understood causes and consequences without which the routine textual instance could not emerge.

In addition, causal connections often remain implicit rather than explicit, and there may even be a deliberate narratorial effort to conceal or erase causal connections. Conversely, there may be an equally disruptive narratorial campaign to bolster or distort a dis-course with unsubstantiated and implausible assertions of causal relation, lending sense and purpose and design to events which the reader may discover or judge to be unrelated. We need also to recognize that clauses of reason are an indeterminate semantic-syntactic category. There may be a large degree of coincidence of, on the one hand, clauses introduced by *because*, *for*, and so on, with, on the other hand, the disclosure of information concerning the causes or results of actions or states. But on many occasions that expected coincidence does not arise. Furthermore we often only convey, in the information of the subordinate clause, a very loose or partial account of the true cause, purpose, or result of an action or state. In a natural language the status of the instruments of causal connection is thus highly problematic (Hendricks 1976: 54–9). Causes may be expressed elsewhere than in causal clauses; clauses introduced by *because* etc. are not always causal, as will be examined below; and claimed causes may, intentionally or otherwise, be at variance with actual and evident causes.

The connectives that introduce causal clauses are of particular interest, since they appear to straddle the distinction between grammatical and lexical items. They occupy a well-defined slot in the structure of the sentence, yet are a less closed system than, for example, prepositions or pronouns. Also, by contrast with a truly closed system, they frequently require the speaker or writer to choose from a range of distinct choices in a particular context (e.g. *because* versus *since* versus *so* versus *as*, etc.). Some of these options may be inappropriate in the larger interactional context but are nevertheless syntactically and semantically unexceptional. This contrasts with typical closed-system items: there is no choice, standardly, in the selection of the pronoun that can corefer with a human, male, and singular antecedent; nor, owing to usage and pragmatic factors, may we typically choose freely from a range of prepositions in certain contexts:

He put the sugar [in/inside/on/within] his tea.

A simple example of the choices between equally grammatical but semantically contrasting connectives and clause sequences may emphasize this point:

1 He was bruised because he had fallen over.   + CAUSAL
2 He was bruised and he had fallen over.   +/− CAUSAL
3 He had fallen over and he was bruised.   ? CAUSAL
4 He had fallen over because he was bruised.   + CAUSAL

The *because* of sentence 1 is clearly causal: there is the simple assertion that it was the falling over that bruised him. By contrast, in sentence 2 there is no explicit assertion that the event of falling over was caused by his bruises, although this may well be inferred, on the basis of the order of presentation of the two clauses. In sentence 3 the reader is drawn to consult the co-text in order to see whether *and* is being used here merely in its additive function, conjoining two statements 'in parallel', or whether it has some resultative force – *and* as if it were a contracted form of *and so*. Sentence 4 does, on one reading, claim a causal connection between its two propositions; but it is a claim to which the reader applying his or her experience of events in the everyday world is immediately resistant (as he or she is of the causal reading of sentence 2: bruising does not typically cause falls). On these grounds alone this final sentence would be important to bear in mind when we consider the actual sentences of the narrative of *Go Down, Moses*, since it is a clear reminder of the ease and lack of grammatical disruption with which a speaker can make highly suspect claims about causes.

On another reading, however, often relevant to the novel under discussion, sentence 4 contains a type of causal connective that is not at all suspect. This would be the case if the sentence were taken to be reporting, in free indirect discourse, first a character's judgement ('He must have fallen over') and then the grounds for that judgement ('because [I can see] he is bruised'). This 'explanatory' use of *because* – quite common in both spoken interaction and argumentative writing – is discussed in Halliday and Hasan (1976: 256 ff.), Brown and Yule (1983: 227), Martin (1983), and Toolan (1988: 222–4). Sentence 4 above (on the FID reading) is related to sentences such as the following:

5 John was at the shops this afternoon, because I saw him there.
6 Dinner is ready, if you'd like some.
7 I'm fixing the socket downstairs so don't turn the power on.

Brown and Yule note that in such uses of *because* as in sentence 5 'the structure . . . is not that normally associated with *because* as a logical connector (P because Q), but is as follows: "I mention/ask P because Q."' (Brown and Yule 1983: 228). In cases like 5, they suggest, we assume that 'a reason is being expressed for an *action* performed in speaking' (229). In Martin (1983: 21) essentially the same contrast is identified as a distinction between external and internal conjunctive relations: '*External* conjunctive relations make connections between propositions about the real world. *Internal* relations make rhetorical connections between speech acts.' The internal conjunctions in 5–7 link adjacent speech acts, and in each case one clause provides some kind of justification or grounds for the performance of the speech act carried by the other clause. External conjunctions, by contrast, as in

8 I'll prepare dinner, if you'd like some.
9 I inadvertently turned the power on, so the breaker tripped.

introduce clauses expressing conditions, causes, and results in the conjured world external to the text, the world upon which the text is a commentary. External conjunctions, world-oriented, are common in narratives, while internal conjunctions, speaker-oriented, are common in argumentative or expressive text. But there is much scope for crossover, with, for example, internal conjunctions dispersed through narrative writing, and some instances of this will figure in subsequent discussions of Ike's represented speech and thought. At this point it may suffice to note that frequently there is an evident deference, tentativeness, or defensiveness apparent in a speaker's recourse to internally conjoined clauses such as those in sentences 5 and 6.

An important general contrast that underlies much of the discussion so far in this chapter is that between sequentiality and consequentiality, that is between temporal and causal succession. Perhaps an initial impulse is simply to record events, capturing the state or action. Subsequently, a number of events may be temporally ordered to create a developmental perspective. A greater interpretative step – often less open to empirical verification – involves the ascription of causality and interdependence between states and events. The degree of sophistication of modern human systems of interpretation and causal explanation of the world is a key hypothesized contrast with the state of human civilization in its primitive stage. And this contrast between primitive and sophisticated man has often issued, in fiction, in the depiction of an individual's or community's ability to develop working hypotheses of causal connection. Of particular note here, since it both dramatizes this theme and has also attracted much stylistic attention, is the novel *The Inheritors* by William Golding (see Halliday 1971; Lee 1976).

Absence of explicit causal connections (due to a speaker's inability, reluctance, or refusal to recognize causal links) is common in *Go Down, Moses*. Consider, for example, p. 23 of 'Was', where a sequence of actions by Mr Hubert is reported as if Cass (the covert narrator) is mesmerized by them:

> Mr Hubert blinked at Uncle Buck. Then he stopped. Then he went and took the candle from the table and went out. They sat on the edge of the bed and watched the light go down the hall and heard

Mr Hubert's feet on the stairs. After a while they began to see the light again and they heard Mr Hubert's feet coming back up the stairs. Then Mr Hubert entered and went to the table and set the candle down and laid a deck of cards by it.

In fact Hubert simply goes to fetch some cards – in the middle of the night, admittedly – so that he and Buck can gamble on Sophonsiba and Tomey's Turl. Such reticence – as in this passage – on questions of cause, purpose, and result fosters the impression of narratorial alignment of the narrator with Cass and the latter's view of events as they happened (this even in a report further removed from the scene than usual, being a report of Cass's report to Uncle Buddy). Such reports, neither omniscient narration nor detached retrospective reordering of events, even in these fairly unimportant areas of the story, transfer the onus on to the reader to adduce a causal interpretation of the narrative.

Such passages are also a preparation for the larger questions and confrontations in the novel, where the reader is compelled to contribute interpretations for the text to be fully meaningful. Of course a basic level of interpretative work is necessary in the construal of any text. But in many texts – even literary ones – most if not all the causal connections are ready-supplied in the surface structure. Such depthless readerly texts require only that the reader adequately process those overtly encoded interpretations. Among such information-oriented texts we may include much everyday factual literature and most pulp romantic fiction. Mystery, detective, and thriller novels, however, present a different case: there is often a practice of supplying a surplus of alleged causes and explanations, so that it appears that every character has good reasons for having killed the victim. Many literary narratives are much less prodigal in their explicit disclosure of causes. However, since viewpoints of characters and the narratorial perspective on those characters is central to critical interpretation of such texts, study of the presence and absence of ascribed causal connections and their subtypes should be an important strand of literary-linguistic analysis.

The grammar and meanings of causal clauses and the subordinators which introduce them may at first glance seem fairly straightforward. The causal subordinators (*for, so that, because, since, as*, etc.) generally imply that we can apply the labels 'cause' (intentional or unintentional) and 'effect' to the two connected propositions. In the case of the subordinator *so that* the intended relation may be either resultative or purposive. However, the order of the clauses connected by *so that* is fixed if the relation is resultative, while it is free if the relation is purposive: *so that* with resultative force can never be sentence-initial, while with purposive force it may.

When examining the wider network of causal relations within a text, ellipted causal connections merit consideration, together with any result connectives that occur at the opening of a sentence and signal a condition–result relationship between that sentence and prior text. As Quirk *et al.* note (1972: 669), the logical resultative connection may appear even more remote in form from the simple causal subordinators if it is cast as a framing clause such as 'The result is that . . .'. In the terms of Halliday's functional grammar (Halliday 1985a) such a construction is a 'grammatical metaphor', representing what would standardly be cast as a projected enhancement as if it were a non-projecting identification, and with 'The result' now in the role of a participant.

Purpose clauses are often infinitival, and are semantically distinguishable from result clauses by the fact that they state a putative intention rather than the factual consummation presupposed by a result clause. The occasional difficulties of distinguishing purpose and result clauses, and the concomitant difficulty of interpreting events as consciously intended or arbitrary, are a source of ambiguity in a text where ascribing of intentions and the authority or motivations of the character or narrator making those ascriptions are cruces of literary-critical interpretation.

SHOWING AND TELLING CAUSES: PATTERNS AND DEPARTURES

It is worth stating again that there can be no unchanging context-free basis in the forms alone for asserting the presence of causal force: the reader, engaged with the text, actively participates in constituting causal connectivity, just as s/he is co-participant in all the other text-constituting dimensions of the activity of reading. The stylistician's position must be that, while such facts give rise to problems in analytical procedure, they are not utterly disabling. It remains the case that causal connectives constitute a particularly explicit and institutionalized invitation to the reader to understand that a causal link is being asserted between the propositions so linked. Even though the reader or analyst may wish to question or reject that invitation, s/he cannot merely ignore it and still be said to be reading carefully. In short, while reading is a constructivist activity, involving faculties and materials that lie outside the text (they are 'in' the reader), this in no way sanctions the view that the construction can proceed reasonably, as a communicative community practice, if there is wilful disregard for the contingent but established significations and values of the various kinds of material contained in the text.

A preliminary count was accordingly made of all those interclausal junctures where a causal connective actually occurred, or where punctuation of a form such as *and* helped locate an implicit but absent causal connective. The data on causal connectives so defined, analysed into those which are actual and those which are ellipted, and

Table 9 Causal connectives in *Go Down, Moses* (norms in parentheses)

	actual	ellipted	total	reason	result	purpose
'Was' I	6(3)	2(1)	8(4)	5	2	1
'Was' II	34(27)	8(5)	42(32)	14	20	8
'Was' III	9(10)	5(3)	14(13)	2	9	3
'Was' IV	5(1)	0	5(1)	2	3	0
'Fire/Hearth' 1, I	27(20)	11(6)	38(26)	14	14	10
'Fire/Hearth' 1, II	24(31)	12(11)	36(42)	7	17	12
'Fire/Hearth' 1, III	11(19)	1(7)	12(26)	1	2	9
'Fire/Hearth' 1, IV	3(3)	0(1)	3(4)	1	2	0
'Fire/Hearth' 2, I	1(3)	1(1)	2(4)	1	1	0
'Fire/Hearth' 2, II	12(14)	5(4)	17(18)	1	10	6
'Fire/Hearth' 2, III	0(1)	0(1)	0(3)	0	0	0
'Fire/Hearth' 3, I	26(30)	10(9)	36(39)	15	10	11
'Fire/Hearth' 3, II	8(10)	2(3)	10(13)	3	5	2
'Fire/Hearth' 3, III	0(1)	0 0	0 0	0	0	0
'Pantaloon' I	30(33)	12(9)	42(41)	10	25	7
'Pantaloon' II	1(2)	2(0)	3(2)	1	1	1
'Old People' 1	23(28)	12(9)	35(41)	12	15	8
'Old People' 2	13(10)	5(3)	18(13)	6	7	5
'Old People' 3	2(2)	1(0)	3(2)	2	1	0
'The Bear' I	25(36)	3(10)	28(46)	12	10	6
'The Bear' II	22(27)	7(8)	29(35)	5	12	12
'The Bear' III	35(45)	10(14)	45(59)	10	19	16
'The Bear' IV	135(80)	28(25)	163(105)	70	45	48
'The Bear' V	32(27)	10(7)	42(34)	16	11	15
'Delta Autumn'	45(40)	13(12)	58(52)	29	12	17
'Go Down, Moses'	17(19)	1(5)	18(24)	5	10	3
Totals	546	161	707	244	263	200

further analysed into the categories of reason, result, and purpose, are set out in table 9.

On the basis that an estimated 67 per cent of the book is narrative (238 of the 357 pages) rather than dialogue, we can posit norms of approximately 2.2 actual and 0.64 ellipted causal connectives per page of narrative over the novel as a whole, hence a combined average of 2.85 causal connectives per narrative page. By multiplying these norms by the calculated length of the narrative, in pages, of each section, we can arrive at text-based norms of frequency of occurrence for the three categories (actual, ellipted, and actual + ellipted causal connectives). Table 9 therefore includes these norms, set alongside the actual frequencies, so as to highlight any marked scarcity or abundance of occurrence.

The table reveals markedly high frequencies of actual causals in 'Was', sections I and IV, and 'The Bear', section IV, and markedly low frequencies of actual causals in 'The Fire and the Hearth', chapter 1, sections II and III, and in 'The Bear', section I. In view of the inevitable uncertainties in identifying ellipted elements, I shall limit the following discussion to the more noteworthy of the six cases of abnormal frequencies of actually occurring causals. (We may even wonder in passing whether, save for brevity, it is wise to use the syntax-derived term 'ellipted' when a more reader-oriented one – e.g. 'imputed' – might be more appropriate.) The high number of actual causals in 'Was', section I, is almost entirely due to a high frequency of reason clauses. In addition, the reason clauses always co-occur here with relative clauses. There is a recurring sequence which runs as follows:

> But Isaac was not one of these . . . who owned no property and never desired to since the earth was no man's but all men's . . . (p. 3)

In the case of 'Was', section I, we may see the location of the reason clauses, late in their respective sentential sequences, as part of the Faulknerian strategy of delayed disclosure. The effect here is one of supplying a considerable body of important characterizing information via the finite and non-finite relative clauses, the full interpretation of which information then becomes conditional upon the postposed reason clause. The second reason clause in 'Was', section I, gives some indication of this latent potential of reason clauses to supply generalizing causal principles for series of events:

But Isaac was not one of these – a widower these twenty years, who in all his life had owned but one object more than he could wear and carry in his pockets and his hands at one time, and this was the narrow iron cot and stained lean mattress which he used camping in the woods for deer and bear or for fishing or simply because he loved the woods. (p. 3)

In my making sense of this passage, I understand there to be an implicit temporal particle (e.g. *when*) between *used* and *camping*. What I thus take to be a non-finite temporal clause is followed by two severely abridged clauses of purpose. That is, Ike was not camping 'for deer' or 'for fishing', but was camping 'when he was deer-hunting or fishing'. These paraphrases indicate that in the structurally co-ordinate series 'for x . . . or for y or simply because z' the first two clauses are not only purposive but supply temporary contingencies to explain Ike's act of camping. In contrast to these local contingencies realized by dynamic verbs, the third justification, 'he loved the woods', is not a contingency at all, but a permanent cause, realized by a stative verb. As a reason for camping it is wholly different in kind from the two co-ordinated contingent purposes: camping has become an end in itself rather than a means to something else. In this instance, at least, it seems that the syntactic structure of the sentence is striving to conceal the dichotomy between contingent purposes, which require an agent motivated by some specific occasion, and enduring causes, permanent conditions which can only be acknowledged or denied.

A consideration of such topics is germane to an assessment of the main characters. For the novel presents a series of crucial experiential trials in their lives where, it seems, they must choose between becoming (or remaining) wilful agentive shapers of events, men exerting what power or skills they have (less destructively, it is to be hoped, than L. Q. C. McCaslin); or becoming (or remaining) submissive patients or witnesses, at best responding to deeply felt 'timeless' causes, rather than to spatio-temporally and materially specific social and contingent purposes – at worst, perpetrating shameful repudiations of responsibilities, and reduced to apathy and impotence by their own self-deluding rhetoric.

Sections II and III of 'The Fire and the Hearth', chapter 1, have low frequencies of reason clauses, and their particular contextual impact deserves further note. As we have seen above in the first section of chapter 6 and the last section of chapter 9, 'The Fire and the

Hearth' is centred on Lucas, the shrewd and cunning old share-cropper of McCaslin blood who is distinguished also by a certain youthful energy and credulousness. Section I of chapter 1 is a relatively lighthearted portrayal of the old man hiding his whisky still, stumbling upon a buried pot containing a single gold coin, and devising plans to search by night for further treasure. In the course of all this, he catches his own daughter spying on him; but, even confronted with this development, Lucas is found extending and adjusting his plans so as to turn this to his own advantage. In the entirety of the section, then, Lucas remains in control.

In considerable contrast to all this, section II contains a long flashback to a time forty years earlier, when Lucas and Edmonds's father (Zack) had a violent confrontation. The confrontation was ostensibly over the fidelity of Lucas's wife Molly, Zack Edmonds being suspected by Lucas of having slept with her. The flashback covers fourteen pages, from p. 45 to the end of the section on p. 59. Thus the section falls into two distinct parts: (a) 3.5 pages of immediate narration, then (b) 14 pages of more distant recollection (not, one should note, given solely from Lucas's point of view). I set out below the frequencies of explicit causal connectives in these two subsections, set against the norms of frequency we can expect in the respective lengths of narrative text:

	(a)			(b)		
	reason	result	purpose	reason	result	purpose
actual	7	7	4	0	10	8
norms	3	3	2	11	12	9

It would seem that the opening 3.5 pages of the section are stylistically akin to the preceding section, with rather high frequencies of all three types of causal connective. The markedly low frequencies (which, derived from table 9, drew our attention to this section in the first place) are limited to subsection (b), the extended flashback. Here, very specifically, we find that the abnormal scarcity of causal clauses is due not to lack of purpose or result clauses, but solely to absence of even a single reason clause. The motivations for this negative foregrounding will be probed in the final section of this chapter, a comparative treatment of various linguistic features and their collective role in character presentation.

The eleven narrative pages of 'The Fire and the Hearth', chapter 1, section III, have distinctively low frequencies of reason and result connectives. The section resumes the story interrupted by the four-teen-page flashback. But the explanation for the low frequency of reason clauses here has little to do with reasons for their absence in the preceding section, and is rather more compatible with the low frequency of reason clauses in section II of chapter 2 of this story (discussed in chapter 6 above). Like the latter, chapter 1, section III, records a successful deception or outmanoeuvring (here, of Edmonds and the judge, by Lucas and others). As such its effect depends crucially on concealing from the reader at least some of the evidence, just as this is concealed from the outmanoeuvred victims. The reader's final wry, amused acknowledgement of Lucas's cunning depends on this. Thus, although there are various indications that the section is predominantly a FID report of events from Lucas's perspective, this vaguely intimated collusion between Lucas, narrator, and reader is undercut by narratorial suppression of various facts and causes.

DISTINCT CAUSAL CONNECTIVITY IN 'THE BEAR'

Besides the absence of reason clauses in 'The Fire and the Hearth', chapter 1, section II, to be discussed in the next chapter, the other sections with the most interesting deviant frequencies of causal connectives are both in 'The Bear' – sections I and IV. The former has markedly low frequencies of reason, result, and purpose clauses, while section IV has high frequencies of reason and purpose ones.

Section I is the extensive record of Ike's personal reflections on his various hunting and wilderness inheritances. These reflections are presented in heavily embedded sentences. Much of this embedding is right-branching, and takes the form, almost exclusively, of relative and adverbial clauses. The following seems structurally typical of sentences in this section:

It [the bear] loomed and towered in his dreams before he even saw the unaxed woods where it left its crooked print, shaggy, tremendous, red-eyed, not malevolent but just big, too big for the dogs which tried to bay it, for the horses which tried to ride it down, for the men and the bullets they fired into it; too big for the very country which was its constricting scope. (p. 193)

Yet few of the adverbial clauses are ones of cause. The passage quoted, rather, is exemplary of the 'additive' style noted by Ohmann (1964).

247

Although the opening of 'The Bear', section I, speaks of Ike as being 'sixteen now', the events recorded in the section happen in his tenth and eleventh years. The emphasis is on Ike as a novice acquiring the code of hunting and of the wilderness. Perhaps here more clearly than elsewhere in *Go Down, Moses* we can see the operation of narratorial empathy with Ike without the standard linguistic indicators of free indirect thought. This is because Ike has, as it were, no reorganizing consciousness at this stage: he more passively receives and stores his sense-impressions. The very fact that Ike is presented as not recasting his experience, as not inserting personal evaluations and interpretations between himself and events, may be a kind of confirmation of the sincerity of his quest for the values of the true hunter, the true wilderness-dweller: especially, patience and humility.

Among the interpretative tools Ike ignores are those claiming causal connections between events or states. Ike, for most of this section, is the totally innocent novice, submitting to the wilderness, and as a result experiencing a series of profound epiphanies which, through their very nature or the youth of the boy, belie rational explanation. This prevailing trend is broken in only one passage – one of the most vivid and arresting of the whole book – during the denouement at the close of the section, when Ike relinquishes totally to the wilderness and, having divested himself of gun, watch, and compass, comes finally face to face with the mythic bear.

The single page of narrative relevant here (p. 208) reveals a density of causal connectives far higher than the norms not only for the section as a whole but also for the entire book. I quote an extract:

He had not been going very fast for the last two or three hours and he had gone even less fast since he left the compass and watch on the bush. So he went slower still now, since the tree could not be very far; in fact, he found it before he really expected to and turned and went to it. But there was no bush beneath it, no compass nor watch, so he did next as Sam had coached and drilled him: made this next circle in the opposite direction and much larger, so that the pattern of the two of them would bisect his track somewhere, but crossing no trace nor mark anywhere of his feet or any feet, and now he was going faster though still not panicked, his heart beating a little more rapidly but strong and steady enough, and this time it was not even the tree because there was a down log beside it which he had never seen before and beyond the log a little swamp, a seepage of moisture

somewhere between earth and water, and he did what Sam had
coached and drilled him as the next and last, seeing as he sat down
on the log the crooked print. (p. 208)

This single page has two reason, four result (two of these are ellipted),
and two purpose connectives. This brief passage of narrative centres
on detailed presentation of Ike's ratiocinative response to developments. Coming at the close of the account of his novitiate proper, this
is peculiarly appropriate. For at this very point in the story Ike ceases
to be a novice, and becomes a true hunter and spiritual son of the
wilderness. He has just relinquished the last of his town and civilization tools for taming the wilderness, the watch and compass (in
effect, has said of the wilderness what Sam will say of Lion: 'I dont
want him tame'). Much of the motivation for Ike's reactions here,
trying to loop back on his own tracks, are prompted by a natural
human sense of fear as he comes to realize that he is utterly lost. But
the actual procedures enacted are a woodsman's, ones learnt from
Sam.

Nowhere else in 'The Bear', section I, is there such a frequency of
causal connectivity, since nowhere else in the section is there such an
acute tension between Ike as submissive experiencer and Ike as the
seeker after coherence and sense. He is, for the first time, independently embracing the wilderness code (as he sees it) of relinquishment
and anonymous brotherhood. In doing so he also reveals an enduring
characteristic and weakness of his own: a compulsive search for and
ascription of causal connections even when such ascriptions are
implausible or irrelevant. This masking or obscuring of inadequacies
is hinted at here, and amplified in 'The Bear', section IV.

It should be acknowledged, however, that the entire closing
passage of 'The Bear', section I, can be read in a rather different way,
as a dramatization of the contradictions within Ike. When Ike puts
down the gun, watch, and compass, he may be becoming a child of the
wilderness, but arguably he is also relinquishing (and even
repudiating?) the predetermined role of the (white, farm-dwelling)
hunter. Simply put, there are two kinds of hunting: hunting for food
and subsistence, and hunting for recreation. In the story, the former is
associated with Indian values, the latter – parasitic – activity is
associated with the white men who gather for sport each November.
With this contrast in view, the passage becomes one of the most
'Indian' moments in the book, a moment when a nexus of Indian
values and beliefs (belief in the animate spirits of the natural world; in

the sufficiency of that which man has available to him; in stewardship) inspires Ike.

It is little surprise to find that 'The Bear', section IV, has high frequencies of purpose and (especially) reason clauses, and so reveals a stylistic similarity with 'Was', section I, in this respect as in others previously noted. 'Was', section I, is certainly the section with which it begs comparison; but it should also be related to 'Delta Autumn' which, despite an unexceptional frequency of causals taken as an aggregate (58 against a norm of 52), has a rather high frequency of reason clauses (29 against a norm of 18).

It is in just these two sections that Ike, in his mature years, undergoes the fullest exercises of self-examination, self-justification, and self-discovery. They are distinguished from many other sections ostensibly focused on Ike where in fact he is not an agent, but an individual submitting to external forces and influences. In these two sections, above all, we see events unfolding as a result of Ike's conscious choices and decisions in his adult life. If 'The Old People' and sections I to III of 'the Bear' chiefly portray Ike as the child of innocence, he has now become the child of experience. In his own confused way, he ceases to be merely a passive submitter to external guides and tutors (Sam, the old buck, Cass, the wilderness, etc.). With Sam's death at the end of 'The Bear', section III, Ike has (in one possible interpretation of the book) matured into a distinctive world-view, and begins to act, as agent and causer and shaper of events. That world-view or mind-style and the actions that issue from it remain disablingly confused and limited.

High frequency of causal connectives in 'The Bear', section IV, seems confined to particular crucial passages highlighting, from Ike's own perspective, his compulsive quest for rationalization and self-justification. The multiple causal clauses of pp. 311–12 will be discussed in the next chapter; the other pages revealing density of causal ascription are 254, 269, 270, 271, 289, 291, 294, and 296. Some of these scarcely require extended comment, for they come within Ike's extended recollection of the contents of the ledgers and their significance (that recollection spans pp. 263–82). The causal connectives within that recollection – the most commonly used is *because* – are generally character-aligned reflexes of Ike's laborious efforts to interpret and comprehend the cryptic announcements in the ledgers:

> *Tennie Beauchamp* . . . *Marrid to Tomys Turl 1859* . . . and no date of freedom because her freedom . . . derived . . . from a stranger in

Washington and no date of death and burial, not only because McCaslin kept no obituaries in his books, but because in this year 1883 she was still alive . . . (p. 271; italics in original)

More illuminating are the multiple causal clauses which are not attributable to the sense-making effort involved in interpreting the ledger: those occurring on pp. 254, 289, and 294.

The particular significance of the causals on p. 194 is that they relate to the action and motivation not of Ike but of his grandfather, L. Q. C. McCaslin. If 'The Bear', section IV, is predominantly narratorially aligned with Ike, it is not thereby barred from discussing the actions and principles of other individuals. Rather, such discussions are enriched because, as in this case, the character discussed is evaluated from Ike's viewpoint. It is Ike who ascribes to his grandfather a series of tyrannous and outrageous arguments for the vain but ruthless principles by which he chose to live:

Old Carothers McCaslin his grandfather had bought [the land] . . . and believed he had tamed and ordered it *for the reason* that the human beings he held . . . had removed the forest from it . . . *in order to* grow something out of it . . . which could be translated back into the money he . . . had had to pay *to* get it and hold it and a reasonable profit too: and *for which reason* old Carothers McCaslin . . . could raise his children . . . *to* believe the land was his *to* hold and bequeath *since* the strong and ruthless man has a cynical foreknowledge of his own vanity and pride and strength . . . (pp. 254–5; my emphases)

Ike's implicit repudiation of his grandfather is clear in his characterization of him as a ruthless autodidact with his own crude and illogical design, who is said to have believed he had tamed and ordered the land simply because his slaves had managed to make it commercially viable. Carothers McCaslin's supposedly great design is thus exposed as a vicious circle of debased reasons and purposes. It is worth noting that Ike's bitter and hostile narratorially cast ascriptions of motivation here co-occur with the sort of generic sentence which is almost a hallmark of his own thinking by the close of 'The Bear', section IV – 'the strong and ruthless man has a cynical foreknowledge of his own vanity' and so on.

On pp. 289 and 294, however, in narrative presented from Ike's viewpoint, the causal ascriptions must be treated, like those in the ledger passage, as Ike's own. It is Ike who provides explanations and justifications when contemplating negro 'licence' during the Reconstruction period –

> who misused it [freedom] not as children would nor yet *because* they had been so long in bondage and then so suddenly freed, but misused it as human beings always misuse freedom, *so that* he thought . . . (p. 289; my emphases)

– or when contemplating the values of the ordinary Southern soldiers:

> who had fought for years and lost *to* preserve a condition . . . not *because* they were opposed to freedom as freedom but *for the old reasons* for which man . . . has always fought and died in wars: *to* preserve a status quo or *to* establish a better future one to endure for his children; (p. 290; my emphases)

Here too are generic sentences with their foreclosing half-truths: human beings always misuse freedom, man has always fought in wars to preserve a status quo or to establish a better future. And what strikes the reader here is Ike's apparent urgent need to formulate adequate explanations, yet the palpable inadequacy of the reasons supplied. (Note also Ike's explicit admission, just two pages earlier, that he is indeed 'formulating' – a style of talk identified and discussed by Schegloff (1972).) The explanations Ike provides are rhetorical rather than historical, and both the abundant causal connectives and the generic sentences are a flimsy mask attempting to conceal the limitations of Ike's analysis, but in fact drawing attention to them. The causals reflect Ike's pursuit of the unshakeable ground of rational explanation, just as the generic sentences are a striving for the firm foundations of 'universal truth'. Such passages thus also highlight the troublesome power of generic sentences: they purport to remind us, merely, of that which we can take on trust, that which can be uncontroversially presupposed. Their format invites us to 'treat them as Known', a form of structural discouragement of the critical reception that they may need.

The vulnerability in Ike's rationalizations, in his relinquishment of the farm, and in his relations to both L. Q. C. McCaslin and black people is more apparent still in a passage peppered with causal clauses:

> 'They will outlast us because they are –' it was not a pause, barely a falter even, possibly appreciable only to himself, as if he couldn't

252

speak even to McCaslin, even to explain his repudiation, that
which to him too, even in the act of escaping (and maybe this was
the reality and the truth of his need to escape) was heresy: *so that*
even in escaping he was taking with him more of that evil and
unregenerate old man who could summon, *because* she was his
property, a human being *because* she was old enough and female . . .
because she was of an inferior race . . . than even he [Ike] had feared.
(p. 294; my emphases)

The racist slur at the conclusion here – 'an inferior race' – whether
attributable to Ike or to his grandfather, is beyond comment. But the
passage opens on an entirely different note, with Ike pausing or
faltering just as he is about to declare (as he goes on to do) that the
negroes are better and stronger than the whites. Such inverted racism
strikes the reader as a rhetorical excess, and is understandably an
almost blasphemous heresy not only to Cass but to Ike himself. Yet it
is a heresy Ike finds himself driven to asserting, notwithstanding his
almost instinctive fleeting resistance to the claim. As a result this is a
passage characterized by what may be described as acute narrative
turbulence, as, from Ike's perspective, the narrative rather abruptly
switches focus to old Carothers McCaslin while apparently inadvertently disclosing crucial assumptions made by Ike himself.

Having faltered in his assertion, Ike evidently feels a need to
provide explanations and sources (external to him) for that faltering.
His explanation involves citing once again his 'evil and unregenerate'
grandfather, with (it is alleged) all his debased justifications. But the
four reason clauses (quoted above) relating to the grandfather are all
subordinate to the resultative one – 'so that even in escaping he was
taking with him more of that . . . old man . . . than even he feared'.
They are thus subordinate to Ike's *own* compulsive searching out of
(quite controversial) explanations.

This particular explanation, furthermore, carries a number of
assumptions, which Ike has earlier been seen to deny, concerning the
nature of his relinquishment. Ike had earlier contested Cass's judgement that the relinquishment was in fact a repudiation (p. 256), yet
here the Ike-oriented narrative apparently discloses Ike's underlying
assessment, in referring to the act not only as 'his repudiation' but also
as 'the act of escaping'. This passage is, understandably, singled out
by Hunt in the course of his discussion of the novel: 'He [the narrator]
allows us to see that Isaac is not so fully divested of inherited evil as he

likes to believe, and he shows that privately Ike thinks of his act as an escape through repudiation' (Hunt 1965: 159 – 160). This disclosure is triggered by the quite self-conscious hesitation on Ike's part, and is the narratorial expression, through character-aligned narrative, of what (as Hunt puts it) Ike privately thinks.

On p. 294, then, as on certain earlier ones in the section, and as on pp. 295 and 296, high frequency of causal connectives draws attention to rhetorical excess in Ike's interpretation of events, his compulsive urge to ascribe reasons and justifications, even when the information supplied in the causal clauses does not amount to plausible or sufficient explanation. Such causal connectives are often a signal of a more thoroughgoing stylistic turbulence, reflecting the turbulence and the involuntary revelation of Ike's deepest evaluations. On pp. 295 and 296, for example, Ike is once more airing his obsession by piling up causal interpretations of the behaviour and qualities of the bear and the fyce. Thus the bear seems deliberately to put its freedom in jeopardy 'in order to savor it and keep his old strong bones and flesh supple and quick to defend and preserve it' (p. 295); while the little dog

> couldn't be dangerous because there was nothing anywhere much smaller, not fierce because that would have been called just noise, not humble because . . . not proud because . . . so that all it could be was brave even though they would probably call that too just noise. (p. 296)

In both cases there is an elaborate rhetorical working out of the analysis which draws attention to the analyst; and in both cases the persistence of the anthropomorphism draws us to see these claims as purely conjectural in relation to the animals described, but directly relevant to the values and asserted ideals of Ike himself. After the close of 'The Bear', section I, Ike never again conspicuously puts his own freedom in jeopardy, nor demonstrates true bravery. In the terms of the analysis provided at the top of p. 296, Ike's failure of bravery and courage entails an incomplete acquisition of humility and pride. The implications of such a failure as it directly affects Ike are drawn with grim vividness in the novel's next and penultimate chapter, 'Delta Autumn'; the broader context and consequences of that failure are at least intimated in the final chapter, 'Go Down, Moses'.

11

SYNTACTIC CHARACTERIZATIONS

THE STYLES OF CHARACTERS UNDER STRESS

This chapter demonstrates one way of 'reading' the three central characters of the novel (Ike, Lucas, and Roth Edmonds) through stylistic analysis of their narrative rendering. I have chosen to focus on three key passages of the text, each about seven pages in length, which report from the contrasting perspectives of these three characters. The passages are:

1 p. 45, 1. 22, to p. 52, 1. 9, of 'The Fire and the Hearth', chapter 1, section II: (from 'He would never forget it . . .' to '. . . and took his razor from the drawer'), on and about Lucas;
2 p. 112, 1. 8, to p. 118, 1. 25, of 'The Fire and the Hearth', chapter 3, section I: (from 'Henry didn't move . . .' to '. . . all blood black, white yellow or red, including his own'), on and about Roth Edmonds;
3 p. 308, 1. 10, to p. 315, 1. 12, at the close of 'The Bear', section IV: (from 'except that he didn't hear McCaslin' to 'her back to the rented room, laughing and laughing'), on Ike.

I shall henceforth refer to these passages as the Lucas-text, the Roth-text, and the Ike-text, respectively.

I have chosen these passages in particular since each involves its main character (reported indirectly) in extended reflection on past events and personal experiences, and evaluation of other characters. Thus the Lucas-text is a dramatic flashback to that time when Lucas and Molly's marriage was nearly wrecked by the woman's absence, caring for Zack Edmonds's motherless child, and Lucas's tormented sense of usurpation and cuckoldry. The Roth-text reviews Roth's harrowing stumbling, as a boy, upon his white 'overclass' heritage (his rejection of, and subsequently by, Henry); it then presents an extended evaluation of Molly and Lucas. The Ike-text assesses, in turn, Cass, Ike himself, and Ike's wife. All three texts are marked by empathetic alignment of narrator and central character, often confirmed by the presence of formal indicators of free indirect discourse; and all three texts are centrally concerned with questions of personal identity, the articulation of personal values, and the complex shading into each other of the following traits: possession, ownership, repudiation, sharing, partnership, and compassion. My assumption is that detailed stylistic interpretation of the syntax of these passages, passages portraying the characters from their own partial viewpoints, may identify those characters' strengths and weaknesses even as, 'from within', they are disclosed.

The analysis of these passages will consider not only the deployment and function of progressive verbal forms, personal and demonstrative pronouns, proper names, causal connectives, and subordination, but also trends in the use of relative clauses, in Hallidayan transitivity, and in assertions of animacy and agency in clause subjects. The discussion is, then, something of a synthesis attending to all the major linguistic foci of this study. As has been argued previously, the selective attention to just the linguistic features listed above, and neglect of others, is an operational necessity in much the same way that all interpretation involves placing greater store by some aspects of a discourse rather than others. But this necessary selectivity of stylistic attention here is emphatically not arbitrary; each of the linguistic properties to be examined has an established value (in a Saussurean sense) within the grammar of the language and, more specifically, within the grammar of extended fictional narrative. Progressive aspect, pronouns and proper names, causal clauses, and so on, each have an essential (rather than peripheral) role to play in the construction of the complex texture of literary narrative. (The very non-arbitrariness of attention to these textual features contrasts with what sometimes seem to be the more obscure motivations of the interpretative attentions in some literary criticism.) Furthermore, while progressivization, pronouns, and so on, are separable elements of a text, it should be increasingly clear that they function interdependently in actual text construction.

OBSESSIVE RELATIVIZATION

As an initial lexicogrammatical manoeuvre, the main and finite subordinate clauses of each passage were examined, and analysed in terms of their transitivity into the broad types of process (material, mental, relational, and so on). The primary categorization is set out in table 10 and will be discussed later. Table 10 also presents numbers of occurrences of relative pronouns and causal connectives in the texts, and analysis of relativization trends may be a useful place to begin the stylistic examination. For the Roth-text reveals a high frequency of relative pronouns – 36 in 6.5 pages, against a narrative norm of 3 per page. The relativization in the Roth-text is particularly prominent, since all but two of these 36 relative pronouns occur on pp. 115–18.

The relative clauses first proliferate in those passages where the Roth-aligned narrative discusses Lucas and his activities. The narrative shift into a syntactic style in which multiple relativization predominates is arguably a structural miming of the maddened, obsessional nature of Roth's preoccupation with Lucas. In addition the content of these multiple relative clauses maintains the focus on Lucas. Roth is explicitly reported as seeing Lucas as antagonist in 'one long and unbroken course of outrageous trouble and conflict': the inordinately long sentences that follow this observation, carefully progressing from one 'outrageous' detail to the next by means of relative clauses, are a structurally iconic representation of that long and unbroken course.

Table 10 Selective structural analysis of the Lucas-, Roth-, and Ike-texts

	Lucas-text	*Roth-text*	*Ike-text*
Narrative clauses	161	170	168
Material-process clauses	103	85	100
2-participant	45	42	59
1-participant	58	43	41
Mental-process clauses	30	52	38
Relational clauses	28	33	30
Narrative clauses with main characters as subject	89	63	77
Material-process clauses with main character as subject	51	22	44
Other clauses with main character as subject	38	41	33
Relative pronouns	22	36	17
Causal connectives	12	19	28

But the relativization persists. The final paragraphs of this section of 'The Fire in the Hearth' fall into two halves: the first a commentary on Molly, the second a resumption of the commentary on Lucas. In the half-page relating to Molly, the frequency of human relative pronouns is quite noteworthy (*who/whom* occurs on seven occasions, while *which* appears only twice). This entire commentary on Molly, by contrast with the preceding bitter recognition of Lucas's ramifications of antagonizing influence, is a compassionate testimony to her nurturing qualities ('the only mother he [Roth] ever knew'). Molly's influence is presented as entirely on the personal level of what she has been 'in herself'. This is mirrored in the sequence of relative clauses on p. 117, which convey Molly's tireless personal influence on Roth by repeatedly designating her as clause subject:

who had been the only mother he ever knew
who had raised him
who had surrounded him always with care
who had given him, the motherless
who had no other kin save an old brother in Jefferson

This tribute to Molly suggests that Edmonds's transcribed feelings towards her are intimate, personal, and emotional. But a concealed motivation may also be present: Roth expresses affection and sympathy in his portrait of Molly (the woman upset by Lucas's incorrigible tendencies), so that by extension and analogy some of those transferred and legitimized feelings of pity and sympathy can be directed back to the other victim of Lucas's activities – Roth himself. Roth acknowledges that Molly had been the only mother he ever knew, that he had been motherless, and that she had given him that love 'which existed nowhere else in this world for him'. In the very next line, we turn from contemplation of the motherless, kinless, love-lacking Roth to focus on Molly, 'who had no other kin save an old brother in Jefferson'. Other details of content point to this implied shared condition: Molly taught Roth to be 'generous to the weak'; she, earlier, had mothered him 'without stint or expectation of reward'. Additionally, the association of Roth's experience with Molly's is invited by the repeated references to Roth within each relative clause.

In fact much of the information in the passage relates to Roth rather than to Molly, so that we are increasingly drawn to expect at least one of these *who* pronouns to refer to Roth. Each of the intraclausal references to Roth draws the reader to consider Roth as referent of the next following use of the pronoun *who*. We briefly entertain such an interpretation in particular since the linearity of serial right-branching is common elsewhere in Faulkner's mammoth sentences, in contrast to the parallel right-branching that obtains here – a 'stacking up' of discrete characterizations of Molly. (On readers' necessary reprocessings of complex sentences in Faulkner and other writers, see especially Dillon (1978).) Perhaps precisely because no such topic switch to Roth does transpire, since this Roth-oriented passage remains nominally an outpouring of concern for Molly, the latent workings of self-pity on Roth's part are more strongly suspected. Roth is seen registering sympathy for Molly in the two senses of the term: he expresses his affection and concern for her, but also claims a common plight with her, as fellow victim of Lucas and the world.

On p. 118 there is a style of relativization in stark contrast to the above. Here the non-human pronoun *which* predominates (six out of seven relative pronouns). Of those in the narrative proper (i.e., prior to the italicized closing lines which are Roth's direct thoughts), all but one refer to Lucas's face:

> It seemed to Edmonds . . . that he could actually see Lucas standing there in the room before him – *the face which* at sixty-seven looked actually younger than his own at forty-three . . . – *the face which* was not at all a replica . . . of his grandfather McCaslin's but *which* had heired . . . – *the face which* . . . was a composite of a whole generation of fierce and undefeated young Confederate soldiers, embalmed and slightly mummified. (p. 118; my emphases and ellipses)

The repeated clause subject and relative pronoun reflect the fact that Roth's relations with Lucas are of a very different order from those he claims with Molly. Here is a detached and impersonal grappling with Lucas not as *the man who* but as *the face which*, a reduction of Lucas from human individual to inanimate face – 'embalmed and slightly mummified'. That, in short, is how Roth regards Lucas at this point in the story, at the close of the first section of chapter 3 of 'The Fire and the Hearth'. By the close of the third and final section, however, when Lucas renounces any further use of the divining machine, a more tolerant and even affectionate attitude emerges, in a sentence of relativized descriptions that is an important counterpoint to the one examined above:

'Well,' Edmonds said. 'Well.' He thrust his chair back from the table and sat looking up at the other [Lucas], at the old man who had emerged out of the tragic complexity of his motherless childhood as the husband of the woman who had been the only mother he ever knew, who had never once said 'sir' to his white skin and whom he knew even called him Roth behind his back, let alone to his face. (pp. 130–1)

EXPLAINING AWAY BY ROTH AND IKE; SUPPRESSION OF REASONS BY LUCAS

In addition to significant patterns of subordination through relativization, subordination with reason clauses is also foregrounded in the texts, as the high frequencies of causal connectives in the Roth-text and the Ike-text indicate (see table 10). In the Roth passage that characteristic seems to relate to Roth's discursive review of his early experiences, his attempt to order and rationalize events in an explicit way. By contrast Lucas is reflective but often anti-rational, either declining to admit causal connections, or preferring to state what for him are facts, true accounts, as the results of vaguely specified causes. The Ike-text, however, has even more causal connectives than the Roth-text: 28 in all, including 11 of reason. This seems to reflect Ike's temperament and mind-style: he is a compulsive explicator and preacher. It is not enough for him to formulate reasons to himself; he must also convey them to those around him – Cass in section IV of 'The Bear', the men (and the woman) in 'Delta Autumn'. The causals come thick and fast where Ike is narratorially represented as excited by his own rhetoric, as on pp. 309 and 311–12:

> [Ike became a carpenter] not simply *because* he was good with his hands *because* he had intended to use his hands and it could have been with horses, and not in mere static and hopeful emulation of the Nazarene as the young gambler buys a spotted shirt *because* the old gambler won in one yesterday, but . . . *because* if the Nazarene had found carpentering good enough . . . (p. 309; my emphases)

In the Lucas-text, as is reflected by 'he hadn't intended to say this' and 'When he discovered suddenly that he was going now, this moment' (with the latter's startling switch from indirect report to free indirect discourse), Lucas does not rationally respond to events by weighing evidence, reaching a conclusion, and acting upon it. His

responses are often disordered and irrational, instinctive and prejudiced; and his actions are often embarked upon without conscious
intention. Often a physiological stimulus beyond his control – e.g. his
strained breathing on p. 48 – is presented as triggering a response in
terms of action which he has not decided upon, but finds himself
doing, as a driven participant. Then, as on p. 47, Lucas suddenly
'discovers' what his active response already is.

The reluctance or failure to give reasons is implicitly ascribed to
Lucas himself by the chosen narrative means of depicting that
character's views. Explanations for it are not hard to find: tormented
with jealousy, it is as if Lucas fears to enunciate his own worst
suspicions (of his wife), lest that procedure help to substantiate them.
Not only is there an obsessional suppression of causal links: the
well-formedness of some of 'Lucas's' sentences is also disrupted. Thus
on p. 46 we encounter the following turbulent passage:

> It was as though the white woman . . . had never existed – the
> object which they buried . . . a thing of no moment, unsanctified,
> nothing; his own wife, the black woman, now living alone in the
> house which old Cass had built for them when they married,
> keeping alive on the hearth the fire he had lit on their wedding
> day . . . – thus, until almost half a year had passed and one day he
> went to Zack Edmonds and said 'I wants my wife. I needs her at
> home.'

The sudden shifts of grammatical subject and discourse topic are the
source of difficulties. Focus switches sharply but manageably (for the
reader) from the white woman to the black woman. But it then
switches again, quite unpredictably, from Molly to Lucas himself: the
referent for the long postmodifying clause describing someone 'now
living alone in the house which old Cass had built for them' is not
Molly but Lucas. This discovery draws us to re-examine the sentence,
whereupon it becomes quite evident that the appositional noun
phrases *his own wife, the black woman* have no structural relation to their
co-text. They constitute a syntactic breakdown at precisely the point
in the report of Lucas's early married life when Lucas himself faced
a threatened breakdown of marriage and self. In this disrupted
grammaticality we encounter a passage that modulates subtly and
economically towards stream-of-consciousness.

If causals are suppressed in the Lucas-text, one particular 'pseudo-
causal' is prominent: the adjunct *until*. This conjunction often conveys

resultative or purposive force – 'the creek out of banks until the whole valley resembled a river choked with down timber' – but on p. 47 we find recurring use of *until* signifying merely 'up to when' rather than, in addition, 'so that then':

> the fire which was to burn . . . until neither he nor Molly were left to feed it, himself sitting before it night after night . . . until one night he caught himself standing over it . . . the cedar water bucket already poised until he caught himself and set the bucket on the shelf . . .

Stylistically, there seem parallels to Lucas's psychological state in other features of the reporting of the action. For in the report here adverbial phrases and clauses of time and place seem strikingly prominent, frequently the orientationally key initial and final places in sentences. By contrast the specific plot-advancing actions which Lucas 'finds himself engaged upon' are often embedded in the much less prominent medial material of sentences.

Consider, for example, the passage on p. 46, quoted above, where Lucas's visit to Edmonds is the crucial plot-developing action (*he went to Zack Edmonds*), but is submerged by surrounding, and apparently framing, circumstantial detail. The presentational reversal, in which situation is foregrounded while actions are backgrounded, reflects and conveys Lucas's own chaotic state: any gestures by him towards considered, rational reaction are overwhelmed by the oppressive net of circumstances and their apparent power to compel particular responses.

Lucas is often not only compelled to act in a certain way: he is also, relatedly, dehumanized:

> She was sitting before the hearth where the supper was cooking, holding the child, shielding its face from the light and heat with her hand – a small woman even then, years before her flesh, her very bones apparently, had begun to wither and shrink inward upon themselves, and he standing over her, looking down not at his own child but at the face of the white one . . . not his son but the white man's who had been restored to him, *his voice* loud, *his clawed hand* darting towards the child as her hand sprang and caught his wrist. (p. 49; my emphases)

Upon discovering that it is Edmonds's child who is being suckled, Lucas is dehumanized in the report (not an individual, but a voice and a clawed hand), and his intervention is recorded with a non-finite verb, *darting* (he does not choose to act in this way: the action is simply already in progress). There is a stylistic continuity here with the even more agentive and animate voice and hand of Ike's wife, on pp. 312–15, discussed below. As remarked earlier of Lucas's agonized breathing, he is seen driven to act by irrational compulsions rather than by any enunciated intentions. At key moments, as in the Ike-text also, the character's actions are rendered as often by participles as by finite verbs. In this way the narrative conveys the judgement that in moments of great stress Lucas and Ike tend to be driven by compulsions which render them very much less than full and conscious human agents.

ACTION, POWER, AND CONTROL

Repeatedly, the characters are presented undergoing – or recalling undergoing – experiences in which they are now actors, now acted upon. At one moment they appear to have wittingly instigated a series of events, consciously caused some development; the next moment they may be bewildered participants, propelled on courses by forces external and beyond their control, an experience analogous to the literal propulsion of the convict on the Mississippi flood waters in *The Wild Palms*. It is arguable that, in their switches from conscious control to impotent submission to experience, these passages objectify Faulkner's views on man's perennial and problematic grappling with varieties of subjection and freedom. In *The Wild Palms*, through curious circumstances, the convict is free of the penitentiary; yet he is also quite trapped – by the flooding river, and his sense of obligation to the pregnant woman with whom he shares his boat. More subtly, the characters of *Go Down, Moses*, struggle with conflicting forces of independence and entrapment.

While non-finite clauses are prominently deployed in the depiction of characters as powerless, compelled actors, we can also see the fluctuations between character control and submission correlating with patterns of finite-clause structure, when such patterns are elucidated through a Hallidayan transitivity analysis. Characters in control of events are normally depicted as actor or causer in two-participant, transitive, material-process clauses, in which there is a stated goal or affected participant. Where the character is submitting to external direction, we may expect an increase of intransitive (one-participant) clauses, with the character as affected participant (not acting upon or in relation to another participant), and of passive-voice, transitive clauses (in which the character remains syntactic subject, but the cause of the process is postposed or deleted).

Actual frequencies of clause types in the three texts are presented in table 10. In practice, while Lucas and Ike are the subject in twenty-seven of the two-participant (transitive) material-process clauses of their respective texts, Roth is so in only eleven clauses in his passage. And with regard to all types of clauses, Roth is infrequently the subject (and 'senser') of mental-process clauses, relative to the other two passages and characters. Frequencies of various clause patterns thus vividly express the differing mind-styles of Lucas, Roth, and Ike. In particular the scarcity of two-participant material-process clauses with Roth as subject/actor – i.e. of clauses which could report Roth's effect upon the people or things in his environment – is stylistic testimony to his ineffectuality, his inability to influence or direct events, and his failures of personal connection with Lucas, Molly, and others. Similarly, the relative preponderance of mental-process clauses in the Roth-text is expressive of Roth's withdrawn introspection: Roth's preferred 'activities' here are those of looking, listening, seeing, knowing, and thinking.

Passivity and control are particularly vividly encoded stylistically in the seduction scene within the Ike-text. The woman's power and control are reflected in post-positioned non-finite clauses in which the apparently agentive element in subject position is a part of the woman's body, exerting forces or constraints on Ike. Ike notices 'her face strained and terrible, her voice a passionate and expiring whisper', after which they enter into a dialogue in which all the woman's utterances are the initiatory moves in the 'transaction', brief instrumental statements, questions, and directives aimed at achieving specific perlocutionary effects in the addressee (on speech acts and conversational analysis in relation to literature, see especially Pratt (1977) and Burton (1980)):

> 'I love you. . . . When are we going to move? . . . No! No! . . . When? . . . Stand up and turn your back and shut your eyes. . . . Lock the door. . . . Take off your clothes. . . . Promise. . . . That's all from me. . . .'

To these Ike responds in his characteristically confused and hesitant way. The woman in turn reacts to Ike's prevarications not with words but with actions: 'The hot fierce palm clapped over his mouth'. These actions do not, it seems, emanate from the woman as individual, but from animate and independent parts of her body: 'the fingers themselves seeming to follow through the cheek the impulse to speech as it died in his mouth'.

Presented from Ike's perspective, the woman is physical, mechanical, inhumanly detached – looking at nothing, thinking of nothing – like the dog Lion. There seems a particularly alarming gothic disjunction between 'the woman' and 'the hand', reflected in such phrases as 'then she was gone, the hand too . . .' (p. 312). It is not even *the woman* or *she* who usually speaks, but simply *the voice* or *the whisper*. And it is a hand which controls Ike: as he approaches the bed, he encounters 'her hand moving as though with volition and vision of its own, catching his wrist' (p. 313). With lethal hand and wrist, Ike's wife (never given a personal name, any more than the white salesman in 'The Fire and the Hearth') is woman-as-castrator become woman-as-lyncher: 'only the light increasing pressure of the fingers as though arm and hand were a piece of wire cable with one looped end, only the hand tightening as he pulled against it.'

By contrast with the hypotactic clause patterns evident in the Lucas- and Roth-texts, paratactic chaining predominates here. *And* links finite clauses on thirty-five occasions in the Lucas-text, is rare in the Roth-text, but occurs fifty-seven times in the Ike-text. On pages such as 313–14, in particular (where inter-finite-clause *and* occurs twenty-six times), *and* seems to function, along with such temporal qualifiers as *still* and *now*, as a pulse embodying the intense particularity of the remembered encounter, as if Ike can vividly recall the sequence of events in which he was chiefly witness, but is unable or reluctant to hierarchize (that is to say, interpret or judge) those events.

Although this Ike-oriented narrative reports that the woman's 'steady and invincible hand' tames Ike, we may feel that the narrative says more about Ike (his failed commitment) and his view of women (as seductive but alien sexual animals, inhuman, machine-like, Lion-like) than it does about the woman herself. Ike is, after all, a rhetorician and a confused, logic-chopping idealist (cf. the causals of pp. 309 and 311–12), and the passage incidentally highlights Ike's failure to act consistently, his moral weakness. His powerlessness before the woman's controlling hand compares ill with Lucas's self-assertion on p. 50, in breaking free (however brutally) of Molly's grasp.

'IT' IN THE ROTH-TEXT: STRATEGIC VAGUENESS

Further intertext variation is apparent in usage of *it* as relational clause subject. The pronoun fulfils this role in seven relational clauses in the Lucas-text, nine in the Ike-text, but fourteen in the Roth-text. Again, the feature's deployment in the Roth-text is distinctive in both frequency and function. For while relational-clause *it* in the Lucas- or Ike-texts either corefers straightforwardly with a recently mentioned noun phrase (i.e. substitutionary *it*), or else functions as existential or 'empty' subject, the situation is very different in the Roth passage. Here *it* regularly denotes a vaguely specified element of Roth's personal and cultural inheritance, one for which he is in part responsible. Besides clearly substitutional or existential use of *it* in relational clauses, there are also the following:

> so that it would be gone forever (it = the rift, or the shame and grief of the rift??)
> as if it had never happened (it = the whole rift)
> since it did not exist (it =some vague tension)
> it was shame now (it = what he felt?)
> it was grief (it = what he felt?)
> it was shame also (it = what he felt?)
> he said it the best he could (it = an apology/reconciliation?)
> it would be gone forever (it = the rift)

The cumulative impact of the recurring items is most evident when they are encountered in context:

> Then one day he [Roth] knew it was grief and was ready to admit it was shame also, wanted to admit only it was too late then, forever and forever too late. He went to Molly's house . . . he said it the best he could for that moment, because later he would be able to say it all right, say it once and forever so that it would be gone forever. . . . But it was too late. (pp. 112–13)

Thus nine of the thirteen uses of *it* as subject in the Roth-text refer to a vaguely defined but crucial state or condition in the strained relations between Roth and the black McCaslins.

There may be good pragmatic reasons here for use of an indeterminate-reference pronoun to report the traumatic rupture in personal and familial relations as experienced by the young boy (a young boy who is upset yet aloof – 'lordly . . . peremptory'). But the thematic motivation for the use of *it* here is more important.

Up to this time, Roth has experienced unquestioned intimacy (anonymous communal brotherhood) with Henry, Molly, and Lucas. They have been his family, in no way alien or impenetrable to him. But in his triggering and then experiencing of a racial, familial, and personal gulf we encounter the pattern of all Roth's subsequent dealings with all blacks, including these, his own relatives. Characteristic of that pattern of dealings is the presence of a barrier of impenetrability and inscrutability, of what Faulkner might have called 'tranquil hostility'.

Just as Molly's voice, on p. 113, had seemed to Roth to be as it formerly had been, Roth will always afterwards be vulnerable to his inability to penetrate the calm masks of the blacks. He recurringly fails to discern the true feelings and motivations of Lucas and others until he has been presented with *faits accomplis*. His tragic personal inheritance is to know that he is incapable of understanding his black relatives' subtle motivations. As a consequence he is driven to designate those motivations by the pronoun of vaguest, most general potential reference, *it*. What is perhaps chiefly a self-defence mechanism in this passage of remembered childhood humiliation becomes an integral element in Roth's attenuated and depersonalized relations with the blacks who surround him. Thus 'The Fire and the Hearth', chapter 3, opens with Roth barely recognizing old Molly, though he apparently leaves her candy every month; and his relations with his former lover and the bearer of their child in 'Delta Autumn', in which Ike is used as intermediary, are ruthlessly impersonal.

GENERIC SENTENCES IN THE IKE-TEXT

The Ike-text is in sharp contrast with the other two texts with regard to its numerous generic sentences. There are nine of these within the passage, all playing a significant part in the covert characterization of Ike. They include:

1 At the last, fathers and sons are no kin. (p. 308)

2 How much it takes to compound a man. (p. 308)

3 Those who serve you even for pay are your kin. (p. 311)

4 Those who injure you are more than brother or wife. (p. 311)

5 The new country [of love and marriage?] . . . was the heritage of all. (p. 311)

6 Each must share with another in order to come into it. (p. 311)

7 In the sharing they become one. (p. 311)

Generic sentences are usually the preserve of intrusive narrators and are a means of inserting general evaluative templates or standards of worldly wisdom against which the behaviour of characters within a novel can be set. But in *Go Down, Moses* generic sentences are rare outside 'The Bear', section IV, where they are regularly part of the temporary narratorially aligned disclosure of Ike's values.

As has often been noted, the switch from report of particular facts to a general statement entails a claim of a very much enhanced authority (see e.g. Fowler 1977). The reader's response to such sentences depends very much on the quality of the insight and freshness of the judgement or observation. Even when the sentences carry only clichéd prejudice, however, they may have a literary function within the discourse. Ike's narratorially cast generic sentences in 'The Bear', section IV, in general and at its close in particular, are often romantic and over-rhetorical half-truths about human nature which highlight his idealistic distance from a willingness to grapple with the complexities of ordinary life. They are also, like his compulsive ascriptions of causal explanation, indicative of his fondness for withdrawing to a detached perspective from which he can escape from the inconsistencies in his own behaviour by diverting attention to supposedly profound or noble sentiments. Thus we are presented with the profound half-truths that fathers and sons are finally no kin, while your paid servants are, and the noble injunction that love and wholeness come through sharing.

> and they were married, they were married and it was the new country, his heritage too as it was the heritage of all, out of the earth, beyond the earth, yet of the earth because his too was of the earth's long chronicle, his too because each must share with another in order to come into it and in the sharing they become one: for that while, one: for that little while at least, one: indivisible, that while at least irrevocable and unrecoverable . . . (p. 311)

Our suspicions concerning Ike's true commitment to submissive sharing should already be aroused by the past tense of generic statement 5. That statement claims that 'the new country . . . *was* the heritage of all' (my emphasis). The past tense here suggests that this millenarian new country is viewed by Ike as irrevocably past, removed from present experience. The validity of the claim is thus limited to some past era, and its falsifiability is thereby equally attenuated. And, as the repeated phrase *that while at least* emphasizes, the temporal extent of validity of Ike's claims about that sharing, in his own experience, is decidedly limited.

NAMING

A final point of reference in comparison and contrast of the three texts and their main characters will be naming practices, which often function as an index of the narrator's or character's respect for the named individual. The major trends in the naming of participants in the three texts are detailed in table 11. That naming can disclose evaluation is well recognized by Roth Edmonds, who recalls how Lucas so often addresses him with insulting carelessness:

> the old negro who in his case did not even bother to remember not to call him mister, who called him Mr Edmonds and Mister Carothers or Carothers or Roth or son or spoke to him in a group of younger negroes, lumping them all together, as 'you boys'. (p. 116)

Roth himself, of course, shows no great respect or affection for Lucas in referring to him here as *the old negro*.

Within the Roth-text, the stylistic turbulence concerning naming in the second half of p. 116 (co-occurring with the prominence of

Table 11 Varieties of naming in the sample texts

	Lucas	Zack	Zack's wife	Molly	
Pronouns	108	2	10	30	
Proper names	5	5	0	3	
Definite descriptions	0	15	5	5	

	Roth	Henry	Lucas	Molly	Zack
Pronouns	78	8	19	13	7
Proper names	4	14	15	5	0
Definite descriptions	9	0	4	1	0

	Ike	McCaslin	Ike's wife		
Pronouns	119	1	55		
Proper names	5	8	0		
Definite descriptions	0	0	3		

269

relativization and subordination, as noted earlier) merits attention. Here the narrative, though cast from Edmonds's perspective, is drawn to refer to Edmonds as *Edmonds*, and to Lucas as *he*, in order to present a clear version of the latter's assumed reasoning:

> [Lucas has an account] which Edmonds knew he would never pay for the good and simple reason that Lucas would not only outlive the present Edmonds as he had outlived the two preceding him, but would probably outlast the very ledgers which held the account. Then the still which Lucas had run almost in his, Edmonds', back yard for at least twenty years . . . (p. 117)

The formulations *his, Edmonds'* here, and *he, Edmonds*, a few lines later, are laborious but necessary devices in order to 'reinstate' Edmonds as the dominant perspective of narration. Adopted after extended discussion of Lucas, they are a clumsy delaying of the informational flow of the text, while he whose viewpoint is being presented (Edmonds) reasserts his presence: another linguistic symptom of the 'trouble and conflict' (p. 116) Lucas always causes Edmonds.

Plural pronouns, by contrast, function in the Roth-text to promote a sense of shared experience among so-denoted participants. Thus, for all the hostility of the confrontation of Lucas and Zack over Molly, the two men are repeatedly referred to by the pronoun *they* in the course of Roth's reflection on p. 115, and are thereby united in a bond of particular closeness, sharing 'something which nobody but they knew and would ever know if the telling depended on them'. More poignant is Roth's ill-judged assumption of renewed community with his black relatives, at the top of p. 113, in which he believes himself to have been accepted back as an equal by Henry and Lucas, so that the narrative refers to the three of them as *they*: 'Then they were busy in the yard in the dusk.'

Generally, in both the Roth- and Lucas-texts, variation between pronominal and proper naming is subtly done, while adoption of definite description is a much more overt manoeuvre. This is fairly clear in the Lucas-text, where Zack Edmonds is most often referred to as *the white man*. The description, the reader may infer, is really Lucas's; it is one that establishes narratorial detachment from Zack, while making the reader fully aware that Zack is a white man and that in the narrative context his whiteness is significant. Indeed, in the Lucas-text, every major character besides Lucas himself is named at one point or another by a definite description specifying their skin colour. Thus Zack Edmonds's wife is *the white woman*, Roth is *the white child* or *the white man*, and even Molly is once referred to as *the black woman*.

Predictably, there are no distancing definite descriptions denoting Lucas himself in the Lucas-text. The only passage in which some narratorial withdrawal from Lucas's perspective may be detected is in the first half of p. 50. As has been in part noted in my discussion of transitivity and animacy, this Lucas-oriented narrative shamefacedly strives to mask Lucas's culpability for the physical assault on Molly:

> his clawed hand darting towards the child as her hand sprang and caught his wrist. . . . He broke his wrist free, flinging her hand and arm back; he heard the faint click of her teeth when the back of her hand struck her chin and he watched her start to raise her hand to her mouth, then let it fall again.

The initiation of the assault is reported in a non-finite clause with a part of Lucas's body (hence only the instrument), itself ascribed the non-human attribute 'clawed', in the subject and actor position of the clause, while the true intentional actor remains unstated. Subsequently, the causal connection between Lucas's flinging back of Molly's hand and its striking her on the chin is suppressed. Rather the two events are sharply separated by a semicolon and by the placing of the second event in a clause subordinated to one in which 'what Lucas heard' is the informational focus of the main clause. In this way the textual reporting leaves the impression of lamely attempting to attribute responsibility for the assault simply to *his clawed hand* and *the back of her hand*, rather than to Lucas himself, as intentional participant.

In comparison with the narratorial distancing of Lucas from that action of which he is no doubt ashamed, it is much easier for the Ike-oriented narrative of pp. 312 ff. to convey emotional distance from the apparently dehumanized manipulations effected by Ike's wife. Some of those means have been noted already. They are reinforced by two alienatory appositional definite descriptions of the woman at that point where, implicitly, Ike finds her behaviour most grotesque. She has already been repeatedly reduced from an animate individual to *the voice* and *the hand*; by p. 314, not looking at him, her whole body reportedly altered, she is further distanced and generalized as 'the chaste woman, the wife'.

The other intriguing characteristic of the naming in the Ike-text relates to Ike himself, who on five occasions on pp. 308–9 is alluded to as *Isaac McCaslin*. This happens in passages where the Ike-oriented narrative considers the 'case' of Isaac McCaslin – as if it were one on which detached and objective judgement, as from a non-aligned narrator, were possible here. In practice it appears to be a further textual expression of Ike's mannered intellectualization and egocentricity:

> and he [Ike] looking at the bright rustless unstained tin and thinking and not for the first time how much it takes to compound a man (Isaac McCaslin for instance) and of the devious intricate choosing yet unerring path that man's (Isaac McCaslin's for instance) spirit takes among all that mass to make him at last what he is to be, not only to the astonishment of them . . . who believed they had shaped him, but to Isaac McCaslin too.

SUMMARY

In this chapter I hope to have demonstrated how variable deployment of a range of syntactic features and patterns serves to further, and in part constitute, narrative characterization. From a purely linguistic viewpoint, relativization, causal connectivity, transitivity, vaguely referring *it* pronouns, generic sentences, patterns of naming, and so on, may seem a miscellaneous set of topics. But they are united by being foregrounded in the distinct narrative styles we can associate with the three characters. We can relate the grammatical elements taken separately, as well as the three clusters of patterns and features taken as wholes (i.e. treated as three distinct syntactical styles), to implicit narratorial evaluations of the presented characters. In this way the stylistician-as-critic can connect the identified linguistic patterns, the syntactical styles, to such fundamental interpretative touchstones of Faulknerian criticism as the themes of community, solidarity, alienation, (ir)rationality, self-deception through bogus intellectualization and rhetorical excess, passive submission, active control, freedom and entrapment, and so on. In a writer as evidently concerned with uniqueness of expression as Faulkner was, close attention to varying syntactical styles in the presentation of characters may enrich critical awareness – as well as potentially contributing to the wider discussion of character in critical and narrative theory.

12

MONOLOGUE AND DIALOGUE

ANALYSING SPEECH, FICTIONAL AND REAL

This chapter turns attention away from narrative, which has been the focus of much of this book, in order to demonstrate that literary linguistics can have useful things to say about the direct-speech portions of novels too. Most of this chapter will look at the structure of particular conversations in *Go Down, Moses*, but in the next section I offer some observations within an older tradition of analysis of direct speech, one which focuses on the sometimes varying rendering of the dialects (standard or otherwise) of characters, relating such dialectalism both to sociolinguistic claims about their significance (e.g. as expressions of covert prestige, upward social mobility or otherwise, power, solidarity, identification or exclusion) and to the author's thematic purposes.

Traditionally stylisticians have rarely addressed themselves to the logic, structure, or dynamics of the talk in novels, reflecting in this the tardiness in the parent discipline, linguistics, to take ordinary speech interaction as its subject-matter. But emphases have changed, within some species of linguistics at least, and the recent abundance of linguistic and sociolinguistic analyses of speech, in both institutional and casual settings, affords stylisticians a greatly enriched repertoire of models and descriptions to adopt and apply in the domain of literature.

These broadly linguistic models and hypotheses concerning the structure and logic of talk include the following, which is far from an exhaustive listing:

1 An ethnomethodologically oriented conversation analysis (henceforth, c.a.) tradition, offering detailed descriptions of the work

273

done by co-conversationists in mutually performing certain tasks within talk (e.g. getting started, or closing a conversation), with its emphasis on such notions as 'repair', 'recipient design', 'displayed understanding', and 'preference organization'.

2 Birmingham (UK) discourse analysis: a model positing a structured hierarchy of elements forming a quasi-grammatical descriptive taxonomy, especially useful in identifying the regularities within institutionalized interactions (formal teacher–pupil, doctor–patient, and lawyer–witness exchanges). Key works in this tradition include Sinclair and Coulthard (1975), Coulthard and Montgomery (1981), and Burton (1980).

3 Proposals which relate language behaviour to sociology and social psychology, identifying aspects of the content and form of individuals' conversational contributions as heavily shaped by concern for the maintenance of an appropriate image of self and other or addressee. Two central notions here are 'face' (most fully explored in Goffman (1981)) and 'politeness' (on which see especially Brown and Levinson (1978)).

4 A fourth tradition, popular with literary analysts in relation to other topics besides conversation, has developed from Grice (1975), a seminal paper on what we logically expect from our co-conversationists, such that absence of the overt fulfilment of these expectations prompts us to make various inferences, in a principled way, about what has been covertly intended to be conveyed. The fundamental claim is that individuals are ordinarily co-operative in their talk, saying neither more nor less about a subject than they believe is required, and saying only what they believe is true and relevant, in a brief and orderly fashion. Among those works that have developed Grice's propositions along lines that should be of interest to stylisticians are Pratt (1977), Leech (1983), and Sperber and Wilson (1986).

Having listed these four distinct but often overlapping orientations, all of which seem of great potential value in the stylistics of fictional conversation, I must emphasize that in this chapter, using aspects of these models or hypotheses in focusing on the dynamics of particular dialogues in *Go Down, Moses*, I shall draw less on the Birmingham tradition and the face/politeness literature than on c.a. and Grice. Burton (1980) has developed the Birmingham model in interesting ways, so as to render it applicable to both casual conversation and drama text analysis – a development which has championed the very valuable notions of 'discourse framework' and 'supporting and challenging moves' (see Toolan (1985 and 1987), for further applications to literary texts, and discussion). But the broader ambitions of the model, its commitment to matching talk to a finite set of acts and moves (the standard assumption of speech-act theory) and to a hard-to-achieve replicability of description, are confronted by particularly acute problems in the face of ordinary conversation. Any structurally inclined linguist will be attracted to the aspirations of this model, but many argue that the model is premature if not fundamentally mistaken (see Levinson 1983).

It needs to be acknowledged at the outset that fictional dialogue is an artificial version of talk, partly shaped by a variety of aesthetic and thematic intentions and conventions. The artifice emerges in many ways, but perhaps pre-eminent is the continued presence behind the direct-speech dialogue of fictional characters – though we often ignore this in the reading – of a teller addressing the reader. That teller (author or narrator) will have his or her own aesthetic and thematic goals, and will intend to highlight this, conceal that. Perhaps for this very reason, the more routine aspects of talk that have attracted much analytical attention are precisely those that tellers often omit. Prosody, overlaps, and closing, opening, and repair sequences, for example, much focused upon by analysts, are rarely prominent or fully rendered in fictional dialogue. While c.a. focuses on everyday conversational routines, fictional dialogue is often non-routine. If it were so, could we bear to read it? Embedded in and contributory to a story, fictional dialogue is part of what author and reader take to be extremely tellable material. And it may well be designed (in ways that make it less like a transcript of ordinary talk) so as to enhance its 'tellability' (on tellability, see Sacks (1975) and Polanyi (1981)).

Nevertheless it seems incontrovertible that many crucial structural and functional principles are at work just as much in fictional dialogue as in natural conversation. It is hard to see how we could recognize and respond to the former as a version of the latter if this were not so. Accordingly, my interest is in developing a stylistics of fictional conversation, drawing eclectically on the work mentioned above. While these theorists represent different perspectives, their views are often compatible and can be made to converge on the data, so as to provide mutual support for a particular assessment of a particular dialogue. Underlying much of my descriptive analysis will be the conviction that it is simply not possible to specify a finite set of rules governing conversational practice – as one perhaps can in the description of the syntax (though hardly of the meaning) of standard written language. Indeed, it has perhaps been stylisticians' awareness of conversation's 'overflowing' of all attempts at 'capture' by rules, hence by orthodox linguistic treatment, that has led them to neglect literary dialogue.

To reiterate a thread of argument that has run through this book, the assumption here will be that, though there can be no finite grammar of talk, yet talk discloses an important degree of structure and organization: it is neither random nor devoid of coherence, a coherence that speakers work mutually to achieve, on both conscious and unconscious levels. Rules of talk hold only in a less formalizable Wittgensteinian sense – rules as signposts or helpful maxims, principles that organize our proceeding towards incompletely specified goals. And those goals are themselves locally determined by the current interests of conversationalists (the emphasis on local relevance emerges in many of the discussions mentioned above). That is why the theoretical emphasis of c.a. is so attractive:

> Conversational analysis is concerned with the social organization of conversational interaction, and conceives of the various situated manifestations of this organization as a set of methodical solutions to locally occurring technical problems that conversationalists must 'solve'. The orderliness of conversation is thus seen to be an *achieved* orderliness, and accomplishment of conversationalists on actual occasions of their talk. (West and Zimmerman 1981: 506)

Throughout Faulkner, what gets done conversationally is very much more than what actually gets said. This is soon evident in *Go Down, Moses*, as the reader struggles to grasp the overt connections between the remarks of Buck, Buddy, and Hubert during the card-games of 'Was', as well as the covert import (does Buddy win, or must Buck marry Sophonsiba – as he eventually does anyway?). Both the fictional conversationists and we readers are obliged to work very hard at deriving intended but elliptically specified inferences. Faulkner seems not to have put much faith in the tactic of dispensing with such hard work by simply stating things baldly and 'on record'. Usually (e.g. given the unequal status of interactants, or the delicacy of the topic – the skirting of taboo subjects, and so on) this is not a permitted option. Even were it a possibility, Faulkner seems to have shared Addie Bundren's distrust of words *per se* (in *As I Lay Dying*) and constantly focused his attention on the 'what was meant' behind the 'what was said'. But before exploring these issues further, from an analytical standpoint, the function of the various dialects rendered in the novel will be considered.

DIALECT AS SOCIAL SEMIOTIC

Dialect in fictional dialogue is both important and problematic. The problems have been charted in valuable detail in Page's (1973) pioneering study, but see also Chapman (1984), Shapiro (1984), Golding (1985), Cole (1986), and Macafee (1986). Many readers, we may suspect, remain impatient of rendered speech that departs to any appreciable degree from standard colloquial speech, or even from standard written English. The reasons for this intolerance or resistance may be many: a normative familiarity with standard language; an attachment to the prestige of standard speech; an expectation that novels, in all their aspects, should be 'improving' – an expectation established by a school diet of novels by Austen, Thackeray, James, and Forster, in which the standard dialect is particularly dominant. Most of us have on occasion arrived at that minority of pages in Dickens, Melville, Hardy, or Lawrence where some other dialect is rendered, and felt a spirit of enforced labour descend. We struggle through the barbarous spellings (barbarous since they are foreign in relation to the standard orthography), the plethora of apostrophes, the sheer unrecognizability of it all, and feel the truth of the near-tautology that alien forms alienate.

But dialect in the English novel of the last 150 years or so has often been intended to do something other than alienate, to be something other than quaint or comical. It is generally agreed that, in earlier periods during which a standard dialect prevailed, rendering a character's speech by means of forms that purported to be a transcription of some low-prestige dialect was typically a way of intimating the uncouthness, ignorance, stupidity, or even criminality of that character. However, beginning with Dickens and Mrs Gaskell, new motivations were tapped. For these novelists begin to present characters (such as Stephen Blackpool in *Hard Times*) who speak non-standard dialects but are intelligent and independent-minded. Their speech deviates from the norm not so as to prompt the reader to consign them to a notional periphery of deviancy in the moral universe, but so as to assert a counter-norm. Such alien dialects are an index of the character's adherence to standards of behaviour and values positively opposed to the normal and conventional. Increasingly, the personal and social significance of dialect informs and meshes with the thematic significance of literary works.

Even a cursory glance at the direct speech of *Go Down, Moses* will reveal that virtually all speakers adopt a fairly colloquial mode of utterance. Exceptions to this are the indirectly reported genteel speech of Sophonsiba in 'Was', the educated speech of Gavin Stevens, the ornate formalism of the black clergyman in section IV of 'The Bear', and the extraordinarily discursive styles of Ike and Cass in that same section. Within the dominant colloquial mode, however, there are varying degrees of non-standardism, and it is in inspecting those degrees of distinctiveness of speech that we may find an expression of the differential status, evaluation, independence, and credibility accorded to particular characters.

Below I list a series of markers of low-prestige non-standard speech, and note their use by the major characters in the novel.

1 *Aint.* This is used by all characters (even Sophonsiba Beauchamp, on p. 12, in the report of her speech relayed by Cass) except Gavin Stevens and the black clergyman stranger who marries Fonsiba. The stranger's prestige dialect and baroque circumlocutions are grotesquely ill matched to his actual destitution, as this is portrayed in the preceding narrative description of his unworked smallholding:

> 'I have a few groceries in the house from my credit account with the merchant in Midnight who banks my pension check for me. I have executed to him a power of attorney to handle it for me as a matter of mutual –'
>
> 'I see. And if the groceries dont last the twenty days?'
>
> 'I still have one more hog.'
>
> 'Where?'
>
> 'Outside,' the other said. 'It is customary in this country to allow stock to range free during the winter for food. It comes up from time to time. But no matter if it doesn't; I can probably trace its footprints when the need –' (pp. 279–80)

2 Irregular first-person present-tense forms (*I wants, I needs,* etc.). These are common in the speech of George, Nat, and Rider,

and intermittent in the speech of Lucas. There is an interesting disparity in Molly's speech (standard in this respect in 'The Fire and the Hearth', except for 'you needs to be in bed' (p. 42), but no longer so in 'Go Down, Moses').

3 Irregular past-tense forms.   These are common in the speech of Lucas, George, Nat, and Rider, though among this group important distinctions can be made. Lucas's past-tense non-standardisms are less 'visible', being forms such as *throwed* and *knowed*, where it seems that the regular past-tense dental suffix has been generalized to irregular verbs. Nat's irregular forms include *seed*, *lef*, and *axed*, while George is reported using *fotch*. Within this category we could also note the irregular 'past-tense' form of *may* used by George and Nat: *mought*. This spelling is not used to convey Rider's pronunciation – *mout* (p. 151) is used – although it is difficult to see a difference in pronunciation between these two forms. The different transcriptions here may carry some sort of evaluative categorization rather than a phonetic discrimination. Both Rider (whose deviant speech may be partly attributed to his increasing drunkenness) and his relatives use markedly low-prestige forms (*dat* and *den* for *that* and *then*, *awready* for *already*, *doan* for *dont*, *mawin* for *morning*, and so on). Typical of Rider's speech is the sequence of non-standardisms in 'Ah'm thu wid all dat' (p. 138).

4 Double negatives.   While rare in Lucas's speech, they are more frequent in that of Sam, Boon, George, Nat, and Rider. Although also absent from Roth's speech, two appear in Ike's speech in 'Delta Autumn', along with a startling triple negative – a strikingly black-vernacular idiom used even in the process of his rejection of his young black cousin: 'Cant nobody do nothing for you!' (p. 361).

5 *Hit* (for *it*), *wuz/uz* for *was*.   These are common in the speech of more lowly evaluated blacks, e.g. Rider and George, but not in that of Lucas, Molly, or Nat.

6 *Be*-deletion from copula or auxiliary position. This is absent from Lucas's speech, rare in that of Nat and George, occasional in Rider's.

As mentioned above, Molly Beauchamp's speech is notably more non-standard in the late story, 'Go Down, Moses', than in 'The Fire and the Hearth'. *Be*-deletion is absent from her speech in the earlier story, except for 'Where you going this time of night?' (p. 42), but is rather frequent in the later one. In the first example below, *be*-deletion is closely followed by non-standard infinitival *be* in auxiliary position:

'And you the Law. . . . I be staying with Hamp Worsham. He my
brother.' (p. 371)

'Sold him to Pharoah and now he dead.' (p. 380)

On the final page of the novel, the newspaper editor relates to Gavin
Stevens what Molly had asked him, using a markedly low-status
speech dialect:

'She said, "Is you gonter put hit in de paper?"' (p. 383)

The editor's version of Molly's speech is far more non-standard (more
Rider-like) than the rendering of it elsewhere by the narrator. Possible
reasons for the variations in these renderings of Molly, who is almost
as near standard colloquial as Lucas in the early story, are several. It
might be simply authorial inconsistency, when recasting the stories
into the novel. Or it might be due to the town setting of this story, and
the greater 'noticeability' of dialect relative to non-rural literates. But,
alone or in addition, the superiority which the white editor seems to
feel could be the rationale. In his reporting to Stevens of the old
woman's words he asserts a gulf between his own dialect and hers
which, again, supports an evaluation of her in other respects too as
alien and bizarre. It is particularly likely that the editor might impute
alien dialect to the old woman, since he regards the content of her
speech also as alien and eccentric.

In broad terms, then, we may propose a loose ranking of the main
characters, in the degree to which they depart from standard dialect:

1 the black clergyman stranger, Gavin Stevens
2 Roth Edmonds, Ike, Cass
3 Sam, Boon
4 Lucas, Molly
5 Nat
6 George
7 Rider

But more interesting than any such ranking is the local impact of
dialectal forms, and here we must look at further specific incidents
such as Ike's encounter with his black kinswoman in 'Delta Autumn'.

Over and above the judgement as to how much unfamiliar dialectalism it is wise to confront a non-local readership with, there is the
difficulty of ensuring that readers accurately 'read off' the sounds that
deviant spellings are intended to signal. The problem is less lexical

than phonological: with dialectal lexis, we know we don't recognize certain words, and know we must resort to a glossary or pure guesswork. With strange spellings of known words, however, we often imagine we do know what pronunciation is intended, if only because we recognize the form that confronts us as a departure from a known, standard form. Our guesses here may be quite mistaken but are less evidently so. Since Sumner Ives's seminal article (1950) on literary dialect, it has been standard to assume that, for accuracy in the reading of literary dialect, we first have to know the author's own dialect, and interpret the rendering of his or her characters' dialects in terms of that dialect. Clearly the work of Ives and many subsequent analysts assumes authorial care in the rendering of dialect (even though, through dialectal selection and generalization, literary dialect is on this view a strategically modified version of real speech). However, given the inescapable fact of the unreliability and inconsistency of English spelling in its representation of English sounds, a rather different tack may be taken, and attributed also to many writers. This would argue that only a limited amount of trouble is usually taken by writers over rendering dialect pronunciation (as distinct from dialect vocabulary). McHale's (1985) arguments, in a fascinating discussion of the status of speech mimesis, seem consonant with this. He advances the hypothesis of 'a *mediated* relationship between the raw material of (linguistic) reality and its literary representation, refracted, as it were, through a linguistic stereotype' (McHale 1985: 362). This subtler theory rejects the rather simple notion of speech copying, of a kind of transcription in novel dialogue. The fact that strict dialectological accuracy is of doubtful relevance to the novelist is one that many have acknowledged but most have been reluctant to confront. Usually, only plausibility, consistency, and a clear sense of the dialect's distinctness are necessary.

More than these minimal requirements may be needed, however, when code-switching is involved, where a character moves, as appropriate, from a home-based local dialect to a public and formal near-standard one (as in Hardy's *Tess of the d'Urbervilles*). And particularly interesting are the cases of a conscious inspection and dramatization of the disparity between standard and local dialect, as in Lawrence (discussed in detail in Leith (1980)) and Dickens and Gaskell (see Fowler 1981). There are clear possibilities of interpreting such clashes, and more acute self-conscious divergences, in terms of Halliday's notion of anti-language (Halliday 1978) and even of

Bakhtin's narrative poetics (see Fowler 1981). In addition, analysis could address the varying syntactic complexity of different characters' speech. In this respect, interestingly, we would find Molly and Lucas no more non-standard than Roth, and at least as complex in their constructions.

Despite these intriguing extra considerations, it has to be conceded that there is nothing in *Go Down, Moses* comparable with the famous sermon scene in section 4 of *The Sound and the Fury*, in which, as the Reverend Shegog is increasingly moved by the spirit of Easter, his speech modulates dramatically and inexorably from standard to black dialectal forms. There is no such richness of dialect exploitation in *Go Down, Moses*: there is simply the previously noted cline of non-standardism (and 'respectability') with Rider at one end, Gavin Stevens and the clergyman at the other, and interesting intermediate cases such as those of Molly and Lucas. Lucas used a fairly low-prestige dialect but remains a highly valued individual, the content of whose speech seems highly valued too. In the revision of 'Gold is not Always' for incorporation into the novel (usefully discussed in Millgate (1964)), various non-standardisms were cut from Lucas's speech, but not from George's. Given this explicit care in the rendering of Lucas's speech, it seems worthwhile to chart briefly some of the changes of dialect – the styles – attributed to Lucas in the course of his canny dealings with those in his milieu.

The first of Lucas's styles encountered is the rhetorical, arrogant, long-winded, self-righteous voice of much of chapter 1 of 'The Fire and the Hearth':

> He, Lucas Beauchamp, the oldest living McCaslin descendant still living on the hereditary land, who actually remembered old Buck and Buddy in the living flesh . . . – he, to share one jot, one penny of the money which old Buck and Buddy had buried almost a hundred years ago, with an interloper [George Wilkins] . . . – a jimber-jawed clown who could not even learn how to make whisky, who had not only attempted to interfere with and jeopardise his business and disrupt his family, but had given him a week of alternating raging anxiety and exasperated outrage culminating in tonight – or last night now – and not even finished yet, since he still had the worm and kettle to conceal. (p. 40)

A crucial ground for the formality and discursiveness of this fanciful narrative (Buck and Buddy were in fact dead five years before Lucas was born, and the idea that they ever buried money is similarly Lucas's invention) is that it is a free indirect rendering of Lucas's thoughts. Since they are embedded within the narrative frame, it is in consequence hard to decide whether the words used are entirely attributable to Lucas. Curiously, the narrative has Lucas describe George with the very same phrase – as a 'jimber-jawed clown' – used by the white judge rather later in the story (p. 74).

Rather more common than the above is Lucas's direct speech, in near-standard language, in chapter 2 of 'The Fire and the Hearth', during his dealings with Roth and the salesman:

> Didn't I tell you about them two strange white men that come in here after dark that night three or four years ago and dug up twenty-two thousand dollars in a old churn and got out again before anybody even laid eyes on them? (pp. 79–80)

From this norm, however, there is a vivid code-switching to a more non-standard 'black' dialect in the brief italicized passages that render Lucas's developing private thoughts on events (thus, a version of free direct thought). When he sees the flashy, seemingly urban salesman resting by squatting down on his heels, Lucas reacts: '*Hah*, he thought, *He mought talk like a city man and he mought even think he is one. But I know now where he was born at*' (p. 80).

Finally, a third style surfaces on the last occasion Lucas speaks in the novel. The speech is delivered at the very close of the story, as a kind of homiletic coda, as Lucas explains why he will now abjure treasure-hunting:

> 'No,' Lucas said. 'Get rid of it. I dont want never to see it again. Man has got three score and ten years on this earth, the Book says. He can want a heap in that time and a heap of what he can want is due to come to him, if he just starts in soon enough. I done waited too late to start. . . . But I am near to the end of my three score and ten, and I reckon to find that money aint for me'. (p. 131)

Is this the authentic Lucas voice, formal and rhetorical (scope for the chiasmus around 'a heap', and framing chiastic mentions of the 'three score and ten years'), weaving detached wisdom with worldly appetite? The style is compelling in its unembarrassed merging of biblical formality and low-prestige usage, a merging that is not in the least incongruous. Like Lucas himself, when he is properly focused upon in the narrative – as in chapter 1 of 'The Fire and the Hearth' – the style succeeds at the risky business of being both vulgar and moving.

THE IKE–CASS DIALOGUE IN 'THE BEAR', SECTION IV

A relatively simple informative act on Ike's part, announcing to Cass upon his coming-of-age that he intends to give up the farm (his inherited material benefit from slavery and exploitation), becomes the basis for an elaborate exercise of self-analysis and of historical, religious, and racial interpretation. Curiously, we have to infer that that initiating topic-establishing turn, announcing his intention to relinquish the farm, has been completed by Ike, since this is not actually rendered. The direct speech begins with what we take to be Cass's reply:

'Relinquish,' McCaslin said. 'Relinquish. You, the direct male descendant . . .' (p. 256)

In the course of this protracted accounting, disparate sub-narratives, too long and detailed to be merely emblematic, are woven into the texture of this verbal and mental dialogue (the seeking-out of Fonsiba's feckless husband, for example, and the story of Hubert's tin-pot 'legacy'). Certain stages of the dialogue quite openly focus on one particular subject or another, but there are also numerous local points where the reader may be extremely puzzled as to quite what the topic of talk is. And examination of how topic, topic resolution, and topic progression are all managed here, by Ike and Cass, will highlight some significant tendencies.

Topic remains something of an intractable notion to analysts. Identification of topic of conversation seems to remain largely intuitive, although one might expect that developments from Keenan and Schieffelin's work on topic as primary presupposition – 'the proposition (or set of propositions) that the question of immediate concern pre-supposes' (Keenan and Schieffelin 1976: 344) – might lead to a more formalized account of topic maintenance and shift. But overwhelmingly studies of topic remain pre-theoretical, and discussions of topic shading and fading, of recycling and reintroduction, are not tied to explicit specifications of what counts as shading or fading. That may be of little embarrassment in many studies; but it does seem that more can and should be done to operationalize these categories by reference to specifiable degrees of difference in the propositions and retrievable presuppositions of adjacent turns of talk. Useful discussions of such issues include Hurtig (1977), Brown and Yule (1983), Gardner (1986), de Beaugrande and Dressler (1981), and Levinson (1983: 308–18).

From a c.a. perspective, however, this approach to topic is likely to seem unhelpfully detached; there the interest is in how participants in a conversation work at mutually identifying, elaborating, and concluding the discussion of any given issue:

> Topical coherence cannot be thought of as residing in some independently calculable procedure for ascertaining (for example) shared reference across utterances. Rather, topical coherence is something *constructed* across turns by the collaboration of participants. What needs then to be studied is how potential topics are introduced and collaboratively ratified, how they are marked as 'new', 'touched off', 'misplaced' and so on, how they are avoided or competed over and how they are collaboratively closed down. (Levinson 1983: 315)

In this spirit it may be useful to examine if, as speakers are generally supposed to do, Ike and Cass in 'The Bear', section IV, work at making their topic introductions, expansions, and divagations relevant to the prior talk; and, if they do not, why they do not.

The very opening of section IV articulates how Ike and Cass (in this, like many non-fictional conversationalists) will jointly focus on the topic of Ike's relinquishing or repudiating of the farm:

> He could say it, himself and his cousin *juxtaposed* not against the wilderness but against the tamed land which was to have been his heritage, the land which . . . (p. 254; my emphasis)

In this long and searching talk with Cass, juxtaposition, setting, all the circumstances that linguists lump together under the heading 'context', make the topic seem, to the reader, almost inevitable. For the first two pages, like so much Ike-oriented reflection that will follow, are a succinct calling to mind of the recent claims on ownership of the land, a rehearsal of the exploitative treatment of the Indians and blacks, of the binding, cable-strong threads of supply and demand recorded in the commissary ledgers. There is no surprise, then, in the reader's being appropriately oriented by the time McCaslin's response comes on p. 256: the reader has been copiously briefed. What is remarkable is the fullness of *McCaslin's* orientation to the topic, reflected in the way in which his lengthy response reviews much of the background that the narrative has just articulated, but in a different, pragmatic light: Ike's forebears took and held the land, 'no matter how', and Ike is the rightful heir.

But then the evidence here of a deep commonality of background and experience, notwithstanding the differences in evaluation of particular events, is characteristic of the entire dialogue. For that reason it increasingly reads like a rehearsed and familiar script, tried out and refined over time by these Southern white kinsmen struggling to elaborate contrasting interpretations from within their shared 'restricted code'. The synchronicity and fluency of this dialogue, with its many examples of the men accurately identifying the projectability of each others' turns, is most immediately apparent at turn transitions. Queries, challenges, revaluations of the other's speech by ironical quotation – all these are economically achieved by brief and pointed repetition of some of the closing words of one speaker in the other speaker's following turn:

> '. . . and the man who bought it [the land] bought nothing.'
>   'Bought nothing?' and he
>   'Bought nothing. Because He told in the Book . . .' (p. 257)

> '. . . or perhaps He would not see – perverse, impotent, or blind: which?' and he
>   'Dispossessed.' and McCaslin
>   'What?' and he
>   'Dispossessed. Not impotent: He didn't condone; not blind, because . . .' (p. 258)

The synchronicity, and its roots in shared knowledge and mutual comprehension, is succinctly captured by the following:

> 'And I know what you are going to say,' he said: 'That nevertheless Grandfather –' and McCaslin
>   ' – did own it. And not the first.' (p. 257)

Such exploitations of projectability (in so far as we can identify these in the artistic 'transcript' we are analysing) persist throughout the dialogue. Interruptions seem never to be violative, but part of a mutually accepted collaborative emphasis, even when the interrupting contribution is ironical or critical:

'. . . [The Southerners in the Civil War must have believed that] all necessary to conduct a successful war was not acumen . . . nor money nor even integrity and simple arithmetic but just love of land and courage –'

'And an unblemished and gallant ancestry and the ability to ride a horse,' McCaslin said. 'Dont leave that out.' (p. 289)

The way in which the talk triggers lengthy narrative flashbacks has already been remarked upon – flashbacks in which the reader is briefed in great detail concerning the incidents and individuals the two men have in mind in their present talk. This is a contextualizing of their utterances far beyond that catered for in most current linguistic-pragmatic models of contextualization. The flashbacks can be seen as a way of coping (in prose fiction) with the dilemma of presenting, 'within' a dialogue, large quantities of AB events and information (for discussion of Labov's notion of AB events – facts already known to both of a pair of conversationalists – see Burton (1980: 13, 30)).

Nowhere is this mechanism more apparent than at the point in the conversation where the talk turns to the length of time and number of individuals needed to make adequate restitution to all those (chiefly blacks) whose ancestors had been exploited:

'Uncle Buck and Uncle Buddy. And they not the first and not alone. . . . Not to mention 1865.' and he

'Yes. More men than Father and Uncle Buddy,' not even glancing toward the shelf above the desk, nor did McCaslin. They did not need to. To him it was as though the ledgers . . . were being lifted down . . . and spread open . . . (p. 261)

So begins the twenty-page narrative recollection of ledger entries, and events and dialogues linked to those entries. On p. 282 the record of the Ike–Cass talk simply resumes, it being quite distinctly understood that all that which Ike has reviewed in his mind has been present in Cass's consciousness too:

that was all: and McCaslin

'More men than that one Buck and Buddy to fumbleheed that truth. . . .' (p. 282)

It would be possible to cite many further instances of the uncannily complete integration of speech, gesture, and shared memory in this dialogue, but one may suffice, where Ike's claim about lack of freedom recalls to both of them the occasion when Ike and Sam had Old Ben bayed, but did not shoot him:

> '. . . because we have never been free –' and it was in McCaslin's eyes too, he had only to look at McCaslin's eyes and it was there, that summer twilight seven years ago . . . (p. 295)

There are also local details of the talk that are amenable to detailed attention. What, for example, is the warrant for Ike's remarkably extended and forensic review, addressed to Cass, of the grounds of his relinquishment? What Ike is doing in general here, and what he says he is doing specifically on p. 288, may be usefully related to what Garfinkel and Sacks (1970) term 'formulating': a developing, inspectable accounting for past and present actions or opinions, through the talk itself.

But a final area of topic management worth mentioning here must be the extraordinary way in which the Ike–Cass dialogue falls away, on p. 300, some pages before the close of the section. There is no proper termination or conclusion, and the whole exchange begins to look more like a therapeutic exercise. At any rate, Ike and Cass's interaction founders on the rock of radically different conceptions of freedom or what it means to be free. The issue is broached on several occasions during the latter part of the dialogue. First there is the recalled assertion of Fonsiba, the young black McCaslin who ran away with the clergyman stranger: 'I'm free' (p. 280). Then, on p. 294, Ike asserts of the blacks that they possess something they had 'from the old free fathers a longer time free than us because we have never been free' (p. 295). Then on p. 299, when Cass makes a final effort to insist on the justness of Ike's inheritance, on the latter's greater claims to the land than either those of Cass himself or the black descendants, Ike cuts across this insistence to assert simply, 'I am free.' This theme is taken up by Cass, critically, soon after, when he raises the question just how long proper reconciliation will take. Ike replies:

> 'It will be long. I have never said otherwise. But it will be all right because they will endure –' and McCaslin
>
> 'And anyway, you will be free. – No, not now nor ever, we from them nor they from us. So I repudiate too.' (p. 299)

And the final exchange of the dialogue has Cass confronting Ike with the argument that, through Sam Fathers, he is the spiritual heir to the land:

'And who inherited from Sam Fathers, if not you? . . .' and he
  'Yes. Sam Fathers set me free.' (p. 300)

This final exchange, like the two cited above, is indicative of the
increasing trouble in the conversation, and the increasingly explicit
divergence of the men's opinions. It is only in such a spirit of
recognition that the difference is intractable, and that Ike will not be
persuaded, that Cass can say 'I repudiate too', putting on record his
rejection of Ike's course of action just as Ike has implicitly done of
Cass's action. These fractured exchanges, with responses tangential if
not openly at variance with their preceding turns, are a faltering
mutual working towards silence, a giving up on talk: not exactly a
breakdown, but a mutual and communicated recognition that there is
no compromise on either side. As elsewhere in the book, Ike's final
turn here (as I interpret it below) can be seen as well designed, even
profound:

  Yes, I inherited from Sam, and what I inherited from him was (an
  understanding of) freedom; that is precisely why I did not 'inherit
  the land' from him.

But whether or not Cass derives all this from Ike's cryptic observation
is doubtful. What is certain is that at this point the dialogue simply
drops away.

CO-OPERATIVENESS

An important starting-point for analysis of dialogue, as noted above,
can be Grice's 'co-operative principle' and its four subsidiary maxims
of quantity, quality, relation, and manner. These are logical bench-
marks, ideals of mutual interactive helpfulness, and what is immediately apparent as we look at novels – with all their dramatization
of characters in conflict, unreconciled, uncertain, groping towards
knowledge – is that speech (even fictional speech) is often perilously
far removed from these ideals. Such distance need not imply complete
absence of relation, however, between characters' actual speech and
these ideals. Outside of Orwell's *Nineteen Eighty-Four*, smear cam-
paigns, framings of innocent parties, and an extreme form of gossip
which lacks substance in reality, people retain a high regard for the
truth, in appropriate detail, told in orderly fashion when relevant.
  The expectation of such rational behaviour is so strong that it

shapes our conversational contributions and our interpretations of others' contributions. Typically, when we find one of the maxims not being evidently observed, we assume not that the speaker is merely violating or disregarding it, but that – still co-operatively – he or she is productively exploiting it, giving rise to some conversational implicature. Conversational implicature denotes the intended meaning of an utterance which is not conveyed by the conventional meaning of the words used, but which is deducible (and is intended to be deduced) from the utterance when the interpreter works at seeing how the speaker might still be being co-operative indirectly.

The literature that purports to question or revise these Gricean principles is now voluminous, and yet the maxims themselves are still widely regarded as a valuable preliminary orientation by many analysts. But one particular feature of the co-operative principle and its maxims, not often highlighted, needs to be emphasized. This is that they primarily concern the expected underlying nature of *non-initial* turns at talk: Grice's principles sketch the rational properties of responses within an already embarked-upon interaction. They are directions as to how addressees should respond, in talk, and presuppose that an addressee has been so identified and designated (i.e. by having been spoken to). This is particularly evident with regard to the quantity and relation maxims, but emerges fairly clearly from Grice's descriptions of non-verbal exchanges which, he argues, adhere to the same logic (Grice 1975: 47). In this passage, examples of maxim observation are attributed to individuals who 'are assisting' or are 'a partner' in an already initiated and mutually recognized activity (such as repairing a car or making a cake). The reactive nature of typical maxim observation is also reflected in *if . . . then* sentence structures: 'If . . . I need four screws, I expect you to hand me four, rather than two or six' (Grice 1975: 47). In the light of this it is reasonable to ask what happens when the assistant doesn't realize that just four screws are what is needed. And this important preliminary difficulty is one outside the brief of the Gricean system. The famous formulation of the co-operative principle – 'Make your conversational contribution such as is required, at the stage at which it occurs, by the accepted purpose or direction of the talk exchange in which you are engaged' – is frank in its emphasis that it concerns talk where conversationists believe that mutual awareness of what is required, of the purpose of the talk, already exists. But how that is achieved remains a mystery.

No doubt, in many instances, such mutual awareness can be assumed. Yet clearly in many other situations individual recognition of a 'mutually accepted direction' (Grice 1975: 45) is far from evident. We can expect that such talk will be more awkward, non-fluent, with overlaps and asynchronicity of turns (Gumperz 1982), and far more liable to breakdown. (Alternatively, we may occasionally find such talk more stimulating, provocative, and path-breaking.) Grice is right to imply that 'mutually accepted direction' is a preferred condition for most talkers; our concern to secure it, if possible, is reflected in the many idiomatic expressions we use to signal success or difficulties in this area: 'What are you driving at?' 'I (don't) see what you're getting at.' 'What are you (trying to) say(ing)?' 'Where does this lead/get us?' 'I see where you're coming from.' 'I'm not sure I'm following you.' 'So what are we saying here?'

If Grice's emphasis is on co-operative negotiation, negotiation is a keyword for c.a. too. However, where Gricean negotiation often seems to focus on the mental calculations of individual participants, working out the likely intended implicatures of utterances, c.a. negotiation is more 'physical' work, done in and through the talk itself.

The foregoing remarks have considerable relevance to *Go Down, Moses*, since a characteristic of the talk therein is the extent to which there is often 'trouble' during its preliminary, pre-Gricean phase, the phase at which mutual orientation needs to be established. In *Go Down, Moses*, over and over again, we find conscious or unconscious resistance to the establishment of mutual orientation, resulting in fractured, asynchronous talk. Topics, goals, interests, and willingness to talk are repeatedly at variance (section IV of 'The Bear' is, as previous discussion should have demonstrated, the most vivid exception to these trends). Talk goes on, of course, but it is constantly troubled by misunderstandings. If we conclude that Faulkner was deeply sceptical of the efficacy of mere talk in achieving understanding and reconciliation, this should hardly be cause for surprise, given his repeated statements that his whole writing career was a repeated failing effort to communicate all and only what needed to be said within the compass of a single sentence.

MUTUAL KNOWLEDGE AND 'UNDERSTANDING EACH OTHER' IN 'WAS' AND 'GO DOWN, MOSES'

The first major instance of topic clash in the novel, of a carefully negotiated conflict over whether there is a mutually known and mutually accepted direction to the talk, is essentially comic. It is one which also highlights just how finely integrated the business of talk is with that of intentional action. When Uncle Buck comes over to the Beauchamps' place in order to retrieve his slave, he finds himself drawn into conversation with Miss Sophonsiba in which he is characterized as eligible bachelor and reluctant suitor. That, at any rate, is the persistent implication of Sophonsiba's remarks:

> Then Miss Sophonsiba said something about a bumblebee . . . something about Uncle Buck was a bee sipping from flower to flower and not staying long anywhere and all that stored sweetness to be wasted . . . or maybe the honey was being stored up against the advent of a queen and who was the lucky queen and when? 'Ma'am?' Uncle Buck said. (p. 11)

Uncle Buck's basic strategy, so as to evade the co-option into talk of love and marriage which Sophonsiba intends, is repeatedly to make on-record statements that he has just come to get his slave, and must then go home. In this way he struggles to dispel any impression that his contributions to the talk are 'doing banter and courtship' rather than simply 'doing neighbourly politeness'. But the placement of these on-record statements (three in all) are also telling and mutually noticeable. When Sophonsiba makes her first grand entrance, greeting Buck with the mock-medieval 'Welcome to Warwick', the text continues:

> He [Cass] and Uncle Buck dragged their foot. 'I just come to get my nigger,' Uncle Buck said. 'Then we got to get on back home.' (p. 11)

Equally noticeable as a non-compliant, redirective response is Buck's reply to her request that the men return to the house early from their slave-hunting, so that she can show Buck her garden:

> Now that she had him, she wanted to show him her garden that Mr Hubert and nobody else had any sayso in. 'Yessum,' Uncle Buck said. 'I just want to catch my nigger. Then we got to get on back home.' (p. 14)

As a response to an implicit invitation this is noticeably improbable. There is a degree of accommodation and compliance in the 'Yessum', but it is hard to see this as a simple expression of acceptance of

Sophonsiba's indirect offer, as soon as we see it is structurally tied (i.e. in the same sentence) to the following modalized informatives. For those informatives are no sort of expression of acceptance (if anything, the opposite). More precisely, they are not tied to Sophonsiba's offer at all. The expectation that an offer will be followed (preferably) by an acceptance is not confirmed here, although, to repeat, the offer is not totally ignored – there is the 'Yessum'.

Thus the informative that follows is a positionally noticeable and highly expressive response to an elicitation that has not occurred. Buck's reply – in its entirety – makes best sense as an elaborate answer to a confimatory query concerning his purposes, as if Sophonsiba had suspected he was at Warwick purely to retrieve the slave, and had been checking this understanding with Buck. The cleverness of Buck's reply thus lies in its imputing to Sophonsiba of understandings that all her own behaviour is attempting to deny. And Buck's reply to the missing elicitation is designed to confirm unequivocally that his purpose is purely to catch Tomey's Turl, that he has no sexual or matrimonial intentions.

What happens here may be structurally typical of what happens within all divergent talk – talk where parties are at odds as to topic of talk, or treatment of that topic. Sophonsiba and Buck contribute turns which are ill-matched first and second pair-parts, since they conventionally belong to quite different pairs: *offer*–accept, and elicit–*inform*. The awkwardness remains manageable largely thanks to that most versatile evaluative preface, *yes*, perhaps the commonest means in English of suggesting supportive accommodation, which yet permits the speaker to continue with content and evaluations that may move in almost any direction.

In the same non-compliant spirit, Uncle Buck declines to make any verbal acknowledgement that he understands the meaning of the ludicrous chivalric red ribbon Sophonsiba sends him as a token of her 'favour' during his slave-hunting. A non-verbal offer-cum-inform is deflected by a verbal elicit or query:

'What for?' he said.
    'She just sont hit to you,' the nigger said. 'She say to tell you "success".'
    'She said what?' Uncle Buck said.
    'I dont know, sir,' the nigger said. 'She just say "success".'
    'Oh,' Uncle Buck said. (p. 16)

And yet it is far from always possible to effect an intentional verbal expunging of an accidental physical action. The 'accepted direction' of some actions – such as that of a man entering the bed of a woman who is not his wife – are just too 'known' and predetermined by the community for individuals, male or female, to be able to claim different motivation (even privately, let alone publicly). When, in the pitch darkness, Buck (and Cass) accidentally enter Sophonsiba's room, and Buck rolls into Sophonsiba's bed, his protestations of denial of mutual understanding count for very little. Actions here, however unintentional or innocent, do speak louder than words. To enter an unmarried woman's bedroom is to imply an 'understanding' between yourself and the woman.

Another route to mutual knowledge adopted in 'Was' is to put things very baldly on record, and this comes to the fore at certain stages of the card-game, understandably enough, since both partici-pants want mutual and public ratification of just what each is committed to, depending on whether they win or lose, whether the hand is called or not. Clearly, card-game talk is highly ritualized, with certain set consequences (as Hubert reminds us, whether he calls or not makes a crucial difference to the outcome) and certain turns realized non-verbally (rapping on the table, for example, to perform a request for a further card to be dealt). Again, however, what is mutually known interweaves with what is mutually suspected. For both players, knowing that Buddy needs the fourth three to win, and discovering that the negro dealing the cards is Tomey's Turl (who has strong reasons for wanting Buddy to win), tacitly suspect and con-clude that somehow Turl will manage to deal that fourth three to Buddy. Since the card is never called for, Hubert instead electing to pass, no one *knows* for certain that that would have happened. But the mutual expectation here is what makes Hubert's action understandable.

Mutual understanding as an achievement, 'done' by one speaker 'to' another, is also amusingly and subtly exploited in 'Go Down, Moses', where Gavin Stevens is tutored or conducted by the old white woman, Miss Worsham, towards a clearer understanding of just what she wants and he must do with regard to the body of Samuel Beauchamp. Miss Worsham's visit to Gavin, and her demands upon him, are in support and protection of Mollie Beauchamp, grand-mother of the executed murderer. Miss Worsham's intimate and evidently lifelong sympathy with Mollie – 'Mollie and I were born in the same month. We grew up together as sisters would' (p. 375) – is in rather eloquent contrast with the attenuated brotherhood of Ike and Lucas, or Henry and Roth Edmonds.

The entire interaction between Gavin Stevens and Miss Worsham seems shaped by Gavin's puzzled and gradual recognition that this is not some conventional lawyer–client exchange, where the powerful professional has the privilege and duty to advise, direct, and organize. Miss Worsham is the essence of smalltown genteel poverty, but it is she who – at first obscurely, but increasingly explicitly – directs Stevens, assigning him the role, to which he submits, of compliant clerk.

The interactional index of this unforeseen pattern of directive and compliant acts is Stevens's repetitions of Miss Worsham's declarations; and these in turn are at least partly prompted non-verbally by the challenging looks she directs at him. He is understandably confused at first when she states that 'She [Mollie] mustn't know [of her grandson's crime and execution]' (p. 375) yet adds 'She will want to take him back home with her':

> 'Him?' Stevens said. 'The body?' She watched him. The expression was neither shocked nor disapproving. . . .
> 'He is the only child of her oldest daughter, her own dead first child. He must come home.'
> 'He must come home,' Stevens said as quietly. (p. 376)

Similarly, when Stevens deliberately specifies an absurdly low figure as covering the expenses of retrieving the body, he explains:

> 'Ten or twelve dollars will cover it. They will furnish a box and there will be only the transportation.'
> 'A box?' Again she was looking at him with that expression curious and detached, as though he were a child. . . . 'Not just a box, Mr Stevens. . . .'
> 'Not just a box,' Stevens said. (pp. 376–7)

This brief exchange highlights how simple repetition of an interlocutor's words, with suitable intonation inferred (signalled in the text primarily by presence or absence of a question-mark), may function either as challenge ('A box?') or as submissive support ('Not just a box') of that interlocutor's implicit and explicit purposes or goals. There is a further charge to Stevens's 'compliance' repetitions. He is being consulted at least partly in a professional capacity, and there is a clear sense that, in a legalistic courtroom manner, where a lawyer will often repeat a witness's answer verbatim, immediately after its delivery, the better to establish it on the record as significant testimony, Stevens knows and intends that his repetitions are, and are heard as, a voluntary 'putting himself under obligation'. This 'voluntary binding commitment' connotation of certain repetitions is particularly highlighted in Stevens's subsequent conversation with the newspaper editor. The latter is being approached (compelled) by Stevens to contribute to the expenses of bringing the killer's body home:

'It will be the first time in my life I ever paid money for copy I had already promised before hand I wont print.'

'Have already promised before hand you will not print,' Stevens said. (p. 378)

In considering possible applications of models of dialogue from Grice and conversational analysts, as well as attending to the implicit evaluative load that disparate and varying dialects may carry, I have inevitably neglected many other approaches. One simple but often surprisingly rich topic for scrutiny is the content of the narratorial frame that immediately surrounds any direct speech.

The verb of communication itself is an important variable here. If *say* constitutes the unmarked option, there may be a cline of increasingly informative verbs describing a response (*reply*, *respond*, *counter*, *deny*, *expostulate*, *storm*, *snap (back)*, etc.) or an initiation (*begin*, *remark*, *blurt*, *burst out*, *splutter*), while many verbs fill both these roles. Popular novels sometimes also resort to the use of expressive verbs which are not conventionally thought to convey verbal communication at all: the 'glared Henry, smiled Lucy' style. Whether the verbs of communication are sentence-initial or parenthetical, and whether they precede or follow their subjects, are subsidiary areas of considerable and sometimes motivated narrative variation. In addition much more detailed attention could be directed to the occurrence and implications of the adverbial expressions, especially of manner, that so often accompany these verbs, as narratorial glosses of the speaker, the content of his or her utterance, and the tone and significance of the encompassing interaction. As part of the terrible diminution of sympathy and compassion we witness in the old Ike of 'Delta

Autumn', his lengthy speech of dismissal of his young black kinswoman is prefaced thus:

> 'Yes,' he said, harshly, rapidly, but not so harsh now and soon not harsh at all but just rapid, urgent, until he knew that his voice was running away with him and he had neither intended it nor could stop it: 'That's right. Go back North. Marry: a man in your own race. That's the only salvation for you . . .' (p. 363)

In this chapter I have tried to show just a few of the potentially rewarding ways in which a stylistics of fictional dialogue might proceed. Obviously, such a stylistics assumes an analyst who is interested in applying accounts of dialogue and conversation that are linguistic (in a broad sense) to the talk that is rendered in plays and novels. That application is undertaken in the interests of elaborating systematic and principled descriptions and explanations of the forms and functions of those verbal interactions. Inevitably proceeding probabilistically and selectively, shuttling back and forth between the pared-down scientistic spirit of linguistic argument and the affective elaborations of literary-critical reception of verbal art, the stylistician of fictional dialogue remains convinced that, like natural dialogue, fictional dialogue is inspectably systematic, ordered, and patterned, and conforms to – or only with conscious creativity departs from – a collectively recognized and inspectable logic.

13

W(H)ITHER STYLISTICS?

INTENTIONS AND GOALS

A major purpose of this study has been the refinement of an under-standing of what *Go Down, Moses* is and how it works. To the extent that these are literary interests, the study has been literary critical. But the particular chosen way that I have argued for – as an enlightening one with some generalizable results – is preoccupied with linguistic description. All readers of Faulkner recognize that *Go Down, Moses*, like all his other fiction, contains striking manipulations of the language of which it is composed. One simple premise here has been that close study of the language strategies in the novel will illuminate, support, and help articulate critical interpretation. Put-ting the case as generally as David Lodge once famously did: 'The novelist's medium is language: whatever he does, *qua* novelist, he does in and through language' (Lodge 1966: ix). While many novels do not palpably draw attention to their language medium, others – including *Go Down, Moses* – arguably achieve their effect, and receive an adequate interpretation, only if the reader responds with great dis-crimination to various linguistic practices woven into the text.

What I have just claimed certainly needs further clarification, if it is not to be dimissed as reactionary polemic. Perhaps the first thing to acknowledge is that a stylistics orientation is neither a necessary nor a sufficient condition for 'linguistically discriminating reader-response'; for some readers and for some texts, however, it sometimes helps. More problematic for many, especially in the light of my rejections of monistic interpretation in early chapters, will be the reference above to (implicitly *proper*) 'effect' and 'adequate interpre-tation'. Neither 'proper' nor 'adequate' is entirely appropriate. But no stylistician interested in relating the idiosyncratic systematicities of a

298

particular text to the public systematicities of the language can entirely dispense with criteria of adequacy or commensurateness. Often the implicit criterion is impossible to meet – for example, the goal that the analytical description should specify and explain all the linguistic aspects of the text that contribute in any way to the analyst's sense of the text.

Even when, as is perhaps becoming more common, a less ambitious criterion of adequacy is the target, for example, accounting for the impression (of a single reader, or a group of readers) that a text is 'densely written' or 'alienating and unfeeling', the enterprise remains open to the attack mounted in Taylor (1980). The independent existence of the effects or impressions, whose assumed textual source the stylistician claims he or she is uncovering, is itself always at least partly taken on trust. We have no unmodulated access to the actual effects on readers of texts, since in their public disclosures readers are always already caught up in the language game of literary criticism and appreciation.

If the upshot of this is that, following Taylor, stylisticians must declare more explicitly that they are not attempting to do the impossible, then so be it. If stylisticians must also recognize that the effects they claim to be explicating, and hence, to a degree, their methods, are not fine, objective scientific ones, but rather internal to the language games of literary criticism and linguistic description, then that is no bad thing. There remain, within this perspective, important explanatory tasks to undertake. The complex mechanisms by which certain discourses become and remain 'Literature', and the remarkable degree to which readers – even from very different communities – attest to similar, often unarticulated, intuitions about a text cannot all be brainwashing and polite accommodation.

Traditionally stylisticians are forgiven, by the more tolerant linguists, for their inexplicit criteria, their deficiencies of scientific method, and their arbitrary positing of something (a claimed prior textual effect) for their machinery to explicate. The stylistician is pitied, when not dismissed, as being in the miserable position of being sure to furnish accounts that are inadequate even to his or her own fuller response – let alone those of others – to even a limited aspect of a text. In linguistics, it is claimed, we do things otherwise.

Yet the burden of my earlier discussion of Taylor (1980) and Harris (1981) has been to the contrary: in normal linguistics, as in normal stylistics, assumptions of fixed-code telementational communication have been much the same. Contrasting the kind of adequacy attended to by stylisticians with the kind of adequacy criterion posited by linguists is usually designed to emphasize the impossibility of the former, the verifiable sense of the latter. But any extended reflection on perhaps the most depended-upon test of adequacy used in syntactic theory – namely, native-speaker judgements of the grammaticality of decontextualized sentences – should suggest that syntacticians have devised for themselves an operational enterprise only by making a number of question-begging assumptions about the fit between their grammatical sentences and speakers' interpretable utterances. A paper waits to be written on the tyranny of the asterisk (or star) in written syntactic argumentation: the symbol that directs readers, before they have read a sentence, to reject it as obviously ungrammatical. The one thing many theorists of syntax hate – and often will not allow – the informant to say, when asked to deliver judgements on the grammaticality or acceptability of sentences, is 'It depends'. In very many cases, however, that is precisely the answer that our actual creative language practice confirms to be nearest the truth.

David Lodge's truism, notwithstanding its suspect emphasis on language as mere medium and its implication that while the novelist *does* things *with* language what he or she actually does is something non-linguistic, articulates the grounding of literary linguistics in common sense. That grounding in itself will ensure that stylistics, in one form or another, will never wither away.

Lodge is far more contentious, however, when he goes on to distinguish linguistics and literature in the following way: 'It is the essential characteristic of modern linguistics that it claims to be a science. It is the essential characteristic of literature that it concerns values. And values are not amenable to scientific method' (Lodge 1966: 57). As Fowler (1984: 172) complains, this applies the key terms 'science' and 'values' as if they were self-explanatory givens, and then trades on these undiscriminating stereotypes. Fowler argues vigorously that stylistics' detractors need to conceive of linguistics in a far less restricted way, while language itself needs to be theorized in a far richer way, one that answers to its social semiotic role. In the following sections I look briefly at some of the current trends in the work of stylisticians, and offer some tentative assessments of just how 'open', or adequately theorized, their conceptions of linguistics, language, and interpretation are.

THE SYSTEMATICITY OF VERBAL ART

One perspective that extends and refines a long tradition of enquiry is that of stylisticians whose primary interest is in what, linguistically, constitutes verbal art. Potentially any linguistic system can be used to probe these issues – and T. Austin (1984) could be discussed here but will be reserved for later attention – but stylisticians working within the systemic linguistic tradition (Halliday 1971; Hasan 1984 and 1985; Butt 1984 and 1985; papers in Birch and O'Toole 1988), are a particularly influential community. Applying the delicate descriptive methodology of systemic grammar, they address anew the questions of foregrounding, prominence, de-automatization, thematic motivation, and so on, that Mukařovský and other Prague formalists grappled with. Systemic linguistics continues to be, in stylistics, perhaps the most popular of the non-traditional grammatical descriptions, no doubt because it has always been resolutely functional. It has always claimed that the systems of choices it identifies at the various levels of text, from sentence to word, are also meaning-choices. And the art in the various verbal artefacts that systemicists study lies in the degree to which there is a 'realizational fit' across three layers of representation:

> The categories of the code of the language are used to symbolize a set of situations, events, processes, entities, etc. (as they are in the use of language in general); these situations, events, entities, etc., in their turn, are used to symbolize a theme or a theme-constellation. (Hasan 1971: 310)

In Hasan's stylistics, then, the consistency of foregrounding of multifarious language patterns, motivated in that they realize the theme (a generalization or abstraction, 'the very governing principle' (Hasan 1971: 310) of a work), is an extra layer of symbolization which is exclusive to literature, and the focus of stylistic analysis:

> Stylistics is the study of literary language for the purpose of showing how it is related to the internal organization of literary texts, how the text is made to cohere into one unity and how the elements of this unity are brought to one's notice. (Hasan 1971: 322)

The attraction of such systemicist manifestos lies in the explicitness with which assumptions and priorities are declared. Various contentious positions are thus helpfully on display – for example, the

301

assumption that literary texts do indeed have single, unifying, regula-
tive themes, that such unity is not simply a standard interpretative
convention of orthodox literary criticism (see Culler 1975: 170 ff.). On
this last point, however, it is worth noting that Hasan's emphasis on a
controlling thematic unity is not fully echoed in Halliday:

> The nature of the language is such that [the writer] can convey, in a
> line of print, a complex of simultaneous themes, reflecting the
> variety of functions that language is required to serve. And because
> the elements of the language, the words and phrases and syntactic
> structures, tend to have multiple values, any one theme may have
> more than one interpretation. (Halliday 1971: 360)

Recent introductory guides to literary stylistics that have adopted
in part a systemicist approach include Carter (1982) and Cummings
and Simmons (1983); but with the latter there are problems of the sort
that seem endemic in stylistic work. Surprisingly, these problems
begin in the Preface to Cummings and Simmons, in a series of
questionable generalizations from, of all people, Halliday himself:

> [The] meanings [of an English literary text] are derived from the
> system of the English language. . . . You will not be able to explain
> 'how it works' if you do not relate it to the system of the English
> Language. (Halliday 1983: xi)

The misdirection here lies in the suggestion that simply knowing 'the
system of the English Language' will bring you to apprehend the
meanings of any particular text, or will bring you to an understanding
of the grounds for positive evaluation of a text, without much further
ado. To be sure, the verbs 'derive' and 'relate' are used, but there
needs to be more attention to the fact that the tasks of deriving and
relating, the central tasks of the stylistician, are always problematic,
provisional, in need of theorizing and coherent motivation. This
curious overlooking of the essential stylistic enterprise itself persists
throughout this introductory stylistics textbook, of which Cureton
comments: '[The authors] write as if no stylistic theory is needed to
intervene to relate grammatical description and aesthetic response'
(Cureton 1985a: 224). On a more positive note, however, Halliday's
Preface valuably reasserts the need for stylistic analysis to be properly
contextualized in relation to factors such as register, genre, intertextual resonance, and metatextual commentary and reception –

contexts which powerfully determine the writing and reading of literature.

By contrast with Cummings and Simmons, the Carter reader (Carter 1982) is more eclectic and diverse (as is its sequel (Carter and Simpson 1988), which concentrates on dialogue and discourse), with contributions from scholars who, despite their differing foci of interest, usually enter into sufficient linguistic detail in their analyses for replicability to be a possibility. As Carter asserts in his Introduction, 'Conclusions can be *attested* and *retrieved* by another analyst working on the same data with the same method' (1983: 6). By the same token, where there are dissatisfactions with an analyst's method or conclusions, the source or sources of the putative inadequacy can be more easily pinpointed when inspectability of grounds and replicability are attended to.

Finally, all those committed to a systemicist linguistic framework have been immensely assisted of late by the publication of Halliday's detailed introduction to the grammar of English (Halliday 1985a). This guide revises and expands earlier discussions of such topics as ergativity, token and value, and grammatical metaphor, and is sure to be the basis for numerous innovative analyses of texts.

The notion of grammatical metaphor, for example, should aid our understanding of the choices available in the manner of narrative presentation of events. Ever since Ian Watt's acclaimed essay on the style of the opening of James's *The Ambassadors*, stylisticians have pondered over the rationale(s) and effects of James's chosen way of beginning:

> Strether's first question, when he reached the hotel, was about his friend; yet on his learning that Waymarsh was apparently not to arrive till evening he was not wholly disconcerted.

Smit (1988: 119–29) contains the latest – and one of the most judicious – assessments of the stylistic implications of James's choices. As others have done, Smit acknowledges the significance of the fact that Strether's utterance is (very) indirectly reported in the opening sentence. Halliday's account of grammatical metaphor highlights a source of the indirectness, the reificated timbre: the first main clause recasts an implicitly verbal process (Strether asked . . .) as a relational process with the substance of Strether's query represented as a circumstantial attribute of a 'thing', his question.

LITERARY LANGUAGE AS SOCIO-HISTORICAL DISCOURSE

One of the contributions to Carter's collection stands out for its radical critique of orthodox stylistic goals:

> In that a substantial body of literary criticism in general (stylistics in particular) colludes in [the] construction and maintenance [of the dominant ideology] by 'appreciating' and 'describing' texts which hide the problems, conflicts and oppressions in that ideology, this polemical introduction is a plea for a radical rethinking of the contribution that stylisticians could be making to society. (Burton 1982: 198)

Burton proposes that stylistics should help uncover the ideology-laden 'constructedness' not only of literary texts, but also of all the texts of everyday 'reality', so that perceptions of that constructedness might give rise to recognition of potential *re*-construction. Something of this emphasis lies at the heart of two other, chiefly British, stylistic enterprises focused around the works of Colin MacCabe and Roger Fowler respectively.

One of MacCabe's premises is that language study at the level of meaning cannot be divorced from situation (as, he is prepared to concede, they may be at the levels of phonology and grammar): 'At the level of meaning . . . the relation of the meanings of a text to its socio-historical conditions (of both production and reception) are not secondary but constitutive' (MacCabe 1981: 77). His actual exemplifying of sociohistorically inscribed meanings sometimes boils down to a treatment of particular words, whose shiftings of sense at the time of their use in the text are claimed to be especially noticeable; such words become pegs on which to hang lengthy and abstract interpretations. In fact, MacCabe's keywords (he explicitly states he is working in a tradition made more visible by Raymond Williams) are not always even pegs but rather triggers. Thus a brief speech from Falstaff (*Henry IV, Part 2*, IV. iii.18–23), in which he asserts that 'my womb undoes me', prompts MacCabe to alert us to the fact that at the end of the sixteenth century both the sexual 'uterus' sense and the asexual 'stomach' sense of *womb* were current. And this functions as preface to a longer conspectual discussion of language and the social order – 'Falstaff's body constitutes a polymorphously perverse threat to the possibility of representation' (MacCabe 1981: 91) – and so on.

With all the merits of this refreshingly historicized philology, it has to be admitted that it is a long way from stylistics as usually understood. There is no special concern here with method, pattern, cumulative emphasis, text-*pervasive* foregrounding, or craft and technique. More generally, again for good or ill, there is none of the 'interpretative parsimony' which stylisticians usually maintain: a linguistic detail triggers an elaborate interpretative assessment in a way which disregards the conventional stylistic concern for elaborate and specific evidential substantiation of claims. It might appear that my reservations with this approach are, ironically, that it is a way rather than a method (see my chapter 1 and 2); but the reservation is rather that nothing even so systematic as a way seems to be adopted.

What stylisticians might see in MacCabe, then, is an admirably theorized treatment of literary (and, by implication, any) language – his rejection of the existence of *langue* at the level of meaning, for example, is well argued – but little demonstration of a procedure for practical analysis. Just this complaint is levelled at contemporary critical theory in general in Peter Widdowson's introduction to a controversial collection of essays entitled *Re-reading English* (1983), although it has to be said that many of the contributions gathered therein evince the same tendency.

MacCabe's philology in a new key is thus a stimulating fusion of British (Richards, Empson, Williams) and European (Saussure, Benveniste, Jakobson, Foucault, Lacan) linguo-cultural studies. It currently has something of a 'home base' in the English Department of the University of Strathclyde in Scotland. There, courses in this literary linguistics which differ rather markedly from more orthodox stylistics courses are offered to (chiefly foreign) graduate students. And in 1986 Strathclyde hosted a potentially sparkling conference on 'The linguistics of writing' and on where poetics has got to in the quarter-century since the seminal Indiana conference on 'Style' (Sebeok 1960). A spectrum of theorists of poetics and stylistics held parliament – Derrida, Fish, Halliday, Culler, Hollander, Jameson, Pratt, and others (some of these papers, collected in Fabb *et al.* (1987), have been cited elsewhere in this study). A number of those conferring, however, consigned to the voiceless Strangers' Gallery, seem to have been disenchanted with the monologic version of 'representative democracy' adopted: form and function ill aligned once again.

However, it is the other 'school' of politicized stylistics, associated with the approach of Fowler (1981, 1986), Kress and Hodge (1979)

305

and Kress (1985), that most stylisticians find more amenable. This approach is also systemicist in its linguistics, and continues to attract students despite the considerable theoretical and descriptive problems with published work so far (see critical reviews in T. Taylor (1983), Taylor and Toolan (1984), Pateman (1983), Frow (1985), and Richardson (1987)). Fowler *et al.*'s 'linguistic criticism' looks at the patternings of syntactico-semantic phenomena such as nominalization, passivization, and types of clause process, with the goal of laying bare aspects of the shaping ideology or assumptions of various discourses – literary texts, regulatory instruments, newspaper stories, and all the other more palpable bearers of ideology. The broad belief is that the encoding of meanings (including ideological meanings) in discourses always involves refraction, such that some meanings become particularly obscured, hence in need of skilled stylistic retrieval: '[The reader] is continually coerced into taking the surface form as the real form; and that surface is a radically transformed version of the originally chosen linguistic form' (Kress and Hodge 1979: 28). Or so the authors would have us believe. The chief problem with all this (see T. Taylor 1983) is that the analysts claim to be teasing out the veiled ideological force of texts made up of certain formal linguistic structures, but build their account on axiomatic assumptions about the ideological impact of those formal features. These texts contain those forms, and those forms carry these ideological assertions and evasions, hence the text necessarily carries these ideological marks. Like much stylistics of the 1960s, such analyses can very easily succumb to the fixed-code bi-planarity view of language (where meanings – ideology – are mechanistically read off forms) that I rejected in chapter 1. It has then retreated to assertion rather than demonstration (we know the forms carry the ideologies we say they do . . . because we're skilled readers).

On the other hand the vicious circularity of fixed-code bi-planarity can be resisted, I believe, and linguistic criticism can be made sensitive and responsive to questions of genre, irony, and other contextual determinations. More recently Fowler restated the interests of linguistic criticism thus:

We want to show that a novel or a poem is a complexly structured text; that its structural form, by social semiotic processes, constitutes a representation of the world, characterized by activities and states and values; that this text is a communicative interaction between its producer and its consumers, within relevant social and institutional contexts. Now these characteristics of the novel or poem are no more than what functional linguistics is looking for in studying, say, conversations or letters or official documents. (Fowler 1984: 175)

One objection to this will be that it gives no *particular* attention to the sort of phenomena Jakobson subsumed under his poetic function: enquiry into the textual bases of the 'verbal art' that, for Hasan, Epstein, Freeman, and others, distinguishes literary work. On the other hand, it is not clear that Fowler would accept Taylor's objections in their strong form. He is (perhaps increasingly?) conscious of the tendency in functional stylistics for a circular 'reading off' of functions from forms:

> There is not an invariant relationship between form and function. So the linguistic critic, like the ordinary reader or hearer, cannot just recognize the linguistic structure and, consulting this pragmatic competence, assign a significance to it. . . . We process text as *discourse* . . . rather than as structure with function attached. We approach the text with a hypothesis about a relevant context, based on our previous experiences of relevant discourse, and relevant contexts: this hypothesis helps us to point an interpretation, to assign significances, which are confirmed or disconfirmed or modified as the discourse proceeds. (Fowler 1984: 181)

This passage captures the stylistician's effort to adopt and adhere to a plausible model of meaning-making, which is neither telepathic nor entirely pre-programmed, nor a seeming impossibility. One has to say, however, that earlier stylistic analyses by Fowler, Hodge, and Kress displayed less of this consciousness of negotiation and provisionality, and more of the confident assertive style, where the agentless passive, for example, is always taken to be culpable mystification.

It may be important to conclude these remarks on circularity of argument in stylistics by stressing the need to distinguish kinds of circularity, and to distinguish all of these from informed intuition.

Thus I believe Smit (1988: 24) is right to defend some orders of circularity as more permissible than others – if not, quite simply, inescapable. However, just as the 'circularity' of traditional grammatical definitions has been erroneously asserted, so it may be that the alleged circularities in stylistic description have been too liberally claimed, with 'circularity' functioning as (ironically) a grossly inaccurate cover-term for alleged faults of impressionism, unfalsifiability, and vagueness. Lyons (1968: 317–18) and Harris (1981: 66–7) are rightly critical of careless dismissal of allegedly circular traditional grammatical definitions (e.g. of nouns as the names of persons or things), and Harris concludes with an analogy that should be borne in mind as we consider stylistic descriptions and interpretations:

> What the argument is really directed against is not the circularity of the notional definition (for there is no circularity), but rather the difficulty of applying the definition in particular instances. This, however, is quite a different matter. Judges or juries may occasionally find it difficult, on the basis of the legal definition of a certain crime, to decide whether or not defendants are guilty of it. That does not show that the legal definition is circular. Nor does it mean that the definition is inadequate. It may simply be in the nature of the offence that the kind of evidence available is often likely to be contentious or inconclusive. *Mutatis mutandis* the same problem may arise for grammatical definitions. (Harris 1981: 67)

We may conclude this section by simply noting that stylisticians particularly interested in ideological analysis can draw on many other germane contributions besides those reviewed above. A very partial listing might include work by Fairclough (1985), Pateman (1980), Chilton (1985), Said (1982), Pratt (1986), Gumperz (1982), Atkinson (1984), Smitherman-Donaldson and van Dijk (1987), Birch and O'Toole (1988), Fabb *et al.* (1988), Carter and Simpson (1988), and Hickey (1989). Particular mention would also be made of several exemplary papers by Weber (1982a, 1982b, 1986) which, drawing on current trends in the pragmatic and semantic analysis of text-processing, plot various strategies of inference-making, frame construction, and distancing in samples of ideologically complex modern fiction.

APPROACHES TO SYNTAX AND INTRADISCIPLINARY CRITIQUE

This brief survey, reflecting my own background has focused to excessive extent on the newer trends in stylistics in Britain. I shall now attempt to remedy this imbalance somewhat, for even a cursory inspection shows literary linguistics to be alive and well in many parts of the world. That liveliness was reflected in the informed critical responses that greeted a stylistics article, 'The case for syntactic imagery' (Ceci 1983), in the widely distributed generalist journal *College English*. The article argued that we can postulate a degree of calculated contrivance, in certain texts, of a mental experience in the reader that is mimetic of the (usually troubled and disturbed) experience or perspective articulated in the text itself. To revise a computer slogan, 'What you get is what you read'. Inspecting passages from Faulkner, Yeats, and Eliot where particularly creative exploitations of syntax are evident, Ceci suggested that 'there are certain inherent properties of syntax, that writers can and often do take advantage of these properties, and that the foregrounding of these properties produces effects in the mind of the reader which I shall call *syntactic imagery*' (Ceci 1983: 432). The sense in which Ceci wants the term 'imagery' to be understood remains a little obscure, although he turns to discussion of the figurative 'mental impact' of syntax: 'a [textual] representation which uses syntax and the processing of syntax to stand as a *metaphor* for the experience' (438). More specifically, Ceci wants to see certain uses of syntax as mimetic of original, not yet verbalized and comprehended 'lived experience' that is the text's theme.

All this, it may be argued, recapitulates emphases that have recurred in the stylistics literature – and are particularly prominent, let it be admitted, in many of our undergraduate stylistics courses. The blended influences of Ohmann, Fish's affective stylistics, and Dillon, are openly acknowledged. A wide-ranging and informative piece, the essay is, however, weakened by its mistaken belief that it refutes Fish's arguments for interpretative relativism, by a few oversights in its linguistic descriptions, and by an uncritical dependence on both a metaphoricality of expression and psycholinguistic speculation.

This latter dependence is perhaps the most problematic. As Richard Cureton writes in a response to the article: 'There is precious little solid evidence about the exact nature of the psychology of speech production – about "prephenomenal experiencing", "experiential chunking", and "verbalizability"' (Cureton 1985b: 426). The conclusion we should perhaps draw from this airing of differences is that the use of psychological and psycholinguistic evidence in stylistic analysis remains problematic – though by no means intrinsically valueless. When the theory or assumptions are themselves flimsy, they undermine any stylistic work in which they are applied. But it seems extreme to deny the potential usefulness of all such research. Van Peer (1986), for example, is a stimulating application of statistical methods in the analysis of readers' perceptions of foregrounding in texts; Dillon (1978) contains many useful speculations on the often strenuous processing-cum-guesswork involved in making sense of text that is opaque, oblique, or dense; and a wide range of research on the mechanisms of text production and reception is summarized in de Beaugrande and Dressler (1981).

The more general reason for referring to the Ceci article and its reception is to highlight the simple, heartening fact that it shows stylisticians critiquing fellow stylisticians in an informed way, which is yet comprehensible to literary critics and theorists. This has been something rather lacking in the field in the past. Stylistics has had its detractors, of course – F. W. Bateson, E. D. Hirsch, Barbara Herrnstein Smith, Stanley Fish, etc. – but the discipline has lacked the internal corrective and focusing effects which are evident in more established areas of language study, whether that be Old English morphology or 'government and binding' theory, and which are themselves a good indicator that here are issues academics deem worth arguing for, worth getting straight. A heterodox clash of voices within stylistics is a welcome development, and helps us stay alive to new developments in literary and linguistic studies. For those reasons Barry's responses to various stylistic papers (one of these was discussed in chapter 4; see also Barry (1986)), for example, or Frow's critique of Kress and Hodge, and his proposal for a sociological stylistics more attentive to universes of discourse and registers (Frow 1985), are both very welcome.

One tradition of stylistics that seems, latterly, to be sure of an alert critical reception is generative stylistics. (Within this tradition, the impressively developed sub-field of generative metrics continues to refine its descriptions of poetic metre – see Attridge (1983), Youmans and Kiparsky (1989), and, for a non-generativist treatment, Cureton (forthcoming) – but falls outside the scope of this book.) The most noted recent contribution here has been Banfield (1982), discussed briefly in chapter 3, which has prompted considerable critique from other stylisticians interested in narrative discourse. Banfield's book is impressive on two counts: in its detailed attention to what she takes to be the contrasting syntactic options realized by narration and discourse respectively; and in its discursive commentary – however open to challenge – on the consequences of narration. The grammatical descriptions are not so very different, essentially, from those of previous students of represented speech and thought: what is different is the insistence on the rule-governed well-formedness of some sentences, the inadmissibility of others, and the confident identifications of who speaks (or does not speak) particular sentences, and of whose subjectivity is being expressed. The ultimate test of such sharp prescriptions must be whether they answer to readers' grasp of narrative texts, and whether the explanations they proffer seem relevant to their literary experience. The task of validation by application awaits the attention of stylisticians, although McHale (1983) and Mittwoch (1985) contain negative reports on aspects of Banfield's theory. According to McHale, it has no adequate account of the place of history, genre, register, context, all the extra-grammatical determinants of – or at least influences upon – narration and the interpretation of narration.

More recently has come Austin's 'linguistic theory of poetic syntax' (1984). This is a carefully delimited and clearly presented account of how specific syntactic operations (often ungrammatical structures, by the standards of present-day written English) have been exploited by particular writers or particular literary periods – chiefly Augustans and Romantics. The syntactic operations are claimed to have particular aesthetic characteristics, and these syntactic-aesthetic pairs are themselves said to correlate with 'essentially independent interpretations of . . . content' (T. Austin 1984: 14). But as may be already evident, in order for Austin's delimited account to get started, it seems, a host of troubling questions are put to one side. Thus deconstruction constitutes 'too strong a disagreement' with stylistic method, and so is simply ignored; the separability of technical description and interpretation, and of aesthetic statements and interpretative ones, are simply asserted; a 'broad-based unanimity about language, its structure, and its meaning' (1984: 11) is assumed; and the view that perception of propositional structure is 'based on' grammatical analysis is expressed without clarification of how direct or loose or prone to adjustment this 'basing' is.

In his first technical analysis, Austin examines that much knocked-about poem, cummings's 'anyone lived in a pretty how town'. He argues that the 'distribution of syntactically acceptable and unacceptable contexts for the word *anyone* in the poem corresponds strikingly with the narrative's account of the fluctuating fortunes in love of the character Anyone' (T. Austin 1984: 32). Though Austin does not in fact formulate syntactic rules by which to determine acceptability, we might say informally that in the standard dialect, setting aside certain exceptions, *anyone* must be preceded and commanded by some negative particle, while *no one* must not be so preceded and commanded. The 'exceptions' we must set aside include various kinds of generic sentence ('Anyone can learn to windsurf', 'Anyone who damages these trees will be prosecuted'), and sentences involving doubt, conditionality, counterfactuality, and questioning ('Is anyone there?', 'That anyone survived was amazing'). What unites all these exceptions is the fact that, by one criterion or another, they are at some remove from canonical narrative-sentence form (e.g. a past-tense main clause with a dynamic verb; on this topic see Labov (1972) and Toolan (1988), chapters 2 and 5). This is important, since we take the cummings poem to be a narrative, and assess the use of *anyone* and *noone* therein accordingly. Thus 'anyone lived in a pretty how town' is unacceptable, and, in Austin's reading, the sentence reports Anyone's hard times when 'he is an outsider' in the town. Soon, however, Anyone meets Noone and, since harmonious syntax allegedly reflects the harmonious circumstances, it comes to pass 'that noone loved him [sc. anyone] more by more'. In short, 'Distribution of syntactically acceptable and unacceptable contexts for the word *anyone* in the poem corresponds strikingly with the narrative's account of the fluctuating fortunes in love of the character Anyone' (T. Austin 1984: 32).

This is an ingenious reading of one feature of the poem's syntax, but it very noticeably fails to address other aspects of the syntax, to say nothing of non-syntactic influences on interpretation. Only the acceptability of *anyone* is inspected, and former favourites for commentary (*he danced his did*) are set aside. And for some readers, it should be acknowledged, *anyone* and *noone* are primarily names of individuals and only coincidentally, as it were, indefinite pronouns. Their dual status (with the definiteness of the name, however, submerging the indefiniteness of the form) gives rise to uncertainty in the reader, with regard not so much to the acceptability of sentences as to their interpretability. These are the kind of difficulties that confront any claim, such as Austin's, that the technical and interpretative phases of analysis are quite distinct, and any assumption that all readers ground or partially ground their apprehension of the poem in the question of grammaticality, given the multiplicity of other patterns and emphases evident in other areas of the syntax, to say nothing of semantic patterning, lexical cohesion, and rhythm. The attention to acceptability or grammaticality of sentences comes directly from generativist linguistics, where it is an obsessional question, motivated by the particular interests of generative theory (all and only the well-formed sentences . . .). There is no intrinsic reason why accept-ability, thus narrowly conceived, should be a touchstone of analysis in literary stylistics, where texts have the licence to do just about anything, phonologically, syntactically, semantically. The extrinsic influence of generativism has drawn Austin to promote grammatical acceptability as a shaping interpretative strategy, regardless of his protestations of the independence and 'purely syntactic' nature of his technical phase of analysis. Interestingly, a recent essay by Austin argues elegantly for the need in stylistic analysis to take into con-sideration quite 'remote' possible ambiguities in texts, ones that orthodox linguistics simply would not entertain when a simpler disambiguating reading of a sentence is already available (T. Austin 1986). In effect, the essay involves a (convincing) argument against assigning standard generativist notions of ambiguity and grammati-cality any privileged status in interpretation.

Nevertheless, within a tradition of formalist syntactic stylistics, Austin writes with acuity of particular poets' grammatical styles. Often his concern is to elucidate non-standard syntactic preferences (e.g. in Pope and Shelley) using a generative-grammatical framework. Where he attempts to identify a distinct supratextual level of aesthetic functioning he clearly moves away from formalism towards a functionalism which faces the same difficulties of estab-lishing independent motivation faced by other versions of functional stylistics.

STYLISTICS IN ENGLISH TEACHING

I have only intermittently touched on the broad topic of pedagogical stylistics, but it certainly requires attention. For one thing, it remains the case that most stylisticians continue to spend most of their time, in stylistics, teaching the standard practice of it to their students, rather than pursuing original theories and models to be presented to their academic peers. Nor would many of us want things arranged dif-ferently. Most stylisticians accordingly take the business and prob-lems of teaching the subject very seriously. They do so not least because they are so commonly perceived and treated as an irritation (rarely, these days, a threat) to their colleagues comfortably within 'normal' disciplines – traditional literary studies or standard core and 'hyphenated' linguistics.

A question often asked both of and by stylisticians is 'What specific use is stylistics in the nurturing of discriminating literary response?' But the formulation of this question is loaded with such a heavy freight of limiting assumptions about the purposes of literary studies, and with such negative expectations of stylistics (stylisticians themselves are sometimes more pessimistic about the relevance of their work than are their critics), that it cannot be answered without clarification and critique of those veiled assumptions. One rationale has always been invoked: enhanced awareness of the workings of the language of texts is always cited as an index of sensitive literary response, even in quite traditional circles, so that a role for stylistics to fill, in this respect at least, seems already fashioned.

But it is also necessary to insist that stylistics has other functions besides facilitating literary response. There is the still neglected process of literary production, of understanding the craft of writing, in which stylistics can be an invaluable aid. And the uses of stylistics in advanced foreign- and second-language environments, in all sorts of activities aimed at enhancing comprehension and production skills in both spoken and written language, and in strengthening awareness of register and pragmatic constraints (Thomas 1983), are particularly to be noted. In such environments, the student often already has a formal learned awareness of grammar and grammatical description waiting to be harnessed. Having said so much in favour of stylistics, it should be stressed that its application has to be a considered one, properly integrated, relevant to the particular needs and abilities of particular students. Varying degrees of attention are given to these issues in the stylistics textbooks alluded to earlier (Leech and Short 1981; Traugott and Pratt 1980; Carter 1982; Cummings and Simmons 1983). Rather more direct assessment of the problems and their resolution can be found in Carter and Burton (1982), Brumfit and Carter (1986), and D'Haen (1986).

The topic of pedagogy should not be closed without a restatement of the claim, articulated in one domain by Fish (1981), that teaching in general and the profession of literature and linguistics in particular are inescapably prescriptivist, normative, directive. More accurately, they are so to varying degrees, depending on the subject, the teacher, the school, and the wider community. Not only are things so but, it may be argued, they are better so.

Eagleton's emphasis on rhetoric (Eagleton 1983), noted in chapter 2, is again relevant here. Rhetoric in one aspect is simply the elaborated classification of compositional prescriptions. And it is easy to argue that the open acknowledgement of partiality, of the intent to persuade the reader, challenge other positions, and so on, of prescriptive texts is ultimately far less insidious than the impact of those texts which claim to be interpretation-free, pure descriptions. A more direct consequence is that, in a rhetorical-prescriptive tradition, very many topics in text composition which are not amenable to delimited formal methodology return to the stylistic agenda. For these reasons, Nash's work on the language of text creation and humour (Nash 1980, 1985), and Dillon's on the rhetorical construction of interpersonal codes in popular advice books (Dillon 1986), are particularly to be valued. With Taylor, I have elsewhere argued:

> It has always been the case that, whether they like it or not, we look to stylisticians (and others professionally concerned with language) to tell us how to read certain texts and how to write 'with greater style'. It may be that the current trend in stylistics indicates that stylisticians will soon acknowledge their normative role. (Taylor and Toolan 1984: 78)

The foregoing perilously brief sketch of (some) current and developing trends suggests, I hope, that stylistics or literary linguistics is consolidating its standing as a coherent branch of enquiry and theorizing concerning the workings of language, and that the likelihood of its withering away is slim. Some small index of its continued influence can be derived from the following (alphabetical) list of journals, all of which are sympathetic to stylistics in some of its forms, and many of which continue to publish the kinds of discussions of language interaction which can enhance our critical models: *Applied Linguistics*; *Discourse Processes*; *Dutch Quarterly Review of Anglo-American Letters*; *English Studies*; *Journal of Pragmatics*; *Language and Style*; *Poetics*; *Poetics Today*; *Semiotica*; *Style*; *Text*.

By way of conclusion to this section, I wish simply to note a number of invaluable recent books on language and linguistics which I would hope to see informing the stylistics of the early 1990s. Stylistics proper still cannot 'go beyond its linguistics' (cf. Whitehall 1956). The good news for stylistics is that among recent publications the linguistic contributions to which stylisticians can turn are far more accessible and relevant to our concerns than the intensely abstract formalism that seemed the sole preoccupation of linguists in the 1960s and early 1970s. The books I mention below either explicitly address the 'big issues' (gender, class, power, race) to which I alluded at the close of chapter 2, or can reasonably be applied in the analysis of such issues. It is not that only these issues should be addressed by stylisticians – most of the analyses in this book are an argument to the contrary. But by and large literary linguists today are more concerned than ever to enlarge the context of their analyses, so that more delicate accounts of both the verbal art and the sociological assumptions of a particular discourse can be achieved. My hope is that each of the following books might have the impact on thinking, theorizing and practice in literary linguistics that, for example, Pratt (1977) recently had. The books I have in mind are listed below alphabetically by the name(s) of the author(s); the list naturally reflects my own particular interests.

G. Brown and G. Yule, *Discourse Analysis* (1983)

E. Goffmann, *Forms of Talk* (1981)

M. A. K. Halliday, *An Introduction to Functional Grammar* (1985)

R. Harris, *The Language Myth* (1981)

R. Hasan, *Linguistics, Language, and Verbal Art* (1985)

S. B. Heath, *Ways with Words* (1983)

G. Lakoff, *Women, Fire, and Dangerous Things* (1987)

S. Levinson, *Pragmatics* (1983)

G. Smitherman-Donaldson and T. van Dijk (eds), *Discourse and Discrimination* (1987)

D. Sperber and D. Wilson, *Relevance: Communication and Cognition* (1986)

AN APOLOGY TO FAULKNERIANS

I should like to close with an acknowledgement – however inadequate – of the substantial body of critical work on Faulkner's *œuvre* in general and *Go Down, Moses* in particular, in the last few years, which I have neglected to discuss in this study. My defence must partly be insufficiencies of time, space, and energy. However, even were I not subject to those constraints, I hope that those things I have set out to do in this book can stand on their own as specific exercises not directly dependent on or necessitating lengthy attention to contemporary Faulkner scholarship. Those exercises have included a defence of stylistics, and particularly stylistics of fiction, as a principled and informed way – however partial, provisional, and corrigible – into lengthy and complex texts. Only secondarily, by way of facing the methods of literary linguistics with a challenge likely both to reward its own lengthy and sometimes pedestrian procedures and to highlight some of the discipline's many gaps and inadequacies of textual comprehension, was attention focused upon *Go Down, Moses*.

Although I have not directly addressed recent Faulkner studies, I have been aware of many invaluable contributions that shed light on aspects of his art. There have been important and original discussions of voice, narrative motivations, and the interplay of personal and literary obsessions from, respectively, Ross (1981), Krause (1984), and Zender (1980, 1981, 1984). Bakhtin has accented the discussion at several points of the present study: I am delighted to see that Tangum (unpublished dissertation, 1986) provides a full-blown application of Bakhtinian dialogism to the engaged voices and reader in *Go Down, Moses*. There has also been Waegner's study (1983), informed but not stifled by reader-response theory, of the rhetoric of character presentation in several of the novels. Her view of the manipulative misdirections of the reader in *Go Down, Moses*, such that the reader is caught up in a trouble-ridden effort after sense, is largely consonant with my reading of the work. From a more narratological perspective, Kuyk (1983) is a painstaking demonstration of the structured patterns and unity of the novel. More directly concerned with Faulkner's language are Rubin (1983), on his complex blendings of vernacular and high dialects or styles; Esau *et al.*'s (1982) review of sociolinguistic aspects of the direct speech, and, similarly, Hoffer (1979), on Faulkner's acute use of a range of quite specialized registers (legal, military, and so on); Stewart (1981), on language and vision in 'The Old People'; and Matthews's challenging deconstructionist analysis (1982) of absence, loss, and desire as the dynamic of all Faulkner's fiction.

Bunselmeyer (1981) identifies two pre-eminent narrative styles in Faulkner's works, the comic and contemplative styles, and supports this binarism by reference to the syntax of particular passages. Though admirably focused on specific instances, such a compartmentalization tends to ignore many delicate distinctions which would suggest that, rather than hypostasizing styles, we should attend to the complex interaction of a multiplicity of 'ways of speaking' in particular contexts of situation.

While a binarist approach to the syntax is questionable, more persuasive is the argument in Millgate (1983) that there are (always) two voices in Faulkner, in so far as 'dialogue, debate, and opposition' are pervasive. Faulkner's novels are:

> town meetings of the imagination, loud with the rhetoric of advocacy, complaint, and self-justification. . . . And by the time he wrote *Go Down, Moses* Faulkner was ready to integrate a whole series of apparently distinct oppositions within a single contrapuntal structure, pivoting the whole network of cross-references upon the fourth section of 'The Bear' and specifically on that debate in the commissary [between Ike and Cass]. (Millgate 1983: 76)

Such an assessment, were circumstances otherwise, could serve very well as the starting-point of a literary-linguistic study of *Go Down, Moses*, rather than occurring, as here, in an endnote. It is just one of the most recent and most eloquent literary-critical observations that would seem to endorse the kind of close attention to the language(s) of narration that I have attempted. Often that attention was directed very specifically to temporary narratorial alignments between narrator and characters, alignments which sometimes took the explicit form of free indirect discourse. Recurringly, marked distributions and uses of selected language features could be attributed to local narratorial manipulations of perspectival alignment and FID.

But all such asserted correlations are only one stage of interpretation: their wider significance lies in the fact that they entail distinct but varying empathy with different characters. The critical but unironic FID which operates so widely through *Go Down, Moses* is a particularly effective vehicle for the promotion of narrator–reader 'compassionating' with so-revealed characters. No concern, I believe, was more foundational to Faulkner as man and artist than the desire to tell the stories of characters as individuals – not as objects of discussion, to be analysed and explained away, but as independent subjects worthy of respect, containing complex and unresolved impulses towards (among other values) untrammelled personal freedom and commitment to the interests and good of the community.

Troubled consciousness as processing rather than product is thus his subject-matter, and is reflected in his technique. Kinney (1978: 39) has written that Faulkner writes 'in the syntax and the grammar of the growing consciousness', and that readers 'must come to understand' the characters' own formulations of their worlds. Further, defending Faulkner's elaborate sentences, Beck has argued that they are often 'the representation of a character's consciousness in turmoil, as it wrestles and feints under immediate circumstances' (Beck 1976: 60). Such observations, representative of the views of many critics, indicate that various aspects of my broader interpretation of the novel have long held currency in Faulknerian critical circles.

Mention should also be made of three scholars whose studies seem particularly consonant with my approach. The first of these is Reed, who writes that 'the book throughout is an exercise in varieties of third-person narrative' (Reed 1973: 188). Even some of the terminology Reed uses, writing of narrative freedom and characterological control, implicitly probes the issues I have considered concerning exercise or relinquishment of narratorial power. Millgate, relatedly, has written of the novel as an interaction of competing viewpoints without a conclusive adjudication – instead we are offered, by way of resolution, 'the fact of complexity itself' (Millgate 1973: 187). More contestable, but still thought-provoking, is the thesis of Slatoff (1960) that various verbal mannerisms such as oxymoron are an index of Faulkner's divided mind and his chronic failure to choose (the same failure as is seen in Ike). The problem here is the old intentionalist one of being sure we know what Faulkner really did intend; one can speculate that Faulkner might have retorted, using a word he was rather fond of, that he did not fail to choose, he just *declined* to choose. Whatever we assert of Faulkner, there seems little substance to the suggestion that Ike fails to choose. On the contrary we see him making numerous stark choices; whether he proceeds to live out those choices, and whether those choices are mutually consistent and coherent, are other questions.

The quotation from Millgate (1983) used above contains the memorable description of Faulkner's novels as 'town meetings of the imagination'. Perhaps it needs emphasizing that in the attenuated narrative style of *Go Down, Moses* the imagination invoked is not just that of the author, but that of the reader too, who must actively work at making sense of the many-voiced gathering. Some critics have deplored such attenuated narrative as not so much a liberation of enslaved characters as a dereliction of authorial responsibility, leading to anarchic texts which readers will reject as riddled with unreliability and moral uncertainty. My own sympathies are rather with those who see multiple-viewpoint narrative as a rich probing of an insoluble dilemma: the search for the most just relation between personal freedom and social responsibility, between commitment to others and personal independence, between wildness and tamedness.

The narratorial strategy we have seen revealed in the stylistic evidence is itself a dramatization of one of the novel's themes. This is the variousness of freedom and enslavement, whether of black men by white; men by women; women by men; animals by humans; humans by ancestry, environment, or experience; characters by narrator; or reader by author. Faulkner's narrator, as it were, responds to the plea contained in the spiritual from which the novel's title is taken: from his pre-eminent, pharaoh-like narratorial position he lets his enslaved people, his characters, go. In that spirit the narrator declines to be a presiding judge, and the narrative declines to foreclose the issues by unequivocally endorsing the values of any one of the characters. Rather, practising what it preaches, it presents an object-lesson in tolerance and compassion.

BIBLIOGRAPHY

Aiken, C. (1939), 'William Faulkner: the novel as form', *Atlantic Monthly*, November, 650–4.

Allen, R. L. (1961), 'The classification of English substitute words', *General Linguistics*, 5, 7–20.

Allen, R. L. (1966), *The Verb System of Present-Day American English*, The Hague, Mouton.

Altenberg, B. (1984), 'Causal linking in spoken and written English', *Studia Linguistica*, 38, 20–69.

Anderson, B. (1983), *Imagined Communities*, London, Verso.

Armstrong, P. (1983), 'The conflict of interpretations and the limits of pluralism', *PMLA*, 98, 341–52.

Atkinson, J. M. (1984), *Our Masters' Voices: The Language and Body Language of Politics*, London, Methuen.

Attridge, D. (1983), *The Rhythms of English Poetry*, London, Longman.

Attridge, D. (1987), 'Closing statement: linguistics and poetics in retrospect', in N. Fabb *et al.* (eds), *The Linguistics of Writing*, New York, Methuen, 15–32.

Austin, F. (1982), '*Ing* forms in *Four Quartets*', *English Studies*, 63, 23–31.

Austin, F. (1985), 'Making sense of syntax: a reply to Peter Barry', *English Studies*, 66, 167–8.

Austin, J. L. (1962), *How to Do Things with Words*, Oxford, Oxford University Press.

Austin, T. (1984), *Language Crafted: A Linguistic Theory of Poetic Syntax*, Bloomington, Indiana University Press.

Austin, T. (1986), '(IN)Transitives: some thoughts on ambiguity in poetic texts', *Journal of Literary Semantics*, 15, 23–38.

Bache, C. (1985), *Verbal Aspect: A General Theory and its Applications to Present-Day English*, Odense, Odense University Press.

Bache, C. (1986), 'Tense and aspect in fiction', *Journal of Literary Semantics*, 15, 82–97.

Bakhtin, M. M. (1973), *Problems of Dostoevsky's Poetics*, trans. R. W. Rotsel, Ann Arbor, Ardis.

Bakhtin, M. M. (1985), *The Dialogic Imagination: Four Essays*, Austin, University of Texas Press.

321

Bal, M. (1985), *Narratology: Introduction to the Theory of Narrative*, Toronto, University of Toronto Press.

Banfield, A. (1982), *Unspeakable Sentences*, New York, Routledge & Kegan Paul.

Barry, P. (1984), 'Making sense of syntax, perhaps', *English Studies*, 65, 36–8.

Barry, P. (1986), 'The limitations of stylistics', *Essays in Criticism*, 38:3, 175–89.

Beaman, K. (1984), 'Coordination and subordination revisited', in D. Tannen (ed.), *Coherence in Spoken and Written Discourse*, Norwood, Ablex, 45–80.

Beaugrande, R. de, and Dressler, W. (1981), *Introduction to Textlinguistics*, London, Longman.

Beck, W. (1976), *Faulkner*, Madison, University of Wisconsin Press; first published 1941.

Benveniste, E. (1966), *Problèmes de linguistique générale*, Paris, Gallimard.

Berger, P., and Luckmann, T. (1967), *The Social Construction of Reality*, Harmondsworth, Penguin.

Birch, D., and O'Toole, M. (eds) (1988), *Functions of Style*, London, Francis Pinter.

Bloomfield, L. (1935), *Language*, London, Allen & Unwin.

Blotner, J. (1964), *William Faulkner's Library: A Catalogue*, Charlottesville, University Press of Virginia.

Blotner, J. (1974), *Faulkner: A Biography*, 2 vols, London, Chatto & Windus.

Bolinger, D. (1977), 'Pronouns and repeated nouns', *Lingua*, 18, 1–34.

Brinton, L. J. (1985), 'Verb particles in English: aspect or Aktionsart?', *Studia Linguistica*, 39: 2, 157–68.

Bronzwaer, W. J. M. (1970), *Tense in the Novel*, Groningen, Wolters Noordhoff.

Brooks, C. (1963), *William Faulkner: The Yoknapatawpha Country*, New Haven, Yale University Press.

Brown, G., and Yule, G. (1983), *Discourse Analysis*, Cambridge, Cambridge University Press.

Brown, P., and Levinson, S. (1978), 'Universals in language usage: politeness phenomena', in E. Goody (ed.), *Questions and Politeness: Strategies in Social Interaction*, Cambridge, Cambridge University Press, 56–311.

Brumfit, C., and Carter, R. (eds) (1986), *Language and Literature Teaching*, Oxford, Oxford University Press.

Bunselmeyer, J. (1981), 'Faulkner's narrative styles', *American Literature*, 53, 424–42.

Burelbach, F. (1986), 'Names as distance controllers in literature', *Literary Onomastics Studies*, 13, 171–82.

Burton, D. (1980), *Dialogue and Discourse*, London, Routledge & Kegan Paul.

Burton, D. (1982), 'Through glass darkly: through dark glasses', in R. Carter (ed.), *Language and Literature*, London, Allen & Unwin, 195–214.

Butler, C. (1984), *Interpretation, Deconstruction, and Ideology*, Oxford, Oxford University Press.

Butt, D. (1984), 'Perceiving as making in the poetry of Wallace Stevens', *Nottingham Linguistic Circular*, 13, 124–45.

Butt, D. (1985), 'Wallace Stevens and "willful nonsense"', *Southern Review*, 18, 279–97.

Cain, W. (1981), 'Constraints and politics in the literary theory of Stanley Fish', *Bucknell Review*, 26: 1, 75–88.

Capps, J. L. (ed.) (1977), *Go Down, Moses: A Concordance*, Ann Arbor, The Faulkner Concordance Advisory Board.

Carden, G. (1982), 'Backwards anaphora in discourse context', *Journal of Linguistics*, 18: 2, 361–8.

Carson, J. A. (1972), 'The linguist and literature: a critical examination of contemporary theories of stylistics in America', unpublished PhD dissertation, Indiana University.

Carter, R. (ed.) (1982), *Language and Literature*, London, Allen & Unwin.

Carter, R. and Burton, D. (eds) (1982), *Literary Text and Language Study*, London, Edward Arnold.

Carter, R., and Nash, W. (1983), 'Language and literariness', *Prose Studies*, 6, 123–41.

Carter, R. and Simpson, P. (1988), *Language, Discourse and Literature*, London, Unwin Hyman.

Cassirer, E. (1953), *The Philosophy of Symbolic Forms*, vol. 1: *Language*, New Haven, Yale University Press.

Ceci, L. (1983), 'The case for syntactic imagery', *College English*, 45, 431–49.

Chafe, W. (1982), 'Integration and involvement in speaking, writing, and oral literature', in D. Tannen (ed.), *Spoken and Written Language*, Norwood, Ablex, 35–53.

Chafe, W. (1984), 'How people use adverbial clauses', in C. Brugman and M. Macaulay (eds), *Proceedings of the Tenth Annual Meeting of the Berkeley Linguistics Society*, Berkeley, Berkeley Linguistics Society, 433–49.

Chaika, E. (1987), review of D. Tannen (ed.) (1984) *Coherence in Written and Spoken Language*, Norwood, NJ, Ablex, in *Journal of Pragmatics*, 11: 2, 249–54.

Chapman, R. (1984), *The Treatment of Sounds in Language and Literature*, Oxford, Blackwell.

Chastain, C. (1975), 'Reference and context,' in K. Gunderson (ed.), *Language, Mind and Knowledge*, Minnesota Studies in the Philosophy of Science, vol. VII.

Chatman, S. (ed.) (1971), *Literary Style: A Symposium*, London, Oxford University Press.

Chatman, S. (1978), *Story and Discourse*, Ithaca, Cornell University Press.

Chilton, P. (ed.) (1985), *Language and the Nuclear Arms Debate*, London, Pinter.

Chomsky, N. (1965), *Aspects of the Theory of Syntax*, Cambridge, Mass., MIT Press.

Clancy, P. (1980), 'Referential choice in English and Japanese narrative discourse', in W. Chafe (ed.), *The Pear Stories*, Norwood, Ablex, 127–202.

Clark, H. (1977), 'Bridging', in P. Johnson-Laird and P. Wason (eds), *Thinking: Readings in Cognitive Science*, Cambridge, Cambridge University Press, 411–20.

Clark, H., and Marshall, C. (1981), 'Definite reference and mutual knowledge', in A. K. Joshi, B. L. Webber, and I. Sag (eds), *Elements of Discourse Understanding*, Cambridge, Cambridge University Press, 10–63.

Cleman, J. (1977), '"Pantaloon in Black": its place in *Go Down, Moses*', *Tennessee Studies in Literature*, 22, 169–80.

Cole, R. (1986), 'Literary representation of dialect: a theoretical approach to the artistic problem', *The USF Language Quarterly*, 24: 3/4, 3–8, 48.

Comrie, B. (1976), *Aspect*, Cambridge, Cambridge University Press.

Coulthard, M., and Montgomery, M. (eds) (1981), *Studies in Discourse Analysis*, London, Routledge & Kegan Paul.

Creighton, J. (1977), *William Faulkner's Craft of Revision*, Detroit, Wayne State University Press.

Crymes, R. (1968), *Some Systems of Substitution Correlations in Modern American English*, The Hague, Mouton.

Crystal, D. (1966), 'Specification and English tenses', *Journal of Linguistics*, 2, 1–34.

Crystal, D., and Davy, D. (1969), *Investigating English Style*, London, Longman.

Culler, J. (1975), *Structuralist Poetics*, London, Routledge & Kegan Paul.

Culler, J. (1981), *The Pursuit of Signs*, London, Routledge & Kegan Paul.

Culler, J. (1983), *On Deconstruction*, London, Routledge & Kegan Paul.

Cummings, M., and Simmons, R. (1983), *The Language of Literature*, Oxford, Pergamon.

Cureton, R. (1985a), review of M. Cummings and R. Simmons, *The Language of Literature*, (1983), in *Language and Style*, 18.

Cureton, R. (1985b), comment on L. Ceci, 'The case for syntactic imagery' (1983), in *College English*, 47, 424–7.

Cureton, R. (forthcoming), *Beyond Metrics: Rhythmic Phrasing in English Verse*, London, Longman.

Davis, W. (1984), 'Offending the profession', *Critical Inquiry*, 10, 706–18.

D'Haen, T. (ed.) (1986), *Linguistics and the Study of Literature*, Amsterdam, Rodopi.

Dijk, T. van (1977), *Text and Context*, London, Longman.

Dik, S. (1968), *Coordination*, Amsterdam, North Holland.

Dillon, G. (1978), *Language Processing and the Reading of Literature*, Bloomington, Indiana University Press.

Dillon, G. (1981), *Constructing Texts*, Bloomington, Indiana University Press.

Dillon, G. (1982), 'Whorfian stylistics', *Journal of Literary Semantics*, 11:2, 73–7.

Dillon, G. (1986), *Rhetoric as Social Imagination: Explorations in the Interpersonal Function of Language*, Bloomington, Indiana University Press.

Dowty, D. (1986), 'The effects of aspectual class on the temporal structure of discourse: semantics or pragmatics?', *Linguistics and Philosophy*, 9, 37–61.

Dry, H. (1981), 'Sentence aspect and the movement of narrative time', *Text*, 1, 233–40.

Eagleton, T. (1983), *Literary Theory: An Introduction*, Oxford, Blackwell.

Edgren, E. (1985), 'The progressive in English: another new approach', *Studia Linguistica*, 36, 67–83.

Ehrlich, S. (1987), 'Aspect, foregrounding and point of view', *Text*, 7: 4, 363–76.

Esau, H., Bagnall, N., and Ware, C. (1982), 'Faulkner, Literary criticism and linguistics', *Language and Literature*, 7, 7–62.

Fabb, N., Attridge, D., Durant, A., and MacCabe, C. (eds) (1987), *The Linguistics of Writing*, London, Methuen.

Fairclough, N. (1985), 'Critical and descriptive goals in discourse analysis', *Journal of Pragmatics*, 6, 739–64.

Faulkner, W. (1942), *Go Down, Moses*, New York, Random House.

Faulkner, W. (1967), *Essays, Speeches and Public Letters*, ed. J. B. Meriwether, London, Chatto & Windus.

Fehr, B. (1938), 'Substitutionary narration and description: a chapter in stylistics', *English Studies*, 20, 97–107.

Fish, S. (1981), *Is There a Text in this Class?*, Cambridge, Mass., Harvard University Press.

Fish, S. (1982), 'With the compliments of the author: reflections of Austin and Derrida', *Critical Inquiry*, 8, 693–721.

Fish, S. (1985), 'Consequences', *Critical Inquiry*, 11, 433–58.

Foucault, M. (1972), *The Archaeology of Knowledge*, London, Tavistock.

Fowler, R. (1971), *The Languages of Literature*, London, Routledge & Kegan Paul.

Fowler, R. (ed.), (1975), *Style and Structure in Literature*, Oxford, Blackwell.

Fowler, R. (1977), 'The referential code and narrative authority', *Journal of Literary Semantics*, 8, 47–60.

Fowler, R. (1979), 'Linguistics and, and versus, poetics', *Journal of Literary Semantics*, 8, 3–21.

Fowler, R. (1981), *Literature as Social Discourse*, London, Batsford.

Fowler, R. (1984), 'Studying literature as language', *Dutch Quarterly Review of Anglo-American Letters*, 14, 171–84.

Fowler, R. (1986), *Linguistic Criticism*, Oxford, Oxford University Press.

Fox, B. (1987), 'Anaphora in popular written English narratives', in R. Tomlin (ed.), *Coherence and Grounding in Discourse*, Amsterdam, John Benjamins, 157–74.

Freedman, A., and Kaplan, H. (1967), *Comprehensive Textbook of Psychiatry*, Baltimore, Williams & Wilkins.

Freeman, D. (1975), 'The strategy of fusion. Dylan Thomas' syntax', in *Style and Structure in Literature*, ed. R. Fowler, Oxford, Basil Blackwell, 19–39.

Freund, E. (1987), *The Return of the Reader*, London, Methuen.

Frow, J. (1985), 'Language, discourse, ideology', *Language and Style*, 17, 302–15.

Gardner, R. (1987), 'The identification and role of topic in spoken interaction', *Semiotica*, 65, 129–41.

Garfinkel, H., and Sacks, H. (1970), 'On formal structures of practical actions', in J. McKinney and E. Tiryakian (eds), *Theoretical Sociology*, New York, Appleton-Century-Crofts, 338–66.

Genette, G. (1980), *Narrative Discourse*, trans. J. Lewin, Ithaca, Cornell University Press.

Gibson, W. (1969), 'Tough talk: the rhetoric of Frederic Henry', in G. Love and M. Payne (eds), *Contemporary Essays on Style*, Glenview, Scott Foresman, 227–36.

Giddens, A. (1979), *Central Problems in Social Theory*, Berkeley, University of California Press.

Gilbert, S., and Gubar, S. (1979), *The Madwoman in the Attic: The Woman Writer and the Nineteenth Century Literary Imagination*, New Haven, Yale University Press.

Ginsberg, M. P. (1982), 'Free indirect discourse: a reconsideration', *Language and Style*, 15: 2, 133–49.

Givon, T. (ed.) (1983), *Topic Continuity in Discourse: A Quantitative Cross-Linguistic Study*, Amsterdam, John Benjamins.

Goffman, E. (1971), *Relations in Public*, New York, Harper & Row.

Goffman, E. (1981), *Forms of Talk*, Philadelphia, University of Pennsylvania Press.

Golding, R. (1985), *Idiolects in Dickens*, London, Macmillan.

Greenblatt, S. (1987), *Shakespearean Negotiations: The Circulation of Social Energy in Renaissance England*, Berkeley, University of California Press.

Grice, P. (1975), 'Logic and conversation', in P. Cole and J. Morgan (eds), *Syntax and Semantics*, vol. 3: *Speech Acts*, New York, Academic Press, 41–58.

Grimes, J. (ed.) (1978), *Papers on Discourse*, Dallas, Summer Institute of Linguistics.

Gross, M. (1979), 'On the failure of generative grammar', *Language*, 55, 859–95.

Guerard, A. (1976), *The Triumph of the Novel: Dickens, Dostoyevsky, Faulkner*, New York, Oxford University Press.

Gumperz, J. (ed.) (1982), *Language and Social Identity*, Cambridge, Cambridge University Press.

Gwynn, F. L., and Blotner, J. L. (eds) (1959), *Faulkner in the University*, Charlottesville, University of Virginia Press.

Halliday, M. A. K. (1964), 'Descriptive linguistics in literary studies', *English Studies Today*, III, 25–39.

Halliday, M. A. K. (1967), *Grammar, Society and the Noun*, London, London University.

Halliday, M. A. K. (1971), 'Linguistic function and literary style: an inquiry into the language of William Golding's *The Inheritors*', in S. Chatman (ed.), *Literary Style: A Symposium*, London, Oxford University Press, 330–68.

Halliday, M. A. K. (1978), *Language as Social Semiotic*, London, Edward Arnold.

Halliday, M. A. K. (1983), Preface to M. Cummings and R. Simmons, *The Language of Literature*, Oxford, Pergamon, 1983.

Halliday, M. A. K. (1985a), *An Introduction to Functional Grammar*, London, Edward Arnold.

Halliday, M. A. K. (1985b), *Spoken and Written Language*, Deakin, Deakin University Press.

Halliday, M. A. K., and Hasan, R. (1976), *Cohesion in English*, London, Longman.

Hamburger, K. (1973), *The Logic of Literature*, trans. M. Rose, Bloomington, Indiana University Press.

Hankamer, J., and Sag, I. (1976), 'Deep and surface anaphora', *Linguistic Inquiry*, 7, 391–426.

Harris, R. (1980), *The Language Makers*, London, Duckworth.

Harris, R. (1981), *The Language Myth*, London, Duckworth.

Harris, R. (1987), *The Language Machine*, London, Duckworth.

Hasan, R. (1971), 'Rime and reason in literature', in S. Chatman (ed.), *Literary Style: A Symposium*, London, Oxford University Press, 299–326.

Hasan, R. (1984), 'The nursery tale as a genre', *Nottingham Linguistic Circular*, 13, 71–102.

Hasan, R. (1985), *Linguistics, Language, and Verbal Art*, Deakin, Deakin University Press.

Hatcher, A. G. (1951), 'The use of the progressive form in English', *Language*, 27, 254–80.

Hayes, C. (1969), 'A study in prose styles: Edward Gibbon and Ernest Hemingway', in L. Dolezel and R. Bailey (eds), *Statistics and Style*, New York, American Elsevier, 80–91.

Heath, S. B. (1983), *Ways with Words*, Cambridge, Cambridge University Press.

Hendricks, W. (1976), *Grammars of Style and Styles of Grammar*, Amsterdam, North Holland.

Hickey, L. (ed.) (1989), *The Pragmatics of Style*, London, Routledge.

Hinds, J. (1977), 'Paragraph structure and pronominalization', *Papers in Linguistics*, 10, 77–99.

Hirsch, E. D. (1967), *Validity in Interpretation*, New Haven, Yale University Press.

Hirsch, E. D. (1976), *The Aims of Interpretation*, Chicago, University of Chicago Press.

Hirsch, E. D. (1983), 'Against theory?', *Critical Inquiry*, 9, 743–7.

Hoffer, B. (1979), 'The sociolinguistics of literature: Faulkner's styles and dialects', *Linguistics and Literature*, 4, 212–23.

Hogan, M. (1981), 'Grammatical tenuity in fiction', *Language and Style*, 14, 13–19.

Hopper, P. (1979), 'Aspect and foregrounding in discourse', in T. Givon (ed.), *Discourse and Syntax*, New York, Academic Press, 213–41.

Hopper, P. (1982), 'Aspect between discourse and grammar: an introductory essay', in P. Hopper (ed.), *Tense-Aspect: Between Semantics and Pragmatics*, Amsterdam, John Benjamins, 3–18.

Hopper, P. and Thompson, S. (1980), 'Transitivity in grammar and discourse', *Language*, 56, 251–99.

Huddleston, R. (1984), *Introduction to the Grammar of English*, Cambridge, Cambridge University Press.

Hudson, R. (1980), *Sociolinguistics*, Cambridge, Cambridge University Press.

Hunt, J. (1965), *William Faulkner: Art in Theological Tension*, Syracuse, Syracuse University Press.

Hurtig, R. (1977), 'Toward a functional theory of discourse', in R. Freedle (ed.), *Discourse Processes*, vol. I: *Discourse Production and Comprehension*, Norwood, Ablex.

Hymes, D. (1983), *Essays in the History of Linguistic Anthropology*, Amsterdam, Benjamins.

Itkonen, E. (1984), 'Concerning the ontological question in linguistics', *Language and Communication*, 4, 241–6.

Ives, S. (1950), 'A theory of literary dialect', *Tulane Studies in English*, 2,

137–82; reprinted in J. Williamson and V. Burke (eds), *A Various Language: Perspectives on American Dialects*, New York, Holt, Rinehart & Winston, 1971.

Jacobsson, B. (1970), 'English pronouns and feature analysis', *Moderna Sprak*, 64, 346–59.

Jakobson, R. (1957), *Shifters, Verbal Categories, and the Russian Verb*, Cambridge, Mass., Harvard University Press.

Jakobson, R. (1960), 'Closing statement: linguistics and poetics', in T. Sebeok (ed.), *Style in Language*, Cambridge, Mass., MIT Press, 350–77.

Jefferson, A. (1980), 'The place of free indirect discourse in the poetics of fiction: with examples from Joyce's "Eveline"', *Essays in Poetics*, 5: 1, 36–47.

Jeliffe, R. (ed.) (1956), *Faulkner at Nagano*, Tokyo, Kenkyusha.

Jespersen, O. (1922), *Language, its Nature, Development and Origin*, London, Allen & Unwin.

Jespersen, O. (1929), *The Philosophy of Grammar*, London, Allen & Unwin.

Johnson, B. (1981), 'The frame of reference: Poe, Lacan, Derrida', in R. Young (ed.), *Untying the Text*, London, Routledge & Kegan Paul, 225–43.

Joos, M., (1964), *The English Verb: Form and Meanings*, Madison, University of Wisconsin Press.

Kaluza, I. (1964), *The Functioning of Sentence Structure in the 'Stream of Consciousness' Technique of William Faulkner's 'The Sound and the Fury'*, Folcroft, Folcroft Press.

Kantor, R., Bruce, B., Green, G., Morgan, J., Stein, N., and Webber, B. (1982), 'Many problems and some techniques of text analysis', *Poetics*, 11, 237–64.

Kazin, A. (1942), *On Native Grounds*, London, Jonathan Cape.

Keenan, E., and Schieffelin, B. (1976), 'Topic as a discourse notion', in C. Li (ed.), *Subject and Topic*, New York, Academic Press, 335–84.

Kennedy, C. (1982), 'Systemic grammar and its use in literary analysis', in R. Carter (ed.), *Language and Literature*, London, Allen & Unwin, 83–99.

Kinney, A. (1978), *Faulkner's Narrative Poetics: Style as Vision*, Amherst, University of Massachusetts Press.

Kiparsky, P., and Youmans, G. (eds) (1989), *Rhythm and Meter*, New York, Academic Press.

Knapp, S., and Michaels, W. (1982), 'Against theory', *Critical Inquiry*, 8, 723–42.

Koerner, K. (1983), 'The Chomskyan "revolution" and its historiography: a few critical remarks', *Language and Communication*, 3: 2, 147–69.

Krause, D. (1984), 'Reading Bon's Letter and Faulkner's *Absalom, Absalom!*', *PMLA*, 99, 225–41.

Kress, G. (1985), *Linguistic Processes in Sociocultural Practice*, Deakin, Deakin University Press.

Kress, G., and Hodge, R. (1979), *Language as Ideology*, London, Routledge & Kegan Paul.

Kuroda, S.-Y. (1973), 'Where epistemology, style and grammar meet: a case study from Japanese', in S. Anderson and P. Kiparsky (eds), *A Festschrift for Morris Halle*, New York, Holt, Rinehart & Winston, 377–91.

Kuyk, D. (1983), *Threads Cable-Strong: William Faulkner's 'Go Down, Moses'*, Lewisburg, Bucknell University Press.

Labov, W. (1972), *Language in the Inner City*, Philadelphia, University of Pennsylvania Press.

Lakoff, G. (1968), *Pronouns and Reference*, mimeo, Bloomington, Indiana University Linguistics Club.

Lakoff, G. (1987), *Women, Fire, and Dangerous Things*, Chicago, University of Chicago Press.

Lakoff, G., and Johnson, M. (1980), *Metaphors We Live By*, Chicago, University of Chicago Press.

Langacker, R. (1969), 'On pronominalization and the chain of command', in D. Reibel and S. Schane (eds), *Modern Studies in English*, Englewood Cliffs, Prentice-Hall, 160–86.

Lanin, I. (1977), 'You can take the sentence out of the discourse but you can't take the discourse out of the mind of the speaker', in W. Beach *et al.* (eds), *Papers from the Thirteenth Regional Meeting of the Chicago Linguistic Society*, Chicago, University of Chicago Press, 288–301.

Leaver, F. (1958), 'Faulkner: the word as principle and power', *South Atlantic Quarterly*, 57, 464–76.

Lee, D. (1976), '*The Inheritors* and transformational generative grammar', *Language and Style*, 9, 77–97.

Leech, G. (1969), *A Linguistic Guide to English Poetry*, London, Longman.

Leech, G. (1983), *Principles of Pragmatics*, London, Longman.

Leech, G., and Short, M. (1981), *Style in Fiction*, London, Longman.

Lees, R., and Klima, E. (1963), 'Rules for English pronominalization', *Language*, 39, 17–28.

Leith, R. (1980), 'Dialogue and dialect in D. H. Lawrence', *Style*, 14, 245–58.

Le Page, R., and Tabouret-Keller, A. (1985), *Acts of Identity*, Cambridge, Cambridge University Press.

Levinson, S. (1983), *Pragmatics*, Cambridge, Cambridge University Press.

Limon, J. (1986), 'The integration of Faulkner's *Go Down, Moses*', *Critical Inquiry*, 12, 422–38.

Linde, C. (1979), 'Focus of attention and the choice of pronouns in discourse', in T. Givon, (ed.), *Syntax and Semantics*, vol. 12, New York, Academic Press.

Ljung, M. (1980), *Reflections on the English Progressive*, Göteborg, Acta Universitatis Gothoburgensis.

Lodge, D. (1966), *Language of Fiction*, London, Routledge & Kegan Paul.

Lodge, D. (1977), *The Modes of Modern Writing*, London, Edward Arnold.

Love, N. (1981), 'Making sense of Chomsky's revolution', *Language and Communication*, 1, 275–87.

Love, N. (1988), 'Ideal linguistics', *Language and Communication*, 8: 1, 69–84.

Lust, B. (ed.) (1986), *Studies in the Acquisition of Anaphora*, vol. I: *Defining the Constraints*, Dordrecht, Reidel.

Lyons, J. (1968), *Introduction to Theoretical Linguistics*, Cambridge, Cambridge University Press.

Lyons, J. (1977), *Semantics*, 2 vols, Cambridge, Cambridge University Press.

Macafee, C. (1986), 'Dialect vocabulary as a source of stylistic effects in Scottish literature', *Language and Style*, 19, 325–37.

MacCabe, C. (1981), 'Language, linguistics and the study of literature', *Oxford Literary Review*, 4: 3, 68–82.

McCawley, J. (1968), 'The role of semantics in a grammar', in E. Bach and R. Harms (eds), *Universals in Language*, New York, Holt, Rinehart & Winston, 125–69.

McCawley, J. (1970), 'Where do noun phrases come from?', in R. Jacobs and P. Rosenbaum (eds), *Readings in Transformational Grammar*, Waltham, Mass., Ginn, 166–83.

McHale, B. (1978), 'Free indirect discourse: a survey of recent accounts', *Poetics and Theory of Literature*, 3, 249–87.

McHale, B. (1983), 'Linguistics and poetics revisited', *Poetics Today*, 4: 1, 17–45.

McHale, B. (1985), 'Speaking as a child in *U.S.A.*', *Language and Style*, 17, 351–70.

McKay, D., and Fulkerson, D. (1979), 'On the comprehension and production of pronouns', *Journal of Verbal Learning and Verbal Behavior*, 18, 662–73.

McLain, R. (1977), 'The problem of "style"', *Language and Style*, 10, 52–65.

Macleod, N. (1984), 'More on backward anaphora and discourse structure', *Journal of Pragmatics*, 8, 321–8.

Mailloux, Steven (1979), 'Learning to read: interpretation and reader-response criticism', *Studies in the Literary Imagination*, 12: 1, 93–108.

Mailloux, S. (1982), *Interpretive Conventions: The Reader in the Study of American Fiction*, Ithaca, Cornell University Press.

Mandelbaum, D. (ed.) (1949), *Selected Writings of Edward Sapir*, Berkeley, University of California Press.

Mann, W., and Thompson, S. (1986), 'Relational propositions in discourse', *Discourse Processes*, 9, 57–90.

Martin, J. (1983), 'The development of register', in J. Fine and R. Freedle (eds), *Developmental Issues in Discourse*, Norwood, Ablex, 1–40.

Matthews, J. (1982), *The Play of Faulkner's Language*, Ithaca, Cornell University Press.

Meyer, N. L. (1971), 'Syntactic features of William Faulkner's narrative', unpublished PhD dissertation, University of Nebraska.

Milic, L. T. (1967), *A Quantitative Approach to the Style of Jonathan Swift*, The Hague, Mouton.

Millgate, J. (1964), 'Short story into novel: Faulkner's reworkings of "Gold Is Not Always"', *English Studies*, 45, 310–17.

Millgate, M. (1966), *The Achievement of William Faulkner*, New York, Random House.

Millgate, M. (1973), 'William Faulkner: the problem of point of view', in L. Wagner (ed.), *William Faulkner: Four Decades of Criticism*, Michigan, Michigan State University Press, 179–91.

Millgate, M. (1983), 'William Faulkner: the two voices', *Southern Literature in Transition*, 2, 73–85.

Milroy, L. (1981), *Language and Social Networks*, Oxford, Blackwell.

Mitchell, W. J. T. (1982), Introduction to special issue of *Critical Inquiry* on 'The politics of interpretation', 9: 1.

330

Mittwoch, A. (1983), 'Backward anaphora and discourse structure', *Journal of Pragmatics*, 7, 129–39.

Mittwoch, A. (1985), 'Sentences, utterance boundaries, personal deixis and the E-hypothesis', *Theoretical Linguistics*, 12, 137–52.

Modleski, T. (1982), *Loving with a Vengeance: Mass-Produced Fantasies for Women*, Hamden, Archon Books.

Moi, T. (1985), *Sexual/Textual Politics*, London, Methuen.

Nash, W. (1980), *Designs in Prose*, London, Longman.

Nash, W. (1985), *The Language of Humour*, London, Longman.

Nehls, D. (1978), 'The system of tense and aspect in English: a structural-functional approach', in D. Nehls (ed.), *Studies in Descriptive English Grammar*, Heidelberg, Gross, 45–62.

Norris, C. (1982), *Deconstruction: Theory and Practice*, London, Methuen.

Norris, C. (1988), *Paul de Man: Deconstruction and the Critique of Aesthetic Ideology*, London, Routledge.

Nunberg, G. (1978), *The Pragmatics of Reference*, mimeo, Bloomington, Indiana University Linguistics Club.

Ochs, E. (1979), 'Planned and unplanned discourse', in T. Givon (ed.), *Syntax and Semantics*, vol. 12, New York, Academic Press, 51–80.

Ogden, C. K., and Richards, I. A. (1923), *The Meaning of Meaning*, London, Routledge & Kegan Paul.

Ohmann, R. (1964), 'Generative grammars and the concept of literary style', *Word*, 20, 423–39; reprinted in G. Love and M. Payne (eds), *Contemporary Essays on Style*, Glenview, Scott Foresman, 1969, 133–48.

Ohmann, R. (1969), 'Literature as sentences', in G. Love and M. Payne (eds), *Contemporary Essays on Style*, Glenview, Scott Foresman, 149–57.

Ohmann, R. (1971), 'Speech, action, and style', in S. Chatman (ed.), *Literary Style: A Symposium*, London, Oxford University Press, 241–54.

Ohmann, R. (1972), 'Instrumental style: notes on the theory of speech as action', in B. Kachru and H. Stahlke (eds), *Current Trends in Stylistics*, Edmonton, Linguistic Research, Inc., 115–41.

Ota, A. (1963), *Tense and Aspect of Present-Day American English*, Tokyo, Kenkyusha.

Page, N. (1973), *Speech in the English Novel*, London, Longman.

Partee, B. H. (1975), 'Deletion and variable binding', in E. Keenan (ed.), *Formal Semantics of Natural Language*, London, Cambridge University Press, 16–34.

Pascal, R. (1977), *The Dual Voice*, Manchester, Manchester University Press.

Pateman, T. (1980), *Language, Truth and Politics*, Lewes, Jean Stroud.

Pateman, T. (1983a), 'What is a language?', *Language and Communication*, 3, 101–27.

Pateman, T. (1983b), 'Linguistics as a branch of critical theory', *UEA Papers in Linguistics*, 14–15, 1–29.

Peer, W. van (1986), *Stylistics and Psychology: Investigations of Foregrounding*, London, Croom Helm.

Polanyi, L. (1981), 'Telling the same story twice', *Text*, 1, 315–36.

Postal, P. (1969), 'On so-called "pronouns" in English', in D. Reibel and S.

Schane (eds), *Modern Studies in English: Readings in Transformational Grammar*, Englewood Cliffs, Prentice-Hall, 201–24.

Pratt, M. L. (1977), *Toward a Speech-Act Theory of Literary Discourse*, Bloomington, Indiana University Press.

Pratt, M. L. (1986), 'The ideology of speech act theory', *Poetics Today*, 7, 59–72.

Pratt, M. L. (1987), 'Linguistic utopias', in N. Fabb *et al.* (eds), *The Linguistics of Writing*, New York, Methuen, 48–66.

Quirk, R., Greenbaum, S., Leech, G., and Svartvik, J. (1972), *A Grammar of Contemporary English*, London, Longman.

Quirk, R., Greenbaum, S., Leech, G., and Svartvik, J. (1985), *A Comprehensive Grammar of the English Language*, London, Longman.

Radomski, J. L. (1974), 'Faulkner's style: a stylistic analysis', unpublished PhD dissertation, Kent State University.

Ramsey, V. (1987), 'The functional distribution of preposed and postposed "if" and "when" clauses in written discourse', in R. Tomlin (ed.), *Coherence and Grounding in Discourse*, Amsterdam, John Benjamins, 383–408.

Raybould, E. (1957), 'Of Jane Austen's use of expanded verbal forms', in S. Korninger (ed.), *Studies in English Language and Literature Presented to Prof. K. Brunner*, Vienna, Wilhelm Braumuller, 154–74.

Reed, J. (1973), *Faulkner's Narrative*, New Haven, Yale University Press.

Reinhart, T. (1983), *Anaphora and Semantic Interpretation*, London, Croom Helm.

Riedel, F. C. (1957), 'Faulkner as stylist', *South Atlantic Quarterly*, 56, 462–79.

Richardson, K. (1987), 'Critical linguistics and textual diagnosis', *Text*, 7: 2, 145–63.

Riffaterre, M. (1959), 'Criteria for style analysis', *Word*, 15, 154–74.

Riffaterre, M. (1960), 'Stylistic context', *Word*, 16, 207–18.

Riffaterre, M. (1973), 'Interpretation and descriptive poetry: a reading of Wordsworth's "Yew Trees"', *New Literary History*, 4, 229–56.

Romaine, S. (1983), 'Variable rules, OK? Or can there be sociolinguistic grammars?', *Language and Communication*, 5, 53–67.

Romaine, S. (1988), *Pidgin and Creole Languages*, London, Longman.

Rorty, R. (1982), *Consequences of Pragmatism*, Minnesota, University of Minnesota Press.

Ross, J. R. (1969), 'On the cyclic nature of English pronominalization', in D. Reibel and S. Schane (eds), *Modern Studies in English: Readings in Transformational Grammar*, Englewood Cliffs, Prentice-Hall, 187–200.

Ross, S. (1981), 'The evocation of voice in *Absalom, Absalom!*', *Essays in Literature*, 8, 135–49.

Rubin, L. (1983), 'The mockingbird in the gum tree: notes on the language of American literature', *Southern Review*, 19, 785–801.

Russell, B. (1948), *An Inquiry into Meaning and Truth*, London, Allen & Unwin.

Rynell, A. (1952), *Parataxis and Hypotaxis as a Criterion of Syntax and Style*, Lund, Gleerup.

Sacks, H. (1975), 'Everyone has to lie', in M. Sanches and B. Blount (eds), *Sociocultural Dimensions of Language Use*, New York, Academic Press, 57–80.

Said, E. (1982), *The World, the Text, and the Critic*, London, Faber.

Sapir, E. (1929), 'The status of linguistics as a science', *Language*, 5, 207–14; reprinted in D. Mandelbaum (ed.), *Selected Writings of Edward Sapir*, Berkeley, University of California Press, 1949, 160–6.

Sapir, E. (1931), 'Communication', *Encyclopedia of the Social Sciences*, 4, 78–81; reprinted in D. Mandelbaum (ed.), *Selected Writings of Edward Sapir*, Berkeley, University of California Press, 1949, 104–9.

Scheffer, J. (1975), *The Progressive in English*, Amsterdam, North Holland.

Schegloff, E. (1972), 'Notes on a conversational practice: formulating place', in D. Sudnow (ed.), *Studies in Social Interaction*, New York, Free Press.

Searle, J. (1979), *Expression and Meaning*, Cambridge, Cambridge University Press.

Sebeok, T. (ed.) (1960), *Style in Language*, Cambridge, Mass., MIT Press.

Shapiro, M. (1984), 'How narrators report speech', *Language and Style*, 17, 62–78.

Sinclair, J., and Coulthard, M. (1975), *Towards an Analysis of Discourse*, London, Oxford University Press.

Slatoff, W. (1960), *Quest for Failure: A Study of William Faulkner*, Ithaca, Cornell University Press.

Smit, D. W. (1988), *The Language of a Master: Theories of Style and the Late Writing of Henry James*, Carbondale, Southern Illinois University Press.

Smitherman-Donaldson, G., and van Dijk, T. (eds) (1987), *Discourse and Discrimination*, Detroit, Wayne State University Press.

Sosa, E. (ed.) (1975), *Causation and Conditionals*, Oxford, Oxford University Press.

Sperber, D., and Wilson, D. (1986), *Relevance: Communication and Cognition*, Oxford, Blackwell.

Spitzer, L. (1948), *Linguistics and Literary History*, Princeton, Princeton University Press.

Stewart, J. (1981), 'Structure, language, and vision in Faulkner's "The Old People"', *Ball State University Forum*, 22: 3, 51–7.

Stoneback, H. (1976), "Faulkner's blues: "Pantaloon in Black"", *Modern Fiction Studies*, 21, 56–65.

Tangum, M. (1986), 'Voices in *Go Down, Moses*: Faulkner's dialogic rhetoric', unpublished PhD dissertation, University of Texas, Austin.

Taylor, R. C. (1979), 'Semantic structures and the temporal modes of Blake's prophetic verse', *Language and Style*, 12, 26–49.

Taylor, T. (1980), *Linguistic Theory and Structural Stylistics*, Oxford, Pergamon Press.

Taylor, T. (1983), review of G. Kress and R. Hodge, *Language as Ideology* (1979), in *Journal of Literary Semantics*, 12, 92–5.

Taylor, T., and Toolan, M. (1984), 'Recent trends in stylistics', *Journal of Literary Semantics*, 13, 57–79.

Theroux, P. (1985), *Sunrise with Seamonsters*, London, Chatto & Windus.

Thomas, J. (1983), 'Cross-cultural pragmatic failure', *Applied Linguistics*, 4, 91–112.

Thompson, S. (1984), 'Subordination in formal and informal discourse', *Georgetown Roundtable on Language and Linguistics*, 85–94.

Thompson, S., and Longacre, R. (1985), 'Adverbial clauses', in T. Shopen (ed.), *Language Typology and Syntactic Description*, vol. II: *Complex Constructions*, Cambridge, Cambridge University Press, 171–234.

Thorne, J. P. (1965), 'Stylistics and generative grammars', *Journal of Linguistics*, 1, 49–59.

Thorne, J. P. (1970), 'Generative grammar and stylistic analysis', in J. Lyons (ed.), *New Horizons in Linguistics*, Harmondsworth, Penguin, 185–97.

Thornton, W. (1975), 'Structure and theme in Faulkner's *Go Down, Moses*', *Costerus*, new series, 3, 73–112.

Thurley, G. (1983), *Countermodernism in Current Critical Theory*, London, Macmillan.

Tick, S. (1962), 'The unity of *Go Down, Moses*', *Twentieth Century Literature*, 8, 67–73.

Tomlin, R. (1985), 'Foreground–background information and the syntax of subordination', *Text*, 5, 85–122.

Toolan, M. (1985), 'Analysing fictional dialogue', *Language and Communication*, 5: 3, 193–206.

Toolan, M. (1987), 'Analysing conversation in fiction', *Poetics Today*, 8, 393–416.

Toolan, M. (1988), *Narrative: A Critical Linguistic Introduction*, London, Routledge.

Toolan, M. (ed.) (forthcoming), *Essays in Contextualized Stylistics*, London, Routledge.

Traugott, E., and Pratt, M. (1980), *Linguistics for Students of Literature*, New York, Harcourt Brace Jovanovich.

Trilling, L. (1942), 'The McCaslins of Mississippi', *Nation*, 30 May, 532.

Twaddell, W. F. (1960), *The English Verb Auxiliaries*, Providence, Brown University Press.

Ullmann, S. (1965), 'Style and personality', *A Review of English Literature*, 6, 20–5.

Uspensky, B. A. (1973), *A Poetics of Composition*, Berkeley, University of California Press.

Vickery, O. (1959), *The Novels of William Faulkner: A Critical Introduction*, Baton Rouge, Louisiana State University Press.

Volosinov, V. N. (1973), *Marxism and the Philosophy of Language*, trans. L. Matejka and I. R. Titunik, New York, Seminar Press.

Waegner, C. (1983), *Recollection and Discovery: The Rhetoric of Character in William Faulkner's Novels*, New York, Peter Lang.

Weber, J.-J. (1982a), 'Inferences and ideological point of view in Joyce's "Eveline"', *UEA Papers in Linguistics*, 16/17, 1–25.

Weber, J.-J. (1982b), 'Frame construction and frame accommodation in a Gricean analysis of narrative', *Journal of Literary Semantics*, 11, 90–5.

Weber, J.-J. (1986), 'Inferential and evocational processing of literary texts', *Grazer Linguistische Studien*, 26, 173–85.

Weinreich, H. (1964), *Tempus: Besprochene und erzählte Welt*, Stuttgart, Kohlhammer.

Wells, E. (1969), 'A statistical analysis of Fitzgerald and Hemingway', in M. Bruccoli (ed.), *Fitzgerald/Hemingway Annual*, Washington, Microcard, 47–67.

West, C., and Zimmerman, D. (1981), 'Conversation analysis', in K. Scherer and P. Ekman (eds), *Handbook of Methods in Nonverbal Behavior Research*, New York, Cambridge University Press, 506–41.

Whitehall, H. (1956), 'From linguistics to criticism', *Kenyon Review*.

Widdowson, P. (ed.) (1983), *Re-reading English*, London, Methuen.

Williams, E. (1977), 'Discourse and logical form', *Linguistic Inquiry*, 8, 101–39.

Youmans, G. and Kiparsky, P. (eds) (1989), *Rhythm and Meter*, New York, Academic Press.

Young, R. (ed.) (1981), *Untying the Text*, London, Routledge & Kegan Paul.

Zender, K. (1980), 'Reading in "The Bear"', *Faulkner Studies*, 1, 91–9.

Zender, K. (1981), 'Faulkner at forty: the artist at home', *Southern Review*, 17, 288–302.

Zender, K. (1984), 'Faulkner and the power of sound', *PMLA*, 99, 89–108.

Zink, K. (1954), 'William Faulkner: form as experience', *South Atlantic Quarterly*, 53, 384–403.

Zoellner, R. (1959), 'Faulkner's prose style in *Absalom, Absalom!*' *American Literature*, 30, 486–502.

INDEX

INDEX

Cowley 71
Creighton 226
Crymes 127–8, 130, 132
Culler 18, 21, 61
Cummings and Simmons 302–3
Cureton 302, 309
Crystal 102
Crystal and Davy 63

Davis 13–14
deconstructionism, and stylistics 46–53
deixis 126–9, 177–90
'Delta Autumn' 199–200, 205–6
De Man 30
demonstrative pronouns and adjectives 177–90
Derrida 2, 11, 22, 48–9
dialect in fictional speech 277–84
Dik 215
Dillon 20–1, 98, 209, 211, 220, 223, 226, 310, 315
Dowty 100

Eagleton 29, 31–3, 35, 41, 49, 315
Ehrlich 103, 122
enough and *not enough* 202–6

Faulkner: assessments of his style 54–9; and freedom of the individual 81–2
Fehr 110–13
'Fire and the Hearth, The' 107–9, 129, 157–66, 177–81, 198, 255–72
Firth 51
Fish 3, 12–13, 14–25, 29–31, 33, 191
fixed code, language as 7
Foucault 13
Fowler 1, 14, 37, 50, 53, 68, 300, 305–7
Fox 137–8, 139
free indirect discourse 73–81, *et passim*; *v.* stream of consciousness 172–6
Freedman and Kaplan 202
Freund 21
Frow 310
Frye 21
functional relevance 41

generativist linguistics 2, 4
generic sentences 267–9
Genette 74, 111, 172
Gibson 217–18, 219
Giddens 13
Gilbert and Gubar 22

Ginsberg 74, 78
Go Down, Moses: interpreting the novel 71–4, 89–93; merged voices in 78–81; Isaac McCaslin in 82–4, 87–93, 186–90, 200, 247–54, 255–72, 203–6, 284; Lucas in 85–6, 157–66, 177–81, 203–4, 230–4, 255–72, 282–4; Roth Edmonds in 86–9, 230–4, 255–72; compositional history 90; progressives in 104–24; pronouns in 143–76; demonstratives in 177–90; lexical patternings in 191–206; dialogue in 273–97
'Go Down, Moses' 146–8, 196, 229, 291–7
Goffman 13
Grice 128, 274, 289–91
Gross 2, 4
Guerard 89
Gumperz 291
Gwynn and Blotner 82, 223

Halliday 13, 14, 15–16, 25, 39, 69, 71, 95, 212–14, 230, 234, 242, 281, 301–3
Halliday and Hasan 61, 129, 131–7, 156, 239
Harris 2, 3, 5, 7, 8, 33, 36, 42, 46, 61, 308
Hasan 301–2
Hatcher 102
Hayes 217
he 171–6
Hirsch 22–5, 30, 36
Hodge and Kress 53
Hogan 102
homogeneity, linguistic 4–5
Hopper 103
Hopper and Thompson 138
Huddleston 130, 132
Hudson 3
Hunt 254
Hymes 52

intentionality 30–1, 36
interpretive communities 12–13, 17–19
inter- and intratextual analysis 62
intuition 63–4
it 166–71, 266–7
Itkonen 2
Ives 281

Jacobsson 131
Jakobson 6, 14, 20, 23, 64, 127

337

INDEX